"In this outstanding work, Adda Bozeman has brought her incomparable knowledge of international cultural history to bear on pressing issues of intelligence policy. . . . In the range and rigor with which she addresses them, Dr. Bozeman demonstrates that she is the most distinguished analyst in this field in the United States. Her book could not have come at a better time. For now, with the collapse of the Soviet empire, there is real danger that our nation will slip back into the simple universalism that has been the source of such costly foreign policy failings in the past—and this just when the ancient cultures of the Middle East, Asia, and Africa are coming to play an increasingly assertive role in international politics. Adda Bozeman's work is an indispensable corrective to these parochial tendencies in both the governmental and academic worlds. Her masterful book is one of the most important—and surely one of the most needed—of the decade."

> —Whittle Johnston
> Professor, Government and
> Foreign Affairs
> Woodrow Wilson Department of
> Government and Foreign Affairs
> University of Virginia

"Adda Bozeman's knowledge of the history of intelligence—ancient and modern, Western and Eastern—is unrivaled. *Strategic Intelligence and Statecraft* brings together her most wide-ranging and most provocative essays . . . handily and elegantly collected."

> —Ernest R. May
> Charles Warren Professor of History
> Harvard University

". . . Professor Adda Bozeman takes the intellectual strands of politics, history, and culture and weaves them into an incomparable and brilliant mosaic that reveals the actual nature of the intelligence game as it has been played against the broad expanse of world politics. Her penetrating insights and bold departures from what passes for conventional wisdom in the field of international relations . . . establish[es] . . . both a theoretical position and standard of scholarship that those who follow her will do well to emulate."

> —Abraham H. Miller, Chair
> Intelligence Studies Section
> International Studies Association
> Professor, University of Cincinnati

Strategic Intelligence
& Statecraft

Other Volumes in Brassey's Intelligence & National Security Library

Jaubert MAKING PEOPLE DISAPPEAR: AN AMAZING CHRONICLE
OF PHOTOGRAPHIC DECEPTION
Shulsky SILENT WARFARE: UNDERSTANDING THE WORLD
OF INTELLIGENCE
Stiller with Adams BEYOND THE WALL: MEMOIRS OF AN EAST AND WEST
GERMAN SPY

Related Journals*

Armed Forces Journal International
Defense Analysis
Survival

*Sample copies available upon request

Strategic Intelligence & Statecraft

Selected Essays

Adda B. Bozeman

BRASSEY'S (US), Inc.

A Division of Maxwell Macmillan, Inc.

Washington · New York · London

U.S.A. (Editorial)	Brassey's (US), Inc. 8000 Westpark Drive, 1st Floor, McLean, Virginia 22102, U.S.A.
(Orders)	Attn: Brassey's Order Dept., Macmillan Publishing Co., 100 Front Street, Box 500, Riverside, New Jersey 08075
U.K. (Editorial)	Brassey's (UK) Ltd. 50 Fetter Lane, London EC4A 1AA, England
(Orders)	Brassey's (UK) Ltd. Orders Headington Hill Hall, Oxford OX3 OBW, England
ASIA/PACIFIC	Maxwell Macmillan Publishing, Singapore Pte., Ltd., 72 Hillview Ave., 03-00 Tacam House, Singapore 2366, Singapore
AUSTRALIA/NEW ZEALAND	Maxwell Macmillan Pergamon Publishing, Australia Pty., Ltd., Lakes Business Park, Bldg. A1, 2 Lord St., Botany, New S. Wales, 2019 Australia
JAPAN	Maxwell Macmillan Japan, Misuzu S. Bldg. 2F, 2-42-14 Matsubara, Setagaya-ku, Tokyo 156, Japan
CANADA	Maxwell Macmillan Canada, Inc., 1200 Eglinton Ave. E., Ste. 200, Don Mills, Ontario M3C 3N1, Canada
LATIN AMERICA EXPORT	Maxwell Macmillan International Publishing Group, 28100 U.S. Hwy 19 North, Ste. 200, Clearwater, Florida 34621
EUROPE	Maxwell Macmillan International Publishing Group, Ferievagen 15, S-161 51 Bromma, Sweden
UNITED KINGDOM/ EUROPE/MIDDLE EAST/AFRICA	Maxwell Macmillan International Publishing Group, c/o Nuffield Press, Hollow Way, Cowley Oxford OX4 2PH, United Kingdom

Copyright © 1992 Brassey's (US), Inc.

Brassey's (US), Inc., books are available at special discounts for bulk purchases for sales promotions, premiums, fund-raising, or educational use through the Special Sales Director, Macmillan Publishing Company, 866 Third Avenue, New York, NY 10022.

Library of Congress Cataloging-in-Publication Data

Bozeman, Adda Bruemmer, 1908–
    Strategic intelligence & statecraft : selected essays / Adda B. Bozeman.
        p.   cm.—(Brassey's intelligence & national security library)
    ISBN 0-02-881009-0
    1. Intelligence service. 2. International relations. I. Title.
II. Series: Brassey's intelligence & national security library.
JF1525.I6B69   1992
327.1'2—dc20   91-46454
                                            CIP

Printed in the United States of America

10 9 8 7 6 5 4 3 2

CONTENTS

PREFACE

The essays collected in this volume examine politically and culturally different orientations to statecraft and political intelligence. Also, they focus on greatly various intelligence-related themes. Nonetheless, they are conceptually unified in the following ways.

All are carried by the dualistic conviction that successful statecraft is always and everywhere dependent on good intelligence, but that the United States will not be able to promote its vital interests effectively in the 21st century unless it upgrades this particular dimension of policy formation by widening the field of intelligence collection, deepening levels of data analysis, and—above all—by fashioning a reliable national consensus in support of strong intelligence services.

Next, the essays are closely linked since they are grounded in the same perceptions of world politics and international history, and draw on the same multi-disciplinary approaches to learning. Specifically, they are held together by the commitment first, to uncover and analyze the uniqueness of each system of statecraft and intelligence and second, to compare the separate case studies with a view to locating discordant as well as congruent themes. In other words, the essays are not carried by trust in the universal validity of one particular code of norms and theories.

Last, it should be noted in this Preface that the present volume is a derivative as well as an extension of my earlier work, particularly of *Politics and Culture in International History,* which I began writing in the late 1940s (publ. 1960). At that time political intelligence was not the object of common scholarly concern in the West. Indeed, the topic had not been brought up in either of my seminars and courses at the Section Diplomatique of Ecole Libre des Sciences Politiques from which I graduated in 1934. But my interest was aroused a few years later when I immersed myself in comparative studies of classical Persian, Chinese and Indian statecraft in the context of both my teaching and my writing programs and thus had occasion to do my first reading (in translation) of the Chinese Legalist treatises on the arts of war, espionage and deception, Indian arthasastras on that subject, and the Persian and later Islamic manuals on statecraft and the functions of intelligence.

The present book incorporates my mature understanding of these Asian legacies. But it is relevant to note that these matters were already discussed in *Politics and Culture in International History* and thereafter in *The Future of Law in a Multicultural World* (1971), because it is there, in prefaces, footnotes, textual references, and bibliographies, that I acknowledge my lasting indebtedness to Jean Escarra, *Le Droit Chinois* (1936), and Arthur Waley, *Three Ways of Thought in Ancient China* (1939), who introduced me to the Legalist philosophers; and to Rudrahatha Shamasastry, editor of *Kautilya's Arthasastra* (1915), and Heinrich Zimmer, *Philosophies of India* (ed. Joseph Campbell, 1951), who brought me to the sources of Indian statecraft, as well as to numerous other pioneering scholars who worked in different fields and lived in different ages and places.

All helped me consolidate my belief in the primacy of mind over matter; the co-existence of diverse cultures and mind systems in the world, and the necessity therefore of accentuating the study of ideas and ways of thinking. I thus want to thank them again today because they provided key intelligence for writing the essays included in this book; for developing new academic approaches to teaching statecraft and intelligence on undergraduate, graduate and post-graduate levels; and for enabling me to join like-minded American scholars in concerted efforts to promote the nation's security by anchoring it in a vitalized system of strategic intelligence.

Reflections on the record of my most recent work under these headings leave no doubt in my mind that it could not have been carried out effectively had it not been for the pioneering achievements of the late Dr. Frank N. Trager. It was he, after all, who was instrumental in establishing national security studies as an academically legitimate subject in American political science; and to him, then, this book is a special tribute.

Further, I am indebted to Dr. Roy Godson for suggesting that I should select some of my papers on security and intelligence in book form; to Mr. Jeff Berman for helping me cope with many procedural problems; to Ms. Vicki Chamlee, the production manager for Brassey's (US), who was unfailingly helpful in furthering the publishing process; and to the publishers and editors of seven essays who gave permission to re-publish them here. However, now as many times before, I thank my husband Arne Barkhuus, M.D., for his steadying support, his thoughtful criticisms, and above all his inspiring presence.

Introduction

WHAT IS STRATEGIC INTELLIGENCE?

A case can be made for the general validity of the following propositions. Intelligence in its primary or generic sense is everywhere a property of the mind. It stands for the human being's inborn capacity to come to terms with life by engaging in thought and acquiring, developing, and investing knowledge. However, no universally applicable answer can be given to the further question—namely, just how men and women actually engage or commit their mental capabilities. This uncertainty stems from the fact that ways of thinking and orientations to knowledge are, and always have been, greatly various in the world because they are expressions of different languages, cultures, moral orders, and political systems.

Intelligence in its derivative political sense is a component of statecraft that centers upon the need of one politically unified community to have reliable information, knowledge, or "intelligence" about other societies in its environment. Intelligence "2," then, is by no means a wayward offspring of intelligence "1." The records suggest rather that the elementary idea was nowhere and at no time expunged when it was drafted into vocabularies of domestic and international politics to serve the security interests of any given politically independent organism. What has always been in issue, though, are the particular meanings and functions assigned to this norm under the auspices of culturally and politically disparate forms of statecraft.

The term "statecraft" as used in this book stands for the sum total of human dispositions, doctrines, policies, institutions, processes, and operations that are designed to assure the governance, security, and survival of a politically unified human group. Although we appear conditioned today to recognize only entities called "states" in this context, it should be borne in mind that greatly diverse politically active societies have always coexisted in the world, and that they continue to do so now. Apart from ethnically homogeneous or ethnically divided states, commonwealths, and empires, these include churches, ecclesiastical orders, and commercial conglomerates; openly transnational political parties and cosmopolitan ideological movements as well as secret societies; sub-rosa governments; and closely knit groups of like-minded people such as racial, tribal, linguistic, or religious associations that are lodged within the orbit of greater ensembles while often functioning

1

as antistate bodies. Last but not least, account must always be taken of ruling dictatorial regimes or individual personages whose power in political decision-making proves to be so absolute as to become incontestable internally as well as externally.

Further, one finds in either of these disparate contexts that the jurisdiction for policy-making is either territorially fixed, or floating, or totally unbounded; that ruling purposes and patterns of administration are too various to allow for accurate classification; and that the legitimacy of political organizations is sustained by altogether different, often mutually incompatible mind-sets, moral persuasions, and worldviews.

In short, the world is divided, conflicted, and anarchical by definition. This circumstance explains why no theory—be it a world-encompassing religion, ideology, utopian dream of world conquest, or law of nations—has been instrumental in bringing forth globally unifying normative references in terms of which international actors and their respective modes of internal and external statecraft can be identified reliably from one day or one century to the next.

Security-conscious governments in all ages and places appear to have accepted these persistent complexities as standing challenges in their conduct of foreign affairs by collecting, processing, and institutionalizing their own political intelligence. But we also learn from past and present records that responses to the challenge of evaluating the human environment, defining vital security concerns, and setting directives for intelligence services have been greatly various, being in each case faithful reflections of culture-specific mental dispositions, moral values, and political systems.

MAPPING INTELLIGENCE DESIGNS

In light of the complexities and uncertainties that have marked the world environment throughout time, it is not surprising to find that successive generations of security-conscious governments and intelligence scholars have converged on two separate yet closely linked tasks. One calls for identifying the diverse foreign schemes, ideas, and operations, each in its discreetness; comparing the norms and functions they accentuate; and distinguishing that which is unique to one or just a few intelligence programs from what is widely shared. The other—and it should be viewed as the ultimate test of successful statecraft everywhere—consists of fashioning a comprehensive intelligence design for one's own political community. Ideally this should be uniquely fitted to facilitate the steady pursuit of long-range policy objectives even as it also provides guidance in the choice of tactically adroit ad hoc responses to particular occurrences in foreign affairs. Wherever or whenever such designs are in place, one deals in my estimation with "strategic intelligence." Needless to say, not all "political intelligence" qualifies for this rating.

Next, but as suggested earlier, no general intelligence schemes or particular intelligence agendas can be either constructed or deciphered unless one has come to terms with the political system and the cultural matrix in which the intelligence matter is enclosed.

It is thus important to identify component elements of culture such as language, race, religion, shared historical experiences and ways of thinking, or attachment to a particular spot on earth, if one wants to learn, for example, whether a given intelligence design is authentic and apt therefore to be a constant factor in foreign affairs or whether it has been installed, decisively influenced, or surreptitiously captured by forces from without—in which case it may well be perceived by knowledgeable outsiders as unpredictable but malleable. And the same preparatory homework is required if one is challenged to come to politically or academically successful terms with such particular manifestations of a given intelligence scheme as deception, terrorism, or covert action. In either instance the intelligence specialist must tap the sources of such operations in the mind-sets of the counterplayers on the world's intelligence board. That is to say, he must be familiar with their basic beliefs, values, and behavior patterns as these have become registered over time before he can reliably estimate a threat, or chart a realistic counter policy or course of action. In short, the study of political intelligence requires resort to what we in the West call multidisciplinary research. And in this context, again, history must be accepted as the primary and indispensable tool of political analysis—a commitment openly avowed by spokesmen for some of the most accomplished intelligence systems in the West and in the East. (Exemplars here are the Adriatic Republic of Venice and Maoist China.)

The essays collected in this volume were originally presented as small but comprehensive monographs that addressed rather specific intelligence-related issues. They are unified in their new appearance not only by my particular scholarly interest in this dimension of statecraft, but also by my persuasion as an American citizen that it is very much in our nation's public interest today to deepen and extend the knowledge of which Sherman Kent spoke when he wrote in the Preface to *Strategic Intelligence for World Policy* (1965), "Strategic intelligence is the knowledge upon which our nation's foreign relations, in war and peace, must rest."

PRE-TWENTIETH CENTURY LEGACIES OF INTELLIGENCE AND THEIR RELEVANCE FOR UPDATING AMERICAN UNDERSTANDINGS OF THE CRAFT

Kent's concept of strategic intelligence was to sink into limbo, neglect, or irrelevance in the last decades of our century, in terms of American scholarship, the nation's civic consciousness, and foreign policy-making. As suggested in some of the following chapters, this retrogression may well be an expression of the ever latent American impatience with the past *per se*. At any rate, it coincided with the dramatic downgrading of history and other disciplined studies of past phenomena in our institutions of higher learning at just the time when all other political entities, be they states or nonstate bodies, chose to recover the legacy of the past in search of vitality, security, and better intelligence. Soon they were to return transformed to the stage of world politics, but we were and continue to be unable to recognize them on their new merits, and therefore we do not as yet know the rules of engagement in the new intelligence games.

Let me illustrate this proposition briefly. Although Mao Tse-tung's works were "soft sources" in our libraries from the 1950s onward, readers in academe and the intelligence community simply did not care to note that the Leninization of China— and therewith also of several historically Sinicized societies—had been carefully programmed by Mao Tse-tung to proceed in tandem with the revitalization of China's own Legalist precepts for totalitarian statecraft as these had been formulated two and a half millennia earlier. In light of these realities it is reasonable to suggest that American intelligence assessments of Chinese Communism in the era of the Sino-Japanese War, the Chinese civil war, and the Second World War might well have led to more accurate insights and more successful foreign policies than the ones that were to climax in the Maoist victory, our defeats in Sinicized Korea and Vietnam, the diplomatic cop-out of the Shanghai Communiqué, and our optimistic overtures to Peking in the late 1980s had our analysts indulged the pleasure of reading the treatises of such Legalists as Lord Shang, Han Fei-tzu, and Sun Tzu, or had they come to appreciate the lessons for winning projected in China's ancient game, Wei-ch'i, a favorite pastime for Chinese strategists throughout the ages, including those successful in our times.

Likewise, it looks as if humanist historians have been consistently missing at American intelligence desks in charge of continental Europe, and that from the First World War onward. At any rate, no adviser in the last seven decades has led U.S. decision-makers to the awareness that the long-range security of the West is inextricably bound up with the solidification of this geopolitically and culturally crucial European space. Indeed, not even the idea of Europe could survive as long as American policies focused single-mindedly on improving relations with the Eurasian Soviet Union.

Observations such as these do not disregard the revolutionary impact of Marxist-Leninist ideology and statecraft on the twentieth-century world. To the contrary, it is precisely the study of this impact which confirms the necessity of a *renvoi* to the past. A return to Lenin's and Djershinskiy's explicit blueprints for the counterintelligence state and the tactics of subversive or revolutionary takeover is thus mandatory if the West's intelligence communities are to devise effective ways of rehabilitating cultures and political systems that have long been despoiled by the impact of Leninism.

Further, but in the same Soviet context of analytical intelligence, we learn from European, Asian, African, and Latin American case studies that the ultimate strategic objective of military or psychological takeover required in each case determined, usually protracted preparatory tactics. These aimed at nullifying or muddying the human target's memory and mind-set—the target might have been a state, a civilization, a group, an institution, or a particular personage—and at discrediting the trusted past, undermining cultural self-confidence, and uncovering vulnerabilities, all with a view to weakening the target's will to resist.

It goes without saying that neither of these complex operations could have been launched or sustained if generations of Soviet intelligence scholars had not been thoroughly schooled in the languages and culture histories of scores of different peoples. And it should have gone without saying that U.S. intelligence establishments were capable of parrying the Leninist input of this type of intelligence. However, the records do not bear out that trust. The United States was not prepared intellectually to dissolve, lessen, or preempt the Marxist-Leninist impact on world affairs. It just confined itself to reiterating its unresearched trust in the universal validity of such basically Western values as law, democracy, and peace.

These incantations—and they were simplified rather than elaborated in response to steadily intensified Leninist thrusts—did not eliminate Maoism in mainland China. Nor did they obstruct Peru's Leninist-Maoist "Shining Path" terrorists; El Salvador's armed guerrillas; Nicaragua's Sandinista regime, which continues in 1991 to wield total power over the state's military and policing forces even though it was officially ousted by elections; or Cuba's hard-core Leninism in the conduct of government and foreign affairs. Rather, studies of post-1987 developments in this region as in Communist-controlled Vietnam, Laos, Kampuchea; in Iraq and Syria; or in South Africa and adjoining states leave the contrary impression. Consumer economies may be in shambles, but there has been no serious letup in ideological fervor and commitment in ruling circles.

Further, it has to be admitted that the Soviet mentor nation has kept faith with its dependents and surrogates. Although its economy has long been bankrupt and its citizenry in a state of insurgency, the Gorbachev administration was to remain steadfast in the pursuit of basic Soviet foreign policies: witness its "secret" preparation of Iraq's military forces prior to the outbreak of the Persian Gulf war and its "open" role in planning and directing the 1987 military offensive in the Angolan war that was to overrun and eliminate the Savimbi forces, thus tightening the ANC stranglehold on the Republic of South Africa. (The South African Defense Force foiled the attempt.)

In sum, conflict will no doubt remain the paramount theme for non-Western societies in the twenty-first century—whether described as "political," "unconventional," "secret," or "cold" war, or as plain low-intensity conflict. Also, it will be more variegated than it was in the past for the following reasons. The crisis of the international states system has deepened in the last decades as ethnically or culturally discreet components of the state seek secession and independence or engage in revolution; and as the number of nonstate decision-makers such as state-transcending religious factions (e.g., the Shi'ite complex), Communist parties, and terrorist networks increases. Further, it is significant that not even powerful states have been able to deal decisively with either of these trends. Indeed, no one knows today just what the Soviet Union, the leading non-Western state in the world, will be like in human, political, and geographic terms when we enter the third millennium.

These new realities and uncertainties in the world environment require careful shifts of U.S. foreign policies, and therefore shifts also in the program of collecting and assessing intelligence data. In the Eurasian orbit of the former U.S.S.R., for instance, we need new files of information not only about Ukraine but also about each of the empire's Asian "republics" if we are to come up with timely, effective responses, on the one hand to regional secessions and revolutions, on the other to Moscow's countermoves. Here as everywhere else in the non-Western world, the

U.S. government can no longer rest content with pushing its version of a "new world order" and the basic values that have sustained the Euro-American West. Rather, the time has come to insist that intelligence analysts provide precise information on two interrelated concerns, and to act accordingly:

First: Which traditionally trusted institutions characterize the established foreign state? Would they be strengthened or weakened by grafts of American institutions?

Second: In which respects are non-Western or semi-Western states, groups, or ruling personages vulnerable to Leninist or Maoist penetration? Do comparative studies authorize us in some instances to count with affinities in thoughtways and personality traits that favor such penetration as well as willing connivance or allied action?

Questions such as these relate to practical, everyday problems in present-day international relations. But not even strategically astute political intelligence can answer them without a searching exploration of the past.

Item: What precisely is the mix of Leninist Maoism and the reconstructed mythical remembrance of Peru's Inca culture that makes for the savagery of the Shining Path?

Item: The African National Congress has been authoritatively defined in U.S. documents as a terrorist organization, and the findings are unequivocally to the effect that it has long been operating under Soviet patronage and in close alliance with the Communist parties of South Africa, Cuba, and Ethiopia. But has the Leninist apparatus been the ultimate or only source of the well-organized "necklace burnings" and lynchings of nonradical blacks in South Africa? Or should allowance be made for the resurgence throughout Africa of traditional tribal orientations to death and its infliction?

Item: Just how should we take the measure of Qaddafi? Is he a uniquely irrational personage, and would far-flung terrorist networks and training camps vanish automatically with his death? Or would it help the cause of analyzing, fighting, or deterring terrorism were we to think of this fanatically hegemonic Libyan leader as yet another reincarnation of those ever-warring Fulani Muslim divines, chief among them Dan Fodio in the nineteenth century, whose perpetual slave raids and *jihads* were the scourge of West and North Africa, and whose territorially overstretched "states" have always been best understood as extensions of biographies?

POLITICAL INTELLIGENCE EAST AND WEST

The past, then, is a useful data bank because it can be expected to furnish some missing keys in such intelligence and counterintelligence jobs as assessing enemies and tracing linkages between them; identifying different actors as well as their differing motivations in transnational terrorist conspiracies, disinformation campaigns, guerrilla wars, and other hostile combinations; or just uncovering "truth" behind some camouflage.

Further, historically accumulated knowledge is valuable for present-day American intelligence on purely intellectual grounds. After all, this nation had a very short history before it was drawn into the welter of contending cultures and systems of statecraft in which Asians, Europeans and North Africans have been at home for millennia.

Removed from the Eurasian and Mediterranean centers of international relations in the context of both time and space, our nation could not actually experience the standing "otherness" of the multifarious political entities in its world environment before the twentieth century. This circumstance helps explain why Americans tend to cast their worldview and their vision of destiny in essentially futuristic terms, why they know very little about the role of political intelligence in non-American statecraft, and why they have been so very slow and hesitant even in the late twentieth century to accept and institutionalize the principle as a vital component of their country's national defense establishment.

Throughout Asia and in most parts of Europe, by contrast, where the past has always been accepted as an organic and important component of existence, we find that all intelligence-related thought and practice is safely encrypted in historical records to which timeless significance is usually affixed. These, then, should now be studied and compared in the United States with a view to learning just what it is that makes foreign nations often "tick" in unexpected foreign ways, how diverse systems of statecraft and intelligence have always been, and how we should structure ours to best advantage.

ASIA AND AFRICA

The panorama unfolds in Asia between the seventh and fourth centuries B.C. when the Indians, the Chinese, and the Persians succeeded in inventing and systematizing strategic intelligence in three totally different ways and in deference to strikingly divergent ultimate objectives.

The Hindu wisdom that was well captured in the fourth century by Kautilya's *Arthasastra* for the benefit of the Maurya rulers had its ultimate and historically enduring sanction in sacred Hindu texts which tell us that only divine surveillance can assure the deft management of cosmic and earthly affairs of state.

The Chinese sages, by contrast, who steered the Ch'in kingdom to total victory over all "warring states" between the seventh and third centuries B.C. in order then to become the architects of China's first unified empire, scoffed at religion, morality, and established Confucian beliefs as they built a secular totalitarian police state that had most of the attributes nowadays associated with the Leninist-Maoist "counterintelligence state."

The originality of Indian and Chinese approaches to statecraft will never be in dispute. However, in the context of comparative studies in strategic intelligence as conducted at the very end of the twentieth century A.D., the focus should be on the Achaemenid kings of the Persians who had burst upon the Near East in the seventh century B.C. This is so, it is here suggested, because the pre-Islamic Persians were the first in history and the only Asians ever to set the parameters for political intelligence along humanistic lines. True, Persian strategists, like their counterparts elsewhere, knew how to facilitate conquest by fomenting dissidence and treachery within target nations. It is also true that a strong army was always in readiness; that the empire reaching from the Nile to the Aegean in the West and to the Indus and

Jaxartes in the East was intersected by well-planned roads; and that elaborate networks of police and espionage were everywhere on the "qui vive." But "the king's eyes and ears" were also under strict instruction to learn about and respect the traditional languages, belief systems, and institutions of all conquered or otherwise dependent non-Persian peoples so as to cast heterogeneous African, Asian, and European communities into a morally unified international society, symbolized and led by "the king of kings."

Persian statecraft and intelligence, then, were informed by a strategic design that was buttressed by a definite worldview. Although the latter accorded with considerations of political expedience, it had the imprimatur of the Zoroastrian faith to which most royal Achaemenian administrators subscribed. And the central tenets here were Zoroaster's projection of religious universalism and his distinctions between "good" and "evil" and between "the better" and "the bad."

Iran's comprehensive conception of a multicultural empire was introduced into the history of Occidental statecraft by Alexander the Great after he had defeated the Persians and begun building his own culture-transcendant commonwealth. Thereafter it was to have resonant echoes in the Hellenistic successor states, the Roman Empire and the Eastern Christian (Byzantine) empire. However, it failed to move the Orient. True, Persia was acclaimed by friends and foes alike as the "prestige state" throughout its long existence (700 B.C.–700 A.D.). But in Northwest India (long a Persian satrapy), Central Asia, and North Africa the prestige was associated almost exclusively with Persian ways of buttressing secular executive power, chief among them the imperial court system, public architecture, and political intelligence.

This accentuation was to harden between the seventh and sixteenth centuries when Asia's Islamic forces knocked out not only the Persian Zoroastrian and Eastern Christian empires but also scores of other political systems in Europe's Mediterranean region (specifically important provinces of Spain and Italy), in North, East, and Saharan Africa, and in West, Central, South, and Southeast Asia. However, and for reasons detailed in subsequent essays of this book, no Mohammedan conquerors, with the possible exception of the Turks, could come up with frameworks of governance that were capable of assuring stabilization of all that arms and ideology had won while also qualifying as "legitimate" in the eyes of those administering Islam's own religious law.

The resulting vacuum of authoritative guidelines explains—partially at least— why all new Islamic polities, whether Arab, Persian, Afghan, Indian, Mongol or black African, settled down as personal despotisms; why the sophisticated Persian and Byzantine models of statecraft and intelligence were ground down to the nuclear Asian notion of absolute executive power, and why all rulers of the new polities, whether benign or tyrannous in disposition, were particularly keen to institutionalize Iran's systems of espionage and postal communication as shields for their own personal security, power, and survival.

The implications of this development have been far-reaching in several respects. The advent and diffusion of "the personalized state" in Islamic societies and in communities dominated by Islamic superstructures (as in a host of Africa's traditional folk societies), and the corresponding eclipse of the ethnically, culturally, or territorially bounded state, have had the general effect of constricting the range of foreign policy concerns to the limits set by one biography. True, all rulers are morally committed to advance Islam throughout the world, but actual military or political service in this cause does not stipulate the need for the kind of long-range strategic thinking that is requisite in behalf of a state's or nation's security and survival. In the Islamic context then—which diverges greatly from classical Persian, Indian, and Chinese patterns of statecraft—one has to conclude that political intelligence does not usually qualify as strategic intelligence.

A CONGRUENCE OF ORIENTATIONS IN ASIA AND AFRICA

Comparative case studies and surveys of political intelligence in non-Western societies—many of them not included in this volume—have persuaded me that there has long been a congruence of basic orientations on the following themes, both supportive of institutionalized intelligence.

1. The prevalence of different types of despotism and the absence of pronounced concern for the principle of individuation in thought, behavior, and social status combine to foster mistrust, fear, insecurity, and conflict in the ranks of the rulers as well as the ruled. These dispositions make for indirect modes of communication, fifth columns, secret societies, police surveillance, and dense networks of surrogates, undercover agents, and a rich assortment of spies.

2. Authoritative religions, ideologies, philosophies, and other regulatory codes sanction the stern principle of "rule by the rod." They also make full allowance for the paramountcy of conflict in life, the legitimacy of hatred in human relations, and the essentialness of war for the security and well-being of society. Peace, by contrast, is at best a metaphysical reference. It does not emerge from the records either as a politically significant concept or as a well-defined actual condition.

In these circumstances it is not surprising that inconvenient or unfamiliar "others" in the human environment—be it in the immediate family or in distant foreign quarters—are readily cast in the role of enemies who have to be rendered harmless by overt or covert means. The art of warring is thus highly developed as well as variegated throughout Africa and Asia, under the headings of both military and psychopolitical operations. Moreover, no holds are barred in either of such transactions since equivalents for Western notions of peace and international or humanitarian law are missing. However, none—whether directed at threatening personages at home, enemy generals on battlefields, or civilian subjects in foreign nations—is undertaken without foreknowledge of the human target's mind-set.

INTELLIGENCE REQUIREMENTS FOR MILLENNIA

Knowing "the other" who is likely to be or become your enemy or counterplayer in one life situation or another has thus been the primary intelligence requirement for millennia. And indeed how can either military or psychopolitical campaigns to disorient, distract, deceive, subvert, penetrate, encircle, and ultimately capture or destroy individual or national mind-sets succeed without this kind of human understanding? Nor can any understanding be reached without relevant information, and this was supplied—also for millennia—by well-trained and usually highly respected scouts, spies, proxies, covert agents, or enemy hostages. (Xerxes, king of the Persians, was one of many master strategists who had the key to such winning combinations. He was determined, during the onslaught on Greece, to finish off that country and therewith banish the perplexing idea of Europe once and for all. Quizzing a royal Greek held hostage in the Persian camp, he asked: "You once ruled some of those Greeks; so tell me how do those people think?")

Intelligence requirements such as these could assure the integrity and durability of most non-Western systems of statecraft because they were in each case authentic expressions of ruling moral orders. And since the latter were not inactivated during the period of European dominance (the nineteenth century) in world affairs, the former, too, remained in place, albeit often under wraps. This has changed drastically in the twentieth century under the impact of Leninist diplomacy and intelligence as managed by the Soviet Union, mainland China, and leading surrogates of these superpowers. The steady goal here has been to denature the underlying moral orders and thus induce atrophy in independent ruling institutions. And the winning tactics have invariably included the task of identifying the acupuncture points of human targets; accentuating and exploiting affinities between Marxist-Leninist and non-Western orientations to political power, government, society, the individual, and to all manner of conflict and warfare; hyping awareness and hatred of designated enemies; loosening traditional discipline in thought and behavior; brutalizing locally acceptable modes of killing as, for example, in Communist-controlled terrorist operations, and shaping mental dispositions favoring clandestinity and deception so as to make them serve Communist causes of conquest and subversion.

POLITICAL INTELLIGENCE IN THE WEST: STRENGTHS AND WEAKNESSES IN EUROPE AND THE UNITED STATES

What marks the West in counterpoint to the East? Which nations are Western in juxtaposition to those assembled today as non-Western nations? and where are the relevant lines of geographic and cultural separation? Europe is no doubt the original and hence quintessential West, but where in Asia does it take off territorially and culturally? And just how "Western" or "European" have the Americans been in the last five hundred years?

Comprehensive time-transcendent answers to these questions cannot be given because boundaries between East and West—be they territorial, political, or cultural—are known to have fluctuated in the course of international relations, perhaps never more so than in our times. However, in distinguishing Western from other modalities of statecraft and intelligence I feel confident in identifying the irreducible substance of the European West—and therewith also of Western civilization—with classical Greek thought, Roman jurisprudence, and Christianity. These three interdependent orders of ideas deviate from those stressed by non-Western and Communist societies in the following ways—each relevant to an appreciation of the strengths and weaknesses implicit in modern Western systems of political intelligence.

1. The norms set by Greek ways of thought, Rome's secular law, and the New Testament's moral precepts are equally universalist in that they recognize the individual as the measure of life rather than the group to which he belongs. It is the steady impact of this principle upon different European peoples that explains why their civilization has been more inventive and industrious than any other in the world in all fields of life, including those pertaining to political intelligence.

   Thus it is a matter of record that successive generations, beginning with those of ancient Greece, have been so tireless and successful in seeking, collecting, analyzing, and storing new "intelligence" about the earth and its peoples that they ended up creating the world's first and only "academic universe"—the primary and indispensable data bank upon which all intelligence services, be they Western, non-Western, or Communist, go on feeding.

2. The standing Occidental commitment to individualism presents challenges to organized political society not faced in the Orient, Africa, and modern twentieth-century Leninist realms. Since it is axiomatic that neither ideas nor their consequences are easily predictable, it has always been harder in the West to maintain constancy in public order systems than it was and is in places where human beings are programmed to play the roles assigned them by policy or tradition. This explains why it is at times difficult in the West to know just when the exercise of personal freedom infringes upon national security or actually turns into treason, and when, by contrast, freedom is put in jeopardy by undue governmental power.

   The framework for maintaining domestic peace and order and resolving conflicts such as these was set in continental Europe by Rome's secular law as supplemented by Germanic customs, and in England by the common law. In other words, political societies in the West were not conceived either as conflict systems or as closed public orders, and the laws upon which they rest are therefore not secret codes or assemblages of arbitrary rulings but open, readily accessible books.

   On the levels of domestic jurisdiction, then, it is reasonable to suggest that Europeans have had little room, impetus, or opportunity to develop arts of camouflage, deception, and covert action, or, for that matter, to engage seriously in all-out political intelligence.

3. A related measure of the West's distinctiveness that continues to affect dispositions germane to political intelligence is that the moral-religious and the political-secular spheres in society do not coincide in the Christian West as they do in non-Western and Communist societies. The New Testament speaks to man the individual and to his search for inner peace and salvation. Con-

trary, for example, to the sacred teachings of Hinduism, Islam, and Judaism, no claim is made here to regulate domestic politics and direct foreign policies in respect of war and peace. Further, whereas the Old Testament and the Koran instruct their faithful to hate and extinguish their enemies by open, covert, or other surreptitious types of warfare and to prepare such assaults by espionage and prior penetration of the target land, Christians could not find any political or military guidelines in their gospel when they entered the arena of world politics in the fourth century A.D.: all leading references were to love and peace.

THE MATRIX OF POLITICAL INTELLIGENCE IN EAST AND WEST IS WAR

As we know from the long history of politically organized Christendom, remarkable adjustments were made to harmonize relations between religion and statecraft by calling on the time-tested secular legacies of Greek and Roman thought on philosophy, ethics, and law as well as on the arts of war. The morality and propriety of war were duly affirmed under these auspices as was the necessity for knowing and manipulating the enemy general's mind.

Military intelligence was thus firmly incorporated as a vital aspect of warmaking in the West, but the tactics of the battlefield were not supposed to spawn or in any way affect normal—i.e., peaceful—relations with other peoples, and peace as defined in secular law remained the primary value in human relations, whether on domestic or international levels. War, also defined in terms of law, was accepted as an open military confrontation or relationship that disturbed the peace on condition that it be fought lawfully and for just causes. In short, "peace" and "war" are conceived as opposites in the West, and in law as well as in religion—quite in counterpoint to non-Western mind-sets in which these concepts interpenetrate.

LAW AS A BARRIER TO THE DEVELOPMENT OF STRATEGIC INTELLIGENCE IN THE UNITED STATES

This constellation of lead values and ideas has important implications for the cause of the West's strategic intelligence today, nowhere more so than in the United States.

For one thing, it seems to make it theoretically nonsensical to cultivate enmity or awareness of it and to engage in close surveillance and assessment of "others" in peacetime on the mere assumption that war may come sooner or later. Likewise, while camouflage, deception, disinformation, and other diversionary tactics are accepted as legitimate ruses in the context of war, resorting to them in peacetime is readily viewed today as illogical, immoral, or illegal. Not surprisingly, uneasiness intensifies at the mere thought that a covert action or psychopolitical operation might be carried out by recourse to physical violence, or worse, that it might lead to entanglement in what is often described in present-day American scholarship as "secret war."

Now these kinds of war were and continue to be commonplace and "open" in non-Western cultures as well as in all regions, states, and societies decisively controlled by Leninist statecraft. Although they are breaking up states, consuming scores of people in the world, and gravely affecting the national security interests of the United States, they do not qualify officially as "real" war in our view for two reasons. First, these wars do not openly involve adversary states (the subjects of traditional international law) and are never openly declared or announced. And second, a strong wish prevails in the nation to save our concept "peace" from being swallowed by uncongenial concepts of "war"—an eventuality that would threaten the integrity of international law since it is anchored in the distinction between "peace" and "war."

At any rate, claims on behalf of this particular cause keep proliferating in our era. Indeed, as Americans distance themselves from the realities of war, they tend to assign the whole field of foreign relations—and therewith the nation's basic security interests—to the tender mercies of the rule of law, domestic as well as international. The dynamics of diplomacy and policy-making are thus locked out from realistic assessment by static legal or pseudo-legal propositions which tell us as a matter of theory rather than good intelligence findings that war "X" should not be undertaken because the vocabulary of law does not provide for it; that covert action "Y" should be aborted because it actually also *proves* to be covert and thus liable to be judged illegal or criminal; that political or moral commitments to strict confidentiality or secrecy in human relations must be betrayed so that they may be accommodated in what present-day exponents of law have staked out as their exclusive intellectual preserve; or that psychopolitical operations and cold wars of nerves or ideas just make no legal sense, do not damage the nation, and can therefore be disregarded with impunity. Yet this nation surely is at risk today, and that partly at least because events bear out Charles Dickens's dictum that law is or at times may become "a ass—an idiot."

FURTHER IMPEDIMENTS ON THE AMERICAN ROAD TO STRATEGIC INTELLIGENCE: THE LIMITATIONS OF THE WILSONIAN WAR/PEACE DIPLOMACY

In the context of this brief introduction to the place of political intelligence in statecraft some additional comments are appropriate. One is to the effect that the hold of law over diplomacy, foreign policy-making, and national security concerns has been unduly—in this writer's view unconstitutionally—extended. Another suggests that the very idea of law—which is here viewed as a major sustaining element of Western civilization—has suffered serious bone loss in the United States as a result precisely of this kind of arbitrary ideological tampering. A third argues that not even situational or tactical intelligence has a chance to live up to its *raison d'être* as long as law is conscripted to screen off today's diverse modes of warfare from principled assessment so as to focus single-mindedly on the globally irrelevant notion of peace. And the last maintains that strategic intelligence cannot be effective in a democracy when it is micromanaged in public by scores of legislators, prosecutors, and judges, and that it is not even fathomable unless it has the full support and respect of the nation it serves.

Further, but in the same context of inhibited intelligence, it looks at times as if this craft is widely conceived today as a one-shot or ad hoc effort that can be switched on and off at will. Yet it should surely be self-evident that all intelligence work—be it theoretical or practical—is "process" and that it must therefore be continuous and systematic if it is to sustain basic intelligence requirements. Indeed it is questionable whether the United States can ever find the way back to *strategic* thinking, and therewith to the kind of strategic intelligence that marked statecraft in the early years of its existence, unless it retraces its brief journey through world politics with a view to locating the crucial error that got it to the present straits.

In my view we can identify this turning point with two interrelated factors: the war/peace diplomacy as announced in the Woodrow Wilson era and the academic rendition of this subject matter in our institutions of higher learning. Both set the tone for shifting compassless from all-out punitive war and punitive peace in two wars against Germany to an all-out pacificism that calls either for outlawry of war, arms limitation, disarmament, and arms control, or for freezing and destroying weaponry. Indeed, few basic policy decisions responsible for our foreign policy record can be traced either to good intelligence assessments or to geopolitically sound and comprehensive strategic designs.

This mood eventually induced the deliberate decomposition and consequent demoralization of the nation's first modern intelligence community. Not surprisingly, it was responsible also for arresting the evolution of scholarly thought about the intelligence component in statecraft and for flooding academic curricula with "peace studies" that avoid coming to terms with the realities of war and conflict. A review of these offerings and of conflict studies in general also shows that they converge on theoretical, usually ideological musings about the sameness or equivalence of human thought and behavior throughout the world.

FAILURE TO STUDY FOREIGN THOUGHT STRUCTURES

Resolute leveling of this kind led gradually to the widespread conviction that there really are no "others," and that enmity, hostility, and misunderstandings are passing phenomena, always amenable to conciliation or some sort of settlement. In the context of these premises and perceptions it thus nurtured the thesis that political intelligence is not only a superfluous institution but also a rather irritating hindrance in the pursuit of peace. In short, the impression left by the records is to the effect, first, that Americans have been conditioned in recent decades to resist the challenge of examining foreign thought structures, and second, that they have been much too often caught intellectually unprepared and diplomatically off guard by critical shifts of orientation in the ranks alike of friends and foes.

The records of U.S. relations with such openly hostile societies as the U.S.S.R., its East European and Latin American surrogates, mainland China, North Korea, Iran, and Syria thus show convincingly that the nation was easily trapped by deception, disinformation, psychopolitical offensives, and other manifestations of "warrior diplomacy" because it simply did not understand either the mind-sets of culturally different peoples or the mainsprings of Leninist war and conflict theory. It was just as clear in 1989–90, when the United States was taken unawares by the collapse of Leninism in the Soviet Union and the anti-Leninist revolution in Eastern and Central Europe that recent generations of Americans do not even know how Europeans think or what Europe stands for culturally and geopolitically.

THE UNITED STATES MISLAID THE KEYS TO ITS INTELLIGENCE LEGACIES

Several case studies in the present volume illustrate the following general propositions:

- The guardians of statecraft in literate and nonliterate provinces of the non-Western world have been at one throughout the centuries or millennia in viewing the past as the repository of their national and cultural identity and the main source of wisdom and experience in governing "home" peoples and managing relations with "others" in the world.

- Comparisons of these accumulated legacies show a striking convergence on the paramountcy of war and conflict in conceptualizing and conducting international relations and a corresponding absence of commitments to peace, unity, the balance of power, and international law. It goes without saying in light of these historical givens that political intelligence and diplomacy were everywhere allied with "war" rather than with "peace."

- Surveys of present-day wars, revolutions, and violent or low-intensity conflicts as these are being fought, endured, resisted, or compromised in, for example, contemporary India, Sri Lanka, mainland China, Afghanistan, Kampuchea, Myanmar (Burma), Iran, Iraq, Syria, Lebanon, Israel, Peru, Cuba, Nicaragua, and scores of African states, confirm the continuity of local traditions and the corresponding eclipse of recently imported Euro-American norms. In short, the keys to cultural legacies have not been mislaid in Asia and Africa.

- This means in the context of U.S. intelligence requirements in the post-twentieth-century world that non-Western legacies are indispensable data banks also for American statecraft even if some of the recorded thought-ways, images, institutions, and practices appear at first glance too alien to be accommodated by our own conceptual framework.

One of the essays in this book thus suggests that we will not be able to tap the mainsprings of political thought in present-day India and Indianized Asia unless we understand that the principles of war, warrior diplomacy, and intelligence have been hallowed concepts in the region throughout the last two thousand years. Trust in good espionage, for instance, reaches back to the *Rig Veda,* where the spies of the god Varuna are pictured seated around him while the deity holds court over the cosmic universe—much as angels are often rendered in the Christian religious tradition.

Other case studies in this volume follow suit. Since all Asian and African models of statecraft are derivatives or functions of powerful belief systems, U.S. intelligence collection and analysis should be anchored in a thorough understanding of Confucianism, Legalism, and Maoism in China; Shinto and Buddhism in Japan; Islam and Judaism in the Semitic Middle East; and the diverse tribal cults and syncretic creeds in Africa south of the Sahara.

In sum, the American intelligence agenda should call for the acknowledgment that all human contests are in the final analysis mental and psychological, and that they can be won or managed only by those who understand the mind-set of the counterplayer while being absolutely certain also of just who they are themselves and what it is they stand for.

EUROPE'S DATA BANKS ARE CRUCIAL RESOURCES FOR AMERICAN INTELLIGENCE IN THE TWENTY-FIRST CENTURY

This kind of double-knowing is the prerequisite for fashioning strategic intelligence. The challenge facing the United States today is therefore how to acquire it. The first step in that direction should be to move from theory and ideology to history and reality with the firm intention to accept the diverse legacies we find as rich stores of useful ideas about statecraft rather than as dreary records of human shortcomings that are best forgotten. However, and as odd as it may seem, it is usually easier to *dis*cover and come to terms with the past of others than it is to *re*cover and *re*affirm one's own, especially after one has explicitly repudiated that inheritance at some earlier time.

As noted earlier in this introduction, the United States did just that during and after the First World War when its administration recoiled from the entire European States System which it had joined a few decades earlier. The butt of the American displeasure was the concept of "balanced power" and its corollary, secret diplomacy. Overlooked in this reaction was the historically significant fact that *bilancia* in statecraft had been invented and refined by Florentine and Venetian statesmen in Renaissance times when it was being realized, notably by the Venetian republic in the sixteenth century, that continuous bids for unilateral or paramount power were bound to endanger the security of each and all in the Italian commonwealth of associated city-states. And the same concern for collective security and dread of imperial power soon moved the rest of Europe to identify the idea of the balance of power as the mainstay of the all-European concept of separate but independent states and the *sine qua non* of diplomacy and international law, the system's major working references.

ESTRANGEMENT FROM CONTINENTAL EUROPE

The United States had not been present either at the creation of the modern European States System or in the trying centuries during which a very small Europe had gained intellectual ascendancy over Asia, Africa, and America while also managing to survive ceaseless and massive military assaults by Persians, Arabs, North Africans, Turks, and Mongols. This circumstance may explain why Americans did not develop either familiarity with or respect for the intricate modalities of statecraft that account for some of Europe's great achievements in world politics.

Further, it was clear by the end of the nineteenth century that the United States was not only geographically, but also linguistically and hence culturally, too remote from continental Europe—historically the principal stage of just about all crucial transcultural encounters affecting the West—to be able to draw upon the latter's rich fund of accumulated intelligence and experience with protracted wars and conflicts. What the American records show instead is an early predilection for resolving foreign policy problems through reliance on the law of treaties and international peace organizations—two phenomena in diplomacy that also derive directly from continental Europe's heritage of constitutional law and are, in theory at least, unhampered by secret diplomacy and calculations about the balance of power.

This trend was naturally fostered as England became the focus of American dispositions toward Europe in World Wars I and II. Language, literature, and above all the common law were the binding ties that established the United States as the second most important "Anglo-Saxon" country in the world (regardless of its actual composition in the nineteenth century as a "melting pot" of various European peoples), and that conduced on the one hand to a firm Anglo-American compact but on the other to a pronounced estrangement from continental Europe.

Moreover, knowledge of "the other" Europe's culture, geography, history, and law had been sorely missing in Anglo-American war/peace diplomacy already between 1914 and 1945 and was to recede dramatically in the ensuing decades. How otherwise can one explain the ruling notion in American policy-making circles today that Spain, Italy, and Germany have only recently been converted to the rule of law, and that there is really nothing special about constitutionalism and democracy in Europe (never mind the Greek and Latin words)? Actually, we are told, democracy is just as much at home in Fiji and black Africa as it is in "parts of Switzerland."

These propositions and the policies they have come to support would have been dismissed out of hand by the nation's highly educated English-speaking founders. They are patently absurd also today. Put briefly, they attest to the fact that our present leaders—be they diplomats, bureaucrats, scholars, or educators—simply do not know much about the civil law of classical Rome even though it has been the unwobbly pivot of continental Europe's different national legal systems for the last two millennia as well as the nucleus of both the Christian Canon Law and the law of nations. And indeed, recent surveys show that serious civil law studies have long been near-absent in American institutions of higher learning, including law schools, and that they are not offered at the English Inns of Court where they had been introduced by Sir Henry Maine at the beginning of the twentieth century.

THE ACADEMIC NEGLECT OF CONTINENTAL EUROPE'S LAW AND HISTORY AND ITS EFFECT UPON U.S. INTELLIGENCE AND STATECRAFT

This particular gap in education and intelligence "1" in conjunction with the uninhibited trend to overlook or level differences that cannot be readily explained has had desultory effects on American intelligence "2." It was in my view the main roadblock (there were others) when the militarily victorious United States had the historic chance after World Wars I and II to fashion strategically sound designs for continental Europe, the motherland of Western civilization and, in global perspective, the advance base for the protection of American national interests.

The civil law then should be understood as the principal steadying and unifying force in Europe, in times of peace as well as war. Without it there could not have been either the Hanseatic League of separate trading cities or the Grotian law of nations, or—in our times—the European Community and the design for a Europe without frontiers, the latter in many respects a sequence to the medieval Holy Roman Empire. Further, and in stark contrast to the common law which is truly meaningful only to English-speaking peoples, Roman law is conceptually so precise, abstract, lean, and objective that it travels well, at least under good guidance. Records of successful transplantations to non-European environments—as, for example, those relating to Muslim-dominated Spain between the eighth and fifteenth centuries (see the concluding essay in this volume), and to the investment of Roman Dutch law in South Africa, Ceylon and parts of Indonesia from the seventeenth century onward—thus show clearly that the civil law is internationally experienced, as it were, in the context of both internal and external statecraft.

This Roman legacy should have been recognized explicitly as a Euro-American system of ideas for several other politically compelling reasons. It is the core chapter of the transAtlantic community of all Western nations; it generates certain modes of thought, analysis, and communication not fostered by the common law while yet being fully compatible with the latter's lead ideas; and it is a decisive element in the makeup of all continental European mind-sets and institutions.

Next, it is hardly possible to fathom the difference between "West" and "East," or the basic configuration on one hand of Western civilization, on the other of Western Europe, unless one knows the real, albeit invisible, cultural frontier—the line that separates lands and peoples decisively shaped by the law of the First Rome from those long controlled by that of the second or Eastern Christian Rome in Constantinople and its non-European successors. And it goes without saying in the context of the present book that only familiarity with this aspect of Eurasian history can facilitate such requisite efforts in modern political intelligence and statecraft as developing reliable estimates of the qualities, dispositions, and likely alignments of the diverse ethnicities peopling the region; assessing the legitimacy of territorial frontiers; and designing long-range foreign policies for dealing with the region as a whole.

Failure to address these tasks during the embattled twentieth century, joined with failure to recognize the civil law as a rich source of conceptual tools for fashioning winning tactics in the chronic psychopolitical war with the Soviet Union, explains why American policymakers were totally unprepared intellectually and politically for the momentous low-intensity revolution against the Leninist imperium that erupted in 1989 throughout all civil law countries of East Central Europe.

INTELLIGENCE AND THE NEED TO WIN WARS OF IDEAS

Cold wars of ideas consist in essence of nonviolent as well as violent contests between morally and politically distinct collective mind-sets that are designed and carried out as protracted offensive engagements of will power, imagination, intelligence, and tactical astuteness on behalf of values and interests that best symbolize the causes with which the respective protagonists identify.

Warfare of this kind is being categorized today as low-intensity conflict in the United States either because martial violence is normally not called for as, for example, in psychopolitical campaigns of disinformation, deception, and subversion; or because it is deployed covertly and intermittently rather than continuously and openly as in what is termed "real" war in the West.

Such distinctions may be justified in theory. However, they are gainsaid today by the doctrines and tactics associated with present-day enemies of the West as well as by the records of international history.

Comparative studies of low-intensity aggressions as these have been programmed against the West under the auspices of Leninist, Maoist, and Islamic (notably Shi'ite) power centers suggest that our lines of differentiating between "low"- and "high"-intensity wars are too fuzzy to be fully acceptable in the context of realpolitik. For whether conceived in religion or political ideology, wars of words and ideas are meant to provide the necessary backdrop or official *raison d'être* for all strictly military wars. Further, no low-intensity assault on Western values comes to mind that has not either culminated in or merged with armed warfare or terrorist action undertaken on behalf of the very same goals. In short, the low-intensity conflicts here under consideration have been planned, managed, and experienced as high-intensity war operations, and the conclusion is irrebuttable in this writer's view that the West has been kept effectively under siege throughout this century.

Next, logic suggests that wars of ideas are fought in terms of ideas and for the sake of ideas. It follows that ideas, be they on the offensive or the defensive, must be in good fighting shape conceptually if they are to sustain the causes on behalf of which they are enlisted. A survey of twentieth-century contests shows that this has not been the case.

Recent internal upheavals in all major Marxist-Leninist societies confirm what many students of this ideology had long surmised, namely that it had not been designed either as a coherent moral philosophy or a body of well-tested social and economic theories but as a world-spanning aggressive political action program fit to undo the substance and framework of Europe's culture. As such, Marxism-Leninism does not even pretend to deal seriously with values and ideas except when it comes to the task, first, of selecting and analyzing the ruling norms in the enemy camp that require destruction, among them "the independent state," "the free individual," "democracy," and "peace"; and second, of manipulating these ideas by reversing or inverting their original meanings so as to invalidate all of them along with the words in which they are communicated, thus inducing confusion, moral inertia, and political impotence in Western mind-sets.

A preliminary assessment of the Marxist-Leninist cold war offensive as it has been sustained throughout this century allows for the conclusion in 1988–89 that the Communist regime states *had* won what may well be the most significant war of ideas in recorded times. True, there are those in our society who accept massive revolts within these empires as irrebuttable evidence that the Marxist-Leninist ideology is now so cracked and tattered as to be rightly adjudged defeated and defunct. But overlooked in such estimates are the following factors:

1. The Leninist ideology was invented to serve the cause of totalitarian power. The recent removal of the protective ideological camouflage *within* Soviet and in some respects also Chinese orbits was calculated to leave a vast emptiness free even of sham ideas so that it might be filled with nothing but the kind of arbitrary political power that ruling Communist regimes deem necessary for winning the cold war against the West on the *outer* frontiers they claim.

2. The second set of circumstances that explains the Communist advantage in hostile low-intensity conflicts relates to the simple fact that U.S. statecraft is handicapped in this theater of diplomacy and intelligence. Not only are Americans culturally not conditioned to wage relentless semantic warfare for the sake of ruining the thoughtways and ideas of non-Americans, but they do not make a point of linking the conduct of foreign relations to carefully selected and protected concepts and words.

The nation, then, is not really prepared to compete in a type of political warfare in which success hinges on thorough knowledge of two different sets of ideas: those singled out by, for example, Leninist adversaries as inimical to basic American or general Western interests, and those that sustain, protect, and secure the core of the national or cultural "self." Rather, the prevalent disposition in this conflict-ridden century has been a pronounced preparedness to compromise the integrity of American or Western values whenever these seem to counter the nation's stubborn dream images of one world, one type of man, and one kind of moral and political truth in matters pertaining to internal and external statecraft.

This orientation explains why the United States tends to overlook or not contest wrong readings of its value code (and it happens to be rendered in the language of law with which no one outside the Occident is thoroughly familiar); why our legal system is too fractured to provide responsible guidance for clear thinking in foreign affairs; why our intelligence community is often rudderless and immobilized; why our constitutional frame of reference for fashioning foreign policies is in a state of disarray—in short, why the United States has long been trapped in a wilderness of language without compass indicating exits.

COUNTERINTELLIGENCE MUST WATCH FOR WAYWARD MOVEMENTS OF STRATEGICALLY IMPORTANT IDEAS

The vicissitudes that beset the career of the old, once-confident word "democracy" in present-day American statecraft illustrate this debilitating confusion very well in the context of the nation's foreign as well as domestic affairs. Sent traveling throughout the world as the nation's emissary-plenipotentiary, this one word is charged with the mission to tell all other governments and peoples just what the United States stands for morally and politically, and what they, too, are expected to identify with.

But is "democracy" the right word to do battle for the West in its cold war with all Leninist and scores of non-Leninist, non-Western societies? Does the word continue to project the ideas for which it had been coined originally *after* it had been "borrowed" or hijacked with our consent so as to provide suitable cover for all manner of despotisms? And can it mesh or make the needed connections with the thought structures and values that go on sustaining Asian and African peoples?

My answers to these questions are essentially negative for reasons spelled out in several subsequent essays. True, "democracy" may still linger on in some Western and Westernized minds as a convincing code word or metaphor for "political freedom," "the rule of law," and "individual civil liberties." Now these are complex presuppositions for the effective installation of democratic forms of government, but we have cast them aside for purposes of policy formation either in ignorance of their existence or in deference to the transcultural popularity—be it spurious or sincere—of this one particular word. In their stead the United States has come to stress such essentially mechanistic processes as arranging for elections and for a plurality of political parties.

It cannot be concluded from the record that the American "democracy" campaign was mapped well enough to have salutary effects either in the non-Western states to which it addresses itself expressly or in the United States itself. In the non-Western world it founders in my view for the following reasons:

- In its new trivialized version, democracy does not really stand for much that is of substantive value. Rather than revitalizing and solidifying the internal orders of existing states, it has brought moral confusion and political uneasiness to scores of once self-respecting political entities. This impact has been accentuated in the last decade by the realization that the American "model" democracy is fast shedding its prestige and promise as governing American institutions appear incapable of arresting the nation's social degeneration into fields of unrelieved criminal violence.

- On the level of external affairs, meanwhile, the "democracy" campaign has been an unmitigated disaster for the cause of the independent nation-state, and that for one main reason: its American draftsmen seem determined to "democratize" the management of such allegedly low-intensity conflicts as insurgencies, guerrilla wars, and civil wars even when they are actually and knowingly dealing either with foreign military attacks on the state or with determined nationalist countermoves to defend or recover the independence of the state.

- In either case our policy formula suggests the following responses: tone down or negotiate with the enemies; make treaties with them; arrange for occasions to vote; and try to coalesce with them thereafter. And in either case, too, one low-intensity contest after another has been lost on our side in military battles as well as in the minds (and lives) of millions of "freedom fighters" who were let down by "democracy" and by those who contrived new meanings and new uses for this word.

THE IMPORTANCE OF THE ROMAN CIVIL LAW FOR ISSUE IDENTIFICATION IN U.S. STATECRAFT

Reflections on the causes and effects of the American program to democratize not only the governing institutions of non-Communist Asian, Latin American, and African polities but also their ways of conducting foreign relations suggest to this writer that the fateful decomposition first of the democracy concept and thereafter of non-Western societies might not have occurred had our policymakers used their heritage of civil law concepts for purposes of issue identification.

A comparison of the "democracy" drama as it played itself out in China's Tiananmen Square and at Germany's Berlin Wall in the epochal autumn days of 1989 illustrates this proposition.

U.S. statecraft was not prepared to deal expeditiously with either of these momentous yet strikingly divergent developments. Inhibited by regnant doctrines of egalitarianism and universalism, policymakers and their intelligence advisers did not make allowance for culturally quite various traditions and orientations in such closely linked fields of life as law, government, and the dynamics of individualism. True, mainland China and East Central Europe were alike in that both were being ruled by totalitarian Leninist regimes. True, too, that the revolutionary democracy movement has been spearheaded in both instances by the young; and most significantly perhaps that the members of this heroic pioneering age group were born and brought up as Communists in two of the harshest Leninist environments—one in Asia, the other in Europe. Yet there are important differences between the two uprisings, and they may be briefly circumscribed as follows.

The East Germans have the full backing of Europe's civilization in which their nation had evolved. They know its history and the laws it had spawned; they live each day surrounded by its legacies of religion, architecture, literature, art, and music. Therefore they can spell out the many interlocking norms and values that are merely implied in the term "democracy" as it is being heard and used today by freedom fighters elsewhere in the world. This kind of culture consciousness gave them the measure for judging Leninist rule and the self-confidence to reclaim what they knew was theirs. Further, they felt free to remind local German surrogates of Leninism that they, too, "belonged" and should therefore be ready to join in the task of reforming the governance of the state. Lastly, culture consciousness gave the revolutionaries the courage to act resolutely yet serenely and spontaneously on behalf of freedom and democracy by joining in inspired but orderly demonstrations and by staging a dramatic massive exodus into friendly neighboring lands on *their* side of the cultural frontier separating West from East.

The Chinese freedom fighters, by contrast, were all alone. They could not step back into the past looking for cultural sanctions of their daring undertaking. For one thing, their magnificent pre-Maoist civilization simply does not know the concept of democracy and has no equivalent for what the West understands as "law." For another, the Maoist engineers of thought control had spared no effort to purge the history books and anesthetize the human faculty for remembrance. Speaking in the value language of an alien civilization, the revolutionary elite could not communicate reliably with the masses of their less educated co-citizenry. Nor could they count on the effective support of those in governmental strata who were sympathetic to their cause. Further, but again in contrast to the East Germans, the Chinese were trapped in the vast Asian landmass of Leninism from which there is no easy exit any longer. Also, they were programatically deceived by the top brass of China's totalitarian apparatus. In short, whereas the Communist revolution was compelled to let its German children go—at least for the time being—it had no trouble devouring its Chinese progeny in the kind of bloodbath that has typified Leninist statecraft throughout the century.

The significance of these two episodes for U.S. political intelligence may be briefly summarized as follows. Whether viewed as separate low-intensity conflicts or as connected battles in an ongoing transcultural war of ideas, they vividly illustrate certain standing flaws in the American approach to such contests.

Thus we relearned in 1989 what we had already learned in the course of World War II, the Maoist takeover of China and the ill-fated German, Polish, Czech, and Hungarian uprisings against Soviet totalitarianism in the forties, fifties, and sixties, namely:

- that the well-assembled records of European and Chinese culture histories— all "soft" sources—had not been studied;
- that relevant thought systems were not analyzed and could therefore not be compared;
- that reliable estimates of how Marxism-Leninism plays on the one hand in different sectors of Europe, on the other in China, could not be formulated in the existing vacuum of knowledge; and
- that American intelligence services were unable in such circumstances to keep track of shifting trends in the century's historically decisive war of ideas.

Conjointly these negatives explain why the United States has not had either comprehensive policy designs for its global democracy campaign or precise contingency plans for the unfolding of the democracy revolution in each of many separate regional theaters. Indeed, our foreign policy record in both Europe and China leaves the impression that we never knew whether, where, or in which circumstances it would be in our vital interests to render the kind of decisive support that would assure success or at least forestall total failure.

For example, the Tiananmen Square tragedy might not have occurred had we taken pains to persuade the young Chinese activists during the formative stages of their revolutionary program to express their hatred for totalitarianism and their longing for freedom in the rich value language of Confucian China rather than in that of Occidental democracy, and had we coupled this advice with the suggestion that they had a perfect model for their aspirations in the spectacular achievements of the Republic of China (Taiwan).

Such psychopolitical moves might have been forthcoming had the United States subscribed to James Forrestal's strategic vision of Taiwan as "the whole key to the future in the Pacific. He who controls Formosa can oversee the whole coast of continental Asia. It is from bases here that we must maintain a forward posture in a postwar Asia" (Vernon Walters, *Silent Missions,* 1978, p. 111).

This was not to be the thrust of U.S. policy in the ensuing decades during which American scholars and policy planners were totally, and for the most part enthusiastically, absorbed in following the evolution of victorious Maoist China. The hope here was not that the totalitarian regime might be induced to democratize itself but that it would condescend to strike a few reassuring diplomatic bargains with us. The Kuomintang thoughtways and values of the defeated Chinese, by contrast, have not merited serious assessment in American statecraft during the last half century. The nation was therefore as unprepared for the phenomenal socioeconomic and political success of the ROC as it was for the socioeconomic collapse and political betrayals of the PRC—all symbolized by the events on Tiananmen Square.

A few technical observations by way of concluding the opening section of this book: All themes and propositions accentuated in the foregoing pages receive further analysis in the ensuing substantive essays. The Introduction is long because it had to be designed as a unifying frame of reference for eight rather different studies; as a guide to readers; as a synoptic overview of the state of the art in present-day intelligence affairs; and as an open plea for further research.

The book as a whole may be said to carry the following general convictions.

A. 1. Strategic intelligence is the major prerequisite for the successful conduct of international relations.
   2. It is indispensable in anarchical times like ours when the technically unified world society is morally and politically too divided and conflicted to assure a modicum of order and security to its diverse constituencies.
   3. The United States did not develop this dimension of statecraft in the twentieth century. The challenge to do so is peremptory now, at the threshold of the twenty-first century, when it is clear that we can no longer either promote or defend our vital interests by reliance on military preparedness alone.

B. 1. Intelligence and diplomacy are not conceptually autonomous universal givens. Rather, they are derivatives and expressions of the particular society, culture, or ideology in terms of which they are being activated.

2. This means that there are as many modalities of this statecraft as there are actors in world politics at any given time. It is thus axiomatic that the intelligence agencies of any one actor in global politics must know how political intelligence plays elsewhere in the world.

C. Intelligence and statecraft touch all of life, whether experienced vocationally or academically. The subject is therefore studied best by tapping multiple sources of learning.

International Order in a Multicultural World

I

International history richly documents the thesis that political systems are transient expedients on the surface of civilization, and that the destiny of each linguistically and morally unified community depends ultimately upon the survival of certain primary structuring ideas around which successive generations have coalesced and which thus symbolize the society's continuity. This cultural substratum of norm-setting beliefs and linguistic guidelines for thought spawns, supports, or ejects a given society's political system, just as it also determines the general cast of its religions, art styles, social structures, and dispositions to the outside world. In short, then, a culture is all of a piece and careful study is required before one can assess and adequately deal with the political systems of the day.

Next, the inhabited world has been multicultural from the beginning, if only because different languages have brought forth different processes of thought formation and different types of basic norms and ideas. For example, India and China were able to preserve their identities throughout millennia and despite the heavy incidence of political turbulence, natural disasters, and widespread poverty because they held fast to a life-sustaining confidence in the perennial harmony and order of the cosmic universe.

According to the intricate metaphysics of Hindus, Buddhists, and Jains, all things, including humans, come into being as aspects of a single world manifestation. The phenomena of past and future, time and space, life and death are not problematical here since they are perceived to be mere elements of this one great transcendent form of which every part is in accord with all. Further, and for the same reason, no particular importance adheres in biography or ideas of the self. The aim of existence for a believing Hindu is rather to carry out the caste role assigned him at birth so that selfless performance of *dharma* may assure maintenance of cosmic harmony.

Hindu India's stamina throughout its long and troubled history is in large measure a function of the caste system. By providing Indians with religious, moral, and social security, it endowed them with a collective identity that could remain intact despite centuries of alien rule. The logic of these structural norms stipulates further that non-Hindus have to be perceived as outsiders. True, resident groups of Muslims and Christians were casted in later times in terms of their particular occupations. Yet no one not associated with Hinduism could be born a Brahman, a Kshatriya, or

This essay appears here in its original version. It was shortened as Chapter 26 of *The Expansion of International Society*, Hedley Bull and Adam Watson, eds. (Oxford: Clarendon Press, 1984) and is printed with permission of the press.

a Sudra; nor could he hope to gain spiritual merit so as to be able to participate in those cycles of reincarnation that would bring him nearer to Nirvana and release from life. Above all, perhaps, no one not a Hindu could come close to finding meaning in Sanskrit and such sacred texts as the Laws of Mani or the *Mahabharata*—texts that transmit and illustrate all basic Hindu norms and values, and that continue to be mandatory as well as cherished literature for modern Indians in all walks of life.

The pivot in traditional China's normative order as it had prevailed on all levels of thought and society until the mid-twentieth century was belief in the unchanging demands of the heavenly order and determination to maintain this harmony by strict control of human behavior. The main ordering agency was the Confucian family system with its carefully graded relationships, each subject to its own set of unalterable rights, responsibilities, and attitudes, and all held in place by the head of the family, the chief of the clan, the elders of the village, or the superior of the guild. The human being in this culture realm was thus primarily an aspect of the family or other association to which he belonged, a small segment in the intricate web of human relationships that made up society and civilization. The logic of the Chinese worldview therefore required total stress on the person's moral obligations to others; it did not even allow for the conception of individual liberties.

The administration of China was modeled upon that of the natural Confucian family. Conceived as the Middle Kingdom and the abode of civilization writ large rather than as a territorially bounded state, China was deemed to constitute a family of nations. Ruled by the Father Emperor in accordance with Heaven's Mandate, it too consisted of elder and younger sons—all inferior peoples in the sinocentric universe, yet each subject to tutelage through force and persuasion and endowed with special tasks, privileges, and tribute assessments.

In explaining the cast of mind responsible for this entire scheme of multileveled yet organically linked interactions, Sinologists point out that all Chinese thinking is essentially "relational thinking." Influenced by a language which lacks the subject-predicate pattern in sentence structure, the Chinese did not develop the law of identity in logic or the concept of substance in philosophy.[1]

The systems of thought, norms, and values that sustained China and India for millennia as continuing civilizations were radically different from each other in most respects. However, they converged on this: both focused on society viewed as a complex of diverse groups and both stood for preservation of that which was; but neither recognized the individual human being as an autonomous person and the ultimate source of thought. Neither was therefore hospitable to innovation.

Similar factors combined to favor the integrity on the one hand of other literate cultures in the Orient—among them those of Japan, Cambodia, Burma, and the Semitic West Asian realms of the Islamized Arab and Arabized peoples and the Jews; and on the other, of all nonliterate societies—among them those in black Africa. The cultural map of that continent as completed by modern linguists and anthropologists shows more than one thousand small communities, each different from the other, yet all participating in a common heritage marked by the absence of writing and the perfection of compensatory carriers of thought. Here, where human communication required the physical presence of the other, language evolved as a mode of action rather than as an instrument for reflection or a mirror of reflected thought. This circumstance sets definite limits upon the elaboration of theories, systems, generalizations, and the kind of ideas that underlie, for example, Indian metaphysics and European jurisprudence.[2]

Dependence on orality also implies constraints on the control of space. The viable African community thus simply had to be the small linguistically, ethnically, and morally unified community in which each human being was, above all, a representative of the family, absolutely dependent on his "umbilicals" (Noni Jabavu's phrase). In the logic of such a basic setup, other people must be perceived as outsiders, subject to distrust, enmity, and scapegoating as well as to attack and enslavement. Greater unions of ethnically distinct groups evolved in all parts of the continent, usually through conquest; however, most succumbed to fragmentation after the conqueror's death, being too conflicted to endure. Security and order were closely identified with the small folk society. Yet nothing in black Africa's millennial history suggests that peace was included in this constellation of values and norms. The records indicate rather that conflict was accepted on all levels of existence, and that violence and war, whether in the form of regicide, succession wars, civil wars, raids, or full-fledged intertribal wars, were endemic everywhere.

The major sustaining conceptions that distinguish Europe's literate civilization are wholly different from, in important respects even contrary to, those identified with all other literate and nonliterate cultures. Foremost among them is the idea of individuation. This principle, which is rooted in the linguistic and intellectual heritage of Greece and Rome, was to remain the guiding force in Western approaches to the arts, sciences, and letters as well as to religion, ethics, politics, and law. The primary concern in each of these contexts was not the age-set, the family, an economic class or a caste; not "man, the father," "man, the sudra," or "man, the umbilical," but the individual human being viewed here as the exclusive source of thought and the carrier of rights as well as obligations. This is as apparent in such literary forms as the tragedy and the novel as it is in systems of law and government. The English common law certainly differs significantly from the Roman civil law, but both normative orders converge on the commitment to identify the essence of law in counterpoint to other norm-engendering schemes such as nature, religion, or reliance on sheer force; to cast human associations, including those of the state and the church, in reliable legal molds; and to emancipate the individual from the group by defining his status not only as an autonomous person but also as a citizen of his state or city.

Numerous instruments and agencies evolved in the course of European and American history for the purpose of assuring these objectives, among them constitutions and bills of rights. What is noteworthy today about all these norms and models is the fact that they constitute severely abbreviated renditions of the general code of ruling values and beliefs. Just as one has to know that *dharma* is the basic theme in traditional Indian life and thought before one can appreciate the fact that the Indian kingdom, being the patrimony of the warrior caste, is rightly associated with the commitment to wage war, so must one know that the typically European idea of a "law of nature" could not have evolved before "law" as such had been carefully set apart from "nature." Likewise, such phrases as "the rights of man" or "the dignity of man" are meaningless unless one remembers that "man the in-dividual" had been carefully detached from such indeterminate generic references as "mankind" or "humankind." And conversely, it is clear that only this European view of the human being allows for meaningful universalization. Lastly, individu-alism stands for inventiveness, and inventiveness makes for intentional develop-ment. In counterpoint to all other cultures, that of the West has therefore long been identified with risk, discovery, and change. Indeed, and as suggested by Robert Redfield, it may be said to have invented progress and reform.[3]

II

In the absence of a common language, a common pool of memories, and shared ways of thinking, reasoning, and communicating, it is hard to fathom a "world culture" (or for that matter a "world history"), at least if one takes ideas seriously. The evidence points instead to a plurality of frames of reference. Neither of these statements implies that cultures are static or destined to endure for ever. Nor do they suggest that cultures do not interact, or that one set of concepts and institutions cannot be deeply influenced from without. We thus learn from the history of the eastern Mediterranean region that classical Greece was closely linked to Egypt and Persia by commercial, intellectual, and diplomatic relations, but that even after Alexander and his successors merged all three realms into a single Macedonian states system, each of them nonetheless continued to retain its cultural identity.

Studies of trade between Ming China and Japan during the fourteenth to six-teenth centuries enlarge on this motif. Each of these East Asian societies was com-mitted to the promotion of commerce. Yet this convergence proved irrelevant be-cause the Chinese and Japanese understandings of the very idea of trade were incompatible. For the Chinese, trade was just an annoying aspect of the tribute system which they wanted to restrict. They valued the periodic Japanese missions mainly as symbolic confirmations of Japan's willingness to pay tribute. For the Japanese, by contrast, trade was the *raison d'être* of tributary relations—a Chinese conception they viewed as utterly humiliating and undesirable.[4]

Trade, then, in no way narrowed the culture gap. In fact the attempt to engage in it conduced to a widening rather than a narrowing of the distance between two contending worldviews, an impression that gains poignancy when one recalls that Zen Buddhist monks—the elite responsible for introducing Chinese culture to Ja-pan—tried tirelessly to mediate the conflict between these conflicting persuasions. The record of diplomatic relations throughout this epoch thus makes for instructive reading. It is replete with Chinese threats and reprimands on the order of this one: "It is the common rule of propriety that barbarians should respect the Middle King-dom. One principle in both ancient and modern times has been for the small to serve the great. . . ."[5]

The Japanese complied occasionally with China's technical requirements. How-ever, they remained adamant on matters of substance as the following letter (1382) shows:

> I have heard that the Three Emperors established order and the Five Emperors came to the throne each in turn. How should only the Middle Kingdom have her master while

the barbarians did not have their rulers? Heaven and Earth are vast; they are not monopolized by one ruler. The universe is great and wide, and various countries are created
each to have a share in its rule. Now the world is the world's world; it does not belong
to a single person.[6]

Hung-wu's attempt to bring Japan back into his tributary system is reckoned to
have been a total failure, despite strong Buddhist influences on the Shogunate. In
fact the tone of Japan's diplomatic correspondence suggests strongly that Buddhism—one of the world's great religions which addresses mankind as a whole—
was made to cede to Shinto, a specifically Japanese order of norms and values.[7]
And the Buddhist message was similarly blunted, adapted or nationalized in Sino-
Indian relations when the faith was carried from India to China[8] and in India's
relations with Southeast Asia.[9] In the latter context it is interesting to note that
Hinduism, a specifically Indian creed, could be implanted, for example, in Cambodia and Indonesia, albeit shorn of most caste aspects, but that Buddhism was
ejected from its Indian homeland in obvious deference to the sustained force of
Hinduism.

The diffusion of Buddhism, then, did not conduce to "world culture" or world
unity, and neither did that of Christianity or Islam, also universal creeds. Statistics
indicate, to be sure, that x million people profess to being Christians or Muslims.
Observations and scholarly literature, however, provide uncontestable evidence
first, that the meaning of each of these religions differs significantly from region to
region; and second, that the difference is in each case an expression of a given
people's earlier beliefs and values.

However tolerant in accommodating deviations, the faithful in the Arabian
heartland of Islam are thus definitely at odds with certain Iranian or Turkish renditions of their faith, and find much that is entirely alien to them in the beliefs and
practices of, for example, the American Black Muslims or Islamic communities in
black Africa. As J. P. Trimingham remarks in his analysis of the resilience of Bantu
culture, whereas in the Near East peasant beliefs were thoroughly Islamized, in
Africa the parallel elements bear the mark of their African origins. Here, he notes,
where the traditional world remains real, religious life rests on a double structure,
namely the animistic substructure and the Islamic superstructure.[10]

The records of Christianization tell of similar transformations. European Christians, be they Catholics or Protestants, find few affinities with Christianity as experienced, for example, in Dahomey (Benin), Zaire, Uganda, and southern Nigeria,
where the faith is thoroughly Africanized, or in Haiti and the Indian communities
of North and South America. Indeed, and as evidenced in the last centuries by
relations between Russia and most of Eastern Europe, there is a culturally and
strategically important line separating communities Christianized by Rome from
those Christianized by Constantinople. Prominent among the latter are the Russians
who succeeded to the imperial Byzantine Greek Orthodox tradition before experi-
encing that of their Mongolian conquerors, and who remained essentially untouched
by the great movements of the Renaissance and humanism.[11] Prominent among the
former are Baltic peoples, Poles, Germans, Bohemians, Hungarians, Croats, and

others who participated throughout history in the political, legal, and moral systems constituting Western Europe's civilization. Russia's imperial control over these peoples—whether czarist or Marxist-Leninist—has therefore invariably led to revolts and thus to regional instability, since the fundamental sustaining ideas of these two cultures are discordant in their essentials. The ongoing turbulence in that area of the world, officially sanctioned as it were by the post–World War II agreements of Yalta and Helsinki, may therefore in considerable measure be ascribed to the West's misperceptions of cultural realities.

Secular theories and ideologies undergo similar transpositions in their passage from one thought world to another. This was as true of eighteenth-century European interpretations of Confucianism and twentieth-century American understandings of Indian metaphysics as it was of medieval Arab/Islamic attempts to find formulations of classical Greek philosophy that would be compatible with their own traditional truths, and of nineteenth-century Chinese decisions to accept the Occidental law of nations as a useful aid in planning China's border defense while disallowing its validity as a code of meaningful norms.[12]

In short, then, ideas are not transferable in their authenticity, however adept and dedicated the translators.[13] This does not mean, of course, that cultures and conceptual orders (just as nations in this regard) cannot be smashed deliberately by armed force or coercive manipulations of thought and its expression.

III

The world has manifold political systems as it has manifold cultures. One culture realm may consist of diverse politically separate units as evidenced by traditional India, where numerous warring kingdoms were coexisting in the morally unified Hindu order; by black Africa, where ethnically and politically distinct societies are usually hostile to each other while yet complying with the same basic values; by the Islamic Middle East, where relations between different caliphates, sultanates, empires, and states have been marked by endemic strife even as all contending parties are at one in acknowledging the principles implicit in the Dar-al-Islam; and by the medieval Holy Roman Empire and the modern European states system whose separate provinces were similarly engaged in adversary politics while at the same time standing for Europe's unity of thought and experience. Conversely, of course, it needs to be stressed that one and the same political system may comprise a variety of culturally unique fields of thought and experience. Since this was and continues to be true of most empires and international organizations, it is necessary for academic as well as practical political reasons to assess the cultural factor in each case and to monitor its changes over time. In fact, useful comparisons of empires and other multicultural political orders simply cannot be conducted unless one lifts the cover of such generalizing modern trade terms as "empire," "imperialism," "expansion," "order," "state," "law," "bureaucracy," "elite," etc. so as to examine the underlying realities. Only then, it is here suggested, can one proceed to ask: "What was new about the European Empires?" and "In which if any ways did the reactions of dependent peoples to European administrations differ from those registered by dependent peoples in other, i.e., non-European, empires?"

Empires are legion in history. Among those associated with the Orient and parts of Africa one thinks of the Assyrian, the Egyptian, the Chinese, the Mongolian, the Persian, the Turkish, and the Arab imperial systems. In the Americas several expansionist, well-organized Indian imperialisms come to mind, while Europe is identified with the Macedonian, Roman, and later Byzantine empires. All these designs have been carefully studied, assessed, and compared, and it is thus possible to draw attention to some indisputable conclusions.[14] One is that all great non-Western orders, with the possible exception of Achaemenid Persia, have always been despotisms; the other indicates that they were tax-taking rather than legislating empires, and that they did not interfere much in the customs of the communities they ruled if only because they insisted on preserving rigid lines of discrimination between themselves as imperial establishments and all others. Furthermore, none of the Orient's vast political conglomerates could accommodate the image of man as an individual representative of the human species. Cognitive thought about "humanity" or "mankind" was therefore not developed there, and a "world order" regulated by universally valid norms could not be fathomed. Administrative policies were thus aimed exclusively at securing the self-view and interest of the dominant imperial power.

This could be said also of the empires built by European nations, for each of them was permeated by convictions of its own supremacy. The world view, however, informing the Occidental designs was at all times markedly different in the sense that it did not screen out the possibility of recognizing the essential, purely human factor under the trappings of attributes assigning inferiority to certain classes of people. Defeat and spoliation were brought to countless nations in the wake of European conquests, in both classical and modern times. Yet, and in stark contrast to the expansionist thrusts carried out throughout the millennia in the Orient, those originating in the Occident were challenged and at times redeemed in the very homeland of the culture because they were found to violate moral norms to which universal and hence superior validity was assigned.

The millennial Roman Empire was a legislating empire.[15] In that capacity it could introduce the idea of *humanitas* into liberal arts education as the major goal of intellectual aspiration, if only because Roman thinking was decisively guided by Latin (see *supra,* this chapter). Further, it could fashion law and jurisprudence as systems of objectively valid concepts around which men of various origins could rally, and finally, it could institute reforms that altered local customs.

This particular heritage was reinforced in Europe by the New Testament, which is addressed to everyone everywhere and has been consistently interpreted as a severely demanding moral code that commits believers to aid their fellow men— regardless of whether they are friends or foes. Dispositions such as these were activated by the expansion of Europe after the great voyages of discovery and the ensuing establishment of empires in America and parts of Africa and Asia. They thus help explain why European history is so rich in biographies of the kind exemplified in the sixteenth century by the Spanish Dominican Bartolomé de Las Casas and in the nineteenth century by David Livingstone, the Scottish missionary and explorer, and why records are replete with projects to improve the lot of mankind as well as with successful reforms in the actual administration of culturally alien peoples—concerns not dominant in any non-Western empire.

The pacing of these revisionist endeavors was quickened during the twentieth century throughout the world's nonself-governing areas in response to the following developments:

- the spread on the one hand of universalist values, on the other of nationalist movements—both Western in inception;
- the occurrence of two prolonged world wars which had particularly weakening effects upon the European nations;
- the rise to prominence in world affairs of the United States, which is conditioned by its history to think of liberty, equality, and opportunity as the birthrights of men everywhere, and that is inclined therefore to overlook cultural differences;
- the creation, after each of the two wars, of international organizations that were structured in accordance with Euro-American models of constitutional federalism and related Occidental norms and values; and
- the effective propagation of Marxism-Leninism, notably of its combat ideology and its doctrine that "imperialism" is associated exclusively with the capitalist states of Europe and America, and that all colonial peoples, led by the international Communist Party, must rise against these oppressors.

These factors combined to provide the auspices under which one European state after the other proceeded to dissolve its empire and to grant political independence to former dependencies—an unprecedented set of decisions in the long history of empire that was to continue in the annals of the Communist empires of the Soviet Union, China, and North Vietnam.

IV

The responses of the non-Western nations to these developments in international affairs have been greatly various, and the same holds naturally for the impact of the responses upon world society. No assessment can therefore be definitive, least of all one that is supposed to aim at generalization and brevity. The present limited attempt addresses the following questions:

1. Which aspects of Western civilization have proved to be generally attractive, perhaps even irresistible? How were they understood and transposed in non-Western societies by indigenous policy-making elites, and what can be said in this regard about their mediating functions?

2. Which are the critical concepts and institutions—the ones, namely, that were taken for granted in the modern West as incontestably universal norms, but that were misunderstood or dropped altogether by recipient nations?

3. How does Westernization relate to modernization, and what can one say about the effect of these and related processes upon "system" and "order" in world politics?

It seems to have been generally recognized by all elites in the non-European world that Europe's civilization could be made to speak to everyone. Contrary to their own essentially closed conceptual schemes, the intruding alien was an open invitation to explore the unknown, question that which exists, arrive at new truths, aim for intellectual freedom, and thus participate in the universe of learning—a phenomenon openly acknowledged only in the Occident.

The main agency providing access to this life-style was education, and Europe offered it in an entirely new key. Symbolized in later phases of Westernization by the university and its maze of interconnected disciplines as well as by medical schools, law schools, learned societies, and in modern times by education-minded philanthropists, it has been the irresistible magnet drawing aspiring members of local elites into close relationships, first with Europe and later with North America. However, none of these institutionalized intercultural encounters could have occurred, it is here suggested, had it not been for the orientation toward learning that was exemplified in the Orient as well as later in Africa by an altogether unique type of human being, the self-directed individual European whose commitment to learn about foreign lands and peoples was basically personal and voluntary, far exceeding the needs of the colonial administration in whose service he usually stood.

One looks in vain for such public-spirited elites in earlier Asian imperialism. There are those today who maintain that English rule in India, as for that matter all Western imperialism, was in no way different from former exploitation. What is being overlooked by them are two incontestable facts. First, it was the European elite that reconstructed India's history, art, and architecture; rediscovered India's languages, religions, and sacred texts; and identified the region's legal, social, and political traditions in their full complexity, even as it worked out the compromises between local customs and English common law, equity, and constitutionalism that were essential if India were ever to exist as a unified nation. Second, the West, personified in such men as Sir William Jones, called forth Indian nationalism by giving this fragmented land a new sense of its own old cultural values and achievements. Jawaharlal Nehru tended to belittle this achievement, but his contemporary K. M. Panikkar noted explicitly that the uncovering of India's past was mainly the work of Western historians and archeologists, and that it was therefore colonialism that brought into being the sense of history, the *sine qua non* of the spirit of nationalism.[16]

Parallel developments in the propagation of learning, political consciousness, and elite formation were set in motion in the ancient literate cultures of Southeast Asia and the Middle East as well as in hundreds of nonliterate communities in black Africa where even the indispensable infrastructure for intellectual and political emancipation—namely writing—had to be implanted from without by the West's colonial administrators. The general motivations behind these efforts are as complex as the civilizations from which they sprang. Some have been well explained by Sir Henry Maine, himself one of the renowned scholar-administrators in the

Indian service, when he noted that it is difficult for any people to feel self-respect if they have no pride in their own annals,[17] and that those guided solely by the West's social experience are bound to err.

Westernized elites obviously differed from country to country and from epoch to epoch. Yet all stood on the margins of two cultures: they could not belong to the foreign civilization that attracted them intellectually, and they were no longer comfortable in their own traditional society where they were a very small minority, alienated from the majority. The ambivalence of this position was probably least unsettling in the early period of Europeanization during which these marginal men could participate in heady intercultural dialogues, carried by optimism about the future of their nation and unburdened by the responsibilities implicit in the actual administration of their own now split society. All this changed completely with the attainment of statehood when they themselves were required to govern in accordance with Occidental norms and systems upon whose introduction they had originally insisted.

From the mid-twentieth century onwards it thus became apparent that the Westernized elites were not able to Westernize the basic beliefs and values of their nations; that unity and order could not be maintained in the new Asian and African states through reliance on imported Occidental institutions and standards of behavior, and that nationalism was being identified increasingly with commitments to traditional culture. Frustration soon led to doubt and disenchantment about the worth of European precepts and models. Unrelieved by self-criticism, or other analytical reflections, these sentiments grew into suspicion and resentment until the West as a whole was being imagined in many lands as a false prophet or a mischievous sorcerer who had led his apprentices astray deliberately.

The Europeanized reformist elites gradually lost power and influence in this changed social and psychological context. In some societies they became recessive minorities as leadership passed to countrymen who were more closely attuned to prevalent local ways of thought and expectations. In others they changed course by turning against the alien civilization that had awakened them—an option that was facilitated by the effective propagation of Marxism-Leninism.

The main explanation for the attractiveness of this new ideology was the circumstance that it was conceived as an assault upon the West's main sustaining values and norms. In denying the force of ideas and of individual inventiveness, Marxist doctrines of materialism, economic determinism, the primacy of economic classes, and the inevitability of class conflicts thus had the effect of explicitly exonerating non-Western elites from responsibility for failures in administration while sanctioning the perception of the West as a historically near-defunct power complex that is guilty by fiat of theory for all that turns out wrongly in their societies.

A second but related attraction of Marxism is the reductionist view of the European political order, specifically of "the state" and "law," norms that are put down there as mere power manifestations of the economically dominant class. A third, psychologically perhaps decisive appeal is the open invitation to indulge in righteous hatred of the West and to fight the capitalist oppressor so as to help redeem history's promise of freedom and power for the exploited working classes of the world.

Leninism—which is not of the West—transposes some of these propositions and supersedes others. The following theses seem to impress themselves most readily upon the sets of mind of non-Western political elites.

The identification of imperialism with the export of capital, in conjunction with the view that twentieth-century imperialism is the highest stage of capitalism, makes it possible to forget the long inconvenient records of all non-Western empires; to disregard as irrelevant the dissolution of all former European empires as well as the creation, in the twentieth century, of numerous new Communist and non-Western empires; and to indict the United States for the sin of subscribing to the capitalist free enterprise system (with the proviso, however, that the latter must be used as the main source of economic aid and needed export of capital to non-Western states).

The Leninist notion that the economically backward nations have joined the West's proletarian class and are in fact today the "chosen people" in virtue of the imperialist exploitation of their economic conditions gives pride of status where before there had been frustration and uneasiness.[18]

Another tenet, the admission that the revolutionary struggle of classes and nations is of uncertain duration and may well be permanent, is also emotionally satisfying because it puts the emphasis on the dynamics of political action, including fighting, not on the tedious task of peaceful consolidation and development. Indeed, and as seven decades of Communist economics have shown, consumer economics and thus consumer development in general are near-irrelevant in Communist societies, be they states or nonstate bodies. This may be in striking contradiction to the originally declared purpose of Marxist materialism, but it is quite in line with the Leninist conception of the Communist Party as the general staff of the world revolution charged with administering a combat ideology, and the Leninist definition of the Communist state as a totalitarian dictatorship resting directly on coercion and not bound by any laws.[19]

These norms have been and continue to be concretized in a variety of political systems. In the formerly non-Communist societies of Eastern Europe, Afghanistan, and Tibet, communization was accomplished by superior military forces in the service of the Soviet Union and China, both established Marxist-Leninist states. Elsewhere, however, elites have been subscribing voluntarily to the new ideology. This trend is observable particularly in those African, Asian, and Latin American states in which traditional pre-Western patterns of political organization also focus on despotism. To the extent, then, to which the new non-Western elites accommodate Communist precepts by choice, they may well find some anchorage, however shallow, in their own old order of values.

Marxism-Leninism had also swept the Occidental intellectual establishments. It is therefore important to bear in mind first that this order of thought is very definitely part of modern intercultural exchanges, and second that the new dispensation has been communicated to Africans and Asians mainly through the agency of European and American universities.

What is significant for purposes of this particular discussion is the fact that the impact of Communism upon Occidental minds had effects on Western civilization that were the reverse of those imprinted upon non-Western cultures by their Marxist-Leninist elites. As suggested earlier, most of the latter were invigorated by their affiliation with Communist beliefs in the sense that now, having learned to disavow the West and blame it for all that ailed their societies, they had found a way to feel righteous, powerful, and free in their own culture. Scores of Europeans and Americans, by contrast, were taught—and willingly learned—that their Western way of life was all wrong; democracy was depicted as sham, law as too flawed by inequities to merit either respect or reform, and economic norms as mere camouflage for the wanton exploitation of non-Western groups of peoples. In short, they were led to refute, not reconfirm, their heritage.

Further, and following basic Communist understandings of history and politics, the West's new Marxist elites acceded readily to the Leninist definition of imperialism. The sum total of these commitments explains why they were prepared to help dismantle their own civilization and make amends for the sins of their forefathers by building up the cultural identities of non-Western, economically underprivileged peoples—an undertaking that frequently implied active support for revolutions and wars of national liberation.

The touchstone in this sentimentalist yet politically effective revolt is guilt. This theme is more highly developed in Christianity than in any other religion and it is nowhere as strenuously professed as in the United States. Here it merges with strong strains of a deeply rooted antiimperialism and with a peculiar form of economic determinism according to which all underdeveloped people can become "developed," given opportunity and assistance. Traditionally internalized on levels of biography, the guilt complex is so wantonly socialized and politicized today as to constitute a major element in the conduct of the West's foreign relations.

V

It is questionable in the context of the foregoing analysis whether the cultural and political relations between Western and non-Western societies[20] are adequately summarized by such captions as "The Revolt of the Third World Against Western Dominance" and "The Anticolonial Revolution." For one thing, the processes and interactions covered by these terms are too complex, ambiguous, and protracted to justify references to "revolt" and "revolution," all the more so as few colonial peoples had to struggle hard to attain independence. For another, we learn from the multifarious records of responses to the West's challenge that resentment mingles almost everywhere with admiration as well as with frustration and self-doubt. Also, we know of numerous, perhaps particularly talented Asian peoples, from the Japanese to the Turks, who retained their composure in encountering the West because they chose to borrow only those attributes of the alien civilization that could be integrated successfully into their established value-systems and political orders.

The majority of non-Western and non-Communist states—those that were independent to begin with and those that had been non-self-governing territories or trusteeships under Western administration—have not accepted certain crucial European norms. The most important among these relate to constitutional law, penal law, and the whole complex of ideas that sustain the cause of self-determination and development and that make it mandatory to think of the individual as an autonomous person and a citizen, endowed with rights as well as responsibilities. And since the post-1945 framework for the conduct of relations between states has come to rest on precisely these now embattled Occidental norms, one may also doubt whether "the state" is still a shared experience or reference and whether we can count on the existence of an organically unified system of states.

The preceding sections of this paper identify the major cultural orders and political systems known to recent international history.[21] The following brief references to modern developments are meant to illustrate the continuity of this diversity in our times.

One of the main shared themes in the non-Western realms here surveyed is the reaffirmation of traditional religious beliefs as ultimate norm-setting principles of identity in politics and culture. Shintoism and Buddhism serve this function in Japan,[22] a particularly creative "borrowing" nation whose elites have long known how to shape attractive ideas, be they Chinese, European or American, so that they would not break the form or denature the irreducible essence of that which calls itself Japan. Throughout the twentieth century, surely one of the most severely trying periods in their history, the Japanese could thus assure stability in law and government by adapting select precepts of Occidental law codes and constitutions to their own tested and revered imperial institutions and traditions. Indeed, after their defeat in 1945 they were even able to adjust to the MacArthur constitution which deprived them of "the right to belligerency," abolished all forms of feudalism, and declared that sovereignty henceforth would rest not with the emperor but the people of Japan—a principle unknown in Japan's culture. Buttressed by the discipline of Shinto and Buddhist commitments, the Japanese have now shifted their aspirations toward self-respect and excellence from traditional martial to modern commercial and financial contexts.

Public order in the vast, ethnically and linguistically fractured new Indian nation is also being upheld—although precariously in several regions—by institutions of secular law and constitutional democracy that are of Occidental derivation. However, each organ of India's modern administration—and therewith the very cause of the unified nation—is severely challenged today by orthodox Hinduism and the human dispositions it engenders. The resuscitation of the traditional faith has thus brought a revival of caste consciousness and related social norms that conflict sharply with India's modern systems of constitutional and criminal laws. Two sets of incidents illustrated this collision in the 1980s: the blinding of suspected criminals in some of India's states, and the mass demonstrations of women in Delhi asking for the right to widow-burning, a Hindu practice officially outlawed by the British in 1829. Further, and by way of noting general all-Indian trends, communalism and steadily mounting pressures for secession by disaffected ethnic and religious groups now conduce routinely to widespread civil war, violence, and anarchy.

These social and moral developments, marked as they are by the reemergence of traditional patterns of inequality and animosity in respect of race, religion, social class, and sex, explain, in conjunction with the reappearance of the specter of political disunity, why the federal government, too, has had to resort to repressive measures of rule usually identified with the Hindu past.

The resurgence of religiosity is nowhere as pronounced as in the Islamic world. It is particularly intense in the Middle East, where the faith originated and where relations with the Christian West have been close and conflicted from the seventh century A.D. onward. The history of these interactions—it began with triumphal Arab conquests of one Christian region after another, climaxed in the establishment of politically powerful, culturally luxurious Islamic centers of control, only to ebb into a steady decline of Arab-Islamic fortunes—has never ceased to puzzle the thoughtful among Arab and Arabized elites. To recover the lost dynamic that had brought victory over Christianity, self-confidence, power, and prestige has thus been the standing challenge in modern times. And since the glory of the past is forever associated with Islam, it is the road back to the Koran that is being fervently sought not only in the Near East but throughout the commonwealth of some 600 million believers.[23]

The new longing for this kind of dependable situation implies the refutation of the West's Promethean civilization that an earlier generation had accepted as a promising source of guidelines for the attainment of success. Disenchantment and alienation soon settled in this sector of East/West relations, and explicit statements to that effect became common from the mid-twentieth century onward, especially after the Zionist state of Israel had been installed in formerly Arab territory under the auspices, mainly, of American diplomacy.[24]

Further, states that we tend to distinguish carefully as being either "conservative" or "radical" nonetheless converge today in the judgment that Euro-American principles of constitutional and criminal law, notably those bearing on the status of the individual, are not only irrelevant but also nefarious for the well-being of Islamic societies—a conclusion that has been in the works from the mid-nineteenth century onward.[25] As Albert Hourani notes in a thought-provoking essay,[26] the alien laws, not being rooted in deep convictions and old customs, were simply not accepted by the people as the necessary regulative principles of society. The central problem in the new context has thus been not how to preserve the law and make the community virtuous, but how to preserve the community and make it strong by generating dynamism and a common will.

Comparisons of Islamic states and their respective orientations to existing international orders or systems should therefore be made in different terms. Thus it is the singular distinction of Saudi Arabia that it chose not to emulate Western norms of constitutional and criminal law. For this made it possible to fashion a relationship of mutual trust between the governing royal house, the religious authorities, and the public without undermining commonly shared traditions of justice. This is no longer the case in most other Islamic states, albeit for different reasons. For example, Shi'ite Iran, a prestige nation in the eyes of contemporaries from antiquity onwards, seemed to have fused Achaemenid, Islamic, and Western elements of statecraft so successfully that it could "modernize" to the satisfaction even of Western critics. This proved to be an illusion. For nowhere in the Middle East has the return to Islamic orthodoxy been as decisive and ferocious as here, and in few, if any, states has it created such havoc in normative references to the state, government, and law.[27]

What different groups of liberal supporters of the Ayatollah Khomeini's leadership and opponents of the Shah ignored—both in Iran and in the West—is the confluence of Achaemenid and Islamic thought on the general Oriental belief that despotism is the only reliable form of government and that man the individual is simply not endowed with inalienable rights to liberty.

In modern Syria, Iraq, and South Yemen, meanwhile, government became lawless and capricious after early Marxist-Leninist "waves of socialism" had swept aside indigenous traditions as well as Western reforms, thus creating the vacuum that invites the dynamics of personalized will. And this is the condition also to which the former desert kingdom of Libya was reduced after Colonel Muammar el-Qaddafi's coup d'état. Libya today is Qaddafi's private fiefdom and a base area for transcontinental terrorist operations that aim at the physical elimination of personal enemies at home and abroad and at the expansion and consolidation of his personal power and prestige throughout the world. Such imperial thrusts have been common occurrences in the history of Islam. Also, some of Qaddafi's schemes are similar to those evolved by Gamal Abdel Nasser in modern times. However, most of them recall precedents set between the fourteenth and nineteenth centuries in black Africa by adventurous Islamized conquerors whose forces would regularly sweep over the Sahara and the Sudan, spreading slavery, establishing ephemeral mastery over nomadic and sedentary tribal communities, and generally creating chaos in the regions they struck. Qaddafi's aggressive moves against Chad, Niger, the Gambia, northern Nigeria, and the Central African Republic are best seen in the light of this African heritage, a legacy also relayed by his willful versions of Islamic fundamentalism and his eccentric syntheses of this religion and of Marxist-Leninist ideology.

Nowhere has the reaffirmation of traditional norms and values been as sustained and deliberate in the last decade as in black Africa. In fact, developments on all planes of thought and behavior and the testimony of representative Africans lead to the conclusion that African realities today are not convincingly covered by Western concepts and words. Further, they leave one doubtful whether any important traditional belief or institution has ever been seriously Westernized—and this even though Europeans succeeded in revolutionizing the very premises of thought and communication by introducing writing to hundreds of different African speech communities. This astounding accomplishment in intercultural relations—and it has not yet received the appreciation it deserves—seems to be experienced merely as a technical facility in modern Africa.

Dr. T. Adeoye Lambo has closely analyzed the conflict between tradition and modernism that is disturbing African minds in our times. He notes that Africans have a merely ritualistic admiration for Western civilization, and that it is problematic, to say the least, whether norms and standards can be introduced from without, or whether it is possible to assure a smooth interaction between traditional values and the demands of economic and social growth. The traditional faith in the magic power of certain symbols to produce certain results explains why it was customary in periods of tribal distress—for example, during a famine, drought, or epidemic—to offer expiatory sacrifices. Officially detribalized Africans have not only reverted to this practice under the stress of modern problems, Lambo notes, but have cast it in new and more malignant forms. Further, we learn from this and numerous other observers of the present scene that the prevalence of magico-religious beliefs including witchcraft is as widespread among urban Western-educated Africans as among tradition-oriented non-Western Africans. Over ninety percent of the patients in a large group of Nigerian students thus believed they had been bewitched and regarded their dream life as objective reality.[28] Thinking, then, is not individualized here, and such constellations of ideas as freedom of thought, self-determination, and development are meaningless, all the more so as all values, categories of thought, and significant content of thought are commonly attributed to the group, its forebears, and its tutelary deities.

The recorded work of professional elites strongly reflects this bent of mind. Whereas African jurists showed a pronounced concern for the disjunction between customary and European legal orders in preindependence times, later generations became progressively more relaxed in the search for acceptable syncretisms. It was thus only with the greatest reluctance that Sir Samuel Lewis, a barrister from Sierra Leone, had concluded in one of his reports that one might have to recognize bona fide cannibalism, abandon the jury system in the light of tribal conflicts, and compromise the standards of English law in many other ways. Judge K. Azina-Nartey of Ghana and of Lincoln's Inn in London saw no difficulties several decades later during the trial of a hunter charged with the manslaughter of a fellow hunter in admitting "the wonderful evidence of the mother of the deceased that she killed her son by changing him into that animal which lured the accused to shoot. . . ."[29]

As explained in a subsequent essay, black Africa's states and governments are in a class by themselves also because the very idea of the state is eclipsed by the reality of enduring commitments to kinship and tribal groups. And since relations among the state's ethnic components are marked by mistrust and usually by hostility, national unity remains an elusive goal. Further, all black African polities are either authoritarian or totalitarian despotisms, with some of them run on Communist lines. Power is almost everywhere held by one man who is usually identified as the representative of one ethnic party. Yet government is almost by definition unstable since rivals are always bent on dislodging the incumbent either by intrigue or assassination. Indeed, events as chronicled in postindependence times show that African states are easily reduced to fields of violence.

VI

To sum up, an international system is as solid as the concepts that combine to compose it. Such concepts are solid if they are equally meaningful in the different local orders that are encompassed by the international system. We do not have such a globally meaningful system because the world society consists today as it did before the nineteenth century of a plurality of diverse political systems, each an outgrowth of culture-specific concepts.

Some of these non-Western realms were linked to the Occident and to each other between the mid-nineteenth and mid-twentieth century in an international order that European governments had designed and administered in preceding centuries under the title "the modern states system," and in which member states were juridically equal. The internationalization of this design seemed successful before World War II but proved illusory thereafter. A survey of the world society at the end of this century permits the conclusion that the core concept of the system, namely "the state," is critically embattled everywhere. In some regions, notably in Africa and the Middle East, it has resulted in altogether reductive versions. In others it has degenerated into a protective cover for the dissemination of contra-state ideologies. Internationally relevant decision-making emanates increasingly from scattered, often dissimulated command posts of liberation fronts, terrorist brigades, provisional governments, or international Communist parties. All of these operate across state boundaries and none is recognized in international law as an equivalent of the state.

The integrity of the concept "state" is critically impaired also because it is applied to political establishments that are too different to be comparable or equal in terms of either international law or power politics. The term thus covers today new types of multinational empires, such as those of the Soviet Union and of Communist China and Vietnam, where strategic and ideological doctrines of expansion insist that existing boundaries are provisional only since the proper limits of jurisdiction have not yet been reached. It also covers Muslim regimes that reject the Western concept of a community of states in favor of traditional Islamic concepts. At the same time the word "state" continued, until 1989, to be the unchallenged appellation also for nations whose independence had been canceled through conquest or military occupation. The Soviet Union's satellites were thus not classified as protectorates or dominions in the manner customary, for example, in the former British Empire. Rather, each ranked as a sovereign state and therefore rated a full vote under charter provisions of the UN and other international agencies, even though it was officially deprived of its sovereignty in domestic and foreign affairs by the Brezhnev Doctrine (1968) and a reenforcing sequel enunciated by Brezhnev in the wake of the Soviet invasion of Afghanistan.

In the West, meanwhile, attributes once firmly assigned to the state have been transferred gradually on the one hand to "government," on the other to "the world society," even though both were traditionally perceived in the West as derivatives of the state. A complex process of decomposing the European system has thus been going on for quite some time, without much attention being paid to it by the Occident's scholarly and political elites.

These developments have had adverse effects on international law—the leading European reference for the conduct of relations between states without which "international order" could not even have been imagined in the West. Loosened from the context of Euro-American jurisprudence, history, and ethics, and associated instead with a new freewheeling ideology that proclaims unsubstantiated human rights for everyone, the law of nations is now conscripted to serve the cause of political rhetoric and tactics. More importantly, it no longer provides unifying guidelines for thinking about war and peace. This is so partly because "the rights of war and peace" have ceased to issue from definitions of the state, but mainly because there simply is no consensus in today's multicultural world on the essential meanings of war and peace. Furthermore, as indicated in earlier sections of this essay, war-affirming theories and traditions predominate in non-Western and Communist societies, thus eclipsing the new pacifism that has been sweeping the West in recent times.

The conjunction of these factors explains why today's world can be perceived as a conglomerate of different conflict systems or different theaters of war, some localized, others contiguous and independent. It can therefore not be maintained that the term "international war" refers exclusively to violent conflicts between states. Rather, it now stands also for a broad spectrum of armed belligerence within the state, ranging from sporadic urban guerrilla activities to full-fledged revolutionary uprisings and civil wars, many of them initiated or kept going by foreign principals. This interpenetration of the domestic and foreign environments has had the foreseeable effect of effacing altogether the conventionally accepted lines of separation between legitimate and illegitimate force. Indeed, it puts in question established Western distinctions between peace and war.

The de-Westernization or deconstruction of the norms and institutions that together had sustained the short-lived global international order constitutes a major challenge for European and American diplomacy. For where the distinction between war and peace is blurred; where values supportive of hostility and warfare outweigh those related to cooperation and peace; and where international relations are conceived, in principle, as conflict relations between adversaries, there diplomacy must follow suit. Comparative studies of modern and traditional statecraft indicate that this is the case in most non-Western and all Communist societies today. This means that Occidental diplomacy must henceforth be prepared to function again, as it did before the nineteenth century, in a world that has no common culture and no overarching political order, and that is no longer prepared to abide by Western standards of international conduct.

NOTES

1. See Yu-Kuang Chu, "The Chinese Language," in John Meskill, ed., *An Introduction to Chinese Civilization* (New York, 1973), pp. 601ff. and notes 20–23 for citations of other authorities.
2. See B. Malinowski, "The Problems of Meaning in Primitive Languages," Supplement to C. K. Ogden and I. A. Richards, *The Meaning of Meaning* (New York, 1959). See also Bozeman, *Conflict in Africa: Concepts and Realities* (Princeton, NJ: Princeton University Press, 1976), Part IV, pp. 149–74, "The Role of Conflict in African Thought and Society," and Part V, pp. 175–224, "The Web of War and the Maintenance of Society."
3. *The Primitive World and Its Transformations* (Ithaca, New York, Cornell University Press, 1953; repr. 1958), p. 111.
4. See Wang Yi-T'ung, *Official Relations Between China and Japan 1368–1549* (Harvard-Yenching Institute Studies IX, Cambridge, Mass.: Harvard University Press, 1953), pp. 3, 39, and 53, in particular.
5. *Ibid.*
6. *Ibid.*
7. There is considerable evidence of a revival of Shintoism in present-day Japan, notably in dispositions toward government. While it is fashionable today to allude to this Asian state as "an honorable Western nation" on the ground of its spectacular technical achievements in finance, industry, and trade, such references are off the mark when one examines Japanese modes of decision-making and negotiation in precisely these areas of endeavor.

8. For a discussion of this matter see Bozeman, *Politics and Culture in International History* (Princeton, NJ: Princeton University Press, 1960), pp. 146–61.

9. See Bozeman, *The Future of Law in a Multicultural World* (Princeton, NJ: Princeton University Press, 1971), pp. 21, 121–39.

10. See *History of Islam in West Africa* (London, 1962; repr. 1963), pp. 232ff.; and *Islam in East Africa: Report of a Survey Undertaken in 1961* (London, 1962), pp. 31ff., 43ff.

11. In this context it is undeniable also that Peter the Great's efforts to "Westernize" Russia were found to lead to wholesale ejections of grafts that simply could not and did not "take." See also the Introduction and Essay 4 in this book.

12. See Bozeman, "On the Relevance of Hugo Grotius and *De Jure Belli ac Pacis* for Our Times," *Grotiana,* Vol. I, 1980, pp. 65–124; see p. 79 for bibliographical references to this matter; see also *infra,* Essay 4.

13. See Bozeman, "Do Educational and Cultural Exchanges Have Political Relevance?" in *Exchange, A Publication of the U.S. Advisory Commission on International Educational and Cultural Affairs,* Fall 1969, Vol. V, no. 2, pp. 7ff.

14. It is not in the purview of this particular study to discuss these records in depth, but see subsequent essays in this volume.

15. See Sir Henry Maine, *Lectures on the Early History of Institutions* (New York, 1888), Lecture XI, pp. 329ff. Maine says this on the Hindu law: "There is no reason to suppose that philosophical theory had any serious influence on the jurisprudence of the Hindoos. . . . I believe that none of the remarkable philosophical theories which the genius of the Race produced are founded on a conception of the individual as distinct from that of the group in which he is born." Some of my thoughts in this section of the paper are more fully developed in "On the Relevance of Hugo Grotius and *De Jure Belli ac Pacis* for Our Times," pp. 68ff.

16. See David C. Gordon, *Self-Determination and History in the Third World* (New York, 1971), p. 61, for this reference to K. M. Panikkar, *Asia and Western Dominance: A Survey of the Vasco da Gama Epoch of Asian History, 1498–1945* (New York, n.d.), pp. 492–93.

17. Sir Henry Maine, *Village-Communities in the East and West, with Other Lectures, Addresses, and Essays* (New York, 1880), p. 289. For an appreciation of Thomas Babington Macaulay in this same context, see K. M. Panikkar, *A Survey of Indian History* (Bombay, 1954), pp. 204f; see also Bozeman, *The Future of Law in a Multicultural World* (Princeton, NJ: Princeton University Press, 1971), pp. 135–39.

18. For a full analysis of this psychological tangle, see Alfred G. Meyer, *Leninism* (New York, 1963), pp. 257ff.

19. For a succinct discussion of this issue see Nick Eberstadt, "The Health Crisis in the U.S.S.R.," *New York Review of Books,* February 19, 1981, pp. 23ff. This essay centers on a review of Christopher Davis and Murray Feshbach, *Rising Infant Mortality in the U.S.S.R. in the 1970s.* United States Bureau of the Census, Series P-95, No. 74, September 1980.

20. I am using the terms "Western" and "non-Western" because they relay well the essence of the themes with which this paper deals. By contrast, I avoid "Third World" and "Fourth World" because the implications of these references are quite unclear. The same holds in my view for contrasts or comparisons between "rich" and "poor," "developed" and "underdeveloped" nations, and between "North" and "South."

21. One of several reasons for omitting South and Central America from this survey of the multicultural world is the difficulty of identifying cultural traits that are incontestably common to the states in the hemisphere as a whole or in some of its major regions. A richly suggestive evocation of certain constant themes is Gabriel García Márquez's novel *One Hundred Years of Solitude* (New York, 1970). Affinities between Indo-Iberian societies no doubt exist, but these states, like all other American states, including the United States, originated in rather recent times as racially and culturally syncretic organisms. In regard to the Iberian factor it may be relevant to bear in mind that the conquerors and settlers of the fifteenth and sixteenth centuries were carriers also of Arab/Islamic traditions. After all, the Spanish discovery of America coincided with the final Spanish defeat of Arab and Arabized

peoples that had controlled much of Spain for some eight hundred years. (See *infra,* Essay 8.) Analogies between the political systems of the Middle East and Latin America—and these are readily discernible—may stem from this historical circumstance.

22. See *supra,* this essay.

23. For an extensive commentary on Islamic societies see "Covert Action and Foreign Policy in World Politics" in this volume.

24. Mr. Boutros-Ghali, Egypt's minister of state for foreign affairs, is said to have told his Israeli friends that the establishment of the religious state of Israel had contributed to the vigorous spread of Islamic fundamentalism in the Mohammedan polities. See Flora Lewis, *The New York Times,* December 31, 1979, p. A4.

25. The Ottoman rulers realized already during this earlier phase of modernizing Islamic public law that European notions simply could not be integrated into existing *shari'a* systems. Therefore they decided to construct a new and independent secular legal order on the basis of norms borrowed mainly from Swiss and French models, an effort that led to the creation of several constitutions (e.g., the Tunisian of 1860 and the Turkish of 1876) and in some societies even to the institution of a civil law of personal status.

26. *A Vision of History* (Beirut, 1961), pp. 151ff. For additional illustrations see Bozeman, *The Future of Law in a Multicultural World,* pp. 50–85, especially notes 12, 30, and 51.

27. See Bozeman, "Iran: U.S. Foreign Policy and the Tradition of Persian Statecraft," *ORBIS, A Journal of World Affairs,* Summer 1979, pp. 387–402; see also "Covert Action and Foreign Policy in World Politics" in this volume.

28. Lambo, *loc. cit.* For source material and commentaries on these matters see Bozeman, *Conflict in Africa: Concepts and Realities* (Princeton, NJ: Princeton University Press, 1976). See in particular Chapter 5, "Nonliterate Thought and Communication"; Chapter 9, "Order and Disorder as Functions of Magic, Power, and Death"; Chapter 10, "Fear and the Killing Power of the Spoken Word"; and Chapter 11, "Verbal Aggression and the Muting of Tensions."

29. *The Daily Graphic* (Ghana), August 18, 1977. For other cases illustrative of the ease with which killings are legally accommodated especially when it is possible to link them to witchcraft, sorcery, dream evidence, and the confounding of identities, see Paul Brietzke, "The Chilobwe Murders Trial," in *African Studies Review,* Vol. XVII, no. 2 (September 1974), pp. 361–81; James R. Hooker, "Tradition and Traditional Courts: Malawi's Experiment in Law," American Universities Field Staff, *Fieldstaff Reports,* Vol. XV, no. 3 (March 1971), pp 1ff; and Bozeman, *Conflict in Africa: Concepts and Realities,* Part VI, "The Role of Intermediaries and the Settlement of Disputes," pp. 227–303. On the role of magic in military operations see John Michael Lee, *African Armies and Civil Order, Studies in International Security* (London, 1969); and Kenneth W. Grundy, *Guerrilla Struggle in Africa: An Analysis and Preview* (New York, 1971).

War and the Clash of Ideas

I

"The War of All Against All" is the title of an analytical review of papers that were published in the *Journal of Conflict Resolution* between 1957 and 1968.[1] Within the protective covers of these volumes, contributors contend for different causes; yet the clash of their ideas is significantly muffled by basic accord on two great issues. The scholars are at one, the reviewer notes, in regarding international war as the category of central interest, and they are united also in stressing conflict control rather than conflict itself. Moreover, they are found to be nearly unanimous in assuming that violence is something to be avoided if at all possible, and in attaching connotations of illegitimacy to the phrase "organized violence."

Given these shared dispositions, it is not surprising to learn, then, that arms control is a heavily favored research subject and that the literature on this topic is pervaded by several common impulses, among them the following: repugnance for "untraditional" methods of warfare or for weapons "which a given nation has not yet had a chance either to arm itself with or to develop counterweapons against";[2] disdain for "sham bargaining" and psychological warfare, the latter generally being viewed as sneaky and immoral; the strong conviction that humaneness ought to be accepted as an important criterion in the evaluation of weaponry; a deep commitment to the distinction between "just" and "unjust" wars; and considerable preoccupation with guilt and responsibility in regard to the actual resort to violence or war.

The same exhaustive survey also instructs us that JRC authors have not paid much attention to the relationship between the cause of national survival, on the one hand, and arms control, on the other, and that inquiries into the antecedents of military aggression have been conspicuously absent. In fact, the preferred time dimension has very definitely been the present, amplified by strong overtones of futurist concerns. The historical approach is missing, and statistical treatment is stressed; what is more, the data considered relevant to such statistical processing are drawn almost exclusively from American and European records. And finally, it appears that findings by specialists in military science and strategy have been seldom exploited.

Analogous trends have been found to dominate international relations research. Chadwick Alger, in a research review published in 1970,[3] pointed out that concern with the causes of war had given way to study of the causes of peace and the construction of "alternate futures," and that knowledge of the destructive power of nuclear weapons had sparked a revival of interest in disarmament and arms control. He also noted that the peace research movement has been "international in com-

This essay originally appeared in the twentieth-anniversary issue of ORBIS, Vol. 20, No. 1 (Spring 1976) and is printed with permission of the Foreign Policy Research Institute.

position, being comprised mainly of North Americans and Western Europeans," that these participants have had high value commitments to the nonviolent solution of international conflicts and have endeavored to do work with policy relevance, and that they have stressed "scientific work," including systematic data collection techniques and rigorous methods of analysis. Here, however, as in the field of conflict resolution, the demands of rigorous analysis can obviously be satisfied without methodically utilizing data from non-Western societies.

The processes of theory- and model-building that have been perfected in recent years are certainly impressive, and so are many of the actual mental constructions that have issued from these labors. Yet it is questionable whether objective validity can be claimed for much of this work, if only because it is permeated by paradox. It is necessary, then, to note that most scholarly architects profess to be value-neutral social scientists. This is true even though they admit, directly or indirectly through the medium of their accomplishments, that the major motivation for their sustained efforts clearly originates in the compelling force of their own feelings, impulses, and values, notably those that feed their hopes for, and images of, a peaceful world society.

Now there is no reason why social scientists should not have values; nor is there any reason that they should not be concerned with the improvement of the lot of man. But in this case we discover that personal value preferences have not been checked out objectively before they were judged to be appropriate building blocks for theory. More important, perhaps, few modern theorists in the field of international relations or conflict resolution have bothered to explore the value content of conflict, war, and violence. The configuration of the enemy they profess to fight is thus not clearly rendered—a circumstance that may explain why this "war against war" can be perceived by others as a kind of shadow boxing. Indeed, explicit definitions are missing for both war and peace, perhaps because the ruling supposition is that the one is everywhere known to be the opposite of the other, war being universally disclaimed as a thoroughly bad idea and peace being just as generally accepted as mankind's natural state and birthright.

The clash of ideas over how to control conflict, avoid war, and build the structures of peace seems to have proceeded in the calm of an academic environment within which the clash of arms and the clamor of war-affirming rhetoric are not readily heard. Some future nonacademic parliament of man, however, may well entertain the motion that these theorists fiddled while nations burned. Whether an armed conflict today is classified as an insurrection, a civil war, a war of national liberation, a guerrilla war or a war-by-proxy, a UN war to preserve the peace, an international socialist war to serve the cause of revolution, or a traditional interstate war—and the lines of differentiation are becoming increasingly blurred in response precisely to the high incidence of violence and the steady proliferation of types of warfare—the fact remains that the post-1945 world can fairly be viewed as a conglomerate of theaters of war, some self-contained and localized, others contiguous and interdependent.

A simple inventory of bare and incontrovertible facts is revealing: Irish groups seem bent on changing the political order of the island by resort to indiscriminate violence; relations between Israel and the Arab states and peoples have been characterized from 1948 onward by warfare; factional, national, and international affairs in the Islamic Middle East have been marked by bloody revolutions, armed interventions, takeovers, and ethnic uprisings; several North African Muslim regimes have consistently warred against the non-Islamic populations to their south; Africa south of the Sahara has been convulsed by interstate and intertribal violence, civil wars, coups d'état and political assassinations, as well as by military and paramilitary activities on the part of antiwhite liberation armies and their opponents; Greeks and Turks cannot resist fighting over Cyprus; the armies of the Soviet Union have crushed numerous national uprisings among the allegedly sovereign states of Eastern Europe; India has chosen force over available peaceful methods in order to establish or retain dominion over Hyderabad, parts of Kashmir, Goa, Sikkim, and such non-self-governing territories as those occupied by the Naga hostiles; India and Pakistan have not had any scruples about settling their conflicting claims and interests on the field of battle; there would have been no Bangladesh had there not been ruthless warfare; it was China's armed might that subdued Tibet and successfully asserted control over the Paracel Islands; generations of Koreans have known nothing but the actuality or the threat of civil and international war; the destinies of all peoples in the vast Southeast Asian region have long been molded by war, whether in the form of armed uprisings and revolutions, jigsaw movements of insurgency and counterinsurgency, belligerent confrontations between neighbors, or military interventions by great powers; terrorist organizations of one hue or another operate freely throughout Latin America; the United States, which is the academic center of the search for a warless world, has not only warred against Communist forces in Korea and Indochina but has itself been the troubled scene of terrorist activities by self-styled liberation armies, urban guerrilla bands, and other violence-espousing groups.

War's overwhelming and variegated presence would seem to be at odds with some of the major assumptions relayed explicitly or implicitly by leading theorists of international relations and conflict resolution. Doubt may thus be cast on the proposition that "international war," the category of foremost concern, can be convincingly extricated from the maze of other types of warfare in which modern nations are enmeshed. Likewise, and for the same reasons, it is questionable whether distinctions between combatants and noncombatants, or between humane and inhumane weapons, can be maintained effectively, or whether one can endorse the proposition that clear-cut lines between aggression and defense (and thus between just and unjust wars) are always readily discernible. Specialists in military science have closely studied just such issues; however, as the aforementioned analyses suggest, their findings do not seem to have had a vital impact on present trends in political science, peace research, arms control, or conflict resolution.

Other incongruities between theory and reality are suggested by the raw evidence of modern war and violence. A glance at the embattled and conflict-ridden regions of Africa, Asia, Latin America, and parts of Europe leaves one with the strong impression that human dispositions toward stress, violence, and death are by no means everywhere the same, and that basic orientations toward war and peace are therefore greatly various also. For example, nowhere outside North America and Northern Europe does one encounter the overriding desire to avoid armed conflict and to seek peaceful settlement of disputes that leading peace-minded scholars in our society assume to be generally present.

Furthermore, evidence is totally missing that recourse to armed force evokes feelings of guilt and self-recrimination among the intellectual elites of non-Western societies, or that the high incidence of organized and unorganized violence induces doubts about the appropriateness of ruling moral or political systems. Indeed, the strife-filled records of the past decades, together with the conflict-laden language so often employed by spokesmen for African, Asian and Communist societies, point to the possibility that conflict and violence may well be accepted in most areas outside the Occidental world as normal incidents of life, legitimate tools of government and foreign policy-making, and morally sanctioned courses of action.

Propositions such as these have not been thoroughly tested in the laboratories of peace research, perhaps because they relate, in the final analysis, to values; and values may resist the kind of "rigorous analysis" that has been aimed at by scholars. At any rate, it is noteworthy that eminent theorists in the fields here under review have refrained altogether from probing the mental and psychocultural roots of war, that they have not been much interested in the historical antecedents of actual conflict situations, and that they have not thought of war as a complex of possibly quite disparate, even irreconcilable, norms, values, and ideas. Just why these matters have not surfaced in the mainstream of their investigations is in itself a significant thematic motif in the clash of ideas detonated by modern warfare, and as such it should be scrutinized before going any further.

II

Several learned commentators on conflict and its resolution have drawn attention to the fact that today's scholars are uneasy in the face of all, not merely armed, conflict. They are inclined to view it negatively—as an unfortunate interruption of the normal flow of social life, a failure in communication, an unregulated and hence possibly illegitimate transaction, or an aberration from patterns of rational behavior that should be and can be reduced, transformed, or eliminated because it is situational rather than instrumental, pathological rather than sane.[4] The exact norms, patterns, and models against which motives and actions are judged normal or abnormal are not usually set out. The argument in almost every case appears to be that they are generally known or, to put it differently, that we are here in the presence of some universal givens that need only be implied.

Moreover, and in striking contrast to scholars from an earlier time (notably, Georg Simmel and Robert McIver), conflict today is generally not associated with sentiments, values, or psychic states of being. The stress is rather on concrete struggles or overt episodes in which individuals or groups contend for tangible rewards. Thus conceived in terms of antagonistic poles representing two or more mutually incompatible positions, conflict is suspect at the very start, for it is presumed to spring from some kind of discord that could have been avoided.

This neglect of psychological and intellectual factors in situations of social stress seems to have attached itself almost automatically to scholarly thought about those international conflicts that fall short of military war, known in history as cold wars or wars of nerves. Here again, the premise is widely accepted today that clashes of ideas are somehow either irrational departures from the ground rules of normal behavior or ruses to cover up peace-defying policies. In either case it seems to be supposed, particularly in so-called revisionist academic circles, that the cold war between this country and the Communist states was somehow officially initiated in much the same way that hot wars have been declared, and that it could therefore be called off by political authorities in an equally expeditious manner. In other words, conflict is presented as a willed event, rather than a process or relationship, perhaps in deference to the controlling conviction that "war" and "peace" are always absolutely polarized, mutually exclusive, strictly factual conditions, and that total peace must naturally take over when the fighting stops.

It is difficult to find precedents for this modern, chiefly American orientation toward chronic international discord. The history of Europe, which is very much a history of ideas, and therefore also one of clashing ideas, is replete with such wars of nerves. None has been more protracted or more richly documented than the uneasy coexistence of Christian and Muslim in the lands of the Mediterranean, for which contemporary Spaniards coined the term *guerra fria*. This early model of the clash of ideas in international relations has obviously not been examined by today's schools of peace and conflict studies. Nor have they taken note of the unremitting, politically and intellectually poignant collision of beliefs in the minds of statesmen, scholars, and ordinary citizens that was set off by the French Revolution and continued unabated long after the smoke had cleared. There is thus considerable justification for describing this state of affairs as "the case of the missing historian."[5]

Explanations for the absence of this dimension of inquiry may range from a lack of interest in history and doubt about its relevance for future-directed peace research to the premonition that rigorous historical research would not support some of the theorists' most favored visions. And, no doubt, they also include the related inclination to treat each and every conflict as a clearly discernible, and hence definable, factual circumstance that can be undone as quickly and purposively as it has been conjured up.

At any rate, few present-day specialists in conflict resolution seem prepared to associate conflict with mobility and flux, or to think of it as a process not always easily defined or arrested by decisive action. Not many among them, then, would agree with Jessie Bernard, who in 1949 argued that conflict may exist in latent form for years before there is a formulation of issues, a showdown, or a crisis. Bernard believed that it is therefore a mistake to limit our thinking about conflict to its overt phase; we should instead accustom ourselves to think of conflict as going on day in, day out in varying degrees of intensity, whether the issues are clearly formulated or not.[6] Yet it is this explication of social conflict, rather than the ultramodern one, that can be translated convincingly into the language of international relations to cover that indeterminate continuum of "no war/no peace" commonly known as cold war.

Furthermore, as later sections of this paper suggest, the Bernard concept comes close to explaining the types of discord and disorder most commonly found in the local and international affairs of non-Western societies. Finally, and most important from the humanist's perspective, it captures certain constant motifs in Occidental biography and history, among them the proposition eloquently stated by Ortega y Gasset in his meditations on Don Quixote, namely, that life is uneasiness.

The discomfort experienced by many social scientists in the presence of cross-national ideological strife is paralleled by deep apprehension when their thought turns to what, in the language of the trade, is known as international war. Analysts of research trends in disarmament, arms control, and peace studies see this reaction as a function of their preoccupation with the awesome specter of nuclear war.[7] This preoccupation is understandable; but the fact remains, first of all, that millions of lives have been extinguished since 1945 not by nuclear weapons but by conventional arms employed in all manner of warfare, terrorism, and outright massacre, and second, that political theorists are not nearly as troubled about these actualities as they are about possible future horrors.

To justify their concern, analysts often point to the use of the atomic bomb against Japan in World War II, and their argument is usually heavily encumbered by an insistence on America's "guilt"[8]—an indictment, incidentally, that is seldom softened by the reminder that conventional bombs had in fact visited even greater devastation on some European cities during the same war. Some of this literature thus leaves one with the uncomfortable impression that the fear of that which may be, and feelings of guilt over that which was, have come close to paralyzing analysis of that which is.

Further reflections on the tangle of sentiments and cerebrations in which so much of our supposedly value-neutral work on war is embedded confirm this impression. Thus we see that today's intense academic concern about the morality of military operations was activated by the war in Indochina, and not any other past or present war, and that ever since it has expressed itself almost exclusively in revulsion against the war-related policies of the United States and some of its allies. Nor has this massive volume of accumulated professorial indignation been strained and sifted in an objective, methodical manner in order to salvage those elements germane to theory. In fact, there are indications that the opposite tendency is being favored, in the sense that sentiment is being allowed to drift. For now that the international war in Indochina is officially terminated, and now that it is possible, in virtue of spellbinding legal or moral fictions, to view military activities in Asia as "unofficial" or "illegitimate," scholarly offensives are directed against non-Communist Asian governments, which continue to be embattled.

A group of renowned American experts on East Asian history, government, and culture has thus felt justified, "in the name of humanity and human rights," to protest "the injustice and the inhumanity" of certain judicial and administrative measures that South Korea has taken against some of her citizens.[9] Since similarly severe protests have not been lodged against the dictatorships of North Korea, North Vietnam, or the People's Republic of China, one can only conclude that some private bias is at work here. In this case, as in others,[10] the "missing historian" is an important factor—particularly puzzling here since the charges are formulated with the consent of East Asian historians who must be presumed to know that human rights and civil liberties are not part and parcel of traditional administration in Korea, China, or the states of Southeast Asia.

The overwhelming presence of private sentiments and values that one detects in war-related literature today does not favor the refinement of ideas into reliable, universally applicable theories about the place of war in human existence. Yet it is definitely theory that students of international relations, war and conflict want most fervently. Indeed, the search for this type of intellectual certainty has been so ardent and compulsive in recent decades that the nontheorist is left with the intriguing image of war-weary troops of academics beating a hasty retreat—away from the unnerving uncertainty of life on the fields of battle and back to the secure shelters of ideationally perfect castles in the mind. But here the refugees are also faced with most demanding problems. After all, social science theory is best attained today if the number of variables is reduced as starkly as possible and if only readily quantifiable data are considered. Primary attention is therefore usually directed to specific yet sufficiently simple events that can be counted, compared, and categorized with relative ease.

Is modern war susceptible to this kind of academic processing? If it is true, as the UNESCO Charter states, that "wars begin in the minds of men" and that "ignorance of each other's ways and lives has been a common cause . . . of that suspicion and mistrust between peoples of the world through which their differences have all too often broken into war," should it not follow that one must probe the minds of men in search of all the images, beliefs, sensations, values, concepts, and modes of reasoning that relate to war?

The data thus collected would of course be infinitely various as well as precarious—the kind not easily stored in data banks as these are now constructed. For just how does one quantify pride, prestige, prejudice, moral outrage, insistence on survival, vanity, and vengeance? What does one do with killing in obedience to spirits of the earth or living ancestors? Where in the theoretician's charts and models is there a place for hatred of the enemy or love of country? Are tools available for a rigorous analysis of self-discipline, cowardice, disaffection, or daring? And what are the criteria for an objective, transnational comparison of human inclinations or capacities to inflict violence and sustain war-induced uncertainty, suffering, and death? If we have no answers to questions such as these, should we then assume that the meanings of war carried in the minds of the Sudanese and the Bengalis, the Israelis and the Kurds, the Arabs and the Poles, the Hutu and the Greeks are one and the same? Or would it be more prudent not to wonder what men think of war and why they fight?

The latter course seems to be the favored response today in that intense quest for generally valid norms and standards to which priority is being attached. Ultimately, the challenge implicit in the task of theory-building calls for the reduction rather than the addition of variables; and on balance one can say that this challenge has been met. It may well be that the decision to overlook sentiments, beliefs, and values—in short, the intangibles that resist quantification—explains why international conflict, including war, is now being treated by so many theorists as a special case of social conflict whose paradigm is economic conflict, the category most amenable to data-processing techniques. This choice of emphasis, again, can be traced to the simple but ruling supposition that the norm for the organization of all societies is the modern industrial society of the West, and that the typical human being is therefore rightly envisaged as a man functioning rationally in such an economic environment.

In this kind of theoretical scheme, Hans Morgenthau explains, nations confront each other not as living historic entities, with all their complexities, but as rational abstractions after the model of "economic man"—playing games of military and diplomatic chess according to the rational calculus that exists nowhere but in the theoretician's mind.[11] Nor is it surprising, in light of such pervasive assumptions, that past and present data from non-Western societies have not been analyzed on their intrinsic merits and that a recent volume containing no substantive references to non-American or non-European manifestations of human conflict could yet be entitled *The Nature of Human Conflict*.[12]

This strong trend to constrict the frames of inquiry for the study of modern war has been reinforced in recent years by the steady impact of other firmly held beliefs: trust in the territorial, democratic nation-state as the prototype for political association everywhere on earth; trust, therefore, in the existence of an organizationally unified world society of essentially equal and analogous political units; and trust in the compelling logic and validity of laws of interstate behavior that assign authoritative meanings to all transactions regarding peace, war, neutrality, and conflict resolution.

Now, these propositions have had a rather brief and geographically restricted history. They matured in Europe from about 1648 onward in the vortex, it is interesting to note, of almost continuous war. But there, under the auspices of what later became known as the "modern European states system," they did not carry the fixed, exclusive connotations assigned to them today. International history instructs us, too, that our modern, systematized approaches to war, peace, diplomacy, and conflict resolution have no precedents in classical, medieval, or Renaissance Europe, or in the traditional realms of Africa and Asia. Finally, the actualities of present world affairs strongly suggest that the supposedly pivotal concepts in international relations—that is, the nation-state, the unified world society, and international law—are either in need of radical revision or beyond repair, casualties as it were in the endless war of ideas on which life appears to feed.

The implications of this obsolescence for any reasoned view of war can be seen most clearly by concentrating one's analysis on the state. As suggested in several other essays in this book, it is doubtful indeed whether we are justified in thinking that the territorially delimited, independent nation-state is still universally accepted as the core norm of political organization and, therefore, as the measure by which one distinguishes different types of violence. Surely, nothing comparable to this particular associational form had existed in pre–seventeenth-century Christian Europe, in precolonial Africa south of the Sahara, in the Arab/Islamic realm, or in the different civilizations of South, East, and Central Asia. Lines of demarcation between local and international milieus of conflict, and between internal and international warfare, were therefore not clearly drawn in traditional societies before the installation, from the nineteenth century onward, of nation-states and legal systems modeled on Western prototypes.

These unifying grafts have atrophied in recent decades under the impact of the following developments: the waning of Western influence and power; the reactivation, in the Orient and Africa, of older, locally respected focuses of authority and communal solidarity; and the successful diffusion of Communist doctrines of statecraft, in the context of which the "bourgeois" state is appreciated as a tactical device rather than as a value or norm. In short, the concept of the state as a sovereign community, unified politically, morally, and territorially, is being subjected to processes of erosion in all parts of the world—not excluding Western Europe and North America. Its substance is being worn away by fragmentation and separatism along narrow ethnic or linguistic lines; by civil disobedience and a faltering faith in law; and by internal war, covert foreign interventions, or military aggression from without.

Singly or in combination, these trends account for the dismantlement, division, or satellitization of numerous formerly unified and independent polities, on the one hand, and for the creation of new, fully operational political units, on the other hand, which are antithetical to the state in terms of both intention and activity. This is true, for example, of the national and international liberation front, the "provisional" government that functions year in, year out, or the "independent national authority"—the latter a Middle Eastern guerrilla term denoting the embryo of a future Palestinian state. Each of these organizational types is mobile and fluid in the sense that it has no fixed territorial boundaries and no determinate human substance. Furthermore, each exists in virtue of its commitment to violence and war. In short, the term "international war" no longer refers exclusively to violent conflicts between states.

Next, the erosion of the state as the fundamental, shared norm of political organization, together with general acquiescence in the coexistence of states and antistate bodies as equal actors in foreign policy arenas, has gradually but ineluctably led also to the devaluation of the two state-based superstructures that provide the modern context for official foreign relations: (1) the world society of sovereign, equal states and (2) the law of nations, which stipulates the rights and obligations of these states.

Theoreticians in the field of war and peace studies have made scant allowance for these revolutionary developments. Some proceed as if the situation had not changed at all in past decades, while others, heartened by a belief in progress, retreat into the security of self-made legal and political systems that will be actual, they think, in the future. For as Martin Wight noted in his essay "Why Is There No International Theory?" the conviction usually precedes the evidence in progressivist international theories. "And when the conviction is analysed or disintegrates," he continues, "one is apt to find at the centre of it what might be called the argument from desperation." In modern times, Wight suggested, this may well be the fear of nuclear war.[13] The argument that the hydrogen bomb has made war impossible thus usually contains two propositions: first, war waged with the new weapons will destroy civilization; second, it is therefore too horrible to happen.

Thus confined, discussion cannot move on either to international actualities or to history, where corrective evidence is readily available. For example, the indisputable fact that the flood tide of modern nonnuclear war has washed away the categories reserved for it by international law and the UN Charter is seldom, if ever, recognized by theorists. Likewise, belief in the polarity of war and peace is still widespread, even in policy-making circles, and many thoughtful men believe that every war must end—a proposition negated by the reality of continuous armed struggles. Furthermore, it is astonishing that international theorists, notably those committed to the cause of international law, see no purpose in consulting the records of diplomatic and intellectual history.

The international environment to which American and European theorists address themselves today is certainly more vast and diversified than that of either the seventeenth or nineteenth century, when Grotius and Clausewitz, respectively, reflected on the world. And yet a comparative study of theories then and now leaves the definite impression that war was both being perceived more keenly and explained more accurately by earlier observers, and that the major findings registered in the seventeenth and nineteenth centuries are in harmony with today's reality, whereas those set out most recently are not.

Grotius, writing in a time when the outlines of the modern European states system were becoming apparent, concluded from his reflections on classical, Jewish, and Christian thought and action that war *per se* is not condemned either by the voluntary law of nations or the law of nature; that states may well reduce each other to subjection; that the boundaries of states, kingdoms, nations, or cities can often be settled by the laws of war; that wars must employ force and terror as their most proper agents; and that the arguments in favor of war are as numerous as those for the rule of law. "For where the power of law ceases," he writes, "there war begins."[14]

Enduring international peace, by contrast, is presented by this pioneering theorist of international law as a remote condition. The prophesy of Isaiah that the time shall come when "nations shall beat their swords into plowshares, and turn their spears into pruning hooks," when "nation shall not lift up sword against nation" nor "learn war any more," is in Grotius's opinion (as in that of the Jewish prophet) irrelevant insofar as the justice of war is concerned. In the Grotian perspective, the passage merely describes the state of the world that will result if all nations submit to the law of Christ. Pending consummation of this utopian dream, peace is perforce limited in time and space.

In fact, a significant passage in *De Jure Belli ac Pacis* suggests that it may not always be easy to distinguish between war and peace. War, Grotius notes, is a term for a situation that can exist even when warlike operations are not being carried on. Belligerent powers may agree on a cease-fire or truce in the course of war, and no period need be fixed for the continuance of such an arrangement, described by one of his classical authorities as "a transitory peace, in travail with war." "And I shall add," Grotius writes, "that [truces] are made too for years, twenty, thirty, forty, even a hundred years."[15] In other words, a state of belligerency may well be semipermanent or protracted.

Theorists after Grotius held rather steadfastly to his major axioms. Clausewitz, whose work *On War* laid the basis (in the Occidental world of thought) for the systematic study of war as a field of human knowledge, thus restated Grotius when he defined war as the conduct of political intercourse by other means, a form of human enterprise belonging to social existence, and a conflict of great interests that is settled by bloodshed. But he also inveighed against the folly of viewing war as an act of unrestrained violence, a mere passion for daring and winning, or "an independent thing in itself." To Clausewitz, it was quite clear that war is a serious means to a serious end, only a part of political intercourse, and therefore always subject to the political design. And this design, whether understood as referring to a particular foreign policy or to the realm of politics in general, is here decidedly not being viewed as "war by other means"—a theoretical construct in Communist conflict doctrine that was to be elaborated several decades later by Lenin, when he stood Clausewitz "on his head."

All histories of diplomacy and the law of nations point to the conclusion that modern Occidental war- and conflict-related thought favors the rule of law and peace. However, they also fully bear out Clausewitz's conclusion: "Peace seldom reigns over all Europe, and never in all quarters of the world."[16]

III

The image of the world that is being rendered today by social and political scientists with a strong interest in war, peace, and conflict resolution is one of a global order of states that are structurally alike in essence or destined to become so under the impact of irresistible leveling forces. In the logic of this tight and finite scheme, all international relations—including belligerent confrontations—are seen as manifestations of national interests that converge on three main unifying themes: the survival of the state, the maintenance of the international system, and the avoidance of war. Most of the leading educational texts, syllabi, and gaming or simulation exercises in the field are therefore elaborations of truths and abstractions that the theoreticians have worked out as if with one mind—and that they therefore seldom question. Thus, since there is no essential difference between State A and State B, there can be none between A's war and B's war.

This explains why conflicts and wars can be added up rather simply to yield some grand total that in turn will point to another universally valid, generally accepted proposition—a process of fact-finding illustrated in the following passage by Robert McNamara:

> In the eight years through late 1966 alone there were no less than 164 internationally significant outbreaks of violence, each of them specifically designed as a serious challenge to the authority or the very existence of the government in question. Eighty-two different governments were directly involved, and what is striking is that only 15 of the 164 significant resorts to violence were military conflicts between two states, and not a single one of the 164 conflicts was a formally declared war. Indeed, there has not been a formal declaration of war anywhere in the world since World War II.
>
> The planet is becoming a more dangerous place to live on not merely because of a potential nuclear holocaust but also because of the large number of *de facto* conflicts and

because the trend of such conflicts is growing rather than diminishing. At the beginning of 1958 there were 23 prolonged insurgencies going on around the world. As of February, 1966, there were 40. Further, the total number of outbreaks of violence has increased each year: in 1958 there were 34; in 1965, there were 58.[17]

The exclusive reason for this increase in international violence, we are told, is the obvious fact that so many new states are still economically underdeveloped, a premise evidently no longer subject to verification, as earlier references in this essay have suggested. Again, no allowance is made for the possibility that war-related phenomena are also, perhaps even predominantly, aspects of locally prevalent values, images, traditions, and mental constructions. Indeed, explorations of the ways of thought that make or do not make for war, or the meanings assigned to war and violence in culturally different parts of the world, would quite logically be out of place in the conceptually closed circuit of modern war and peace studies; for how can cultural diversity be perceived if "culture" (or "civilization") is not accepted as a relevant variable or factor?

The student embarking on war and peace studies today will look in vain for rigorous analyses of Occidental, Oriental, or African philosophies, ideologies, myths, and religions. Each volume he consults is likely to contain scores of cross-references to the works of other Western theorists of our era, and scarcely any (in most cases none) to source materials that would tell him how the Chinese or the Indians or the Persians have related to war in the millennia preceding the present moment. Missing, then, are referrals to the writings, for example, of Han Fei Tzu and Mao Tse-tung; to the *Mahabharata,* which our contemporaries in India continue to read with veneration; to the Koran, which is replete with commentaries on warfare that are eternally relevant for Muslims; or, in the case of Africa south of the Sahara, to the memoirs of modern literate Africans, oral history, and the fieldwork of anthropologists.

Anyone interested in uncovering the roots of war-related policies and practices will thus look in vain among today's works on political science or international relations, for access to primary sources is not being stressed anymore. The student in search of authenticity must therefore turn to the humanities, where the uniqueness of men, events, and ideas is still recognized; where clashing ideas on war can still be disentangled; and where he may come to accept the world as a "manifold of civilizations" even as he continues to perceive it as a "manifold of states."[18]

"Culture," or "civilization," if one prefers, has been variously defined. As understood in the present book it comprises those norms, values, institutions, and modes of thinking in a given society that survive change and remain meaningful to successive generations. This point is well illustrated by Paul Verhaegen's discussion of the relation between the "basic psychology" of an African people, on the one hand, and the effects of "cultural transition" on the other. Those characteristics are basic to a culture, he writes, that are dominant in the bush and remain obvious in even the most Westernized Africans.[19] Similar formulations can be devised for the Islamic realm, notably its Middle Eastern nucleus, India, Southeast Asia, China, Japan, and possibly Mongolian Central Asia, including Tibet. Other areas in which distinct norms and values have developed in counterpoint to those brought forth in the West include the Communist orbit of the Soviet Union and the Latin American region.

Several factors combine today in support of civilization as the proper focal point of war research. Not only has the Occidental model of the state ceased to be a reliable indicator or measure of such phenomena as international war and internal war, but it can no longer be viewed as the politically controlling, and hence unifying, organizational norm in international relations. These symptoms of the erosion of the state make it mandatory that we find other or additional ways to determine the configuration of an alien society.

Civilization recommends itself in this respect because it is more comprehensive as an ordering concept than the state: it can cover a host of political formations—armed bands, liberation fronts of empires; anarchies or despotism; transterritorial commonwealths of commodity producers, financiers, or religionists; and multinational political parties. Next, also in contrast to the state, a civilization is more enduring in time, even as it is usually less precisely defined in space. And finally, civilization is today a more neutral reference than the state because, contrary to the latter, it is not associated with typically Occidental norms and values. In short, there continues to be great truth in Alfred North Whitehead's remark that a political system is transient and vulnerable by comparison with the principles and forces of the society and culture that have produced it. These principles and forces require explicit recognition before the elements of the political system—in our case, war—can be understood.[20]

It is much harder for Americans than for other peoples to accept such a worldview because the United States, almost by definition, stands for the denial of cultural differences and the neglect or irrelevancy of the past. In this respect America departed long ago from the European tradition—inaugurated by Herodotus when he explained the Persian Wars as a confrontation between the rival civilizations of Europe and Asia—and is reluctant today to differentiate between wars fought within a culturally unified sphere and those between societies of disparate cultures or idea systems. In fact, after allowance is made for occasional romantic infatuations with insurgencies and wars of liberation in Africa and Asia, it appears that American suspicion of the role of ideas in international relations and foreign policy-making is so widespread that few wars in either category are accepted as reflecting a clash of ideas.

The voluminous literature on war in the traditional world provides some contrasting perspectives on this age-old human contrivance and, at the same time, yields explanations for the incidence and tolerance of war in each non-Western region. The following brief summaries of culturally and historically basic ideas about war are confined to sub-Saharan Africa, the Middle East, India, Southeast Asia, and China.

Sub-Saharan Africa

Since traditional Africa has not produced an organizational form comparable to the Occidental state, "foreign relations" have consisted in interaction among a number of differently organized but self-sufficient units: tribes, clans, villages, and other subgroups or divisions. To the extent that so-called empires, hieratic chief-doms, and kingdoms were merely conglomerates of these communities, they were also the scenes of "foreign relations" in which each socially cohesive group was apt to pit itself against the other, even though the "other" would appear to have been part of the "self" from the non-African point of view. This state of affairs, along with the absence of writing and other reliable communications, explains why the radius of intercommunity relations has always been very limited. Furthermore, no widely shared, regionally valid Pan-African institutions for conducting intercom-munity relations—along the lines of the modern European states system—could develop here, for each small community projected its own social order onto the stage of what we call foreign relations. Black Africa, however, is unified by its culture and a mode of thinking not found elsewhere in the world, and it should therefore not be surprising that we can identify certain uniquely African dispositions with regard to war and peace.

Ethnographers agree that warfare was endemic in all regions of sub-Saharan Africa and that it did not elicit moral qualms. In fact, resort to warfare was logical and necessary in terms of certain deeply held beliefs, among them the following. War and war organization assured the continuous identity of the group as it had coalesced around its own ancestors, origin myths, customs, and rites. War embod-ied the meaning of manhood in tribal life, and war symbolized the workings of the universe, which was envisioned throughout the continent as the abode of constantly contending, essentially malevolent forces.

Two additional factors deserve consideration if the role assigned to war and violence in this culture is to be appreciated on its own terms. First, death was not personalized as it is in thought systems that regard the individual as an entity tran-scending the bounds of the community to which he belongs, and second, death was not objectified as it is in Western causal thinking. In common African understanding it had to be attributable to some superior, surreal cause rather than to the weapon actually used for its infliction because magic, whether associated with ancestral spirits or witchcraft, was accepted as the paramount frame of reference for all of life.

This belief system explains why all traditional structures of African political organization, whether associated with empires, kingdoms, chiefdoms, "anarchies," villages, secret societies, or sub-rosa governments based on fetishism, have been grounded firmly in the view that death is an aspect of society rather than biography, and that conflict, properly staged and manipulated, helps maintain the mythic charter by which a community is ruled. These two motifs and their organic inter-action have found different local expressions, but in certain areas of government the separate records converge on a common pattern of institutionalized hostilities, intrigues, and internal wars. For example, since it was rare in Africa to find rules that clearly indicated a single heir, succession usually raised rival claimants, re-sulting in wars for the kingship after an incumbent's death. Whether in the tribal societies of southern Africa, the conquest states of the Interlacustrine Bantus, the kingdoms of the savanna, or among the Mossi and Yoruba in West Africa—to men-tion just a few of the recognized political systems—ruling circles were rent by quarrels and jealousies that were expected to erupt in dynastic, fratricidal, or civil wars, and to lead to prolonged periods of anarchy, during which the contest for power would be temporarily resolved.

Not only was this violence often preceded by institutionalized regicide, but internal peace did not necessarily follow once the issue of succession had been decided. Since revolts by subordinate princes and chiefs were always expected in East Africa's kingdoms, for example, potential rebels or aspirants to power were routinely murdered or banished. Violent internecine conflict was customary also among the Nuba, the Nuer, the Kamba, the Masai, the Nandi, and other East African peoples, as well as among such territorial groups as the Zulu, the Swazi, and the Barotse in southern Africa. Likewise, war was waged regularly by the central governments of most of the imperial domains of West Africa in order to quell unruly behavior on the part of subordinate regimes.

No agreement exists among specialists in African social organization on just what constitutes rebellion, in which circumstances one can speak of civil war, which episode is properly described as a mere raid or which qualifies as full-fledged aggression. There is general agreement, however, on the proposition that peace was not considered necessary for the maintenance of the inner order in traditional Africa, that conflict was allowed to express itself in violence, and that warfare among component units of a community was accepted as an organic part of the inner law if employed for purposes considered permissible in a given society. But whether the allowable end was cattle, slaves, women, vengeance or punishment, grazing or water rights, aggrandizement, or the allocation or reshuffling of power, the fact remains that violence has been endemic almost everywhere. Sanctioned by basic values and beliefs, violence provided, in one form or another, the structural principles for the education of men and the administration of society. Indeed, one might justifiably conclude that internal war was more likely to sustain than to disrupt existing organizational schemes.

Relations between socially or tribally united communities reflect the same fundamental dispositions. Military power, even when wielded by formidable armies, was thus always closely associated with magical power; although concrete rewards such as the capture of cattle or slaves were as prized in the extended martial contest as in the limited engagement, it was the sensation of success left by the investment of superior power that mattered most. And success, again, savored of the enjoyment of a situation in which the enemy of the day was slain or routed and his habitat reduced to ruin. That is to say, victory here was not controlled by expectations of permanent aggrandizement, redemption of lost territories, the extension of a way of life, or—with a few exceptions—the installation of a moral system. For those who fought, the end of war was war itself.

All this was in strict accordance with the logic of nonliterate, essentially behavioral thought, present-centered time concepts, and the spatial characteristics of African societies. Shrewd calculations of advantage are certainly not missing from the historical records, and particular campaigns, such as the nineteenth-century Ashanti wars, which culminated in the siege of Kumasi, are known to have been planned most methodically. But this sort of comprehensive, long-range planning was not the rule, if only because the future was not seen as separate from the present or the past, and because political identity did not depend on territorial boundaries. Thus strategic thinking, if the term is applicable at all, did not aim at the consolidation of victory by rehabilitating devastated areas, integrating conquered peoples, or establishing definite frontiers.

The same ways of thought naturally obtained in defeat, since the vanquished were at one with the victors in their basic understanding of the meaning of war in life. Generals might be expected to commit suicide if they lost a battle and warriors might have to be instantly dispatched if they returned home without their spears, as was the custom among the Matabele, but the governments for which they had fought were rarely moved by the calamities of battle to refashion their defensive posture or redesign their fundamental orientation. Not every society was as totally confident, for example, as the Sukuma of present-day Tanzania, who believed that a victorious enemy could not defeat the spirits of the conquered group or alter their enduring influence on the land, no matter how great the devastation or loss. Yet all accepted with equanimity the ebb and flow of endless war.

Today, Africans in all walks of life continue to be guided by many of these traditional values and institutions, even as they affirm new interests and commitments associated with the life-style of the modern age. Intellectually persuasive syntheses of the traditional and the new orders are still rare in African politics. In fact, scholarly analyses of coups d'état, mutinies, guerrilla operations, revolutions, and civil wars suggest that the two frames of reference may not be easily reconcilable. As Aristide Zolberg rightly notes, "values, norms and structures have survived to a significant extent everywhere, even where their existence was not legally recognized during the colonial era."[21]

The Middle East

Twentieth-century Jews and Arabs are probably more closely tied to traditional religious beliefs than most other literate peoples. Furthermore, their holy texts are different from other sacred literature in an important way: they are not merely intended to be depositories of religious truth, but also serve as comprehensive manuals of instruction in all secular matters. In other words, they are primary and definitive value references and major sources of normative thinking and policy-making for their respective communities; and in this general context, one cannot read the Old Testament or the Koran and its attendant Islamic traditions without being overwhelmed by the prominence given to the subject of war.

According to the Old Testament, which is accepted by the faithful not only as the official history of the Jews but also as a timeless sanction or constitution for the establishment of a Jewish state, there is only one Chosen People; all others are subservient outcasts, subject if necessary to extermination. In Isaiah, Chapter 60, the tribal deity advises (in its most benign mood) that "the sons of strangers shall build up thy walls and their kings shall minister unto thee." But elsewhere (Deuteronomy 7, 12, 20; Joshua 1–3, 6, 8; Judges 21; II Kings 3; Psalm 135; and Isaiah 61) we find injunction after injunction on how best to cast out, smite, utterly destroy, and extirpate the many "others," great and small, especially those in the region adjoining the River Jordan.

In all the literature exhorting and ennobling war, nothing comes to mind that is quite so chilling as these passages from Deuteronomy, Chapter 7:

> 5. But thus shall ye deal with them: ye shall destroy their altars, and break down their images, and cut down their groves, and burn their graven images with fire;
>
> 6. For thou art a holy people unto the LORD thy God: the LORD thy God hath chosen thee to be a special people unto himself, above all people that are upon the face of the earth.
>
> 16. And thou shalt consume all the people which the LORD thy God shall deliver thee; thine eye shall have no pity upon them; neither shalt thou serve their gods; for that *will* be a snare unto thee.
>
> 22. And the LORD thy God will put out those nations before thee by little and little; thou mayest not consume them at once, lest the beasts of the field increase upon thee.
>
> 23. But the LORD thy God shall deliver them unto thee, and shall destroy them with a mighty destruction, until they be destroyed.
>
> 24. And he shall deliver their kings into thine hand, and thou shalt destroy their name from under heaven: there shall no man be able to stand before thee, until thou hast destroyed them.
>
> 25. The graven images of their gods shall ye burn with fire; thou shalt not desire the silver or gold that is on them, nor take it unto thee, lest thou be snared therein: for it is an abomination to the LORD thy God.
>
> 26. Neither shalt thou bring an abomination into thine house, lest thou be a cursed thing like it: but thou shalt utterly detest it, and thou shalt utterly abhor it; for it is a cursed thing.

These guidelines for methodical genocide are repeated in Deuteronomy (Chapters 12 and 20). With regard to the total destruction of cities delivered by God's will and sword to his people, we read: "Thou shalt save alive nothing that breatheth: But thou shalt utterly destroy them, namely, the Hittites, and the Amorites, the Canaanites, and the Perizzites, the Hivites, and the Jesbusites; as the LORD thy God hath commanded thee" (Deut. 20:17). The same divinely sanctioned policy is given expression in II Kings, Chapters 22 and 23, where King Joshua is told to break down the enemy, reduce the land to desolation, defile the sepulchers, and impoverish all who refuse to acquiesce in the rule of the Chosen Race, and again in Judges 21, where the Chosen are ordered to smite all, including women and children, who do not join them.

Traditional Jewish attitudes toward war and its pursuit must be seen in the context of Near Eastern culture as a whole: throughout the long centuries of ancient history, few if any nations differed from the Jews in their ideas about the conduct of international relations. In other words, war, enslavement and imperialism, unmitigated by considerations of "collective security," "peaceful coexistence" or the "balance of power," combined to make up the real as well as the ideal or preferred system.

In the vast Arab/Islamic domain of West Asia and North Africa, war was idealized and institutionalized in many forms, notably in the *jihad,* or "holy war." Defined in one *hadith* (tradition) as the "peak of religion," the *jihad* is part and parcel of Koranic sacred law. In particular, it denotes the mandate incumbent on each believer to prepare his way to paradise by exerting all his power, including that of the sword, in the service of Allah and the Islamic creed, which is universalist in contrast to the ethnocentric Judaic faith. Consequently, one may view a Muslim's entire life as "a continuous process of warfare, psychological and political, if not strictly military," and conclude that Islamic precepts advance a doctrine of permanent war regardless of whether or not believers are actually engaged in military activities.[22] And, in fact, as the power of the Arabized and Islamized states declined, this doctrine became largely dormant, leaving Muslims in a condition roughly comparable to what is known in international law as a "state of insurgency."

In the context of normative thought, value orientation and foreign policy-making, then, war is a dominant motif in this culture. Peace, by contrast, being associated with essentially otherworldly, metaphysical concerns, has no overriding positive meaning in temporal affairs, except perhaps as a description of that time when the world will have become Islamized. Pending this outcome of the historic struggle, mankind is divided into the Realm of Peace, whose denizens are engaged in rightful combat at the service of Allah, and the Realm of War, which is the abode, by definition, of all unbelievers regardless of their actual conduct or intentions. It follows logically that diplomacy is viewed more readily as an auxiliary to war, a device serving the cause of belligerence and expansion, than as an avenue leading toward peace.

Islamic theory grew out of and confirmed the life-styles of the Bedouin nomads, as shown so convincingly by the biography of the Prophet, the Koran itself, and Charles Doughty's masterful *Travels in Arabia Deserta*. The dominant masculine image or heroic ideal in this harsh world was the warrior, engaged in both great and petty ventures. Camel raids, brigandage, attacks on the despised world of the sedentary and the sown, tribal wars, far-flung military expeditions, and, above all, endless wanderings in a hostile environment—all this epitomized the allure and excitement of life that was to compensate for the stark and tedious task of eking out a livelihood. What could peace on earth mean here except sheer boredom, sterility, and stagnation?

The political history of the Arabic-speaking peoples from the seventh century to the present corroborates the value system that inhabits their life-style and doctrine. Vast expanses of the Dar al-Harb (Realm of War) in Europe, Africa and Asia were conquered by force of arms to become integral parts of the Islamic Realm of Peace. Furthermore, Islamic administrations, civil and military, reinforced and perfected their own understanding of the function of diplomacy, borrowing heavily from the sophisticated "warrior diplomacy" of the Persians and Byzantines. This type of statecraft relied on psychological warfare, espionage, and subversion in its relentless pursuit of victory over neighboring lands and rules. In short, nowhere in this region was "peace" accepted as a realizable goal in the conduct of international relations.

The inner order of the Realm of Peace, meanwhile, has also been rent by continual violence and war, even though the ruling idea-system calls for, indeed assumes, peace and unity. The major source of this incongruity has been, and continues to be, the absence of effective fundamental principles of political organization. The caliphate, vaguely conceived by the Prophet's successors, notably the learned divines trained in Muslim law, as the exclusive, indivisible administrative scheme for the governance of the entire community of believers, actually never got off the ground. Instead, commensurate with the swift extension of the faith and culture, we have had multiple caliphates, sultanates, and emirates; competitive dynasties; ambitious and contentious aspirants to power; plots and counterplots; and assassinations and revolts.

The establishment by conquest of the Ottoman Caliphate in 1453 brought a respite in the divisiveness and anarchy, but its dissolution in 1918–19 returned the Arabized Near Eastern Muslims (Turks, Persians, and Egyptians can draw from cultural reserves in political organization that are not at the disposal of the Arabs) to more familiar patterns of political thought and action. Contemporary possessors of executive power are thus always tempted to foment or condone violence and intrigue in inter-Arab relations in order to protect their tenuous personal positions or to promote their particular dreams of a unity to come.

India

India has experienced the impact of the Middle East (as have parts of Southeast Asia) in a variety of ways, most poignantly perhaps in the fields of statecraft and international relations. Northern India, after all, had been a satrapy of the Persian Empire, and even more extensive portions of the subcontinent were ruled for many centuries by Persianized Mongols. In addition, Islam penetrated through diverse channels to find political expression in the Sultanate of Delhi, the Mogul Empire and, more recently, the Islamic republics of Pakistan and Bangladesh. And yet many prominent members of the Anglicized elite continue to insist in their scholarly discussions of India's political system that the pre-Islamic Hindu order is still the principal influence, despite massive borrowings—first from the Near East and in modern times from Anglo-Saxon Europe. One of the most ardent Indian nationalists, the late diplomat and historian K. M. Panikkar, thus never tired of reminding his contemporaries in the East and the West that "the society described in the *Mahabharata* is not essentially different from what holds its sway today in India," and that if the "Indian administration of today is analyzed to its bases, the doctrines and practices of Chanakya [or Kautilya] will be found to be still in force."[23]

Kautilya's *Arthasastra,* to which Panikkar refers, has been acclaimed as the greatest piece of literature surviving from the Maurya dynasty (322–185 B.C.?). The text is considered exemplary because it explains in systematic fashion how Hindus must think and behave when they are engaged in government, economics, and foreign relations. In all these activities, summarily described as the domain of *artha* (defined by Kautilya as that science which treats of the means of acquiring and maintaining the earth), winning is all that counts. *Artha* norms are thus carefully set apart in Hindu logic and metaphysics from the codes of conduct mandatory in the pursuit of the three other major ends of life: namely, *kama* (pleasure), *dharma* (duty, especially as it relates to caste regulations), and *moksa* (the assiduous quest for release from life and its illusions including *artha* aims). In government and foreign relations, however, the precepts of *artha* are inextricably enmeshed with the *dharma* obligations of the warrior caste, for this caste supplies the kings and other secular officers of state, including the armed forces.

In marked contrast to biographical patterns common in Europe and America which express the aspiration to develop an all-encompassing philosophy of life, Hindus have thus been directed for millennia to live by a plurality of philosophies. And the complexity of these separate commitments grows when one remembers that guidelines for proper behavior also differ for each of the four castes and each of the four stages of life. However, the fundamental question—how should men be governed?—was answered in traditional Indian thought and practice by unqualified recourse to *danda*, the rod of punishment. According to the theory of coercive state authority, the king must wield *danda* if he is to enjoy prosperity and acquire not only this world but also the one to come. The *Dharmasastras*, or *Books of the Law*, notably the remarkable compendium assigned to Manu;[24] the *Arthasastras;* the *Mahabharata* (India's great national epic); and the popular, didactic beast fables (the best known collection of these being the *Panchatantra*) thus converge on the doctrine of *matsyanyaya*—the Principle or Law of the Fishes—in accordance with which the king must enforce his government and punish those who deserve it, lest the strong torment the weak as fish are fried on a pike or as in water they devour each other.

Danda, then, rules all; *danda* is awake while others are asleep; and *danda* insists that warriors fight to acquire spiritual merit. These truths are relayed by all sacred texts (which continue to be widely read), but most eloquently by Krishna's discourse with Arjuna in the *Bhagavadgita* section of the *Mahabharata*. The exchange takes place immediately before the great battle at Kurukshetra. We read that Arjuna, on reaching the battlefield, was so distressed at the thought of having to fight and kill revered members of his family, whom he saw ranged on the opposite side, that he resolved to forsake war. Krishna then turned him from this resolution by reminding him of the inexorable law of his caste: a kshatriya must fight and kill his enemy, and the attainment of victory requires total concentration on the task at hand, including total disregard of other moral or emotional restraints.

The same teachings have been passed on through the centuries by other sages and authorities on *artha* and *rajadharma* (royal duties). The king is created to commit cruel acts, we learn from Bhishma, legendary guru in the *Mahabharata;* whereas ordinary men, not made of such stern stuff, seldom succeed in worldly affairs. Like a snake that devours creatures living in holes, the earth swallows up the king who does not fight and the Brahman who does not go abroad (for study).[25]

The history of inter-kingdom relations before and after the Muslim conquests faithfully reflects the dictates of the *artha* philosophy; its annals speak of endemic anarchy and warfare. True to the law, inequality was postulated as the everlasting condition of political existence, power as the only measure of political worth, and war as the normal activity of the state. On the authority, again, of the *Mahabharata:*

Might is above right; right proceeds from might. . . . Right is in the hands of the strong. . . . Everything is pure that comes from the strong. . . . When thou findest thyself in a low state, try to lift thyself up, resorting to pious as well as to cruel actions. Before practicing morality wait until thou art strong. . . . If men think thee soft, they will despise thee. [Book XII 134:5–7, 2–3; 140:38; 141:62; 56:21].

A king or politician who has no power is a conquered king, the *Arthasastra* tells us, and in such a lamentable state of inferiority he is reduced to peace—defined in the Hindu world as stagnation.[26]

Each king, then, was to chart his course of aggression and withdrawal scientifically and realistically in accordance with the doctrine of the *mandala* (a design symbolic of the universe). This theory—viewed by many Indian and foreign scholars as the most remarkable of many original ideas in the Hindu domain of foreign policy—stipulates that a kingdom is an ally or an enemy according to its geographical position with respect to the intending conqueror. The *mandala* or circle of states usually consists of twelve kings, although the system could be enlarged to include many more. Each king (note that "the state" is not the unit here) is expected to view his own domain as the center or target of the *mandalas* or rings of states. In this context his natural enemies are his next-door neighbors, and his natural friends are in the adjoining circle. The third ring is composed of his enemies' friends, the fourth of friends of his allies, and so forth. Next, the science of *Artha* admonishes the king to be particularly careful in measuring his distance from the dominant power, that is to say from that king in the galaxy of kings who has the capacity to fight without allies and is therefore known as the "neutral" king.

The workings of this principle can be seen throughout the history of Hindu India in the temporary alliances of two kingdoms to accomplish the encirclement and destruction of the kingdoms between them—at which time, of course, the former "friend" becomes automatically enemy number one, that is, the immediate subject of the next attack. However, theory and reality also converge on the proposition that neither the *mandala* nor the particular positions and relations abstracted from it were ever to be trusted completely. An arsenal of intelligence tricks and diplomatic techniques, together with a standing and alert army, was regarded as the best security. *Artha* thus taught the king how to bribe his ally or enemy by gifts, promises, and decorations; how to lull him into a sense of false security through conciliation, negotiation, and other forms of appeasement, while systematically preparing a military attack on him. Simultaneously, he was, of course, expected to sow dissension in the frontier provinces of his enemy in order to soften resistance when he was ready to stage the final armed invasion. In fact, and as illustrated in the following essay, the skills of intrigue were more highly prized by theoreticians and rulers than was material power.

To summarize, war was the normal state of affairs in India's interstate relations until the British unified and pacified the subcontinent. But this episode of Occidental imperialism was a mere moment in the Asian reckoning of time. Hence, many thoughtful and knowledgeable Indians express doubt whether the alien rule of law, including international law, will or should prevail over traditional law.

Southeast Asia

In the course of the fascinating process of cultural diffusion known as the "Indianization" of Asia, the principles of *artha* penetrated much of Southeast Asia. One might even characterize the phenomenon as "cultural imperialism," at least if one were to adopt the parlance currently used by some to describe the impact of European and American culture on the rest of the world. This vast region, which now encompasses Myanmar (Burma), Laos, Kampuchea (Cambodia), Thailand, North and South Vietnam, Indonesia, Malaysia, Singapore, and the Philippines, was previously dotted with separate kingdoms, each remarkable in its commitment to deeply rooted indigenous beliefs as well as in its talent for integrating appropriate motifs from Hindu, Buddhist, Confucian, or Islamic idea systems.

In pre-nineteenth-century times, the most important regionally unifying themes were the cults of the *devaraja,* or god-king, who could do no wrong so long as he was successful, and the acceptance of rebellion, subversion, war, and the threat of war as a normal part of everyday life. Scholars specializing in Southeast Asian history have pointed out that political identity was nowhere a function of secure frontiers, concrete material power, a unifying legal system, or even legitimate royal succession; rather, it depended on an individual ruler's compliance with the cosmo-magical "constitution" of his realm. What mattered in this context was physical possession of the capital, the palace, and symbolically significant royal regalia; and these sources of prestige could be rightfully seized by cunning or by such acts of violence as the murder of an incumbent prince.

The traditional coexistence of the principles of divine kingship and insurrection explains why the usurper was entitled to obedience and respect, why the idea of the state was associated in the final analysis with the successful ruling personality, and why these kingdoms were locked for centuries in combat of one type or another. Full-scale wars, limited invasions, or guerrilla fighting thus marked relations among the rulers of Thailand, Burma, Laos, and Khmer-Cambodia, as well as between those of Java and Sumatra. Kingdoms rose and fell, and empires crumbled, only to be resurrected later in some other form. Cambodia, for example, was once part of a Vietnamese empire; the Mekong Delta was constantly in contention; Assam was part of an aggressive Burmese state; and the Khmers, probably the most martial of all these warrior peoples, tirelessly staked out their claim to what is today Burma. While most principalities and empires were racked by domestic rebellion and subversion, some (notably in present-day Indonesia) are reputed, in modern nationalist texts, to have had vassals as far afield as Vietnam, Cambodia, Thailand, and Malaysia. Other allegedly unified kingdoms—Laos and Burma, in particular—were actually conglomerates of separate, warring states.

In this region, then, as in the Middle East and Africa south of the Sahara, internal war merged with external war to form intricate webs of conflict and violence. Hallowed by myth, sanctioned by religion, accepted by the people, and celebrated in legend, art and architecture, this theme has been oft repeated in recent history as in the 1933 "Royalist Rebellion" of Siam, the reinstallation in Burma of the traditional Buddhist trappings of power politics, the elaborate staging by Indonesia's Sukarno of confrontations with Malaysia and the Philippines, and the complex, ongoing interplay of animosities among Cambodia, Thailand, and Vietnam.

To be sure, one can point to a few nonintervention agreements; for example, in the twelfth century an accord was concluded between Tonkin and the Indianized state of Champa. (It was conceived, by the way, as a reinsurance device that would permit Champa to capture and destroy with impunity the temple of Angkor.) But here, as elsewhere in southern Asia, enmity remained the norm in inter-kingdom relations. This was true even when China's persistently aggressive policies could have been checked by the organization of collective security measures; instead, each kingdom usually offered separate, ferocious resistance when Chinese forces interfered too blatantly. In short, peace had no place as a value either in the metaphysical order of ideas from which these societies derived their identities or in the intricate, artistic processes of statecraft that issued from the royal palaces.

Two thoughts, in particular, impose themselves as one follows the relentless seesaw movements of attack, victory, and defeat that have passed like forces of nature over this culturally complex area. First, in the context of comparative history and religion, there seems to be no doubt that recourse to warfare and palace revolution was hallowed as an integral principle of the ruling cosmic order. And second, this ancient culture complex has indeed been the theater in which numerous rival ideas about war—emanating, above all, from India and China—have clashed throughout recorded time. With respect to modern world politics, meanwhile, it is as irresistible as it is ironic to note that American ideas about war were thoroughly discredited precisely here.[27]

China

The Pax Sinica that in recent decades has been descending on Tibet and elsewhere in Central Asia, on the Himalayan region of the Indian subcontinent, and on parts of Southeast Asia is a function both of traditional Chinese statecraft and of Mao Tse-tung's adaptations of Marxism-Leninism-Stalinism to the needs of revolutionary China. Contrary to the view held in some American intellectual circles, there is no gulf of discontinuity[28] between the old and the new China when it comes to the politics of war and peace.

With respect to ancient China, as with India, Westerners have long pleased themselves in imagining a spiritually superior civilization, anchored in Confucianism and Taoism, in which men shunned violence and all things uncouth, if only because their attention was riveted on etiquette, sincerity, civility, humanism, and the search for harmony. Just why such exalted views of Oriental society would have become so fixed in the Western mind may well be a question that only ethnopsychiatrists can answer as they become adept at dealing with the symptoms of pathology in intercultural relations. Suffice it to say, "[T]here was never a Taoist State as conceived by Chuang Tsu, nor a Confucian State as conceived by Mencius."[29] Indeed, the source materials—which have long been available in excellent translations—teach something else entirely: namely, that China, whatever its geographic configuration and official ideology, has traditionally depended heavily on a judicious investment of war effort, both at home and abroad.

Ping-ti Ho, an authority on Confucian China, and Lucian W. Pye thus agree that the Chinese state has always derived its ultimate power from the army—a circumstance that has largely predetermined its authoritarian character from the days of empire to the rule of Mao Tse-tung.[30] History also instructs us that dynasties usually came to power through armed force; that revolts—and they were commonplace—were staged and smashed by military means; that the science of besieging walled cities was highly developed even in very early times;[31] and that the conduct of all these military operations was organically linked not only to the perfection of weaponry but also, and more importantly, to such official nonmilitary pursuits as the cultivation of crops, the organization of hydraulic works, and the building of walls—occupations without which war could not have proceeded as successfully as it did.[32]

War and agriculture, in fact, have consistently been viewed in China as two fundamental, mutually dependent occupations, perhaps never more so than in the Epoch of the Warring States (ca. 450–221 B.C.) and in the Maoist period. Accounts from the earlier period can thus be cited to the effect that successive generations of Chinese were decimated by war with methodical regularity, that breathing spaces were allowed only so that the peasant armies might be replenished after having been cut to pieces, and that the army was made to labor on public projects and "in the countryside" when not campaigning.

All-Under-Heaven, which consisted of numerous separate provinces, was thus in total disarray during the Epoch of the Warring States; big states ate up lesser ones as systematically as silkworms eat mulberry leaves. Yet China—her contours forever indeterminate—survived mainly, it appears, because the art of war had here reached a mature form by the beginning of the fourth century B.C. By this time, Samuel Griffith notes, the Chinese possessed weapons not at the disposal of other societies and were absolute masters of offensive and defensive tactics and techniques that would have enabled them to cause Alexander the Great a great deal more trouble than did the Greeks, the Persians, or the Indians.[33]

All Chinese schools of thought accepted the idea of war, usually as part of the *fa* dimension of government, which existed to supplement what rule by benevolence (*li*) could not accomplish. As Arthur Waley explains, the duty to punish badly ruled states, or to chastise unruly barbarians on the frontiers of the Middle Kingdom, was emphasized consistently by the Confucians and was acknowledged also by their rivals, the Mohists.[34] Just as the principle of filial piety could rightfully be enforced by the killing or mutilation of offspring who resisted paternal guidance, so might the art of persuasion in the community of unequal states be supplemented by the rod of war. In contrast to the domain of internal and family affairs, however, for which legal codes were periodically promulgated by the imperial keeper of Heaven's Mandate, there was no international law and no court or arbitral commission to indicate which state was "badly ruled," or to compose differences impartially. The principle of the "righteous war" thus usually served as a moral cloak for open acts of aggression, which often occurred after atrocity stories had been spread concerning the society singled out for punishment.

The theoreticians and generals who perfected this side of Chinese statecraft, and who then succeeded in bringing about the first unification of China in 221 B.C., are collectively known as the Legalists, or Realists. The essence of their science, discernible as early as the seventh century B.C., but which is seen fully developed in the fourth and third centuries in the writings of Sun Tzu, Lord Shang, and Han Fei Tzu, is the uncompromising recognition that war and organization for war are the mainstays of government. "How to get the people to die" is the problem that continually occupies the Realists. According to this school of martial thought, it is a misfortune for a prosperous country not to be at war; for in such a state of peace the country will breed the "Six Maggots." In *The Book of Lord Shang,* the parasites that attack in peacetime are enumerated: "rites and music, odes and history, moral culture and virtue, filial piety and brotherly love, sincerity and faith, chastity and integrity, benevolence and righteousness, criticism of the army and being ashamed of fighting. If there are these . . . things, the ruler is unable to make people farm and fight, and then the state will be so poor that it will be dismembered."[35] Vagabonds and draft dodgers, merchants and artisans who deal in nonessential goods, scholars who spread doctrines at variance with Legalist teachings—these are the "Vermin of the State," we learn from Han Fei Tzu.[36] As such, they must be unmercifully quashed so that the people can be kept in ignorance and awe while the king extends the frontiers of the state.

Han Fei Tzu's and Lord Shang's admonitions—that the ruler must make certain everyone within his borders understands warfare, that there can be no private exemptions from military service, and that the people must be concentrated on warfare—were faithfully followed by China's first unifier, Shih Huang Ti. The notorious Burning of the Books in 213 B.C. was thus conceived and executed as "the logical last step in unification," as Derk Boddle puts it,[37] and it may now be seen as the precedent for numerous other "cultural revolutions" in Maoist China.

From time to time, subsequent generations of Chinese scholars have professed to be shocked by these doctrines, but there has never been an age when the martial classics, especially the works of Sun Tzu and Han Fei Tzu, have not been read. Not only did imperial edicts in later dynasties prescribe the study of these works for the aspirant to an army commission, but Sun Tzu's *Art of War* alone stimulated more than fifty commentaries and interpretative studies between 1368 and 1628. Western nations were long ignorant of the treatise's existence, and when it did become known in the West, the reception was one of neglectful scorn. Japan, by contrast, took Sun Tzu's work most seriously, as did Russia after the Mongol Tatars brought it there.

In China proper, *The Art of War* continues to be considered a classic to this very day.[38] Conceptually, Maoist strategic doctrine is closely related to the thought of the great master, and Mao Tse-tung's most elegant maxims and metaphors—which may be found in *Strategic Problems of China's Revolutionary War, On Guerrilla Warfare,* and *On the Protracted War*—recall those formulated in *The Art of War.* Indeed, reflections on the continuity of Chinese history and ideas about war lead to the conclusion that the Sinification of Leninism could proceed as swiftly and smoothly as it did primarily because of the pervasiveness of Legalism.

Legalist and Maoist ideas converge; they do not meet by chance. And Maoist elites make use of Legalist references deliberately, not in a casually metaphorical way. The struggle between the Legalists, openly identified today with progressive forces in China's past, and the followers of Confucius, who stand for all that is reactionary and regressive in the country's affairs, is thus mentioned in the most improbable contexts. For example, a lengthy stricture on the seemingly mundane subject of traffic safety (broadcast in September 1974 from Haikow, Hainan Island) begins as follows:

> In order to raise traffic-safety work in Hainan to a new level, it is necessary first of all to do a good job of criticism of Lin [Piao] and Confucius. It is necessary to study Marxism–Leninism–Mao Tse-tung thought seriously and unfold activities to evaluate [*sic*] the Legalists and criticize the Confucianists.[39]

And nothing in Chinese intellectual history suggests that the Chinese Communist digestive system would be overburdened by this governmental linkage of traffic-safety work to criticism of Lin and Confucius. After all, as one of the foremost students of Chinese military, political, and psychological strategy has pointed out, the present system is only the latest manifestation in more than two thousand years of Chinese strategic thought—a continuity found nowhere in the West.[40]

Chinese commissars, however faithfully schooled in Leninism-Maoism, can thus be expected to use traditional military philosophy to justify both their world-view and the roles assigned them in warfare and society.[41] The easy congruence of these frames of reference is nowhere more impressively demonstrated than in Mao Tse-tung's own writings. Here, elaborate expositions of Communist dialectics and discourses on the tactical and strategic doctrines employed during the revolutionary war mingle freely with allusions to Mao's favorite classical novels, traditional boxing precepts, the rules of the ancient game of Wei-ch'i (in Japanese, Go), and, above all, to the writings of Sun Tzu, the most esteemed of the Legalist philosophers of war. A few illustrations must suffice.

The Maoists and the Legalists share a militarist, militant vocabulary—one that conveys the unqualified thesis that organization, whether of the village or the world, is war organization, to be established and maintained by the same tactical and strategic rules that apply to the battlefield. Mao thus writes: "In China the main form of struggle is war and the main form of organization is the army. Other forms, like organizations and mass struggles are also extremely important . . . but they are all for the sake of war."[42] The pervasiveness of this conviction explains the stress consistently placed by Legalists and Maoists alike on the need to create agro-military communes and to maintain rural base areas under strict military control. It also explains the striking concurrence of certain poetic metaphors: "The people are like water, and the army is like fish," Mao writes, and the tactics of Chinese statecraft "constitute the art of swimming in the ocean of war." The challenge, as Mao sees it, is "to drown the enemy in the ocean of a people's war . . . [to] lure him into the deep,"[43] just as it was when Sun Tzu wrote:

> Now the shape of an army resembles water. Take advantage of the enemy's unpreparedness; attack him when he does not expect it; avoid his strength and strike his emptiness, and like water, none can oppose you. . . .

Just as water adapts itself to the conformation of the ground, so in war one must be flexible.[44]

Whoever or wherever the enemy is, says Mao, he must be moved "to help in his own destruction," or, as the party chairman puts it elsewhere, he must contribute to his own encirclement. Eventually, "a worldwide net will be formed from which the fascist monkeys can find no escape."[45] Just as "tunneling operations"—vividly described in Sun Tzu's and Mao's manuals—are designed to undermine the physical foundations of the enemy's military position, so are psychological offensives meant to subvert his moral and intellectual bases. Confuse the enemy's leaders; if possible drive them insane, advised Sun Tzu. Costly battles would then become unnecessary. And among the techniques employed to achieve these ends, none has received so much careful elaboration in Legalist and Maoist strategy as the art of dissimulation, simulation, and deception. Indeed, as Scott Boorman notes, this concept of stratagem goes far beyond mere attempts to outwit the enemy: it involves the much more sophisticated task of directly manipulating his perception of reality, particularly the values he attributes to various outcomes of the conflict.[46] Sun Tzu's exhortation to "hit the enemy's mind" has thus traditionally been viewed as the prerequisite of victory.

The Legalist master's axiom that "war is based on deception"[47] has been paraphrased often by Mao Tse-tung, who also advocates the intricate, indirect approaches to successful combat and maneuvering outlined in *The Art of War*. Mao's instructions to guerrillas, for example—that they must be as cautious as virgins and as quick as rabbits, mobile and forever changing in appearance—are prefigured in some of Sun Tzu's verses, notably those dealing with offensive strategy and the use of spies and double agents. Furthermore, Sun Tzu's rule that the enemy must be deceived by "creating shapes" or by concealing one's own shape from him is paralleled in Mao's commitment to the consummate skill of creating "illusions":

> Illusions and inadvertence may deprive one of superiority and the initiative. Hence, deliberately to create illusions for the enemy and then spring surprise attacks upon him is a means . . . of achieving superiority and seizing the initiative. What are illusions? "Even the woods and bushes on Mount Pakung look like enemy troops"—this is an example of illusion. And "making a noise in the east while attacking the west" is a way of creating illusions for the enemy. . . . It is therefore extremely important . . . to seal off his information, . . . keeping the enemy in the dark . . . and thus laying the objective basis for his illusions and inadvertence. We are not Duke Hsiang of Sung and have no use for his stupid scruples about benevolence, righteousness, and morality in war. In order to win victory we must try our best to seal the eyes and the ears of the enemy, making him blind and deaf, and to create confusion in the minds of the enemy commanders, driving them distracted.[48]

History suggests that the fundamental ideas in a given civilization are often conveyed better by *Homo ludens*—"man the game-player"—than by "man the theory-maker." In China, the idea of war is eloquently expressed in Wei-ch'i, the game of strategy favored by Chinese statesmen and literati from the early Han dynasty to modern times.[49] Quite unlike the Occidental game of chess, in which the goal is total victory through the capture of a single figure, Wei-ch'i involves a

protracted attempt to extend control slowly over dispersed territory. Play is dif-
fused, and the similarity between this pastime and Maoist guerrilla warfare is quite
obvious. The basic strategy in Wei-ch'i is encirclement and counterencirclement—
all aimed at setting up spheres of influence within enemy territory in order to undermine the opponent gradually by attacks from within. Maoist tactics of "enclos-
ing" or "forming" territory (in the psychological as well as geographic sense) are
thus readily comparable to what counts in Wei-ch'i. Chairman Mao explains:

> Thus the enemy and ourselves each have imposed two kinds of encirclement on the other,
> resembling in the main a game of Wei-ch'i: campaigns and battles between us and the
> enemy are comparable to the capturing of each other's pieces, and the enemy's strong-
> holds . . . and our guerrilla base areas . . . are comparable to the blank spaces secured
> on the board.[50]

In the Maoist theory of insurgency, as in Wei-ch'i, time is long, the grid is
large, and warfare is continuous, shifting from one subboard to the next. In either
case, success in combat hinges squarely on abiding by Sun Tzu's rule: "Know the
enemy and know yourself; in a hundred battles you will never be in peril."[51] Or, if
one prefers to be up to date, by observing Mao Tse-tung's dictum:

> . . . war is nothing supernatural, it is one of the things in the world that follow the
> determined course of their development; hence, Sun Tzu's law, "know your enemy and
> know yourself, and you can fight a hundred battles without disaster," is still a scientific
> truth.[52]

IV

The foregoing reflections on war and the clash of ideas support certain general
propositions in the fields of international relations and foreign policy-making.

1. There are different cultures in the world. Consequently, there are different
   modes of thinking, value systems, and forms of political organization.
2. Within a given society, norms, normative ideas, and notions about what is
   normal evolve from a continuous interaction between the ruling value system, on the one hand, and the society's perception of social and political
   reality, on the other.
3. A society is virile and effective if it can count on stable patterns of perception, judgment, and action. If, by way of contrast, the interaction between
   the commitment to certain values and the common perception of reality is
   seriously disturbed, the normative system becomes unreliable; in such circumstances, the society is apt to be morally confused and politically ineffective.
4. For any society, success in the conduct of international relations turns on two
   characteristics: (a) confidence in the norms and values that control the inner
   order of the society and (b) accurate perception of the world in which the
   national interest must be defined and furthered. Failure ensues when confi-

dence in the nation's integrity is eroded and when the vision of the international environment becomes defective.

5. In the multicultural environment of the twentieth century, foreign policy-makers must recognize and analyze multiple, distinct cultures as well as political systems that differ from each other significantly in their modes of rational and normative thought, their value orientations, and their dispositions in foreign affairs.

6. The fundamental foreign policy–related themes running through the histories of sub-Saharan Africa, the Middle East, India, Southeast Asia, and China converge on conflict and divisiveness as norm-engendering realities. The evidence shows, in particular, that peace is neither the dominant value nor the norm in foreign relations and that war, far from being perceived as immoral or abnormal, is viewed positively.

7. This broad concurrence of non-Western traditions stands in marked contrast to the preferences registered in modern Western societies. It is also at odds with the priorities officially established in the charters of the United Nations and affiliated international organizations. To the extent, then, that the United Nations is supposed to reflect universally valid norms, it is a misrepresentation of reality. And insofar as the United Nations was conceived as a norm-creating agency, it has been unsuccessful, particularly with respect to the incidence of war. What is normal in world politics should in these conditions have been inferred pragmatically from the facts.

The challenge of understanding the multifaceted nature of modern warfare has not been met by the academic and political elites of the United States. This failure in the perception of reality has been aggravated by a widespread acquiescence in essentially irrational trends—the inclinations, namely, to dissociate values from facts, to treat values as if they were general norms, and to assume that privately or locally preferred values are also globally valid norms. These intellectual developments have contributed not only to many recent foreign policy errors but also to widespread uncertainties about America's role in world affairs. Further, they suggest that the United States has begun to resemble Don Quixote: like the Knight of the Mournful Countenance, it is fighting windmills and losing its bearings in the real world.

NOTES

1. Elizabeth Converse, "The War of All Against All: A Review of the *Journal of Conflict Resolution, 1957–1968,*" *Journal of Conflict Resolution* [hereafter cited as *JCR*], December 1968, pp. 471–535.
2. *Ibid.,* p. 479.
3. Chadwick F. Alger, "Trends in International Relations Research: Scope, Theory, Methods and Relevance," in Norman D. Palmer, ed., *A Design for International Relations Research: Scope, Theory, Methods, and Relevance* (Philadelphia: The American Academy of Political and Social Science, Monograph No. 10, October 1970), pp. 7–28. Also see Philip P. Everts, "Developments and Trends in Peace and Conflict Research, 1965–1971: A Survey of Institutions," *JCR,* December 1972, pp. 477–510. Everts shows (p. 499) that "Peace

research itself," "United Nations problems," and "International organization" scored highest as research topics (67 percent, 66 percent, and 65 percent, respectively). Cf. Berenice A. Carroll, "Peace Research: The Cult of Power," *ibid.*, pp. 585–616: "If there is any distinguishing common feature among the highly varied works in the field of peace research, it is an avowed commitment to 'peace' " (p. 599). Carroll's remarks on "conceptions of power" are particularly interesting.

4. See Converse. Also Norman A. Bailey, "Toward a Praxeological Theory of Conflict," *ORBIS*, Winter 1968, pp. 1081–12. Further see Clinton F. Fink, "Some Conceptual Difficulties in the Theory of Social Conflict," *JCR*, December 1968, pp. 412–60. Fink defines social conflict as "any social situation or process in which two or more social entities are linked by at least one form of antagonistic psychological relation or at least one form of antagonistic interaction" (p. 456). For another flexible approach, see Robert A. LeVine, "Anthropology and the Study of Conflict: Introduction," *JCR*, March 1961, pp. 3–15. LeVine distinguishes among intrafamily, intracommunity, intercommunity, and intercultural conflict, and points out that there are pervasive conflict types that spread to several levels.
5. Converse, pp. 476–77.
6. Jessie Bernard, *American Community Behavior: An Analysis of Problems Confronting American Communities Today* (New York: Holt, Rinehart & Winston, 1949), p. 106. For an early commentary critical of conflict theory, see Raymond Mack and Richard C. Snyder, "The Analysis of Social Conflict: Toward an Overview and Synthesis," *JCR*, June 1957, pp. 212–48.
7. Converse, p. 479, Alger, p. 13. See Bozeman, "The Nuclear Freeze Movement: Conflicting Moral and Political Perspectives on War and Its Relation to Peace," *Conflict*, Vol. 5, no. 4 (1985), pp. 271ff.
8. See above, notes 1–4.
9. "U.S. Urged to Cut South Korean Aid: Group Calls for a Protest on Seoul's 'Inhumanity,' " *New York Times*, July 15, 1974.
10. See the scholarly surveys of the literature on war and conflict cited previously.
11. Hans J. Morgenthau, "International Relations: Quantitative and Qualitative Approaches," in Palmer, p. 70.
12. Elton B. McNeil, ed., *The Nature of Human Conflict* (Englewood Cliffs, NJ: Prentice-Hall, 1965).
13. Martin Wight, "Why Is There No International Theory?" in Herbert Butterfield and Martin Wight, eds., *Diplomatic Investigations: Essays in the Theory of International Politics* (London: Allen & Unwin, 1966), pp. 17–34.
14. Hugo Grotius, *The Rights of War and Peace, Including the Law of Nature and of Nations* (Washington: Walter Dunne, 1901); translated by A. C. Campbell; Book 1, Chap. 2, pp. 4, 8; Book II, Chap. 1, p. 2; Book III, Chap. 1, p. 6; Chap. 8, p. 1; Chap. 21, p. 1; Chap. 25, p. 1.
15. Hugo Grotius, *The Law of War and Peace: De Jure Belli ac Pacis* (New York: Classics Club, 1949); transl. by Louise Ropes Loomis; Book III, Chap. 21, p. 1.
16. Karl von Clausewitz, *On War* (New York: Modern Library, 1943); translated by O. J. Matthijs Jolles; Book 1, Chap. 8, p. 57.
17. Robert S. McNamara, *The Essence of Security: Reflections in Office* (New York: Harper & Row, 1968), p. 145.
18. See Harold D. Lasswell, *Psychopathology and Politics*, a new edition with afterthoughts by the author (New York: Viking Press, 1960), p. 240ff., for a discussion of the state as a "manifold of events."
19. Paul Verhaegen, "Study of the African Personality in the Belgian Congo," in F. R. Wickert, editor, *Readings in African Psychology from French Language Sources* (East Lansing, Mich.: Michigan State University Press, 1967), pp. 242–48.
20. For an extended discussion of the nature of civilization and intercultural relations, and of the historical impact of war on the identity of particularly significant cultures, see my "Civilizations Under Stress: Reflections on Cultural Borrowing and Survival," *Virginia Quarterly Review*, Winter 1975, pp. 1–18.

21. Aristide R. Zolberg, "The Structure of Political Conflict in the New States of Tropical Africa," *American Political Science Review,* March 1968, p. 70ff. My own analysis of African orientations to war and conflict is set forth in *Conflict in Africa: Concepts and Realities* (Princeton, NJ: Princeton University Press, 1976).
22. Majid Khadduri, *War and Peace in the Law of Islam* (Baltimore, MD: The Johns Hopkins University Press, 1955), pp. 55ff., 62ff., 144ff.; and compare Essays 3 and 8 in the present volume.
23. K. M. Panikkar, *A Survey of Indian History* (Bombay: Asia Publishing House, 1954), pp. 2, 29.
24. The Books of the Law and the later didactic portions of the *Mahabharata* may be taken to represent the post-Mauryan Brahmanic renascence. Müller dates this code later than the fourth century A.D.; Bühler places it in the second century.
25. Upendra N. Ghoshal, *A History of Indian Political Ideas: The Ancient Period and the Period of Transition to the Middle Ages* (London: Oxford University Press, 1966), pp. 188ff., 235.
26. B. Shamasastry, editor, *Kautilya's Arthasastra* (Mysore: Sri Raghuveer Press, 1951), Book IX, Chap. 1, p. 368. See also John W. Spellman, *Political Theory of Ancient India* (Oxford University Press, 1964); in addition, see the case study of classical India in Essay 3 of this volume.
27. But see *Public Paper of the Presidents of the United States: John F. Kennedy. 1962* (Washington, D.C.: GPO, 1963), pp. 453–54, for the text of a speech in which this interaction of different ideas about war was intimated, albeit faintly.
28. See, for example, John K. Fairbank, "China's World Order: The Tradition of Chinese Foreign Relations," *Encounter,* December 1966, pp. 14–20; also, by the same eminent scholar, "Introduction: Varieties of the Chinese Military Experience," in Frank A. Kierman, Jr., and John K. Fairbank, eds., *Chinese Ways in Warfare* (Cambridge, Mass.: Harvard University Press, 1974). In Professor Fairbank's view, all Chinese warfare, traditional and modern, is strictly defensive, quite in contrast to that waged throughout the centuries by the Occidental nations, especially the United States, which—he alleges—is invariably aggressive and expansionist. The other essays in this collection provide contrasting views. Also see "International Order in a Multicultural World" and "American Policy and the Illusion of Congruent Values" in this volume.
29. Arthur Waley, *Three Ways of Thought in Ancient China* (London: Allen & Unwin, 1939), p. 248; also see pp. 175, 141.
30. Lucian W. Pye, in the foreword to William W. Whitson with Chen-Hsie Huang, *The Chinese High Command: A History of Communist Military Politics, 1927–71* (New York: Praeger, 1973), xiii.
31. Numerous references may be found in Kierman and Fairbank; note especially Herbert Franke, "Siege and Defense of Towns in Medieval China," pp. 151ff., 192, for a summation of the technical, administrative, and psychological aspects of siegecraft and for comments on the continuity of military strategy and technology in Chinese history. In the same volume, see Charles O. Hucker, "Hu Tsung-hsien's Campaign Against Hsü Hai, 1556," pp. 273ff., 305ff.
32. Edward L. Dryer notes that the regions of China were administered from walled cities, which were centers of government as well as places in which large grain reserves were stored. Administrative control of the land was a precondition for further conquest, yet such control could be gained only by capturing the walled cities. These cities thus became the principal military objectives in wars fought within China. The authority of the government over the peasantry, then, extended downward from the walled cities. See "Military Continuities: The PLA and Imperial China," Chapter 1 in William W. Whitson, ed. *The Military and Political Power in China in the 1970's* (New York: Praeger, 1972), p. 15.
33. Sun Tzu, *The Art of War* (New York: Oxford University Press, 1963); trans. and ed. by Samuel B. Griffith, p. 38.
34. Waley, pp. 141, 152ff.

35. Yang Kung-sun, *The Book of Lord Shang: A Classic of the Chinese School of Law* (Chicago: University of Chicago Press, 1928); transl. with introduction and notes by J. J. L. Duyvendak, p. 256. For the proposition that "an intelligent prince . . . strives for uniformity, . . . restrains volatile scholars and those of frivolous pursuits and makes them all uniformly into farmers," see p. 194.
36. Han Fei Tzu, *Basic Writings* (New York: Columbia University Press, 1964); translated by Burton Watson, pp. 96–117.
37. Derk Bodde, *China's First Unifier: A Study of the Ch'in Dynasty as Seen in the Life of Li Ssu 280?–208 B.C.* (Hong Kong: Hong Kong University Press, 1967), pp. 11, 80ff. On this subject see also the Introduction to this book.
38. See Franke, p. 192. Also see Griffith's remarks on the diffusion of this work, pp. 45ff. and Appendix III.
39. Joseph Lelyveld, "In China, It's Politics by Allegory," *New York Times,* September 30, 1974. Further see the laudatory essays on the Legalists in *Selected Articles Criticizing Lin Piao and Confucius* (Peking: Foreign Languages Press, 1974). This collection includes a "Publisher's Note" to the effect that Lin Piao, being "an out-and-out devotee of Confucius," opposed the Legalist school and attacked the "First Emperor" of the Ch'in dynasty.
40. Scott A. Boorman, *The Protracted Game: A Wei-ch'i Interpretation of Maoist Revolutionary Strategy* (New York: Oxford University Press, 1969), p. 182.
41. Whitson with Chen-Hsia Huang, p. 438.
42. Mao Tse-tung, *Selected Works,* revised ed. (London: Lawrence & Wishart, 1958), Vol. II, p. 224. Mao adds: "Every Communist must grasp the truth: 'Political power grows out of the barrel of a gun.' Our principle is that the Party commands the gun, and the gun will never be allowed to command the Party. . . . Some people have ridiculed us as advocates of the 'omnipotence of war'; yes, we are, we are the advocates of the omnipotence of the revolutionary war, which is not bad at all, but is good and is Marxist." *Ibid.,* p. 228.
43. *Ibid.,* pp. 158, 180.
44. Sun Tzu, pp. 89, 43; see Griffith's editorial comments ("Sun Tzu and Mao Tse-tung"), pp. 45ff.
45. Mao Tse-tung, pp. 100, 186ff. The concept of "encirclement," or Wei-ch'i, relates to the physical as well as the psychological annihilation of the enemy; see Boorman, *The Protracted Game . . .*
46. Scott A. Boorman, "Deception in Chinese Strategy," in Whitson, ed., *The Military . . . ,* pp. 313–14. Boorman also points out that current strategic thinking in the United States places comparatively little stress on stratagem. See also Introduction and "Traditions of Political Warfare and Low-Intensity Conflict in Totalitarian Russia and China," and "American Policy and the Illusion of Congruent Values" in this volume.
47. See Sun Tzu, pp. 66–67, 93–94, 97, 106.
48. Mao Tse-tung, pp. 172–75. Also see Samuel B. Griffith, *Peking and People's Wars* (New York: Praeger, 1966), p. 33, for a discussion of Mao's advice to guerrillas that they be as cautious as virgins and as quick as rabbits, and for this general approach to tactics: "When you fight us we won't let you and you can't even find us. But when we want to fight you, we make sure you can't get away and we hit you squarely on the chin and wipe you out." Cf. Sun Tzu, p. 140.
49. Boorman, *The Protracted Game . . . ,* p. 6; for historical references to the pervasive influence of this game, and the suggestion that Sun Tzu's theories bear a distinct similarity to Wei-ch'i dicta, see p. 208 (note 8). Boorman's thesis is significant: Chinese Communist policies and Wei-ch'i, he argues, are products of the same strategic tradition—one without a parallel either in Occidental military tradition or in the Western game of chess—and Wei-ch'i is an important, if little recognized, model of the Maoist system of insurgency.
50. Mao Tse-tung, pp. 151–52.
51. See Sun Tzu, pp. 84, 129.
52. Mao Tse-tung, p. 171.

Covert Action and Foreign Policy in World Politics

INTRODUCTION

Is our understanding of the relation between covert action and foreign policy internationally valid? How relevant to policy-making in the present world environment are our distinctions between different elements of intelligence and our definitions of each of these elements, specifically of covert action?

This paper assumes that U.S. intelligence systems and operations are essentially aspects or functions of the nation's foreign policy. Policies may thus be faulted by ineffective intelligence. However, and conversely, sound intelligence theories and practices may be misused or come to naught by poor policy-making. Any assessment of intelligence therefore requires an assessment also of foreign policy and strategic thought, and any evaluation of the latter must include a close analysis of intelligence.

A second underlying assumption is to the effect that statecraft in its entirety is everywhere the reflection of a given society's sustaining culture and value system. This means that the whole of a culture needs to be mapped reliably before one of its aspects, in this case statecraft, is to be adequately understood. It suggests, further, that foreign policies as well as intelligence projects and actions are apt to fall short of success if this infrastructure of beliefs and dispositions remains unknown.

As mentioned earlier, understandings of this kind are not congenial to the United States, which is conditioned by its own values to believe that people everywhere are basically alike. This disposition was accentuated and sanctioned by the Charter of the United Nations, which borrows heavily from American constitutionalism, and by the swift creation, after 1945, of new states in Africa and Asia whose original laws and constitutions were also modeled on Euro-American precedents.

The successful diffusion of the West's political language and related means of technical communication helps explain why most Americans continued to believe that their own, now internationalized, vocabulary, was actually carrying transnationally shared values and commitments, and why the nation's policymakers were slow in realizing that the rhetoric of communication masked profound discords on matters of substance. By the late 1950s it had become clear that our language of law and democracy had come to cover lawless despotisms of the authoritarian and

This essay originally appeared in *Intelligence Requirements for the 1980's: Covert Action*, Roy Godson, ed. (Washington, D.C.: National Strategy Information Center, Inc., 1981), and is printed with permission of NSIC.

the totalitarian kind; that all aspects of statecraft, specifically diplomacy and intelligence, were being conceptualized quite differently in the world's numerous non-Western provinces; in short that the real identities of foreign states and other international actors were being misperceived.

It is the main thesis of the present paper that most recent U.S. policy and intelligence failures have ensued from these defects in strategic thought and vision. The responsibility here rests primarily with the academic community, not with the intelligence community and not with the Department of State; for it is after all the former that is traditionally charged with providing educational and professional guidance to the latter. It is therefore urgently necessary today to analyze the causes of our policy and intelligence failures, discover ways for avoiding them in the future, and come up with improved methods of learning and teaching the craft of intelligence.

Significant improvements have been made in the last decades when it comes to understanding the Soviet Union and other Marxist-Leninist societies. However, little has changed in our common perception of non-Communist non-Western peoples. Some of their deviations from what we view as transnationally valid standards of reasoning and behavior are simply dismissed as "irrational" or "mindless" actions. Moreover, it continues to be customary to ascribe all their shortcomings to the lack of economic development—a purely temporary condition, so the teaching goes, that will be overcome given material aid and modernization over time. This essay assumes, by contrast, that we are dealing in most instances with very ancient societies and thus with firmly embedded cultural patterns that prescribe or proscribe thought and action, whether in regard to economics or to statecraft.

The present paper should ideally consist of case studies covering all states and cultures in the world. However, limitations of space for the printed version of my findings determined me to focus on the Middle East.

Part I of the study consists of a restatement of current U.S. definitions of the different components of intelligence; a critical review of U.S. norms of covert action and foreign policy; and a commentary on the decay of the moral, legal, and political language that carries our vital norms, values, and interests.

Part II addresses the need for comparative studies. Its core is a draft inventory of propositions or questions that require answers before we devise foreign policies and intelligence projects in regard to a non-Western society.

Part III, together with the preceding four pages, addresses the need for a revision of the parameters within which our intelligence and foreign affairs specialists think about the different societies of the Middle East. Since all peoples in this region are deeply conscious of their histories, and since the craft of intelligence in particular was first perfected between the sixth and fourth centuries B.C. by Achaemenid Persia, in order then to be copied diligently by Arab, Turkish, Afghan, and Mongol caliphates and empires, including the Mogul empire in Northwest India, my analysis follows suit. I chose to include a case study of classical Hindu India because it presents the most systematized Oriental intelligence setup (it too was modeled on the Persian). By contrast, the section closes with the Republic of Venice. This European state endured for a millennium by dint of an intelligence system that I viewed as just about the best the Occident has produced.

I. DEFINITIONS AND U.S. POLICY

A. The Language of U.S. Intelligence

The Consortium for the Study of Intelligence and the colloquia organized under its auspices are joint ventures linking intelligence professionals and academic scholars with a special interest in foreign policy and intelligence. Before writing this paper I therefore reread the records of the colloquia that relate directly to the present topics, noting in particular the following definitions and descriptions:

> Clandestine operations are activities conducted in secret by an intelligence service. They encompass collection of intelligence, counterintelligence, and covert action. Here the term *covert,* though synonymous with *clandestine,* describes an activity or event that generally occurs in the public domain, observable by those who happen to be at hand. It has an identifiable instigator or sponsor, and its covertness lies in the relationship between the latter and some hidden, unacknowledged authority or source of assistance.
>
> Covert action for present purposes thus entails activity in which the U.S. government's involvement is deliberately concealed. Its aim is to get something done in ways that are compatible with U.S. interests. We are taking sides in a local issue, i.e., intervening in a manner that infringes on the host country's sovereignty.
>
> Covert mechanisms are used to supplement diplomatic and other open channels.
>
> The United States has restricted itself to the clandestine collection of intelligence. Covert action no longer figures significantly in the operational posture of the CIA. Covert action in the late 1970s shows all the earmarks of a dying art form. This is regrettable. The U.S. has engaged in various types of covert action since its earliest days and the time for recovering the art is "now."[1]
>
> Counterintelligence, defined as the national effort to prevent foreign intelligence services from infiltrating our institutions and establishing the potential to engage in espionage, subversion, terrorism, and sabotage, is the base for a healthy intelligence system.[2]
>
> It has become apparent in the last years that several components of American intelligence—clandestine collection, counterintelligence, covert action, and analysis—are not functioning well. No nation's intelligence can do well if *any* of these components malfunction.
>
> The CIA's original core, its primary unilateral responsibility, was the clandestine collection of foreign intelligence and covert action in support of U.S. policy.[3]
>
> The term "clandestine collection" is another way of saying "espionage," entailing the use of human sources and technical devices. In other words, it is old-fashioned spying involving the manipulation of people. The use of clandestine collection is costly in terms of time and manpower, unlike covert action, which usually requires a larger expenditure of money as well. Clandestine collection requires a long lead time to identify and recruit those human sources who might have access to the required information. It is a slow and laborious process that is used only as a last resort.[4]
>
> The operations that must be kept secure are of two kinds, clandestine and covert. Clandestine operations consist of two types: espionage and counterintelligence.
>
> Espionage is conducted largely through human (i.e., spies) and technical agents. At the heart of the undertaking and crucial to its success is secrecy.
>
> Counterespionage consists of catching spies and either neutralizing them or compelling them to serve the captor's ends.

Nonclandestine functions as assigned to the CIA since the 1950s are covert action, paramilitary operations, counterguerrilla activity, countering the traffic in drugs, and the rest of it.

Covert action does not strive for invisibility and by its nature it cannot be secret. Its *raison d'être* is to identify the common ground or areas of agreement between the United States and other countries, and to further activity which will support and expand these shared interests. Covert action *programs,* by contrast, need to be kept secret.

Paramilitary operations cannot be kept secret, i.e., they are not clandestine.[5]

These American or Western understandings of particularized intelligence functions provide one set of measures for the comparisons and analyses developed in this text. They are important in my general scheme because they help assure the kind of common thought and discourse between professionals and academic scholars upon which the furtherance of the national interest depends. Other standards of comparison derive from my own studies of foreign affairs in the world society and in international history, and some of them diverge from what may well be orthodox political science in America today. For example, since I am persuaded that there are few if any universally accepted norms and beliefs, I cannot assume that our definitions and understandings of phenomena in international relations and statecraft are ipso facto reliable renditions of reality also in non-American or non-Western societies. Further, and in contrast to many of my colleagues, I believe that all comparative studies, whether of art and religion or of diplomacy, intelligence, and the relation between covert action and foreign policy, can yield tenable conclusions only after one has explored the whole of a given society or culture.

Such approaches are not congenial to the American mind because they conflict with long-established preferred images of one world, one type of man, and therefore one kind of truth. "The men of system" in our universities thus continue to imagine that they can arrange the different members of the world society with as much ease as the hand arranges the different pieces of a chess board. But as Adam Smith observed two hundred years ago, they do not consider that the pieces upon the chess board have no other principle of motion besides that which the hand impresses upon them, whereas in the great chess board of human society every single piece has a principle of motion of its own. This truth is not doubted by students of art, architecture, music, religion, philosophy and even history, but it is definitely being bypassed by scholars working in the social sciences including the sociology of law, international law, and ethics. At any rate, no evidence of diversity in human thought, behavior, and experience has so far effectively discouraged the dominant trend, namely, that of maintaining the universal validity of American-made models and theories of the rational man, democratic government, and human rights as well as of the function of diplomacy, the nature of revolution, or the relation of war to peace and law.

"The men of action," meanwhile, notably those in charge of government and foreign policy, continue to trust these academic models rather than their own powers of observing other men and other models in other places. Failures in policy and intelligence thus continue to be commonplace. Senior officers in the Carter administration are said to have complained that the recent war between Iran and Iraq exposed serious deficiencies in U.S. intelligence-gathering abilities, noting in particular that the United States was poorly informed about specific events in the Persian Gulf area; that it knew next to nothing about political, cultural, and economic trends in the region; and that it was therefore unable to make accurate predictions about the future course of the war, "We are weak in the bazaars, on the campuses, in the streets where the life of a nation takes place" was one comment. Another admitted, "Frankly, we're in the Dark Ages when it comes to knowing what makes these nations tick."[6]

The causes of this intelligence lapse as of all other policy and intelligence failures are no doubt numerous and complex. However, and in light of the fact that "the men of action" have been tutored by "the men of system," I tend to think that the nation's recent and ongoing troubles in international relations are in the final analysis failures of scholarship and learning in our institutions of higher education.

Some of these basic issues in intercultural relations have been addressed succinctly by Dr. Robert Livingston, a well-known neurophysiologist, as when he points out that we act as if there existed a universal common logic of thinking shared by all thinking people; as if there is one metaphysical pool of universal human thought upon which all can draw; and as if we can count on some elementary objective spirit. Such predispositions, Livingston explains, make for the simplistic belief that the persistence of disparities or the failure of communication can be ascribed to the absence of objectivity. Even more important, they totally screen the irrefutable fact that perception is guided by culture, and in culture, especially by language. This is so, he writes, because the logical processes of thinking are everywhere relative to the language learned. If all of us would better understand the biological, psychological, linguistic, and cultural mechanisms affecting perception, judgment, motivation, and action, Livingston concludes, we would be more willing to be tentative rather than hasty in our responses and better able to sort out ambiguous situations correctly.[7]

This strikes me as a fair diagnosis of the blind spot in our national vision. It is also good advice for all Americans in an age in which people in Africa, Asia, Oceania, Latin America, and parts of Europe continue to divest themselves of Western norms of law, government, ethics, education, diplomacy, and other forms of international behavior that they had accepted in an earlier era when Western civilization was deemed prestigious and attractive and when Western power was not as readily challenged as it is today. Yet—and this is the main point here—we in this country do not seem able or willing to adjust our vision to these radically changed circumstances. Dim-sighted in our view of other actors in the world environment, reluctant to distinguish between our domestic and our foreign affairs, or between the concerns of the United States and those espoused by other nations, our government has for quite some time now been unable to fathom a strategic design for long-range foreign policies. Improvisation has therefore been the order of the day in policy-making circles, and rhetoric has come to fill the void left by departed thought.

These developments have had stultifying effects upon our intelligence community. Cut off from Intelligence Writ Large, deprived of concise guidelines for the implementation of coherent policy decisions and left to administer reams of usually contradictory declarations, explanations, retractions, apologies, and strictures emanating from on high, officers have not been able, by and large, to anticipate or frustrate threatening moves by adversaries or to give advance warning of impending events. In such circumstances it is not surprising that coups, revolutions, armed invasions, wars, and shifts in ideological commitment, political orientation, or the distribution of power usually take us by surprise: after all, the forces shaping such events have long been effectively camouflaged by our own rigidly ethnocentric perceptions and commitments.

The foreign policy crisis implicit in such haphazard approaches to the relationship between perception of reality and thought and language is aggravated by the circumstance, first, that the meaning content of our basic vocabulary has long ceased to be internationally valid; and second, that the distance between words—notably those having a universal ring in our ears—and the substantive realities they purport to cover has widened immeasurably.

Studies of non-Western and Communist societies should thus have persuaded us long ago that our conceptions of war and peace, our ideas of the state and sovereignty, our notion of the function of diplomacy, and our values of good faith and contractual ethics in the conduct of international relations are not shared by them. What is being shared throughout the world is the vocabulary of words that has been fashioned in the West to carry these, and only these, ideas but has been conscripted in this century to serve also as protective cover for rival causes advanced by alien and adversary political systems. Keen awareness of the semantic aspects of revolutionary tactics, more particularly of the need for verbal dissimulation, thus explains the stipulation in Lenin's operational code that psychological and diplomatic attack campaigns against the capitalist West must be launched in the value language of the West if they are to reach, confound, and eventually conquer the minds of people targeted for takeover.[8]

These policies and techniques of communication were barely recognized, certainly not seriously contested in America. Molelike in inception and operation, they could therefore be effective as "double agents" in debasing our language, perverting the meanings of some of our strategically most important words and thus in disordering our thought processes. In short, they could penetrate—in Sun Tzu's phrase, "encircle"—our intelligence, which simply does not accommodate the Communist formula that covert thought must spearhead covert as well as overt action.

B.   U.S. Foreign Policy and the Norms of Covert Action

A few brief references to recent policy and intelligence failures will illustrate the rigidities of our general approaches to foreign societies, and therewith also, by implication, the awesome ambiguities with which the minds of individual intelligence officers must wrestle daily, never more so than when pondering covert operations and their implications.

Mr. Colby's account of his life in the CIA[9] is most instructive in these respects. Openly critical of the new breed of systems analysts, Colby came to wonder during his Indochina mission whether their opinions had not become too firmly fixed and whether their objectivity had not come to reflect academia's bias that our programs in Vietnam just could not succeed.[10] Yet at the same time he himself failed to realize that the Vietnam program was bound to fail if it had to be carried out in strict compliance only with American moral and legal standards. The Colby (1969) directive on assassination and "other repugnant activities" related to project Phoenix thus makes strange reading when it states that American personnel are specifically not authorized to engage in assassinations or other violations of the rules of land warfare, but that they are entitled to use such reasonable military force as is necessary to obtain the goals of rallying, capturing, or eliminating the VCI in the Republic of Vietnam. Since the rules of land warfare had not been drafted for the context of combat with irregular guerrilla forces that are bent on terrorizing villages and towns of an allied Asian state, and since assassination was then and continues to be today an integral part of Communist ways of war and administration, it was obviously impossible to comply with both requirements of the directive: on the one hand to oust the enemy, on the other to meet American standards of reasonableness in the use of military force.

Throughout this last tragic phase of our involvement in Vietnam it appears that "decision making" in the matter of norms and standards, whether of reasonableness, rationality, law, or ethics, proceeded exclusively from the vantage point of America's own more recent experiences and expectations. There is no hint in Mr. Colby's volume that our decisions, judgments, and commitments had been made in full awareness of Vietnam's own social and moral infrastructure and historical traditions that had sustained the cultural integrity of this nation for many centuries. In fact, and as Mr. Colby's further comment shows, this infrastructure was deliberately undermined so that "Phoenix ends and our [American] means" would be "well within moral limits":

> When one of my officers reported that a district chief had shot out of hand a woman prisoner and I took the case up with the Prime Minister and had the district chief sacked and punished, the same province officer complained that the district chief was one of the best in the province and should be excused for his action because the woman had been engaged in a terrorist attack on one of the chief's own family.[11]

This episode in our relations with a major, critically embattled Asian ally is particularly significant for purposes of the present inquiry because it shows that we had in no way corrected our earlier misperceptions of reality in Vietnam, namely those that determined us to sanction the elimination of Ngo Dinh Diem and his authentically Vietnamese government on the ground that they represented authoritarian, and thus un-American, principles of rule. The result of this fateful decision, which had ensued from grave errors in thought and understanding, was our own military involvement in the area, its eventual ignominious collapse, the destruction of independent Vietnam, and the establishment of Communist rule over the entire region, including Laos and Cambodia.

The disposition to chip away and thus gradually dissemble the very identities of non-Western nations whose independence we vowed to preserve has now hardened into a policy line, perhaps even a doctrine. This is borne out by the records of our diplomatic relations with, among others, South Korea, the Philippines, Nicaragua, El Salvador, Chile, South Africa, and prerevolutionary Iran. Although these societies surely are radically different from one another, our objective has been the same everywhere: it is the establishment of democracy, the rule of law, and more specifically insistence on respect for human rights—mechanistically conceived, professed, and administered. Meaningful definitions of these references are missing altogether. Dropped from consciousness is the fact, so elaborately explicated in readily available accounts of Asian, Latin American, and African culture history, that "democracy" with its Western connotations of parliamentary or congressional institutions, a multiparty system, elections, constitutional law, and bills of rights is basically alien to each of the non-Western realms. Indeed, this knowledge seems to have left the minds not only of policymakers but also of politically concerned academic specialists and representatives of the media, and that precisely at a time in history when this kind of knowledge should have controlled perception and commitment in strategic thought.

With the nation's general intelligence thus anesthetized, it is small wonder that the KGB and other enemy agencies were successful in executing their strategic deception, covert action, and disinformation programs; that our own intelligence community was often unable to analyze the adversary's mindset, anticipate and detect his operations, and sift factual truth from disinformation; and that reformist congressional legislation such as S.2525 and its successor bills did not require the intelligence community to have a capability for covertly influencing events abroad.

The bills here in issue thus prohibit any employee of any intelligence agency from killing any official of a nation or faction thereof, even if that official happens to be threatening American lives. They also ban any covert action project that might work against a "democratic" government abroad, leaving totally undefined the term "democratic." In fact, and as Michael M. Uhlmann notes in his critical commentary on these legislative efforts,[12] our governing authorities go on assuming that other nations in the world are preparing to play the intelligence "game" in accordance with rules laid down by the United States (see sect. 114(j) of S.2525), and that legal terms of art customary in our political culture cover the universe of human experience. Sec. 137 S.2525 thus explicitly prohibits the U.S. intelligence community from directly or indirectly encouraging or assisting individuals, organizations, or foreign governments to do anything that the American intelligence community itself is prohibited from doing. As Uhlmann writes: "Whatever may be its intention, that language certainly sounds like an attempt to make the rest of the world conform to American law."[13] Indeed, "that language" may even be a faithful expression of the widely current assumption that "law" is the same everywhere, if only because all human experience is essentially the same. Since this persuasion has been cultivated in our academic institutions in the last decades under the covering titles of "empiricism" and a "value-free social science," it is not surprising that it has also come to mark the outlook of the national intelligence community. As Angelo Codevilla explains the matter:[14]

> In intelligence, empiricism's practical tenet is to define what one is looking for in terms of quantifiable units, then to count those units and to monitor their rate of change. What-

ever cannot be counted is deemed not to exist. . . . Moreover, unless something can be counted it cannot be used as currency in bureaucratic controversies. . . .

With regard to evaluating Soviet strategic forces the rule thus seems to have been: "What we've not seen doesn't exist." And since mental calculations of purposes and designs of strategic doctrine cannot be "seen," tabulated, and quantified, they have been seriously neglected by our analysts, with the result that the Soviet's strategic buildup between 1975 and 1978 could proceed virtually without detection.[15]

The same type of malfunction in processes of analysis also explains our misjudgments of the character and intentions of terrorist organizations, "liberation" fronts, and guerrilla forces that have long been active in the Middle East, Latin America (notably Central America), and Africa. As Codevilla remarks in respect to the PLO, our specialists refrained from examining the organizations, behavioral records, and ideological sources, choosing rather to perceive the PLO as the sum total of its public statements that could be read, heard, and tabulated. When the most recent of these declarations were found to be relatively restrained, the conclusion was drawn that the organization was becoming moderate. The fact that rhetoric is often used in radical groups for purposes of camouflaging "real" intentions and operations does not seem to have made much of an impact upon the evaluations.

These new aspects of the American mind-set have been reinforced by other intellectual rigidities also bred in our universities, among them an unquestioning reliance upon models.[16] It has thus become an article of faith that only "socialist" governments can stand in the way of Communist ones.[17] No one seems to mind that the term "socialist" is as undefined in our trade literature as the term "democracy." Further, no allowance is commonly made for the incontrovertible fact that "socialism" stands for Communism in Marxist-Leninist usage. Here, too, one finds that American diplomats and intelligence officers have all too often followed suit. In the early 1960s they thus supported a left-wing government in Italy even though it was clear from the outset that our Communist adversaries would be busy manipulating the Trojan Horse they had introduced for the purpose of concretizing the transition from a "socialist" to a Communist regime.

In later years, our policymakers demonstrated the same Pavlovian reflex reaction to their favorite verbal stereotypes—"socialism," "democracy," and "human rights"—when they treated terrorist guerrillas intent on building Communist-type despotism in southern Africa, Central America, and the Islamic Middle East as if they were freedom fighters intent on building American-type democracies. Deluded by our own theories and models, we thus hardly noticed that the Soviet-Cuban apparatus of subversion was in the process of succeeding to ready the Central American Isthmus and the Caribbean island space for Communist takeovers, and thus for transformation into a staging area for further and more direct, aggressively anti-American designs; and also to radicalize and satellitize several strategically crucial states in eastern and southern Africa, among them Ethiopia, Angola, Mozambique, and Zimbabwe. Nor were we mentally, politically, or militarily prepared to checkmate the Soviet Union in either of its several but interdependent moves to gain control over the Persian Gulf area, the Near East, and the Middle East. As Paul

Nitze explains the Soviet program in a masterful essay, "Strategy for the '80s,"[18] the penetration of South Yemen and Iran led directly to the thrust into Afghanistan. This move, again, advanced the Soviet base structure by five hundred miles so as to outflank the immediacy of a military threat to our now isolated ally Pakistan.

Only one of the societies targeted for takeover or penetration—namely Afghanistan—was openly invaded and occupied by Soviet military forces. Each of the others could be effectively enfeebled and destabilized by reliance first on the type of covert warfare judged appropriate to the society's culture and social structure; second, on the continuous deployment of threat-centered forms of diplomacy and psychological encirclement known in postwar Europe as Finlandization; and third, in my view chiefly, on the incapacity of the United States to deal effectively with both the offensive political processes issuing from the Communist mind-set and the thought world of the non-Western societies with whose viability as independent states we have associated our vital interests since 1945.

II. THE NEED FOR COMPARATIVE STUDIES IN STATECRAFT

Comparative studies in statecraft may help us to clear up the intellectual and political disarray in which we find ourselves today, provided that we ask "the right questions" of the numerous culturally separate societies with which we coexist in the world society. We have done that, by and large, when it comes to the Soviet Union, modern Western Europe, and Israel. However, it has been rightly observed that the United States has not asked the right questions of what for want of a better term is still called the Third World. Unless and until we know more about that, we cannot speculate profitably about the meaning of foreign policy and intelligence, and the place assigned to what we distinguish as covert action in such societies as Uganda, Zimbabwe, Iraq, Iran, Turkey, Brazil, Korea, or India. This means that we are not in a position to devise long-term foreign policies and diplomatic methods or develop intelligence projects that fit the needs in each case.

Further, since we deal everywhere in the Third World with societies that are older than our own and more attached to the past than we are, explorations of history are essential. And in that context again, it is important in each instance to distinguish between substratal indigenous characteristics on one hand, and recent imports from Western and Marxist-Leninist sources on the other. It goes without saying that all such endeavors would proceed best with the aid of linguistically qualified officials.

Next, a reliable inventory of foreign policy–related propositions presupposes familiarity with the domestic order of the society in question. The linkage here is organic, for as we know from our own experience, dispositions toward foreign affairs issue from thoughtways, norms, and institutions developed within society. Moreover, and with special regard to covert and other intelligence operations, most decisive actions take place in the domestic field of a foreign nation. It follows that the latter's inner normative order must be understood on its own terms if we are to recruit the right agents, direct them effectively in desired ways, and evaluate them properly, or if we are to cope successfully with other people's spies and, in general, if we are to know how to estimate the intentions and capabilities of "host" countries, be they allies or adversaries.[19]

Psychology is thus in theory a key discipline. However, it cannot be said that modern texts in this academic discipline shed much light on the problems here under consideration. Not only do they bypass the concerns of statecraft but, more importantly, they proceed from the assumption that human beings everywhere conform to norms encapsulating the life-styles of Americans and Europeans. Patterns of individual and social life, or configurations of "ideal" or "normal" types as these emerge from the records of African and Asian experiences, have so far not found explicit recognition. And similar complaints are justified in regard to disciplines treating of ethics, law, government, and economics.[20]

The following, then, is a draft questionnaire that transcends or crosses academic divisions in order to elicit information on the levels, first, of domestic, and second, of foreign affairs.

A. Domestic Affairs

Which fundamental beliefs, ideas, and values seem to sustain the society in time?

Which purposes and meanings are assigned to life?

How do people think about power, wealth, authority, order, justice?

What are the sources of the basic beliefs, norms, and commitments? religion? ethnic or national customs? ideology? pragmatism? economic acquisitiveness?

How free and self-directed is the individual?

Which personality types are trusted and respected? Which, by contrast, are distrusted and feared? Which are favored for leadership roles?

What is the general core of fellowship? Which hierarchical pecking orders are freely accepted?

How limited or extensive are such feelings as affection, sympathy, and friendship?

How common and accepted are suspicion, hatred, and vindictiveness?

What is the value content of intrigue and conflict?

In which circumstances is violence condoned? What is the ceiling for tolerance of violence within society?

How open or secretive is the society in general, and in such groupings as clans, families, brotherhoods, guilds, or fellowships of friends in particular?

Which dispositions toward oaths and promises or contracts are prevalent?

Are communications between like-minded men direct or indirect and roundabout?

In which conditions is duplicity allowed? When can one count on sincerity and good faith?

Do members of special groups communicate through the use of special politically or socially significant metaphors and symbols?

Which precepts make up the moral order of society?

What do men regard as "law"?

Is law distinct from religion? from the political authority of the day?

In which ways does "law" recognize and protect the individual?

Is citizenship a developed concept?

How is political authority rendered?

Which elements make for stability in society? Which, by contrast, induce disorder?

B. Foreign Affairs

Which political units or organisms should be recognized for purposes of foreign policy and intelligence assessments?

Is our perception too narrowly focused on "the modern state" or "the nation-state"?

Has the time come to admit this modern European form of political organization has ceased being a universally valid norm in international relations, or that it is today effectively de-Europeanized?

What is the actual locus of political decision-making in foreign affairs today?

Which nonstate units merit acknowledgment?

Is territoriality a chief factor in definitions of the nonstate bodies?

Is there an underlying ethic that requires attention when one deals with these non-Western associational schemes, and if so what is it?

What is the prevalent worldview?

How are relations with other independent societies conceptualized?

Do presumptions stress enmity and conflict, or friendship and cooperation?

Is war considered "bad" by definition?

Is war accepted as a norm or way of life, and if so, what do people fight for? When is war activated? Which forms does it take? How is it ended?

How do people think about peace? Is it a definable condition? What is its relation to war?

What distinguishes statecraft in general and foreign policy making in particular?

Are there regionally or culturally accepted rules for the conduct of foreign relations in war and/or in peace?

What is subsumed under the term "diplomacy"?

What is the relation of diplomacy to espionage?

In which ways are existing codes of international or intergroup behavior analogous to or different from those accepted by (a) Occidental democracies; (b) Communist societies?

What typifies the society's negotiating style?

What is the place of deception in the society's conduct of foreign relations? Is it generally accepted in war and peace or is it commonly reserved for specific conditions? If so, which?

What is the place of "political intelligence" in the society's system of foreign operations?

How valid or pertinent are our distinctions and definitions of the elements that make up "intelligence"?[21]

The questions raised in the foregoing draft inventory of propositions may not be relevant for the Soviet Union, and that for the simple reason that the entire Soviet government is marked by the KGB mentality. This judgment also holds for satellite and surrogate states of Soviet Russia; the new Communist Vietnamese imperium in Southeast Asia; and Communist China, where Marxist-Leninist doctrine as reinforced by traditional Legalist principles insists that all organization, whether of the village or the world, is war organization. Superior and inferior units in each of these contexts are therefore garrison states in which the craft of intelligence is the core of both domestic and foreign policies, and in which all moves and operations are mapped in accordance with carefully crafted strategic designs. Although the latter consist of premises and programs to which we do not subscribe, they yet seem to accommodate the particular definitions with which we identify the different elements of intelligence.

The situation in non-Western states that are not penetrated decisively by Communism is, in my view, very different. Many of them, specifically those in the Middle East and black Africa, continue to be ruled by men who do not need, or cannot afford, to conceptualize long-range programs of action of any kind. In all of these cases we may therefore have to answer questions such as the ones raised earlier before we know which if any elements of intelligence are developed and whether our policies and intelligence operations are properly conceived, defined, and implemented. For example:

- If a society is traditionally rent by internecine conflicts between contending personalities, ethnically different units, or rival religious groupings that depend on conspiratorial activities and dissimulation, its foreign relations are apt to be cast in analogous terms.

- If warfare is a socially, morally, and politically accepted course of action, or if hostility to outsiders is a normal disposition, diplomacy is likely to be an adjunct rather of war than of peace.

- If the normal grounds for war are strong feelings such as hatred, religious zeal, insistence on settling old scores or redressing past humiliations, rather than precise calculations of national advantage, references to law or UN Charter provisions are irrelevant.

- If statehood rests upon strong political traditions that do not include the principle of territorially fixed frontiers, lines of demarcation between what in established international law is understood as international war (i.e., war between states) and internal war, as well as between war and peace, cease to carry compelling meanings.

These propositions are well illustrated by recent developments in the Arab-Islamic regions of the Middle East where the identities of some states are continuously shifting while those of others are slowly being erased by war.

Lebanon—admittedly a state with shallow roots in history—is thus a no-man's land today, its capital an open city in which anyone can do whatever he can get away with, and in which scores of private armies and militias operate freely, each financed by outside sponsors and each complete with its own military intelligence service.[22] Jordan, also a fragile creation, continues to exist precariously, its population divided in its basic loyalties, its contours forever questioned alike by Israelis and by Arabs. Syria and Iraq, meanwhile, two other successor states of the Ottoman Empire, continue to alternate between friendship and enmity in their mutual relations, and to shift positions in inter-Arab affairs, especially when it comes to plans for merging states so as to come closer to the ancient goal of creating one great Arab nation.

In short, the state is near-irrelevant in this culture area today. This means, in my opinion, that the American intelligence community, too, will have to transcend the context "state" if it is to do its work effectively in this part of the world.

The case for such a reassessment is hardened by Middle Eastern developments in diplomatic practice. These are exemplified by Colonel Qaddafi's decision to replace Libya's embassies by the same "People's Committees for the Liquidation of Enemies of the Revolution" that are empowered to govern Libya itself. All of the "Bureaus" are instruments of the regime's secret service, a body answering only to Qaddafi and his closest confidants. Its business consists in clearing the land of elements considered undesirable by the chief of state. Arrests and executions thus became mandatory. Indeed the government openly announced that death lists were on file, and that hit teams would be sent abroad to hunt down and kill expatriates, dissidents, and traitors who could be regarded as guilty of corruption and/or opposition to the regime. Numerous assassinations are on record, most perpetrated in the capitals of the West, under cover of Libya's embassies, now transformed into arsenals well-stocked with explosives, false passports, and other necessary tools of the terrorist trade.[23]

It is important to note that Qaddafi rationalizes these revolutionary moves by arguing that "traditional diplomacy" was the invention of imperialist powers in the heyday of colonialism, and that its norms can therefore in no way be expected to bind Third World countries. Foreign embassies in Libya are therefore not considered inviolate, and diplomats, like other foreign residents, are routinely subjected to harassment, even arrest, the latter usually on charges of espionage. Other Islamic nations, among them Iraq and Iran, seem to be in full accord with these policies and dispositions. At any rate, they, too, appear determined to stamp out the form and substance of customary international diplomacy and erase frontiers between sovereign states so as to accommodate terrorism and war.

Lastly, then, and with further reference to the need for a revision of the parameters within which our intelligence community operates today in the Middle East, it is imperative to review the relationship between covert action and war. The war between Iran and Iraq is a case in point.

Iran's theocratic Islamic regime had alarmed neighboring Iraq's secular Islamic government by calling on all Shi'ite communities in the region, in particular that of Iraq, to form a united country without frontiers. It had also invited the faithful to wage a Holy War against the "Satan Puppet" in Baghdad (and therewith, by implication, against the "Master Satan" in Washington). Iraq, in turn, was determined to avenge diplomatic and military defeats that "racist Persian tyrants" had inflicted upon its soil as well as upon its national dignity. These are identified in our times with the Pahlavi monarchs, in past centuries and millennia with the dynasties of the Achaemenids and Sassanians, whose imperial rule had extended over numerous Arab provinces, including some now encompassed by Iraq.

To the astonishment of most observers, this war became almost instantly a total war, with both sides willing and able to attack vital strategic targets, particularly oil and nuclear power facilities, knock out cities without regard for civilian life, and bring ruination upon their respective economies, heedless of future national and regional needs. Such actions struck a White House national security official as "completely irrational" and convinced a State Department specialist that if either or both of the contending states had possessed nuclear weapons, they probably would have been used. Other analysts have concluded that we now have a preview of what future wars between well-armed but otherwise less-developed nations would be like. Pointing to Yehezkel Dror's book *Crazy States,* they cite its warning that conflicts between Third World nations ruled by radical governments and equipped with modern military hardware are likely to degenerate into all-out wars and thus into grave threats to international stability.[24] Whether one finds merit in this general prediction or not, the Iran-Iraq war indicates that covert actions and clandestine operations are neither wanted nor needed here since it is only open war that satisfies.

III.   CASE STUDIES

The following studies of non-American and non-Communist dispositions toward the relations between foreign policy, covert action, and other aspects of intelligence deal with Islamic societies, specifically Iran, and with classical Hindu India.[25] The last study, however, introduces the Republic of Venice, a quintessential European but now defunct state,[26] because it can teach us much about statecraft and survival that is particularly relevant to the challenges facing the United States today.

A.   Persia/Iran

My analysis of the Islamic matter begins with a profile of Persia/Iran, and that for several closely linked reasons. Persia has occupied a pivotal position in world affairs from the sixth century B.C. onward, and its impact on other societies, specifically the later Islamic empires, has been pervasive and indelible, in no field more so than in political intelligence. The case study of Iran is thus intended as an introduction to much of Oriental statecraft even as it illustrates a uniquely creative system of strategic intelligence.

Iran has been and continues to be a central concern for the United States. However, our policies there have been severely tested and found wanting. Indeed, *post-mortem* commentaries on the 1978–79 debacle make it clear that our foreign-policy-making establishment was in no way prepared for the kind of revolution and ensuing turbulence that was to transform the Pahlavi monarchy into a totalitarian theocracy. Nor does anything in the published record suggest that we have been able to upgrade existing methods of intelligence collection and evaluation so as to improve the art of political forecasting in the Islamic world. Rather, what is richly illustrated is the tenacity with which we continue to hold to our prefabricated models and our preconceived, entirely untested truths about this geopolitically, economically, and historically most important region. For example, everyone was aware, Daniel O. Graham notes,[27] that, as the Shah was falling, a score of highly paid CIA analysts were writing that Iran was not in a revolutionary or even a prerevolutionary situation. The base assumption here is obviously that a certain model of "revolution," constructed by Western sociologists and historians with data culled from the records mainly of the eighteenth-century French Revolution, is an accurate measure, and thus also a reliable forecasting device, for the kind of upheaval which has been convulsing Iran in the last years.

Developments have not borne out this assumption. In fact, they also displace several related suppositions that crowd contemporary political science as well as intelligence estimates and analyses. For instance, the Department of State, congressional committees, and representatives of the intelligence community seem to be in broad agreement with Iranian revolutionaries, be they Islamic radicals, Marxist economists, or members of the Tudeh party, that "the Shah" was personally responsible for everything that has befallen Iran and that has gone wrong in U.S. policy. In many commentaries the reasoning is as simplistic as this: "Shah" stands for "king," and "king" stands for "reaction." "Revolution" and therewith "opposition," by contrast, stand for "progress"; and "progress" denotes the coming of "democracy" and respect for "human rights."

Such thought-killing stereotypes have at times also interfered with the task of reliably evaluating other kingdoms and sheikhdoms in the Middle East, notably the monarchies of Iraq, Saudi Arabia, Jordan, Libya, and Morocco. However, it is interesting that they usually do not obsess our thinking about nonroyal dictators in the Middle East, most of them successors to the kings they overthrew or killed. If we had overcome our traditional reluctance to think historically, we would have remembered that modern monarchical regimes in the Middle East have by and large been more moderate, innovative, and progressive in their social policies, and more reliable in the conduct of their foreign relations, notably with Occidental states, than the dictators who followed them. And most importantly, if we had read a little bit more ambitiously in the records of the past, we would have realized that authoritarian rule is the absolute norm in this entire culture realm.

Further, if we had studied Iran in particular we might have realized that the Iranian Revolution is representative of very complex culture patterns; that it cannot be understood solely as a function of events in the past decade; and that the monumental American failure in Iran is ultimately a result of our long-standing misperception of that country's place in the Islamic Middle East and our widespread ignorance of all that has been distinctive about Persian history during the past twenty-five hundred years. In short, we might have come to know that the two twentieth-century Pahlavi shahs had a complex dual commitment on the one hand as Muslims of the Shi'ite persuasion, on the other as culture-conscious representatives of the much older pre-Islamic traditions bequeathed by Persia's classical dynasties and by the Zoroastrian belief system.[28]

It is this second set of references that everyone interested in the relation between foreign policy and intelligence, specifically covert action, should study, for it tells of the principles of statecraft that sustained the multinational Persian Empire throughout antiquity as the "prestige nation" in the Eurasian world. The services that elicited the greatest admiration and emulation in the Orient related to diplomacy, policing methods, espionage, and other clandestine operations for which a group of renowned Achaemenid overseers—the "eyes and ears" of the king of kings—was responsible. No single document attests to this Persian legacy more faithfully than the Indian *Arthasastra*, a manual on the science of government composed by a Brahman adviser for the Maurya king Chandragupta, who founded the first vast centralized state in Northwest India after the region had ceased being a Persian satrapy.[29]

In light of Persia's history, it is not surprising that it was the Achaemenid tradition that provided the Pahlavi regimes with a model for a secular, territorially conceived state; allowed for secular law and secular education, tolerance of ethnic and religious minorities, and the emancipation of women; and stood for the principle of progress and continuity in time, thus inviting future-directed social reforms. These ideas are commonplace in the intellectual history of the West, and Europeans, beginning with the ancient Greeks, have therefore always been aware of their affinities with the Persians, even when their mutual relations were rent by war. But none of this holds for the Islamic Near East, for here each of the clusters of concepts just mentioned is absolutely anathema to the Shi'ite mind and fundamentally uncongenial also to the orthodox Sunni faith. As the Ayatollah Khomeini reminded the Iranians shortly after his ascendancy to power: "There are only two groups: Islam and non-Islam. We are all Muslims, and therefore Iranians have to choose between the Koran and the Book of Kings." (The last reference is an evocation of Persia's non-Islamic heritage of secular rule.)

The religious establishment that represents, after all, the primary cause on behalf of which the Arabs made war on Persia[30] was by definition committed to hatred for the Pahlavi shahs. Each reform, including, of course, the extensive expropriations of land held by the leadership of the religious establishment, was therefore bitterly resented as a betrayal of Islam and an usurpation of the Shi'ite mission in government and society at large. The Pahlavi elites thus had the strenuous task of administering the coexistence in their realm of near-incompatible principles if they were to keep Iran from slipping into the kind of political formlessness typical of neighboring Arab nations,[31] and if they were to succeed, instead, in maintaining Iran as an independent state capable of being effective in domestic and foreign affairs.

By and large the dynasty was able to meet this ongoing challenge. This was so partly because the complexity of Iran's internal and external situation was well understood in Western Europe as well as in the United States. From the 1970s onward, however, amnesia gripped America; and the void left by failing memory or ignorance was swiftly filled with such utopian policy projects as installing "democracy" and "human rights."

It has since been suggested by several analyses of our debacle in Iran that our policy has miscarried because those responsible for its formulation and implementation at State, Defense, and the CIA had not asked the right questions. The main critical data that we missed, it is being argued, were knowledge of the Shah's medical history (namely, the fact that he had suffered from cancer longer than we had presumed), and knowledge of "the opposition." The real failing of fieldwork by State and the CIA is thus said to have been neglect in collecting information about the opposition and therefore failure to communicate the antigovernment elements.

An evaluation of U.S. intelligence performance in Iran by the House Intelligence Subcommittee's staff concludes[32] that close identification with the Shah limited the opportunities for American officials to hear from Iranians who opposed him, thereby causing Iran to resemble a closed society from the U.S. perspective, with even clandestine collection of Iran's politics discouraged.

These judgments and the reasoning that led to them must be rebutted on the ground that they bear no relation to reality. And the same goes for the implicit assumption that there existed in Iran the equivalent of the Republican Party U.S.A. or of Her Majesty's Loyal Opposition in England with which our representatives could have communicated at will if the Shah's regime had not frustrated their attempts to do so. The heart of the matter—and it could have been identified readily—is that Iran is simply not cast in the mold of an "open" society on the order of Western democracies. Neither here nor elsewhere in the Islamic Middle East can we therefore expect to get to know the society's inner social order and its patterns of conflict by discoursing at ease with representatives of an openly organized opposition party. Rather, and as pointed out on preceding pages, the main opposition to the Shah's or any other secular government (the Communist Tudeh party is not considered here) is deeply entrenched, all-pervasive, permanent, and institutionalized in ways that make communication of the kind we anticipate hardly possible.

In short, the "failings" that emerge from all of these postmortem notices were and continue to be failings of scholarship and education that could have been avoided or corrected by collecting information in our libraries. No "assets" and secret contacts were required for that.

Scholarly work of this kind would also have equipped policymakers and their agents with the knowledge that "the opposition" would be at least as authoritarian in the discharge of the functions of government as the Pahlavi monarchy was, even as it would in all likelihood be less capable of maintaining the state. This had already proved to be true of the short-lived, essentially secular Mossadegh regime, which dismissed parliament and ruled without any regard for law, and it should have been forecast also in the years during which the Ayatollah Khomeini and his Shi'ite divines were preparing the overthrow of the Shah. Subsequent developments leave no doubt, unfortunately, that we knew very little, probably nothing, about the nature of Iranian alternatives to Pahlavi rule. For while our governmental agents and representatives of the media fell all over themselves in kowtows before the Ayatollah (widely viewed as another George Washington and, by Andrew Young, as "a kind of saint"), the latter's kangaroo courts and execution squads simply proceeded in a matter-of-fact way with their grisly work of killing Iranians.

The basic American supposition that the ouster of the Shah's "lawless regime" would somehow lead Iran back to the norms of its Western-type constitution of 1906 and thus by implication also to concordance with American commitments to "human rights" simply disintegrated as yet another illusion as Shi'ite Iran returned resolutely to its roots. One is therefore entitled to be surprised that the Carter administration had not been forewarned by its legal advisers and area specialists about the likely consequences for constitutional, penal, and international law of revolutionary Iran's thrust back into the past. As it was, we merely registered consternation when we learned that Iranian citizens pronounced guilty of sundry crimes such as selling alcohol and committing adultery were programmatically buried up to their chests and stoned to death, all to the sound of ceremonial prayers and exuberant acclamations by attending masses. No one in the ranks of our policymakers seems to have been given access to the rich literature (in English) on precisely the issues here in contention that has long been available to every literate person. At any rate it was obviously not expected that the complex of norms that we call "law" and that Westernizing Iranian governments had grafted rather carefully upon the substratum of Islamic precepts and values would be dismantled speedily. This was so, it is here suggested, because no one in authority knew that the term "law" relates to "religion" in the context of orthodox Islam, and that this religious "law" *(shari'a)* is a comprehensive order of precepts that encompasses not only what we call "law" but also what we distinguish as philosophy, ethics, jurisprudence, economics, government, and foreign relations. Lastly, it seems strange to me that our "eyes and ears" abroad—be they journalists or diplomats—had not alerted our policy-making elites to the open comeback of this entire complex of religion throughout the Islamic world.

"Their" law, then, has nothing to do with "our" law, and President Carter's instruction to the intelligence community that its members may not violate the laws of a foreign government would have needed considerable amplification in the case of Iran if they were intended to be meaningful and wise.[33]

The conclusion that comparative studies of law, religion, ethics, and politics had not been conducted by our government when critical decisions in our foreign policy had to be made is particularly relevant in the context of international law and diplomatic methods. As noted earlier, the territorially delimited state had not been a fundamental norm in Arab/Islamic politics before Westernization (Egypt, Turkey, and Iran do not belong in this category for reasons cited earlier). Rather, history tells us in great detail that Islam mandates expansion and the creation of an all-Islamic state, not an international order of multiple sovereignties, and that it does not stipulate the kind of polarization between war and peace that we today consider normative in the conduct of international relations. As most everywhere, cultures in the Middle East accept, even value, conflict, conspiracy, and war. Societies here were thus routinely convulsed by intrigues and bloody power struggles between contesting men or factions and by well-organized religious uprisings that aimed at punishing immorality and at purifying life on earth by resort to war. The Wahabi movement in Arabia is one such illustration. Another is the Order of the Assassins in Iran, an offspring of the Shi'ite sect of the Ismailites that terrorized the land during the eleventh-thirteenth centuries A.D. by meticulously planned assassinations.[34]

Traditions such as these have been reinforced, rechanneled, and in some respects, of course, deformed by twentieth-century Eurasian theories and practices of terrorism and guerrilla warfare. Neither of the two ideological commitments that are joined today makes allowance for the basic norms of international law and diplomacy that we in the United States continue to regard as universally accepted and therefore as universally binding. The quasi-religious pledge to kill the Shah,[35] his children, and his extended family, indeed the entire "opposition" to Khomeini's regime, was thus conceived and openly advertised as a transterritorial mandate, to be carried out without regard whatsoever for the territorial integrity and the laws of other states with which Iran was—from the Occidental viewpoint—at "peace."

This blueprint for murder could be concretized effectively because agents in charge of such covert operations—the reference here is mainly to episodes in the United States, France, and England—can rely on interlocking nets of collaborators in the ranks of Iranian and other Mohammedan radicals who are resident in the host country; on the succor of selected sympathetic Islamic embassies; and on the generosity or weakness of the democratic legal systems within which such actions occur. And the same combination of factors naturally facilitates such related operations as the unleashing of Iranian student mobs in American cities and the dispensing by the Khomeini regime of covert aid for the general purpose of inciting violence in the United States.

These developments have severely tried the institution of diplomacy and its attendant system of norms. Indeed, as so-called students are allowed to storm and occupy embassies in Teheran; as foreign diplomats are being held hostage; as people's committees are replacing Iranian embassies; and as covert action operatives are taking the place of diplomats, the conclusion is not farfetched that diplomacy as we have known it in the last two centuries has been fatally struck. Furthermore, and in the same extended context, the thought is justified that government-sponsored terrorism of the kind made evident here has had the effect of leveling existing distinctions between war and peace. Iran's present foreign policy—and allowance must be made for the fact that it emanates from power centers that are chronically feuding in secret—is thus essentially a covert war policy. Conceived in unmitigated hatred of the West, in particular the United States, it aims solely at humiliating this foe and at exorcising his "satanic," "corrupting" influences from all domains of Iranian life and thought. "We are a superpower," Khomeini declared: "We are not Americans, we do not belong to pragmatism." "Final victory" is therefore officially identified here not with economic development and wealth, nor with nationally secure frontiers, but with the expulsion of the Americans who symbolize the Occident as did the Shah.

It would in my view be a mistake to think of the frenzy of Iran's xenophobia and of the relentless scapegoating in which its spokesmen engage as temporary aberrations of the national psyche, or as expressions of a passing malaise on the part of a hard-pressed, confused revolutionary leadership. After all, Iranians in all age groups and walks of life, whether living in Iran or the United States, whether home-bred ayatollahs and ulemas, or American-educated economists and political scientists, consistently reveal themselves as enthusiastically active participants in these foreign policy orgies.[36]

What needs to be faced in the area of psychology is what has been suggested earlier in this paper in regard to religion, law, history, philosophy, and government: namely, that *there are very few—if any—transnationally valid norms and values.*

Hugh Tovar addressed this matter at a colloquium organized by the Consortium for Study of Intelligence (1979) when he noted:

It is hard for Americans to fathom the turbulent well of Islamic radicalism and its seemingly mindless violence. We are stunned when friendly governments are suddenly en-
gulfed and overthrown in explosive outbreaks that seem beyond our ability to influence,
much less to modulate.[37]

My own response to this American malaise is somewhat sterner: why do we not
accept what the last decades of this century have made manifest in no uncertain
terms—namely, that what is "irrational" in our universe of experience may well be
perfectly rational in that of other, culturally different peoples? In the case of modern
Islam and Iran in particular we should have been well prepared for the likelihood
of the kind of outbursts we are witnessing now. It is thus odd to have to recognize
that those concerned with the Middle East in matters of foreign policy have not
read Gustave von Grunebaum's analyses of the Islamic self-view in history
and international relations in *Modern Islam: The Search for Cultural Identity;* or
H. A. R. Gibb's critique of Islamic modernism in *Modern Trends in Islam;* or J. J.
Saunders's exploration of the factors that have made for the freezing of Islamic
culture in his *A History of Medieval Islam.* These are just three exquisite texts
among many others that deal precisely with the psychological motifs, so prominently displayed today. Likewise, it does not seem plausible that those in charge of
the State Department's Iran desk have missed out on William S. Haas's analysis in
Iran of the Persian mind as molded by Persia's tortured history.

Haas points out that the strong Persian commitment to the dissident Shi'ite persuasion and to Sufism evolved from an admirable but inevitably only partially successful attempt to separate the Persian mind from the Sunni faith of the old empire's
Arab conquerors. Conceived in terms of mental and psychological self-protection
and defense, the effort soon found expression in a peculiar custom, one distinctly
relevant to comparative studies of clandestine and covert operations—namely, the
dissimulation of faith by mental reservation *(ketman).* Under the protective cover
of what eventually became a theological doctrine, a Shi'ite was allowed to pretend
that he was a Sunni, or even a Christian or a Jew, whenever he felt he was in danger
because of the fact that he actually was a Shi'ite and a believer in the eventual
appearance of the Hidden Imam. This fundamentally religious practice communicated itself gradually to other life contexts. In that of statecraft as it had developed
before the twentieth-century reforms, *ketman* gave rise in Persia to a technique of
cunning, simulation, and ruse that Persians in many walks of life learned to master
with rare perfection, nowhere more effectively, Haas notes, than in diplomacy and
in government circles in which "inferiors" evolved a strategy of self-defense
against superiors that allowed them to slip through the meshes of any net thrown
around them.[38]

B.   The Islamic Empires

The great Islamic empires from which numerous nation states have disengaged
themselves in recent times share several characteristics that are relevant for modern
comparative studies of statecraft, intelligence, and covert action. A substantiation
of this conclusion needs the following preliminary information.

The Arab and Arabized caliphates, the Seljuq and Ottoman empires, the Mogul empire, and the Islamized Persian empire were despotisms in which the twin ideas of citizenship and a common public secular law never developed. Each was born of war and organized for conquests; each was a tax-taking, not a legislating polity on the order of the classical Roman and the modern European empires, and each relied heavily on institutionalized slavery. Further, neither empire, excepting that of the Persians, had fathomed or could concretize the concept of the secular state since Islamic religious law had consigned this notion to the realm of illegitimacy, along with that of legislation—the latter on the ground that God, acting through Mohammed, had legislated once and for all.

Next, West Asia's Islamic empires were plural societies, composed of multiple, ethnically and culturally diverse tribes, villages, provinces, and religious sects. Heavily taxed and viewed as conglomerates of subject or inferior peoples, these communities were yet allowed a considerable measure of autonomy in matters of belief and social customs. Totally missing in the Islamic context was a unifying framework for the secular governance of a vast, culturally fragmented international society that would assure stabilization of all that arms and ideology had won.

This standing challenge explains why the Islamic victors borrowed so heavily from the records of statecraft left by the defeated, notably Persia and Byzantium. After all, the latter, too, had been universal empires as well as culturally heterogeneous societies in which religion—Zoroastrianism in one case, Christianity in another—was taken very seriously. But contrary to the upstart empires of the nomadic peoples from the deserts of Arabia and the steppes of Central Asia, Persia (seventh century B.C.–seventh century A.D.) and Byzantium (fifth century–fifteenth century A.D.) had known how to allow for legitimate interaction between institutionalized religion and political organization. This they accomplished by relying on solid bodies of public secular law, stressing the idea of the state as the superior all-encompassing reality, cultivating statecraft through the medium of refined intelligence and communication, and creating specialized bureaucratic services for overseeing affairs of state at home and abroad.[39]

It was the latter aspect of the Persian and Byzantine designs that most intrigued first the Arab dynasties of the Umayyads (seventh century A.D.) and the Abbasids (eighth century A.D.) and later the Turks and Mongols—if only because Islam could not address such organizational challenges. However, it should be noted that the conquering bands of Turks and Mongols—in contrast to the Arabs—had also been vitally influenced by the Chinese and the Tatars of the steppes, and that they had brought with them their own well-tested ideas on how to govern men and nations. After 1258 (the sack of Baghdad) Mongol sovereigns thus relied heavily on their own customary laws, despite their conversion to Islam. This factor explains, authorities note, why their despotisms were never as closely related to the *shari'a* as that of, say, the administration of Suleiman the Magnificent in Istanbul (sixteenth century A.D.), and why the slave system in Akbar's Indian Mogul empire (sixteenth century) was not nearly as harsh and elaborate as that imposed by Turkish rulers upon Christian communities. Yet, and after full allowance is made for the diversity of cultural borrowing processes, the fact is indisputable that it was Persia in each of its multiple incarnations that exerted the paramount influence upon the new Islamic polities. This was so, an Abbasid caliph is said to have explained, because the Persians had ruled for a thousand years and had not needed "us Arabs" even for a day; but "we" (Arabs) have been ruling for one or two centuries and cannot do without them for an hour.

An inheritance that the Abbasids valued particularly was Persia's elaborate system of trunk roads and postal communications—the indispensable framework for all intelligence-related services. In the Abbasid context the postmaster-general was also, indeed primarily, the chief of the espionage system. In this dual capacity he acted as the confidential agent of the central government: all provincial postmasters reported to him or directly to the caliph on the conduct of government officials as well as on the activities of adversaries and foreign enemies. Scores of merchants, peddlers, and travelers were employed as agents in the caliphal espionage network. The records of Al-Ma'mum's rule also show that his particular service included some seventeen hundred aged women, and that spies of both sexes, intricately disguised as traders, journeymen, or physicians, were nowhere more active than in conquered Byzantine territory.

Among the different "Persias" in history it was the one ruled by the Sassanians (third–seventh century A.D.) that recommended itself as the chief organizational model because it had known how to evolve and maintain an elaborate bureaucratic establishment, a highly efficient military system, and an intricate network of diplomacy and espionage—three services that together had assured the security, stability, and glory of the realm. All records of statecraft relating to these Iranian "kings of kings" were thus diligently studied, among them in particular the tenth-century Book of Kings and Firdausi's great epic *shāhnāma* as well as the famous "Mirrors for Princes," composed by men of affairs and letters for the instruction of rulers and their ministers. All of them emphasized the need for gathering intelligence, with some of the later manuals advising that networks of spies should cover the entire realm since a sovereign must know the people's secrets if he is to enjoy a long and successful reign.

Under the impact of this Iranian tradition of "rational statecraft," the Dar al-Islam was early set in the mold of the "power state."[40] This political phenomenon was expounded and analysed by Nizām al-Mulk (d. 1092 A.D.) in *The Book of Government (Seyāsat-nāmeh)*,[41] a remarkable text of timeless significance about which an early scribe wrote that "no king or emperor can afford not to possess and know this book, especially in these days." Anchored firmly in reflections on history and political expedience, the work owes nothing to Islamic theory and religion, even as it aimed openly at protecting the cause of orthodox Islam.

Nizām al-Mulk ("Regulator of the Kingdom") was born into the highly cultured Persian administrating class, became vizier to Alp Arslan when the latter was supreme overlord of the new Seljuq rulers, and advanced to the top post of Grand Vizier ("burden bearer" for the Sultan) when his Seljuq master became sultan over an empire that stretched from the Oxus in the East to Khwarezm and the southern Caucasus and westward into central Anatolia. During thirty years of stewardship Nizām al-Mulk established an unchallenged reputation as the quintessential vizier. Wise, prudent, resourceful, and successful, he was consistently praised by successive generations as an outstanding statesman, and above all as the main architect of an exemplary empire in which prosperity and security were firmly established.

Nizām al-Mulk seems to have stood steadfastly by the following propositions while he recorded these accomplishments. He was determined to upgrade Turkish rule by relating it firmly to Iran's superior traditions of statecraft. He believed that the ruler was chosen by God for the task of preserving stability in the kingdom; that his power had to be absolute; that all administration should be centralized in his person; and that having ultimate ownership of all land, the sultan must be presumed to own the kingship. Furthermore, deep religious convictions combined with considerations of "reason of state" convinced Nizām al-Mulk that it was necessary to maintain the Sunni faith. He was therefore determined to combat all heterodox sects, among them mainly the Shi'ites and the Order of the Assassins they had spawned. (Numerous training schools were thus founded by him for the purpose of countering Shi'ite propaganda.)

Nizām al-Mulk's "power state" could not have realized either of these or any other policy objectives if it had not concentrated its attention upon two particular instruments of rule: a powerful fighting army that could be expected to be always in place and ready to support the momentum of expansion, and a tightly organized, totally reliable network of intelligence *(bārid)* whose officers kept watch over and reported on events taking place in various parts of the empire, thus assuring the speedy transmission of messages between government agents in the provinces and central controls in the capital. The importance attached to this system of communication is well conveyed by the following excerpts from *The Book of Government.*[42]

It is the king's duty to enquire into the condition of his peasantry and army, both far and near, and to know more or less how things are. If he does not do this he is at fault and people will charge him with negligence, laziness and tyranny, saying, "Either the king knows about the oppression and extortion going on in the country, or he does not know. If he knows and does nothing to prevent it and remedy it, that is because he is an oppressor like the rest and acquiesces in their oppression; and if he does not know then he is negligent and ignorant." Neither of these imputations is desirable. Inevitably therefore he must have postmasters; and in every age in the time of ignorance and of Islam, kings have had postmasters, through whom they have learnt everything that goes on, good and bad. For instance, if anybody wrongly took so much as a chicken or a bag of straw from another (and that five hundred farsangs away) the king would know about it and have the offender punished, so that others knew that the king was vigilant. In every place they appointed informers and so far checked the activities of oppressors that men enjoyed security and justice for the pursuit of trade and cultivation. But this is a delicate business involving some unpleasantness; it must be entrusted to the hands and tongues and pens of men who are completely above suspicion and without self-interest, for the weal or woe of the country depends on them. They must be directly responsible to the king and not to anyone else; and they must receive their monthly salaries regularly from the treasury so that they may do their work without any worries. In this way the king will know of every event that takes place and will be able to give his orders as appropriate, meting out unexpected reward, punishment, or condemnation to the persons concerned. When a king is like this, men are always eager to be obedient, fearing the king's displeasure, and nobody can possibly have the audacity to disobey the king or plot any mischief. Thus the employment of intelligence agents and reporters contributes to the justice, vigilance, and prudence of the king, and to the prosperity of the country.

Spies must constantly go out to the limits of the kingdom in the guise of merchants, travelers, sufis, peddlers (of medicines), and mendicants, and bring back reports of everything they hear, so that no matters of any kind remain concealed, and if anything (untoward) happens it can in due course be remedied. In the past it has often happened that governors, assignees, officers, and army-commanders have planned rebellion and resistance, and plotted mischief against the king, but spies forestalled them and informed the king, who was thus enabled to set out immediately with all speed and, coming upon them unawares, to strike them down and frustrate their plans; and if any foreign king or army was prepared to attack the country, the spies informed the king, and he took action and repelled them. Likewise they brought news, whether good or bad, about the condition of the peasants, and the king gave the matter his attention, as did Adud ad Daula on one occasion.

After a lengthy section on the king's need for "boon companions" (these must not be government officials but may serve as body guards), Nizām al-Mulk turns to foreign affairs and diplomacy:

When ambassadors come from foreign countries, nobody is aware of their movements until they actually arrive at the city gates; nobody gives any information (that they are coming) and nobody makes any preparation for them: and they will surely attribute this to our negligence and indifference. So officers at the frontiers must be told that whenever anyone approaches their stations, they should at once despatch a rider and find out who it is who is coming, how many men there are with him, mounted and unmounted, how much baggage and equipment he has, and what is his business. A trustworthy person must be appointed to accompany them and conduct them to the nearest big city; there he will hand them over to another agent who will likewise go with them to the next city (and district), and so on until they reach the court. Whenever they arrive at a place where there is cultivation, it must be a standing order that officers, tax collectors, and assignees should give them hospitality and entertain them well so that they depart satisfied. When they return, the same procedure is to be followed. Whatever treatment is given to an ambassador, whether good or bad, it is as if it were done to the very king who sent them, and kings have always shown the greatest respect to one another and treated envoys well, for by this their own dignity has been enhanced. And if at any time there has been disagreement or enmity between kings, and if ambassadors have still come and gone as occasion requires, and discharged their missions according to their instructions, never have they been molested or treated with less than usual courtesy. Such a thing would be disgraceful, as God (to Him be power and glory) says (in the Koran 24.53), "The messenger has only to convey the message plainly."

It should also be realized that when kings send ambassadors to one another their purpose is not merely the message or the letter which they communicate openly, but secretly they have a hundred other points and objects in view. In fact they want to know about the state of roads, mountain passes, rivers and grazing grounds, to see whether an army can pass or not; where fodder is available and where not; who are the officers in every place; what is the size of that king's army and how well it is armed and equipped; what is the standard of his table and his company; what is the organization and etiquette of his court and audience hall; does he play polo and hunt; what are his qualities and manners, his designs and intentions, his appearance and bearing; is he cruel or just, old or young; is his country flourishing or decaying; are his troops contented or not; are the peasants rich or poor; is he avaricious or generous; is he alert or negligent in affairs; is his vizier competent or the reverse, of good faith and high principles or of impure faith and bad principles; are his generals experienced and battle-tried or not; are his boon-companions polite and worthy; what are his likes and dislikes; in his cups is he jovial and good-natured or not; is he strict in religious matters and does he shew magnanimity and mercy, or is he careless; does he incline more to jesting or to gravity; and does he prefer boys or women. So that, if at any time they want to win over that king, or oppose his designs or criticize his faults, being informed of all his affairs they can think out their plan of campaign, and being aware of all the circumstances, they can take effective action, as happened to your humble servant in the time of The Martyr Sultan Alp Arsian (may Allah sanctify his soul).

Nizām al-Mulk wrote the book shortly before he was assassinated. The murder was probably committed by an Ismā-ili from the castle of the Assassins with the complicity of a court rival, of the queen, and possibly even of Malik-Shah himself. Within a month the sultan, too, was dead, and the disintegration of the great empire was proceeding ineluctably.

The imminence of this development had been predicted by Nizām al-Mulk, who had expressed great anxiety about the sultan's careless disregard for protocol, the decline in prestige of important officials, and, above all, about the neglect of the intelligence service. For contrary to his advice, the sultan had ended up abolishing the *bārid* on the ground that it engendered an atmosphere of mistrust and suspicion among friends and foes alike. This meant that effective checks and controls were missing and that the ruler could not be secured against rebellion, injustice, or extortion by his officials. It was anxiety about this state of affairs that led Nizām al-Mulk to emphasize the need for an efficient system of espionage to be backed by an armed force strong enough to overpower all opposition. The sultan, he advised, now had to have informers and spies throughout the empire and among all classes of the population, including that of the *qādis*.

The pattern of rise, expansion, contraction, and decay, so dramatically illustrated by the Seljuq Empire, continued to mark the histories of Islamic despotisms in West Asia, and foreign relations among established Muslim polities continued to be cast in terms of war relations, with ambitious princes and the dynasties they spawned forever determined to seek new glory and dominion by besting actual or potential rivals.[43] The model of the Perso-Turkish power state that presumed the ruler's omnipotence and required a powerful army as main instrument of statecraft had become firmly established and was therefore reenacted time and time again between the eleventh and the end of the eighteenth centuries, most impressively in the sixteenth-century Ottoman Empire of Suleiman the Magnificent, where government had been deeply influenced by Byzantine traditions from the taking of Constantinople (1453) onward. In accordance with established pattern this empire, too, declined after Suleiman's death, and the main cause here, as in the earlier Seljuq, Persian, and Mongol empires, was the degeneration of the ruling establishment, not any deleterious impact wrought by continuous war.

This was so, it appears, because the sultan's complex court was not just an ordinary government. Rather, it was a direct projection or representation of his identity and biography; of his personality, power, and vitality. And since the sultan personified the state, it was therefore in the final analysis his security and survival that constituted the prime concern in domestic as well as in foreign affairs. Indeed, these two dimensions of statecraft can hardly be disentangled in the Islamic context. Thus when something goes wrong with the ruler and his court, something goes very wrong also with the state. The ruling institution itself, then, was the hub and core of all statecraft, the battleground between contending men and nations, and the uncontested center radiating vitality as well as decay.

The success or failure of a given Islamic despotism at home and abroad was being determined then as it is now—one thinks of Tripolis, Baghdad, Damascus, Teheran, or Algiers—by events unfolding in the immediate entourage of the leading man. This therefore was and continues to be the theater of most intelligence operations, including covert actions.

The dynamics that determined the deployment of clandestine and covert methods were strong and complex feelings on the part of all governing elites, foremost among them fear of treachery, distrust, and vindictiveness. These could be activated at will because enmity, jealousy, and the propensity to engage in conspiracy were generally accepted human traits, and because codes of law and ethics were missing when it came to affairs of state. Sultanates, caliphates, and emirates were thus normally rent by open civil war, rebellion, secession, and above all by internecine strife. More particularly, they were usually prey to one or the other kind of forcible seizure, most of them involving murder.

In the absence of reliable rules of succession, regicide, fratricide, and other forms of assassination were common as were wars between fathers and sons or between elder and younger brothers. For example, Shah Abbas the Great of Persia (seventeenth century A.D.) had two sons blinded and indulged in intricate plots to murder his eldest son because he had become popular. Shah Jehan in the Mogul empire (seventeenth century A.D.) had to contend with four rebellious sons who also fought against each other until the last was able to encompass the death of the others and keep his father imprisoned during the last seven years of his life. Each new sultan in the Ottoman empire had his surviving brothers strangled, usually with a silken bowstring so as not to shed blood. In fact, to avoid the dangers implicit in a disputed succession, the Ottomans adopted a "Law of Fratricide" providing that to whichever son the sultanate might be vouchsafed, it was proper for him to put his brothers to death, so as to preserve the order of the world. Further, and perhaps by way of mitigating the harshness of such destinies, it became customary to keep all princes in the harem. Here they lived a life of gilded imprisonment in the company of their mothers, slaves and eunuchs until they emerged in order to die or reign.[44] As a contemporary chronicler reports, to be born a prince was misfortune of the worst and most embarrassing kind; he must die by clemency, or wade through the blood of his family to safety and empire.

How to induce loyalty and how to locate reliable agents while avoiding security risks were the standing challenges in all Oriental despotisms. The sovereigns in each of the different empires found different ways of recruiting and maintaining appropriate categories of "despotic agents." Yet all, including ancient Persia and China (at times also Rome and Byzantium), relied heavily on eunuchs. The shared natural expectation here was that, having no family ambitions of their own, eunuchs could be made to serve the monarch exclusively, mainly by preventing or uncovering murderous plots and subversive activities. This category of councilors was especially well developed in the Islamic Middle East, more particularly in the Ottoman empire, where "black" eunuchs, "white" eunuchs, and other subgroups were in charge of all essential offices, among them the sultan's harem.[45]

The other major human resource for recruitment was slavery. In the Ottoman empire, slaves were the backbone of the army, the bureaucracy, and the courtly household. Most were Christians, and they were acquired either as prisoners or— until at least the seventeenth century—through the medium of regular levies upon Christian villages. Here, too, the rationale was that the despot needed men without roots, and Christian youths were therefore detached from their families early in life so as to be trained in special palace schools for slaves where their evolution into loyal servants was closely supervised by trusted eunuchs.

Variously defined as a power state and a slave state, the Islamic empire was also a closed society in which clandestine operations and covert actions were called for if the ruling institution was to rule successfully. However, as remarked earlier, it was also a layered society, composed of numerous essentially self-sufficient corporations, guilds, bazaars, sects, and religious brotherhoods. These, too, were closed societies in the sense that each was beholden to its own codes and customs, spurning cooperation with others. But contrary to the state, each could count on the loyalty of its constituency if only because the individual member derived his essential status and identity from the grouping he belonged to. And since most corporate associations were as hostile to the state as the general population, they often did act in concert to resist or defy state authority, sometimes in open rebellion, but usually by engaging in what we today call clandestine and covert operations. These, it is important to point out, were routinely deployed also in relations between rival factions and movements.

In such a context of dispositions, flights into subversive associations were commonplace and "the secret society" became the normative organizational model for religious and political activism, especially in Persia and the Arab lands. The Order of the Assassins, to which reference has already been made, is a case in point. As Brockelmann explains, it was built up in various degrees:

> While the narrowest circle of initiates professed a libertinism which negated any limitations by morality or religion, their agents were trained in the severest fanaticism. The murder of an enemy of the true faith designated by their master was presented to them as a work well pleasing to God, the execution of which would assure them of the joys of Paradise. Such murderers were called Fida'is, "the Self-Sacrificers," or Hashishis (whence Assassins), those intoxicated by hashish. . . .[46]

To destroy in the name of purity was the motivating force also of the Arab Ikhwan ("Sincere Brethren") and the Wahhabites. The latter group, which had been initiated by an Arab tribesman (Muhammad ibn-Abd-al Wahhab) in revulsion against the abuses that had penetrated Islam, notably as practiced by the Turks, swiftly evolved into a great national revival after it had rallied most Bedouin tribes of the

Najd. This revolt, which climaxed in an attack on Mecca in 1803, may be said to have launched the complex and protracted "awakening" process during which the entire Middle Eastern region became honeycombed with secret societies working underground in revolt against Turkish rule.[47]

One of the earliest and most important of these clandestine organisms was the Beirut Secret Society, which began toward the end of the nineteenth century as "a whispered conspiracy" of like-minded opponents to the Turkish regime (all original founders were Christians) until it was emboldened to launch violent exhortations to rebellion, mainly through the medium of placards. These could remain anonymous because their creators had refined the art of disguising handwritings, literary styles, and standards to such an extent that ruling authorities were simply incapable of conjecturing the identities of these subversive elements. Operations were nonetheless endangered by the government's secret agents, and the society dissolved itself voluntarily after a few years' existence, leaving no account of its activities. Its scanty records were deliberately destroyed, and its members emigrated, mostly to Egypt. In short, the secret was well kept to the end, and, as George Antonius concludes from his own exploration of this long episode, the identities of the conspirators never became known either to the government or to the public. What was left was the society's device representing a drawn sword below which there was this line: "By the sword may distant aims be attained: seek with it if you mean to succeed."

This remained the general motto for all societies in the twentieth century that aimed at Arab independence. Most of them unified their membership by common passwords, signals for identification, a clandestine press, a common treasury, and, above all, a total commitment to loyalty and secrecy. Al-Fatāt, the most effective of these Arab societies, was remarkable alike for its objects and methods as for the admirable discipline of its members. A long period of probation preceded admission. Each recruit was introduced by one of the sworn members but was kept in ignorance of the identity of all the other members until he had been tried and proved, when he would be invited to take an oath to serve the ends of the society, to the point of forfeiting his life, if need be, in its service. The society's membership gradually rose to two hundred, the majority being Moslems. The secret of its existence was guarded to the end, Antonius reports. Indeed, the Arab countries had gained their liberation from Turkish rule before it was disclosed. During the war, when the Turks were prosecuting Arab nationalists for treason, one member of Al-Fatāt was driven by physical torture to attempt suicide, and another went to the gallows rather than betray the society's secret.[48] Al-Qahtaniya was similarly organized and equally renowned for discipline. It chose only those whose patriotism was beyond question and who could be trusted to guard a secret. When suspicion of betrayal in their midst arose, members found it impossible to continue work, and the society was allowed to die of willful neglect.

The preceding assessments of Islamic societies as they existed between the seventh and twentieth centuries A.D. relate directly to most of the issues raised in the questionnaire.[49] Reflections on present and historical records suggest that secrecy, dissimulation, and covert activities are part of the general life-style; that social and political relations are marked by intrigue, deception, and conflict; that the image of "the enemy" is highly developed; that fighting is viewed positively as a noble undertaking; and that people tolerate high levels of violence. Trust, loyalty, and peace are valued positively within small fellowships of like-minded men who know each other well. Power and success are respected as attributes of biography; they are distrusted in the arena of government. In fact, government is always suspect, and it is expected to be harsh.

Most if not all of these norms, values, and dispositions are sanctioned by religious texts, foremost among them the Old Testament and the Koran, and by authoritative interpreters of the *shari'a*. Such questions as "Can covert action be just?" would simply not even suggest themselves in the context of Mohammedan law and ethics.

The foreign policies emanating from these societies relay the norms, values, and traditions that are dominant within society. Since neither the state nor the notion of a long-term national interest is fully developed in Arab/Islamic thought and actuality, foreign policy is apt to be as personalized as is the state itself.

The long record of inter-Arab, inter-Islamic, and general international relations shows that war has been and continues to be endemic in this culture realm—a reality explicitly confirmed and approved by theory and religion. As Majid Khadduri explains,[50] the conduct of foreign relations has therefore traditionally been dealt with under the heading of *jihad*. This doctrine of a permanent state of holy war between "believers" and "unbelievers"—and the latter often included Mohammedans as preceding discussions have illustrated—was affirmed and explicated in the fourteenth century by Ibn Khaldūn, the most esteemed Islamic theoretician. It instructed the faithful that defeated Muslims were entitled to hope and plan for a resumption of battle, however long the wait for such a second round, and that the idea of the *jihad* could be rendered in terms of a *guerra fria*, or a psychological war of nerves, rather than in those of continuous physical fighting.[51] In this design, then, peace becomes a state of dormant war and diplomacy an auxiliary or substitute for war. Envoys were therefore naturally suspect as spies, and peace treaties had to be viewed as diplomatic expedients only.

The advent of lively relations among the Ottoman, Mogul, and Persian empires on the one hand and Western European states on the other brought the realization that these traditional Islamic orientations were inadequate and that adjustments to the Occidental law of war and peace would have to be made. This revisionist approach was intensified when Westernization became the watchword in the nineteenth and twentieth centuries. However, and as preceding sections of this essay have suggested, a near-total reversal of orientations set in as soon as Islamic governments discovered toward the end of this century that the West had ceased to press its case effectively.

The clandestine life of the Middle East has obviously always been suffused with "intelligence" and appropriate communication networks. Assassination and related ways of checking enemy lives and activities were common practices. Espionage, being a prerequisite for diplomacy and war, was highly developed in pre-Islamic and Islamic times, among Persians, Turks, and Mongols as among Arabs. And the same holds for military intelligence as the dense records of the great transcontinental invasions, campaigns, battles, and sieges show. For example, the twin causes of war and espionage have been consistently well served in the Orient by "tunneling" the enemy's spatial and psychologial terrain. This particular art, which seems to have originated with the Mongols, was copied and perfected by the Turks, the Chinese (see Sun Tzu's references), and adjacent Asian peoples. In our times it is being exemplified by relentless North Korean attempts to undermine Seoul and take over South Korea by employing this tunneling tactic. In the mid-fifteenth century it was dramatically deployed by the Ottoman Turks during the last phase of their determined yet protracted siege of Constantinople, the Byzantine empire's prize. In fact, and as described by the Venetian ambassador Nicolò Barbaro in his diary of this historic siege, tunneling may well have been the decisive Turkish stratagem; for neither bombardments nor pitched battles on ship were as demoralizing to the spirited defenders of the Christian city as the daily discovery of yet another tunnel undermining the foundations of their walls, and therewith also of their will power and identity.

These and other psychological aspects of intelligence and warfare were developed throughout Asia, most systematically in Achaemenid Persia's statecraft, India's *Arthasastra* world and the records of China's Legalist statesmen, among them in particular Sun Tzu's *Art of War* (probable date 400–320 B.C.), in which the stress in strategy is squarely placed on the need to "encircle" the enemy's mind. The striking convergence of these greatly different Oriental cultures upon affirmation of the need to cancel, neutralize, or subvert the human mind is a function of the fact that all Asian despotisms were, and continue to be, conceived as conflict systems in which human nature is feared and distrusted and in which considerations of war have traditionally eclipsed considerations of peace.

The traditional relation of foreign policy to intelligence including covert action can thus not be covered by our distinctions and definitions which derive from premises altogether contrary to those accepted in the East. Further, developments strongly indicate that Westernization has not displaced the basic norms of statecraft, which have conditioned thought and behavior for more than a millennium and which are widely (and naturally) associated by present generations with the Orient's superiority, in some cases victory, over the Occidental enemy. The American CIA may have been considered worthy of imitation by Westernized ruling elites in Egypt, South Korea, and other states as long as they had reason to associate it with U.S. influence and power. No such reason is perceivable today. The United States has forfeited too much of its power, and the American "model" CIA is discredited, having been knocked out deliberately by the government and nation that it was designed to serve.

In this situation, which has been aggravated for many decades by the tutorial presence of Leninist intelligence advisers, non-Western non-Communist governments should be allowed, if not encouraged, to trust their own modes of perceiving the enemy and of assessing his threats.

C. Classical India

A comparative historical review of political systems justifies the view that the one brought forth by Hindu India in the fourth century B.C. is philosophically the most impressive, even as it may well have been politically the most ruinous. My main reason for presenting this Indian creation in brief outline is twofold: no other system has addressed problems of intelligence, specifically covert action, as comprehensively and methodically; and none stands in greater contrast to American statecraft.

It should be noted by way of preface that the *artha* world of warring kingdoms vanished in the wake of Arab, Turkish, and Mongol conquests, and that the *artha* philosophy of success was officially either subsumed or superseded by non-Hindu strands of thought, among them, after the eighteenth century, English common law and equity. However, and as mentioned in the preceding essay many members of the anglicized Indian elite continue to maintain that *artha* doctrines and practices continue to be in force.[52]

This perspective had already been projected in 1880 by Sir Henry Maine in his comparative studies of Eastern and Western village communities, in which he remarks that Mohammedan influences on Indian institutions and customs had been so slight as to be hardly worth taking into account. And the same theme has been stressed by the Bengali writer Nirad Chaudhuri, as when he notes in a commentary on Mrs. Gandhi's determined policy to weaken Pakistan that all Muslim conquests had driven the Hindu mind back to its roots, leaving nothing but a residue of bitter hatred for these conquerors. Believing that the anglicized Hindus are the recessive, not the dominant, minority in India today, Chaudhuri concludes, regretfully, that a similar "return to roots" is in full swing today and that the effects of Westernization will not last.

The only decisive foreign influence that has been consistently acknowledged in India, usually in terms of praise and particularly eloquently by Jawaharlal Nehru in *The Discovery of India,* is that which Achaemenid Persia exerted on the Maurya state in Northwest India. The case for this special Indo-Persian relationship is strongly confirmed by historians, among them E. J. Rapson:

> If we must seek for any foreign influence in Maurya times, we should think (rather) of the Achaemenids, whose domination extended to the Indus. As is well known, the architecture of the period, and also the style of Asoka's edicts, show definite traces of Persian influence, and the expressions "the king's eye" and "the king's ears," occurring in the *Arthasastra* (p. 175 and p. 328) seem to furnish literary indications pointing in the same direction.[53]

It is further strengthened by the fact, first, that Persian influences continued to reach India during the Afghan and Mogul periods when the Islamic courts were strictly Persianized; and second, that Persian remained the language of court life and diplomacy right up to the British period.

The principles of statecraft with which Hinduism is identified, are set out clearly, precisely, and usually poetically in India's classical literature, more particularly in the *Arthasastras* (of which Kautilya's is the most renowned), the *Dharmasastras,* the Laws of Manu, the *Mahabharata* (India's great national epic), the *Ramayana,* and several collections of didactic beast fables—texts that Indians have been reading, reciting, or memorizing throughout time. All converge on the message that in the domain of *artha*—which comprises the sciences of politics, economics, diplomacy, and war—only winning counts.

As noted in the preceding essay, the *artha* polity was conceived and administered from Maurya times onward as a bureaucratic police state. Its keystone was the monarch who belonged to the warrior caste. This meant that each king—and the subcontinent was dotted with *artha* principalities—had the sacred duty (not a political option) to be at war if he was to gain spiritual merit. Likewise, he was instructed by his *dharma* to keep his subjects in their respective caste places and enforce his rule upon them by wielding *danda,* the rod of punishment, "lest the strong torment the weak as fish are fried on a pike or as in water they devour each other." It is in accordance with this law of the fishes that Kautilya sets out in minutest detail "four kinds of torture, six punishments, seven kinds of whipping, two kinds of suspension from above and the water tube."

All texts are pervaded by the assumption that no human being can ever be trusted, that enemies lurk everywhere, and that the king must know how to distinguish and deal with different battles of intrigues and different groups of troubles, molestations, and obstructions. In deference to the same pessimistic view of human nature each kingdom relied on espionage as its major agency in domestic and foreign affairs. Counseled by religious and quasi-religious texts, the king was to penetrate everywhere by sending his spies to report disloyalty among subjects, ministers and heirs.

The Maurya palace as described by the Greek ambassador Megasthenes and by Kautilya thus remained the model for future kings. Everything here bespeaks caution, we read. The structure of the palace itself includes mazes, secret and underground passages, hollow pillars, hidden staircases, collapsible floors. Everyone has his own apartments here, none of the interior officials are allowed to communicate with the outside, and the king must change his living quarters daily. The kitchen, too, is in a secret place, and a multitude of tasters are at work. The signs of poison in the viands and in the demeanor of persons are carefully noted, and the instruments of the shampooer and others must be handled by the body guard. The royal executive's daily agenda was about as follows:

> Aroused by music at the end of the sixth nocturnal hour, he receives the salutations of his counsellors, and interviews the doctors and kitchen officials, then he reflects upon the principles of polity and forms his plans, after which he sends out his secret emissaries, and hears reports of his military and financial advisors. Next comes the hour for appearing in the Audience Hall or in the Law Courts, and considering the affairs of the public. . . . After this the King retires for his bath and repast; receives those who bear gifts, interviews his inspectors, corresponds by letters with his ministers, and makes plans of espionage. This sixth hour having now arrived, he takes his ease and reconsiders his policy. In the seventh and eighth hours, the cool of the day, he inspects his horses, elephants and arsenal, and consults with the commander-in-chief; at sunset he performs the usual religious ceremony. The first hour of night brings in the reports of spies. Then come the second bath and meal, followed by religious meditation. To the sound of music His Majesty retires for rest.[54]

As this passage illustrates, all modalities of *artha* statecraft and political intelligence were in the final analysis functions of religion. This meant on the level of foreign affairs that each king was obligated to think of himself and his domain as the center or target of different but interlocking *mandalas* (rings) of royal *artha* players.[55] India's interkingdom relations thus came to resemble an endless game of chess, a ritual as it were, in which a player was expected to improve his status by every possible means at his disposal; for as the *Mahabharata* has it, "both kinds of wisdom, straight and crooked, should be within call of the king."

Six major instruments of policy (*Arthasastra,* Book VII) are available to the king so that he may advance from deterioration via stagnation to progress, and each of these has its subdivisions and didactically important illustrations in which the need for covert operations is invariably stressed. Whoever knows the interdependence of the six kinds of policy, we read, plays at his pleasure with kings. The paramount policy is war in the name of *danda.* Its opposite is peace, but the syndrome of peace, negotiation, and conciliation is here understood as appeasement in the way of the snake charmer, by deceit and trickery, or by casting illusions. In short, peace is a tactic of war in Hindu statecraft as shown by the following excerpts from the major texts:

> The whole world stands in awe of the king ready to strike.
> If you have no power, you are a conquered king.
> Only rulers who have no other remedy should seek peace.
> Only weakness calls for conciliation and alliances.
> Like a snake devouring a mouse, the Earth devours a king who is inclined to peace.

However, the advantages of a "double policy" are also pressed (*Arthasastra,* Books 6–14):

> As a fowler, carefully uttering cries similar to those of the birds he wishes to seize or kill, captures and brings them under his power, even so should a king bring his foes under subjection and then slay them if he likes.
> Without trusting one's foe in reality, one should behave as if one trusted him completely. Speak soft words before you smite and while you smite the foe . . . by a sudden pitched battle, by poison, by corrupting his allies, by gift of wealth, by any means you should destroy your foe.
> The enemy should be broken into fragments like an earthen jar on a rock.

The interpenetration of domestic and foreign statecraft to which reference was made earlier is well illustrated by these political maxims, which refer pointedly to the concept of "the enemy" and to the consequent need for intrigue and espionage as main unifying factors. Kautilya thus instructs the king that as between power and skill for intrigue, intrigue is more reliable:

> He who has the eye of knowledge, and is acquainted with the science of polity, can with little effort make use of his skills for intrigue, and can succeed by means of conciliation, and other strategic means and by spies and chemical appliances in overreaching even those kings who are possessed of enthusiasms and power.[56]

The key to successful intrigue is good espionage—a wisdom that reaches back to the *Rig Veda* where the spies of the god Varuna are pictured seated around him in prominent positions while he holds court. This was the case also at the Maurya court where Megasthenes found spies numerous enough to be considered a special class of society. Of them he writes:

The sixth class consists of the overseers, to whom is assigned the duty of watching all that goes on and making reports secretly to the king. Some are entrusted with the inspection of the city, and others with that of the army. The former employ as their co-adjutors the courtesans of the city, and the latter the courtesans of the camp. The ablest and most trustworthy men are appointed to fill these offices.[57]

Assisted by their ministers, who had themselves been tested under espionage, Hindu kings thus proceeded to create spies for every fathomable contingency—spies under the guise of a fraudulent disciple, a recluse, a householder, a merchant, an ascetic practicing austerities, a classmate, or a colleague, a firebrand, a prisoner, a mendicant woman, and near countless other categories of recruits. In fact, no subject in the *Arthasastra* receives as devoted and detailed attention as this one. Under such headings as "Government based on Deceit," "The Administration of Subversion" and "Battle of Intrigues," we learn how spies under the guise of physicians or sauce makers may make a seditious minister believe that he is suffering from a fatal disease in order then to contrive to poison him by prescribing a medication; how suspects may learn through the device of fortune-telling of an impending disaster in their lives—a forecast that is then promptly carried out; and how prostitute spies in the guise of chaste women may cause themselves to be enamored of persons who are seditious and thus "entrap" them. Spies trained to pose as hunchbacks, mendicants, or saints might have the task of luring a prince to kill the king his father, deal secret death to disloyal royal servants, or sow seeds of dissension in an enemy camp. No method of trickery was out of bounds here. Yet the very same type of agent was also sent wandering in the realm so as to report on adulteration of food or on injustice and corruption in the courts.

External spying proceeded in analogous ways. The text advises that foreign spies must be found out by spies of like profession and that one must always conceal one's emotions before the spies of one's enemy. We also read that foreign spies are dealt with best when they are seduced by female spies and then murdered. The main object of sending spies into another kingdom is to sow dissension, seek information, and "seduce wild tribes with rewards of wealth and honor so that they may be incited to devastate the enemy land." Extra credit is given for killing a king, "slaying the enemy's commander-in-chief and inciting a circle of states." These activities fall under the heading of "fiery spies"—Asia's earliest guerrillas. Spies with weapons, fire and poison, are thus dispatched to destroy supply stores and granaries, and in the guise of nightwalkers or firekeepers, to set fires and generally demoralize the population. "Taking advantage of peace and friendship with the enemy,"[58] they penetrate his fort disguised as ascetics, merchants, members of caravans or of processions leading a bride, for the purpose of killing the king, destroying his cattle or his merchandise, and of poisoning his food supplies. All such operations are meticulously prepared as the following passage from Kautilya illustrates:

> The conqueror's spies who are residing as traders in the enemy's forts, and those who are living as cultivators in the enemy's villages, as well as those who are living as cowherds or ascetics in the district borders of the enemy's country, may send through merchants information to another neighboring enemy, or a wild chief, or a scion of the

enemy's family, or an imprisoned prince, that the enemy's country is to be captured. When their secret emissaries come as invited, they are to be pleased with rewards of wealth and honour and shown the enemy's weak points; and with the help of the emissaries, the spies should strike the enemy at his weak points.[59]

The most favored and talked-about category of operatives in this conspiratorial system is that comprising the "shaven heads," monks and holy men who have license to conspire and kill in holy places which the enemy, under the influence of faith, frequents on occasions of worshiping gods or of pilgrimage.[60] And lastly, there were the official diplomats. Numerous categories of envoys are distinguished in the texts, but all seem to have been well integrated in the "system." In fact, an ambassador is described as "but an open spy," and is expected to live with his spies in whatever disguises these are required to function. However, according to the Laws of Manu it is "he alone who makes and breaks the allies of the king."[61]

All types of agents were directed by a regular department of espionage that was in charge of checking incoming information through three separate channels, correlating the reports it received from the agents, and above all seeing to it that there were spies to spy on spies. Discipline was harsh, of course; whoever divulged a secret—by talking in his sleep, for example—"was to be torn to pieces."

Not much would be gained—in fact, the comparative method might be strained to the breaking point—if we were to compare American and Indian approaches to intelligence, or to juxtapose the CIA and the ancient Indian institutes of espionage. From our point of view the entire *artha* order is as irrational as it is pointless. It may even impress some as utterly immoral, since there is nothing here that could be brought in line with what we call law and ethics, or with what we read in the Declaration of Independence about universal human rights. And yet, while Indian kingdoms rose and fell in seemingly endless "times of trouble," Indian civilization soared. And this—it is here suggested—is by no means freakish or coincidental; for the very same ways of thought and perception that made for the *Arthasastra* and the life in which only winning counted also made for sculptured works of art and for the *Upanishads,* which few minds in the West would not judge to be sublime. As Heinrich Zimmer observed in connection with this seeming paradox,[62] the ruthless philosophy of politics and the superhuman achievements in metaphysics represent the two sides of a single experience in life.

D. Venice and the United States

The preceding sections have indicated that Persian, Indian, Arab, and Turkish predispositions to politics in general and the relation between foreign policy and intelligence in particular converge on numerous conceptual and organizational points, and that there are a few elements in each of these Asian systems which have suggestive or didactic value also for us. By and large, however, these records are culturally too alien and historically too distant to be considered relevant in our nation's present quest for better security through better intelligence, even though they do help to explain why we have significantly failed in recent times to locate and assess crucial intelligence-related data in the societies now administering these non-Western traditions.

This kind of judgment does not hold for the old Republic of Venice, which provides the last case study of statecraft for this essay. In fact, the analogies between Venice and the United States are quite numerous. Each took off from Christian Western Europe's law-centered civilization, yet each soon deviated from its heritage and succeeded in fashioning its own destiny as a culturally and politically unique society. The story of the American emancipation is well-known. In respect of Venice one must note that it began its political existence as a small settler nation on the very edge of Italy's northeastern coast, but that it was almost immediately drawn into close relations with the Greek Orthodox Byzantine empire (then in official control of the region) and with the Islamic nations of the Levant, even as it was briefly part also of Charlemagne's West European realm. The territorial home base of the island city-state was thus slight and precarious, whereas that of the United States was an immense landmass flanked by oceans. Yet both were cast by geography into the mold of outward-looking maritime nations, and both were determined from the start to defy all foreign pressures that might compromise the political independence and cultural uniqueness they had won.

At this juncture in time, only two hundred years since its creation, we cannot predict America's future. Of independent Venice we know that it endured from the seventh century to 1797, when its statehood was extinguished by Napoleon. Not unlike Byzantium (its mentor nation in many significant ways), which had also preserved its identity for one thousand years (from circa the fifth century to 1453, when Constantinople was taken by the Turks), but quite contrary to the United States, Venice had always been fully conscious of the fact that it had to maintain its liberty and statehood in a multicultural world environment and that it was encircled by alien, usually hostile peoples. Also like the Byzantines, Venetians knew that they could not rely exclusively on defense through warfare, which would have exhausted available energies and resources, and that they had to perfect systems of diplomacy and intelligence if survival and advance to greatness were to be assured.

The prerequisite for this type of statecraft was a well-developed sense of national identity and knowledge of just what it was that had to be defended and perfected at all cost. The basic dispositions, values, and institutions that sustained this existential mode were distinctly European, having been refined in Italy during the centuries of the Renaissance. They were thus the birthright as it were of all city-states, but it was the Venetian imprimatur they received that stamped them with timeless significance in international history.

For example, the concept of the secular state was taken seriously throughout Italy, but it was only in Venice that the idea rallied all citizens in a spirit of fierce loyalty and patriotism. This was so, Bouwsma explains,[63] because Venice represented to generations of Venetians a realm of unique and abiding values that it was their particular obligation to conserve and to transmit to subsequent generations. Further, this sense of continuity was cultivated deliberately. From the early sixteenth century onward Venice thus relied on an official historian who was charged to guard the state's traditions; for as explicitly noted in a decree, history solidifies the reputation of states even as it instructs rulers in the management of their daily business and assists them "to foresee with greater prudence things to come." Historical analysis was thus generally accepted here as an instrument of statecraft—a fact noted with admiration by the sixteenth-century Florentine historian Guicciardini in his *History of Italy,* as when he comments on the conviction shared by "certain of the oldest and most reputable members of the Venetian Senate that Venice enjoyed a particular advantage in her ability to wait for the opportunity of times and the maturity of occasions."

These ongoing civic commitments explain why Venetian institutions of government, being the organic growth of centuries, aroused pride and loyalty, why Venice was not plagued by the kind of chronic internal dissensions that marred the art of government elsewhere, and why Venetian policies were steadier than those of rival states.

Venice, then, was essentially unified when it had to cope with problems in its far-flung foreign relations—and these were legion in each century.[64] Moreover, it could count on a cosmopolitan citizenry that understood the problems and ever-changing realities in the conduct of foreign affairs. Because Venice was primarily a nation of merchants, seafarers, and travelers, Venetians were conditioned from early times onward to view the world as a complex of ascertainable facts. This meant that they were always keenly aware of the need to sharpen their faculties of observation, appraise their risks and opportunities realistically, and perfect their methods of evaluating the intelligence they got in order to enter their gains and losses on the proper side of the business ledgers they kept.

Realism and objectivity were inbred Venetian qualities, and diplomacy was rightly viewed as a natural calling for Venetians. It was thus expected that any citizen abroad was likely to think of himself as the nation's agent or asset, eager to collect and forward information that might be useful to the national cause. The records tell us, for example, that Venetian physicians whose services were loaned to foreign sovereigns felt morally free to send their home government detailed reports whenever important political and commercial matters would come to their attention. Likewise, it was well-known among contemporaries in Italy that a Venetian cardinal was first and foremost a nationalist who could be persuaded easily to transmit to his government confidential intelligence to which he had access in his capacity as a servant of the Catholic Church in Rome.

However, the fame of Venetian statecraft does not rest on the unofficial ad hoc functions of Venetian citizens abroad, or on the sub-rosa activities of the kind of secret agents and native informers that were used increasingly as the fortunes of the state were declining. Rather, it rests on the official operations of a specifically qualified diplomatic intelligence service and on the systematic supervision of all foreign missions by the home government.

In respect of training and endowment it was generally understood in Renaissance Italy that diplomacy demands "the whole man." A Venetian ambassador was thus expected to live up to this model and know "how to do things well." And indeed, the typical envoy who emerges from biographical and other contemporary records is at once a statesman, a soldier, a man of business, a linguist, and a scholar who spends his leisure hours in literary and scientific studies or in correspondence with artists and authors from many lands. However, all of these gifts and accomplishments were conceived primarily as resources of the state, for it was the envoy's primary function to uphold Venetian interests against the rest of the world by carrying out the government's policies and orders, no matter what they might be. Further, and as carefully set out by Ermaleo Barbaro, a renowned Venetian authority on diplomatic method, ambassadors were supposed to listen, observe, and cultivate the confidence of heads of state and other influential personages. They were admonished not to behave like spies,[65] nor were they to associate diplomacy with conspiracy, assassination, or corruption.

Clandestine operations of all kinds, including hard espionage and counterespionage, gradually accrued to all European intelligence systems from the sixteenth century onward. Two principal factors accounted for this development: the increasingly aggressive policies emanating from France and Spain (the Spanish intelligence apparatus as administered at the English Court by Chapuys and Gondomar appears to have been the most diversified in the sixteenth century); and the spread of resident embassies. Odd as it may seem to us, the latter were generally distrusted.[66] A special—that is, a nonresident—envoy could afford to be an honorable Christian gentleman, we learn, but a resident had to be viewed as at best a kind of licensed spy. At any rate, resident embassies became the norm throughout Europe—with Venice maintaining most of them—and by 1600 undercover agents were employed by just about all of them.

Yet, and after full allowance is made for aspects of intelligence work that contemporaries found unsavory, the fact remains that the resident ambassadors in fifteenth-century Italy—and among them particularly those representing Venice—succeeded time and time again in averting war, preserving or restoring the peninsular system of the balance of power, and thus in assuring four crucially important decades of relative peace during which the civilization of Renaissance Italy could reach its full maturity.

This accomplishment is, of course, a function of the talents, training, and discipline of agents who knew how to detect each shift in power relations and facilitate realignments, and who knew how to communicate swiftly with their home governments. In fact, it is this latter aspect of statecraft, namely the relation between diplomats and the supervising central administration, that accounts for the renown of the Venetian intelligence system.

The sovereignty of Venice resided in the Great Council. At the next level of decision-making was the Senate, which supervised all affairs of state, administered foreign policy, waged war, concluded peace, and appointed ambassadors. Standing somewhat apart from the official hierarchy of governing bodies was the Council of Ten. Established early in the fourteenth century to deal with a particular crisis, it nonetheless became an alternative to the Senate and was regularly asked to deal with extraordinary problems, no doubt because—being small—it could act with speed and secrecy. Its position was strengthened in the sixteenth century by the addition to it of a group of leading senators known as the Giunta.[67] Lest one forget, at the very top of the Venetian administration was the Doge, who was important mainly as the corporeal symbol of the idea of liberty.

All envoys and agents had to report to the Senate, which had given them their appointments and instructions in the first place, and they did so regularly by dispatches—often sent daily—that informed the government of the course of events within the envoy's range of observation. But at the end of their term of duty they were obligated, in accordance with a decree of the Grand Council (1268), to deliver a full viva voce report of their mission; and a later decree (1425) ordered that these "relations" *(relazioni)* be committed to writing. Not all of the *Relations of the Ambassadors* survive, but as Mattingly concludes from his readings of the records,[68] a formal relation was experienced as an intellectual treat by the senators. And the same was true of contemporaries in Italy and the rest of Europe—whether allies or adversaries—who consulted a Venetian report as we would an authoritative text on current international affairs. Manuscript copies thus commanded high prices as early as two years after the report had actually been presented.

The very conception of this mode of collecting intelligence elicited admiration, and it is not surprising, therefore, that the Venetian precedent was soon emulated first by Spain and later by most other European nations. However, it is, of course, the content of these unequaled archives that has earned them time-transcendent significance. What readers found in the *relazioni* were carefully prepared statements of the political situation at the ambassador's post that addressed a wide range of topics. Apart from summarizing recent events and prevalent trends and projecting likely future developments, they drew the government's attention to the area's topography, geography, and economy, and they assessed trade possibilities, local laws, and governmental institutions. Further and above all perhaps, they noted the historical antecedents of all phenomena to which they attached particular importance, and they dwelt in considerable depth upon the biographies and character traits of all leading men. Barbaro's diary of the siege of Constantinople exemplifies the sensitivity and precision of such assessments in conditions of extraordinary stress. And the same holds for the remarkable series of *relazioni* that mirrored the lifestyle, ruling institutions, and policy-making processes of the Ottoman regime—documents without which important chapters in the history of the entire region could not possibly have been written,[69] as well as for the multitude of accounts that analyzed the turbulence in the papal establishment, the policies and plots of Spain, the complex English scenario in which Henry VIII and his successors forged the destiny of their nation, and so on.

One of the tentative conclusions that a comparison of Venetian and American intelligence systems suggests is that diplomatic representation and intelligence work were much more closely linked in Venice than they are in the United States. And in the specific context of intelligence it appears that the integral Venetian approach did not favor the kind of categorization of several distinct elements of intelligence that is institutionalized here. Venetian ambassadors had their publicly declared functions as do ours; but contrary to the latter, they were also supposed to be undercover agents specifically commissioned to shape the thought patterns of men and thus the policies of foreign governments.

In the discharge of this latter task they were given wide leeway as well as reliable protection. One reason for this official disposition was the absence of international accords on the legal status of diplomats (notably residents) and their embassies abroad. And in this respect, the Venetians may be said to have anticipated Grotius, who was to argue that although justice and equity required equal penalties

for equal crimes, the law of nations made an exception of ambassadors because
their security as a class was more important to the public welfare than their punishment as individuals. Their security would rest on a slippery foundation, he concluded, if they were accountable to anyone but their own sovereign. But the main
explanation for the comprehensive nature of the entire Venetian foreign policy establishment is found in the broad national consensus on the nature of foreign affairs
and the purposes of intelligence operations upon which the government and its
foreign agents were able to count for several centuries.

Something approaching this kind of moral unity also marked American intelligence operations after the end of the Second World War. The covert action program
linking the CIA with the National Student Association is a case in point, all the
more so as I think that the Venetians would have viewed it as a normal diplomatic
enterprise. In reflecting on this fifteen-year-long relationship Cord Meyer explains[70]
that this cooperative venture was anchored in a broad agreement as to what the
course of American foreign policy should be and in a shared commitment to support
democratic organizations and oppose Communist attempts to dominate the international student community. But the consensus gradually eroded under the pressure
of student opposition to the Vietnam War until it was extinguished by the *Ramparts*
revelation, an episode that had altogether nefarious consequences for the nation as
a whole. Meyer believes that if the CIA had assessed more realistically and
promptly the shift in student opinion, it could have moved in time to arrange for an
amicable severance of relations with the NSA. However, it is not likely that such a
denouement would have had the effect also of arresting the drift toward demoralization to which the entire intelligence community was more or less deliberately
consigned by its own presiding officers when they chose to elevate their personal
moral scruples of the day into guiding principles for long-range national policies
and operations.

Venice never produced the equivalent of the Schlesinger memorandum (dated
May 9, 1973),[71] which directed every employee and ex-employee to report on past
and present CIA activities that might be construed to be outside the legislative
charter of the agency. Yet in the sixteenth century—a period closely similar to the
era in which we find ourselves—it, too, was buffeted by profound crises of self-
confidence and they, too, were symbolized by leaks and other violations of the
norms of confidentiality. The particular developments in foreign relations that induced the widespread consciousness of the nation's faltering destiny were connected
with the League of Cambrai (1509)—a massive conspiracy on the part of France
and Spain to knock out Venice. Constrained by these continuous threats in the
Christian West to come to terms with the Islamic East, the government (in this case
the Council of Ten) directed its plenipotentiary at Constantinople to try to procure
a settlement on the basis of an exchange of prisoners and territory equivalent to the
arrangement of an ante-bellum status quo. However, the envoy had in reserve the
power of concluding peace on any terms. Knowledge of the latter terms was communicated to the Porte by treachery and the Republic was therefore forced to surrender several places in the Morea.

The shock of this experience (1538–39) and the discovery that the informers,
among them the secretary to the Ten, had been in the pay of France, led in 1539 to

the formal establishment[72] of three Inquisitors into Revelation of State Secrets, whose powers were practically unlimited provided that the three functionaries agreed.

The Inquisitors, in concert with the Decimvirs (members of the Council of Ten), sometimes committed serious mistakes, but scholarly authorities on their recorded operations (1411 to 1793) agree that a weakened Venice was strongly sustained by this institution, if only because diplomacy was the one remaining shield of the Republic in the ensuing centuries.

CONCLUSION

The challenges confronting U.S. statecraft today require many kinds of responses, among them the following:

On the level of strategic thought in general we should remember that sound foreign policies and definitions of the national interest depend upon self-knowledge as well as upon accurate perceptions of other nations. We should therefore recognize that the United States is a culturally unique society with a heritage not shared by other peoples. This means that we should drop or seriously modify the traditional assumption that our primary norms and values are in theory at least valid everywhere. It also means that we should abandon the single-minded search for international systems and such allegedly universally acceptable principles as civil liberties or human rights—a policy course that has preoccupied us in the last troubled decades, and has brought us perilously close to losing our national identity and therewith our bearings in the world environment. The urgent need today is rather to find out just what our truly inalienable sustaining ideas and interests really are so that we may proceed to structure our relations with other states and systems in a realistic way.

This task presupposes a careful stock-taking of all other societies, be they friendly or hostile. It is in my view best accomplished by employing the comparative method, perhaps by reliance on the type of propositional inventory included in this paper. Intelligence gathering of the kind there suggested seems indispensable if we wish to devise and deploy modes of statecraft that are appropriate to each of the greatly various systems, states, and peoples that we are dealing with today, nowhere more so than in contexts bearing on the relation between foreign policy and covert action.

The foregoing case studies of South Asian, West Asian, and North African societies address most of the themes listed in the questionnaire, and a comparison of those findings shows a consensus on the following: traditional and modern patterns of political organization do not accommodate either the Western norm of the territorially delimited nation-state or constitutional democracy. Rather, they converge on expansionism and personalized authoritarian rule. Neither of these polities and ruling establishments is legitimized in terms of local codes of law or ethics. All—be they empires, kingdoms, or modern despotisms disguised as republics—are therefore absolutely dependent upon military force and statecraft, more particularly espionage and covert action.

In the absence of orderly provisions for succession, changes in government are routinely induced today as they were formerly by coups d'état and assassinations. Further, in the absence of fixed state borders, pretenders to power simply strike out from established bases so as to acquire dominion over other lands and nations. What is noteworthy here is this: the tactics in such extended power plays are the same as those employed in conspiratorial operations at the home base, for both situations routinely call for the kind of intelligence and policing work that will assure the ouster of an incumbent or rival claimant. In other words, and as exemplified in history by the seesaw campaigns of Mongol, Afghan, and Persian armies in Central and Southwest Asia, and in our times by the military moves of Libyan and Algerian imperialisms into the vast Saharan and sub-Saharan reaches of Africa, domestic and foreign affairs interpenetrate here in ways not common in the West. This means, mutatis mutandis, that domestic and foreign espionage interpenetrate also, and that our careful distinctions between the functions of the FBI and the CIA have no equivalents there. In short, intelligence actions dominate the government as well as all transactions in foreign relations, thus corroborating the wisdom of India's sacred literature, to the effect that a kingdom is totally dependent on spies and secret agents.

Further, but in the same integral context of Oriental statecraft, we should not forget that "peace" and "war" are not the opposites we perceive them to be. After all, not only is peace traditionally viewed in Asian and African cultures as stagnation or as a tactic of war, but fighting is esteemed everywhere as a natural and noble activity. Also, the conviction rules that there is always an enemy somewhere. The worldview prevalent in the non-Western non-Communist societies surveyed for purposes of this paper allows for "world unity" through conquest or, as in Islam in particular, through conversion to the faith. However, it excludes hope for "a world without war" or for a world of culturally disparate nations, all unified by visions of peace. It is this constellation of values and traditions that explains why diplomacy is related more closely to war than to peace and why it is commonly assumed that diplomats are meant to be spies. Contrary to the United States, then, these two categories of personnel are not held to radically different jurisdictional and behavioral norms. Nor is either hamstrung in its operations by legislative or moral inhibitions.

The traditions of statecraft here discussed could not have settled in such enduring ways had society itself not continued to be a proving ground for their deployment. As suggested in different sections of this essay, generation after generation was tutored in such arts of intelligence as verbal dissimulation, indirect allusive communication, conspiracy, and, above all, confidentiality. Covert thought and covert action are thus rational and normal here where men have come to value the closed, not the open, society.

The point that our modes of perception, thought, organization, and communication are significantly different from those here analyzed, need not be labored in this conclusion. Nor is it reasonable to indulge in the expectation that these non-Western societies will slowly but surely adapt their orientations to ours. In fact, and as developments in criminal law, government, and diplomacy have incontrovertibly shown in the last decades, "progress" and security are being identified with a return to trusted models of their own past, not with our visions of the future. And since it cannot be denied that some aspects of non-Western statecraft are congruous—albeit superficially—with Marxist-Leninist thought and practice, it should be in our interest to focus on these traditions rather than on our preferred visions.

In further elaboration of the need to modify our approaches to these culturally alien societies, it is here suggested that we must relax our commitments to certain theories and systems if we wish our intelligence services to do their work successfully.

Our guidelines for conceptualizing and actualizing intelligence include numerous definitions that distinguish carefully among, for example, covert action, clandestine collection or espionage, counterintelligence, and paramilitary or psychopolitical operations, and that indicate unequivocally what can and what cannot be done lawfully, and which are or are not secret operations. All definitions issue from records of shared experience, and ours are no exception to the norm. They therefore belong to our administrative system. However, they are not meaningful in the societies surveyed in this essay, and they may therefore greatly inhibit our intelligence operations in these foreign fields. Here, where secrecy is the sine qua non of success, the domain of what we call covert action is all-encompassing. Yet it is precisely this element of intelligence that is critically embattled in the United States today.

It is no doubt difficult to revive the dying art of covert action in the present climate of opinion, but it should be possible to loosen the hold of law upon this art and to tighten the rules assuring confidentiality. In reexamining the relationship between foreign policy and covert action we would in general be well advised to return to Dean Acheson's counsel, to the effect that the vocabulary of morals and ethics is inadequate to discuss or test the foreign politics of states.[73]

NOTES

1. Hugh Tovar, "Covert Action" in Roy Godson, ed., *Intelligence Requirements for the 1980's: Elements of Intelligence* (Washington, D.C.: National Strategy Information Center, Inc., 1979), pp. 65–79.
2. Newton S. Miler, "Counterintelligence," in Godson, ed., *op. cit.*, pp. 49–60.
3. Daniel O. Graham, "Analysis and Estimates," in Godson, ed., *op. cit.*, pp. 23–29.
4. Samuel Halpern, "Clandestine Collection," in Godson, ed., *op. cit.*, pp. 37–43.
5. Donovan Pratt, "Operational Security: What Ought to Be the Relationship Between Counterintelligence, Collection and Covert Action?" See Godson, ed., *Intelligence Requirements for the 1980's: Counterintelligence* (Washington, D.C.: National Strategy Information Center, Inc., 1980), pp. 228–45.
6. *New York Times,* September 27, 1980.
7. "Perception and Commitment," *Bulletin of the Atomic Scientists,* Vol. XIX, no. 1, February 1963, pp. 14ff.
8. For an elaboration of this theme see Bozeman, "The Roots of the American Commitment to the Rights of Man," in *Rights and Responsibilities; International, Social and Individual Dimensions,* Proceedings of a Conference at the Center for Study of the American Experience, Annenberg School of Communications, University of Southern California, November 1978, pp. 51–102 (University of Southern California Press, 1980); "Interference or Legitimate International Concern: The Human Factor in U.S.–Soviet Relations," Proceedings

of the National Security Affairs Conference, July 1977, National Defense University, pp. 167–83 (Washington, D.C., August 1977); reprinted as *How to Think About Human Rights* (National Strategy Information Center, New York, 1978); "Law and Diplomacy in the Quest for Peace," in *Virginia Quarterly Review,* Vol. 55, no. 1 (Winter 1979), pp. 1–21; and *The Future of Law in a Multicultural World* (Princeton, NJ: Princeton University Press, 1971).

9. William Colby and Peter Forbath, *Honorable Men: My Life in the CIA* (New York, 1978).

10. See Colby, *op. cit.*, p. 298, in connection with comments on the CIA's Third Culture Analysis.

11. *Ibid.*, p. 275.

12. "Approaches to Reform of the Intelligence Community" in Godson, ed., *Intelligence Requirements for the 1980's: Elements of Intelligence* (Washington, D.C.: National Strategy Information Center, Inc., 1979), pp. 13, 14.

13. See *loc. cit.* in Godson, ed., *op. cit.*, and Arnold Beichman and Roy Godson, "Legal Constraints and Incentives," in Godson, ed., *Intelligence Requirements for the 1980's: Counterintelligence* (Washington, D.C.: National Strategy Information Center, Inc., 1980).

14. "Comparative Historical Experience of Doctrine and Organization," in Godson, ed., *Intelligence Requirements for the 1980's: Analysis and Estimates* (Washington, D.C.: National Strategy Information Center, Inc., 1980), pp. 32ff.

15. *Cp.* Daniel Graham, "Analysis and Estimates" in Godson, ed., *Elements of Intelligence,* (1979), p. 23, to the effect that the malfunction of analysis is potentially the most serious drawback that any nation's intelligence can experience.

16. See *supra,* this essay.

17. Daniel Graham, *loc. cit.*, p. 24.

18. Presented at the Civilian-Military Institute, Denver, Colorado, May 5, 1980; published in *Foreign Affairs,* Fall 1980.

19. Compare Tovar, *loc. cit.*, pp. 68–69.

20. I have dealt with these and other academic aspects of the Consortium's work in a "Memorandum of Suggestions for the Consortium's Program of Studies" (November 1979).

21. See *supra,* this essay.

22. *New York Times,* June 17, 1980.

23. See *Neue Zürcher Zeitung,* May 14, 1980, for a comprehensive analysis of this set of issues.

24. For these accounts see Richard Burt, *New York Times,* October 7, 1980.

25. For analyses of traditional China's international system (which I view as the only rival of the Grotian or Modern European States System), see Essays 2, 4 and 6. See also Bozeman, *The Future of Law in a Multicultural World,* pp. 140–60, and "On the Relevance of Hugo Grotius and *De Jure Belli ac Pacis* for Our Times" in *Grotiana,* Vol. 1, no. 1 (Winter 1980).

26. For commentaries on Byzantine statecraft, see Essay 4 in this volume and Bozeman, *Politics and Culture in International History,* pp. 298–381.

27. Daniel O. Graham, "Analysis and Estimates," in Godson, ed., *Elements of Intelligence,* pp. 23ff.

28. For commentaries on Achaemenian Persia see Bozeman, *Politics and Culture in International History* (Princeton, NJ: Princeton University Press, 1960), pp. 43–56 and authorities there cited; "Iran: U.S. Foreign Policy and the Tradition of Persian Statecraft," *ORBIS,* Vol. 23, no. 2 (Summer 1979), pp. 387–402; also "Civilizations Under Stress: Reflections on Cultural Borrowing and Survival," *Virginia Quarterly Review,* Vol. 51, no. 1 (Winter 1975), pp. 1–18.

29. See *infra,* this Essay Section III C.

30. Today Iraq's main enemy is Iran, and it is interesting that the latter is now referred to by Iraq's press as "Persia." See J. J. Saunders, "The Problem of Islamic Decadence," *Journal of World History,* Vol. VII, no. 3 (1963), pp. 701–702.

31. Egypt and Turkey, like Iran, represent different cultural legacies.

32. U.S. Congress, House. *Iran: Evaluation of U.S. Intelligence Performance Prior to Novem-*

ber 1978 (U.S. House Intelligence Subcommittee Report, 1979). For commentaries on this report, see Richard H. Giza, "The Problem of the Intelligence Consumer," in Roy Godson, ed., *Intelligence Requirements for the 1980's: Analysis and Estimates* (1980), pp. 189–206, and Michael Handel, "Avoiding Political and Technological Surprise in the 1980's," in *op. cit.,* 85–111. See also Bozeman, "Iran: U.S. Foreign Policy and the Tradition of Persian Statecraft," *Orbis,* Vol. 23, no. 2 (Summer 1979), pp. 387–402.

33. See *supra* this chapter for Mr. Colby's misperception of Vietnamese values and norms, and see *infra,* Essay 7, "American Policy and the Illusion of Congruent Values."

34. Iran was doctrinally unified by the Shi'ite faith in the seventeenth century, but it is pertinent to note that the seventeenth-century cities of Safavid Persia were scenes of mass persecutions of large Sunni elements.

35. It is interesting that the anti-Shah groups in the administration, the universities, and the media have made little if anything of the fact that the Shah's government had neither murdered, nor had plotted to murder, either Khomeini or Mossadegh.

36. For the varied backgrounds of some of present-day Iran's political leaders see a report by R. W. Apple, Jr., in *New York Times,* November 11, 1979, Section 4.

37. "Covert Action," in Roy Godson, ed., *Intelligence Requirements for the 1980's; Elements of Intelligence* (1979), p. 72.

38. See also Ann K. S. Lambton, "The Spiritual Influence of Islam in Persia," in A. J. Arberry and Rom Landau, *Islam Today* (London, 1943), pp. 163–77, on the doctrine of *taqiya,* a dispensation from the requirements of religion under compulsion of threat of injury.

39. On Byzantine statecraft, see Essay 4 in this volume; see also Bozeman, *Politics and Culture in International History* (Princeton, NJ: Princeton University Press, 1960), pp. 324ff. For sources of Persian statecraft, see note 28 in this essay. See also Richard N. Frye, *The Heritage of Persia* (New York, 1966), Chapter 6, on Sassanian Persia.

40. See H. A. R. Gibb, "Constitutional Organization," in *Law in the Middle East,* Vol. I, *Origin and Development of Islamic Law,* Majid Khadduri and Herbert J. Liebesny, eds. (Washington, D.C., 1955), p. 21. For the Ottoman empire, see Albert Howe Lybyer, *The Government of the Ottoman Empire in the Time of Suleiman the Magnificent* (Cambridge, Mass., 1913), p. 227, on the influence of Chinese traditions of rule upon the Turks; Appendix IV, "The Government of the Mogul Empire in India." See also Bernard Lewis, *Istanbul and the Civilization of the Ottoman Empire* (Norman, Oklahoma, 1963); and H. A. R. Gibb and Harold Bowen, *Islamic Society and the West,* Vol. I, parts 1 and 2 (London and New York, 1950–57).

41. Reuben Levy, *An Introduction to Persian Literature* (Columbia University Press, New York, 1969), pp. 53ff.; 64ff.; "Nizām al-Mulk," *Encyclopaedia Britannica (Macropaedia),* Vol. 13, pp. 135–36; J. A. Boyle, ed., *The Cambridge History of Iran,* Vol. 5, *The Seljuq and Mongol Periods* (Cambridge University Press, 1968), pp. 76, 80ff., 206ff. James Kritzek, *Anthology of Islamic Literature* (Holt, Rinehart & Winston, 1964), pp. 153ff., for excerpts from *The Book of Government.* For a full English translation of the work, see Hubert Darke, *The Book of Government; or, Rules for Kings* (1960).

42. From Kritzek, *op. cit.,* pp. 154–57.

43. See Carl Brockelmann, *History of the Islamic Peoples,* trans. by Joel Carmichael and Moshe Perlmann (New York, 1949), pp. 240–55, on the aggressive incursions of Turks and Mongols into Persia and adjacent Eastern regions during the twelfth–fourteenth centuries.

44. See Lewis, *op cit.,* pp. 47ff; also authorities on the principle of "The Emirate by Seizure," and *The Book of Counsel for Viziers and Governors of Sari Mehmed Pasha, The Defterdar,* introd., transl., and notes by Walter Livingston Wright, Jr. (Greenwood Press, Westport, Conn., 1971; originally published by Princeton University Press, 1935).

45. See Lewis, *op cit.,* p. 57; Lybyer, *op. cit.,* Appendix I, pp. 244ff. for Venetian reports on the role of eunuchs; Sari Mehmed Pasha, *Book of Counsel . . . , op. cit.,* pp. 21–60.

46. See Brockelmann, *op. cit.,* p. 179; also pp. 250ff. On the authority of Marco Polo, who had passed through the territory of the Assassins in the late thirteenth century, Brockelmann notes that *Fida'is,* while intoxicated by hashish, were placed in a section of the Alamut

gardens fitted out as Paradise, with young women as houris, in order to make the assassins amenable to the orders of the leader by giving them a foretaste of the pleasures awaiting them in the hereafter. See Bernard Lewis, *The Assassins: A Radical Sect in Islam* (New York, 1968), for a full account. Freya Stark, *The Valleys of the Assassins and Other Persian Travels* (London, John John Murray), 1937.

47. The Sanusi fraternity in Cyrenaica (Libya), founded in the middle of the nineteenth century, subscribed to tenets greatly similar to those espoused by the Wahhabi movement. See Duncan Black MacDonald, *Development of Muslim Theology, Jurisprudence and Constitutional Theory* (London and New York, 1903; reprinted New York, 1965) for several chapters dealing with the Ikhwan, the Order of the Assassins, and the Wahhabites; T. E. Lawrence, *Seven Pillars of Wisdom* (New York, 1935), pp. 46ff. on the *Fetah;* Gibb and Bowen, *op. cit.*, p. 285, on religious guilds; and above all, George Antonius, *The Arab Awakening* (London, 1939; 1945), pp. 79, 110, 121.

48. Antonius, *op. cit.*, p. 111.

49. See *supra*, this essay.

50. *War and Peace in the Law of Islam*, pp. 61, 64f., 136ff.; *The Islamic Law of Nations: Shaybani's Siyar*, trans. with Introduction, Notes, and Appendices by Majid Khadduri (Baltimore, Maryland, 1966). Religion and theory confirmed existing life-styles in the Near and Middle East that converged on the principle that war was the major external purpose of any organized society (government being the internal purpose). Among contemporary complimentary comments upon the Turks there is one that says "Turks come together for war as though they had been invited to a wedding." See Lybyer, *op. cit.*, p. 108.

51. Cf. Bozeman, *The Future of Law in a Multicultural World*, pp. 50–85; also, Essays 2 and 8 in this volume.

52. On the classical Indian *Arthasastra* system and the historical context in which it evolved, see B. Shamasastry, ed., *Kautilya's Arthasastra* (Mysore, India, 1923); John W. Spellman, *Political Theory of Ancient India: A Study of Kingship from the Earliest Times to ca. A.D. 300* (Oxford, 1964); Upendra N. Ghoshal, *A History of Indian Political Ideas: The Ancient Period and the Period of Transition to the Middle Ages* (London, 1966); K. M. Panikkar, *A Survey of Indian History* (Bombay, 1954); and authorities listed in Bozeman, *Politics and Culture in International History* and *The Future of Law in a Multicultural World*, pp. 121ff., "India and Indianized Asia." See also *supra*, Essay 2.

53. E. J. Rapson, ed., *The Cambridge History of India*, Vol. 1, *Ancient India* (first Indian reprint, Delhi, 1955), p. 455.

54. See Rapson, *op. cit.*, pp. 444f.

55. See Spellman, *op. cit.*, p. 157, for a graph of such a *mandala;* see also *Kautilya's Arthasastra* and Essay 2 in this volume.

56. *Kautilya's Arthasastra*, Book IX, Chapter 1.

57. J. W. McCrindle, *Ancient India as Described by Megathenes and Arrian* (Bombay, 1877), pp. 85f.

58. *Kautilya's Arthasastra*, Book XIII, Chapter 3.

59. *Op. cit.*, Book XII, Chapter 4.

60. Almost two millennia separate us from ancient India's political order, which was also implanted in Indianized Southeast Asia, notably Cambodia, Java, and parts of what later became Vietnam. Yet readings in Indian political philosophy—as, for example, in the *Arthasastra*—inevitably remind one that "shaven heads" and "pagodas" also combined to create "contrivances" during the Vietnam War, and that our "eyes" and "ears" had not been adequately trained to perceive them in the perspective proper to this Asian culture.

61. See Spellman, *op. cit.*, pp. 141ff.

62. See Heinrich Zimmer, *The Philosophies of India*, ed. by Joseph Campbell (Bollingen Series XXVI, New York, 1951), p. 83.

63. William J. Bouwsma, *Venice and the Defense of Republican Liberty; Renaissance Values in the Age of the Counter Reformation* (Berkeley and Los Angeles, 1968), p. 65.

64. For comments on these aspects, see Bozeman, *Politics and Culture in International His-*

tory, pp. 457–89, and authorities there cited; also Frederic Lane, *Venice and History*, pp. 36–55.

65. See W. Carew Hazlitt, *The Venetian Republic*, 2 vols. (London, 1915), Vol. II, pp. 498ff., for a full account of Venetian practices; also, Garrett Mattingly, *Renaissance Diplomacy* (Boston, 1955), pp. 112ff. and 241ff.

66. Even Grotius expressed skeptical concern about this institution because he could not find a legal way to rationalize the civil immunities that resident embassies required except by resorting to the fiction of extraterritoriality.

67. See Bouwsma, *op. cit.*, pp. 61ff.

68. *Op. cit.*, p. 113.

69. See Lybyer, *op. cit.*, for a listing of the relations upon which his work is based.

70. Cord Meyer, *Facing Reality: From World Federalism to the CIA* (New York, 1980), pp. 103ff. See Chapter 8, p. 259ff. in Peter Collier & David Horowitz, *Destructive Generation, Second Thoughts about the '60s*, (New York: Summit Books, 1989) for Peter Collier's retrospective "Second Thoughts" about the function of *Ramparts*—here described as "a sort of sinecdoche for the New Left"—in the revolutionary program to bring down the U.S. in the Vietnam war. Collins, one of its editors, begins his story by noting that "Ramparts seized the country's attention in 1967 with the first big exposé on the CIA—in this case, the agency's infiltration of the National Student Association. Others followed." The confessional narrative continues with frank reporting of related activities. See Rhodri Jeffreys-Jones, *The CIA and American Democracy* (New Haven, Conn.: Yale University Press, 1989), Chapter 9 (pp. 156ff.), "Helms, Johnson, and Cosmetic Intelligence," for a careful analysis of the *Ramparts* issue and its altogether negative effects on the U.S. and its image at home and abroad. Also, cp. Meyer, *op. cit.*

71. See Meyer, *op. cit.*, Appendix, pp. 410f. and 158ff., in the text.

72. The Inquisitors of State had been temporary officials since 1411. The origin of this office is classical Rome.

73. See Dean Acheson, "Ethics in International Relations Today," *Amherst Alumni News*, Winter 1965. See also "Strategic Intelligence in Cold Wars of Ideas" in this volume.

Traditions of Political Warfare and Low-Intensity Conflict in Totalitarian Russia and China: A Comparative Study of Continuity and Change

I

The organizers of a conference on "Terrorism and Other 'Low Intensity' Operations: International Linkages" (1985) invited me to come to terms with twentieth-century concepts and realities of political warfare and low-intensity conflict by comparing them with antecedents in traditional societies and to respond specifically to the following questions:

1. How did rulers in traditional closed societies employ political warfare and extreme forms of violence against foreign adversaries?

2. Did they also employ surrogates and mercenaries for these purposes?

3. Did these rulers establish guidelines for utilizing these measures?

4. What continuity exists between the ways in which traditional rulers employed these techniques and how they are exercised by present-day governments?

Several premises are implicit in these four questions, and one is communicated explicitly in the following terms: "The direct and indirect use of these techniques by contemporary totalitarian states is not a new development but can be traced back to earlier times."

I shall comment briefly on these assumptions before taking up the substantive questions.

It cannot be denied that international history is dense with records of political warfare, extreme forms of violence, and low-intensity conflict.[1] It is true also that some elements of this conflict syndrome–among them the psychopolitical penetration of adversaries, wars of nerves, limited or irregular military engagements, and

This paper was originally prepared for the International Security Studies Program conference "Terrorism and Other 'Low Intensity' Operations: International Linkages" at the Fletcher School of Law and Diplomacy, April 17–19, 1985. A greatly abbreviated version was published under the title "Political Warfare in Totalitarian and Traditional Societies: A Comparison" and is reprinted with permission by the publisher of Uri Ra'anan, Robert L. Pfaltzgraff, Jr., Richard H. Shultz, Ernst Halperin, and Igor Lukes, eds. (Lexington, Mass.: Lexington Books, D.C. Heath and Company, 1986).

the employment of surrogates and mercenaries—have often been essential ingredients of political and military arsenals in Europe and North America. A noteworthy exemplar from the period of the French and Indian Wars in North America is "Roger's Rules of Rangering or Roger's Standing Rules for Rangering" (1756)[2]— a complete and forthright primer on the craft of covert and guerrilla warfare that stood earlier generations of fighting Americans in good stead, and that would make healthy reading for present-day congressmen and other citizens who go on lapsing into trauma at the mere thought of an American involvement in that so-called illegal, immoral covert war in Nicaragua.

Next, it is a sad but indisputable fact that generations of nations in diverse cultures have known institutionalized terror. However, the sources and forms of this type of extreme violence as well as the actual human experiences induced by its infliction are so strikingly various that they can hardly be covered by any *one* definition. For example, the entry in *Safire's Political Dictionary*[3] identifies "terrorism" with "persuasion by fear; the intimidation of society by a small group, using as its weapon that society's repugnance at the murder of innocents." This definition may be an apt rendition of modern Western opinion even though it does not make allowance for psychological and mental techniques of political terrorism. Further, and like other definitions of the term, it does not come to terms with the heavy incidence of institutionalized yet arbitrary violence in traditional non-Western societies. Killings on an elaborate scale, as, for example, human sacrifices, have thus been essential aspects of statecraft—both religious and secular—in several high civilizations of the Near and Far East as well as in the American Indian empires and Africa's folk societies. But no one knows whether the victims felt terrorized or whether society was intimidated by regime functionaries when scores of living "innocents" were dispatched to the netherland as worthy companions for a dead chief's journey to the ancestors, as required gifts to demanding deities, or as mere symbols of a ruler's omnipotence. What one does learn from available records is that levels of tolerance for conflict, violence, terror, and death have traditionally been higher in the Orient, Africa, and Indian America than in the Occident, and that the identities of near-countless non-Western communities and cultures were assured for centuries, even millennia by the regular enactment of awesomely violent rites and punishments.[4]

In short, I agree with the proposition that precedents for violent statecraft had been set in earlier times. Whether these precedents are relevant for an understanding of modern totalitarian techniques and whether they entitle us to speak of continuities is another question. The answer will be affirmative if we can identify the societies or culture spheres in which these techniques were steadily deployed, and if we can conclude that the present complex of terrorism, irregular armed struggles, insurgency, and so forth repeats patterns set in the past—if not of the same society, at least in the same culture.

It is in regard to this challenging range of thought and speculation that I find myself deviating from the supposition that the techniques advanced by contemporary totalitarian states are not a new development but can be traced back to some "rulers in traditional-closed societies." Definitions and listings for either of the two categories are not given, but the impression is left that today's totalitarian states and their totalitarian modes of statecraft were decisively fathered and mothered by earlier regimes (and here I admit that the phrase "traditional-closed societies" draws a blank in my mind). In other words, it looks as if no identifiable human agents but something called "the past" or "history" is deemed ultimately responsible for totalitarianism and for totalitarian techniques of rule.

My understanding of international history suggests somewhat different premises for this particular discussion. True, non-Western and non-Communist perspectives on time, specifically on the relations between past, present, and future, accentuate the supremacy of the past in ways alien to the Western, Promethean view. However, nowhere in the world has the remembrance or the dominion of the past been absolute so far. Rather, life everywhere has had a way of interpenetrating with the past by bringing forth new ideas or new mutations of old ideas and therewith new approaches to the governance of internal and external affairs.

This has changed with the advent of twentieth-century hard-core totalitarianism which is Marxist-Leninist in essence and constitutes in my view an entirely new development in thought and statecraft.[5] For whether viewed as ideology or political system, Communist totalitarianism stands for the legitimacy of total power over human life and thought as well as for total power over the human past and over human conceptualizations of reality. Two episodes illustrate this proposition. Milan Hubl's reflections on the Soviet Union's relentless campaign to impose Leninist totalitarianism on his Czechoslovakian homeland brought this poignant unassailable judgment:

> The first step in liquidating a people is to erase its memory. Destroy its books, its culture, its history. Then have somebody write new books, manufacture a new culture, invent new history. Before long the nation will begin to forget what it is and what it was.[6]

A young Chinese, buffeted by Maoist "struggle sessions" to recognize as "truth" only what the party leadership established from occasion to occasion, gave this analysis of her experience: "If the leader says of such and such an event, 'It never happened'—well, it never happened. If he says that two and two are five, well, two and two are five. This prospect frightens me much more than bombs."[7]

Further, apart from staking out absolutist control over time, Marxism-Leninism demands total power over space. Communist statecraft has thus been committed to limitless territorial expansion, and therewith to the abolition of bourgeois notions of the sovereign state and distinctions between matters "foreign" and "domestic"; the liquidation of democracy, law, and other non-Communist forms of government; and the invalidation of non-Leninist international systems.

Lastly, the totalitarian ideology was conceived and administered as a combat doctrine, and that on all levels of life and human relations. The "adversary" here is therefore not identified primarily with a threatening or aggressive foreign state. Rather, all human beings—whether within or without the nominal frontiers of former and present Gulag states—are "the enemy" because they may not be trusted by the ruling clique of the day. Throughout this century Leninist totalitarianism has thus stood for hatred, violence, and war. Its logic stipulates that the dictatorial command post, whether embodied in such former Soviet institutions as the Polit-buro, the KGB, the Nomenklatura, or their non-Soviet equivalents in Asia, Africa and several Latin American societies, has the unrestrained right to invent, select, and deploy whichever tactics are best suited for the cause of Communism and the power of its directorate.

A review of the steady realization of these doctrinal theses throughout the world supports the case for the uniqueness of Marxism-Leninism in the international his-tory of political thought. However, it also makes the acknowledgment necessary that certain non-Communist twentieth-century movements have lent considerable momentum to the evolution and consolidation of hard-core totalitarianism. One is the revolution in communication that facilitates territorial expansion and political control. The other is the scientific revolution in biology, genetics, chemistry, phys-ics, medicine, and technology that provides protagonists of totalitarianism with the ultimate techniques to effect the total subjugation of man. The third force that favored totalitarianism in this century is the West's political, moral, and intellectual inattentiveness to the development of Marxism-Leninism in thought and statecraft.

On the level of foreign relations it should have been clear at least since the Second World War that Communist victories, wherever registered, would under-mine the state system, the international law of war, and therewith the very foun-dations of all non-Communist states, big and small. For in Leninist ideology and practice "the state" has tactical significance only, and that chiefly in the context of relations with non-Communist states and their international organizations. In all other respects, it is outranked by the apparatus of the Communist Party in its local and international dimensions and should be viewed as the property of the ruling regime.

This oversight on the part of the West explains why the Soviet Union, acting under the protective auspices of the Modern States System, could go on canceling the independence of states (beginning with those in Eastern and Central Europe) by masterminding low-intensity conflicts, including terrorism; why it could succeed in invalidating international law with its neat distinctions between internal war and interstate war; and why we in the West do not know anymore how to think about war.[8]

II

Hard-core totalitarianism in the post 1989 era is identified with a few provinces of the former Soviet empire, in Europe and Asia; mainland China; the new (North) Vietnamese empire, which includes the formerly independent states of South Viet-nam and Laos, and with Cambodia (Kampuchea); North Korea; Cuba; Nicaragua; Ethiopia; Zimbabwe; Angola; and numerous terrorist nonstate bands that are inter-nationally operative across political frontiers.

Milder, essentially non-Leninist forms of totalitarianism are represented today by Libya, which I view as an emanation of Colonel Qaddafi's personality; the

Shi'ite theocracy of Iran, which is rooted in religious fanaticism rather than in ideology; and the majority of black Africa's despotic states.

What, then, was the incidence of violence, terrorism, low-intensity operations, and war in these provinces of the world before the advent of Leninism? Did ruling establishments employ surrogates or mercenaries in the conduct of their foreign relations? In short, can we speak of continuities in patterns of statecraft or of compatibilities between traditional patterns of statecraft and those fashioned in this century by totalitarian thought and tactics?

Answers to most of these complex questions can only be found in history. But since history is neither science nor ideology, and since it instructs different historical minds differently, it may not provide all the answers we are looking for. The past existence of the Inca Empire in what today is Peru is a well-documented fact, and so is the present-day existence in Peru of the Sendero Luminoso (Shining Path) terrorists. Now this is a Maoist split from the Peruvian Communist Party, which follows totalitarian strategies of terror while fighting the usual Communist-type "protracted people's war" with subsidies from foreign Communist principals. However, the guerrillas also think of themselves as heirs of the pre-Columbian Inca empire, a formidable military establishment administered by a religious bureaucracy wielding awesome powers over men. To "revive" the Inca splendor and prestige after its five-hundred-year lapse, but to do so on the model of Communist totalitarianism, is thus also one of the avowed objectives of the Shining Path.[9]

Whether this opportunity will arise for them or not, a comparison of past and present life-styles, propensities for violence, and techniques of political warfare does point to certain concordances, but in my opinion not to continuities. And the same conclusion suggested itself when I thought about the relation between the totalitarian Khmer Rouge of Kampuchea and their illustrious forebears, the Khmer of Cambodia and *their* immediate predecessors who created the unique civilization of Angkor in Indochina as well as an expansionist yet deeply religious kingdom— one destined to be severely tested throughout its long history.[10]

Do these visions and uses of the past express a genuine longing for continuity in time, or are they tactics of deception and exercises in disinformation on behalf of the totalitarian principle that time and history mean what the Communist apparatus says they mean? Questions such as these illustrate the plurality of time perspectives, the occasional waywardness of the historical imagination, and the near-constant ambiguities of historical references in today's international discourse. Yet they are too important to remain unanswered. For not only do they affect the integrity of history, a strategically vital academic discipline, especially in the West. They are also critically relevant in the context of present-day U.S. decision-making in foreign affairs.

However, and as noted earlier, this dimension of statecraft has been uncongenial to Americans because they tend to identify politically significant time with the last two hundred years—the time span of their own existence as a separate nation-state—rather than with the last twenty-five hundred years. Yet it is the latter time frame that should be our major reference when we speak of "earlier times," since it is the gestation period not only of Western civilization and thus of the main idea systems that sustain the United States today but also of all other culturally distinct contemporary societies with which we are involved, including those of the Khmer and the Inca heirs.

As noted in several essays in this book, it is this decidedly ahistorical American bent of mind that explains why we go on overlooking the obvious fact that all politically organized nontotalitarian societies in the world are older by centuries if not millennia than ours. Further, and in conjunction with the trend to think materialistically about the destinies of nations, it explains why we cannot satisfy the elementary requirement of statecraft—namely, understanding "the other" on his own terms.

"Understanding" the framework of diplomacy and intelligence, means, I suggest, that one knows the mainsprings and patterns of thought in foreign societies and that one is able therefore to assess and influence their plans and movements, detect deception, and distinguish singular occurrences from regularities and continuities in conduct. This kind of challenge is well illustrated by Herodotus in his account of direct and indirect warfare between the Persians and the Greeks.

> "What is the easiest way of breaking these men [the Spartans]?" asked Xerxes. "Tell me, Demaretos, you must know how their minds work after being their king."

And the same advice reaches us through the annals of Venetian history. Since the position of Venice in the world environment of the thirteenth to about the seventeenth century was not unlike that of the United States today, I did not hesitate to follow some Venetian guidelines for probing the relation between "then" and "now" and for tracking international linkages between principal powers and their surrogates. But since my mind does not hold a set of Venetian archives mirroring the whole world, I decided to limit the present inquiry to this century's principal totalitarian powers, namely the Soviet Union and Communist China, and to precedents for their techniques of statecraft in "earlier times."

"Which earlier times?" was the next question. I could not very well relate Moscow's "active measures" or Peking's exercises in psychological and geopolitical "encirclement" and "tunneling" to the Incas and their terrorizing human sacrifices, or the Fulani divines and their fierce jihads in the Sudan and the Sahara, or to the orders of the Shi'ite Assassins and the Hebrew Zealots. These phenomena are relevant for a general understanding of low-intensity conflict and political warfare as well as for the particular problem of coming to terms with the warring ways of specific peoples in the Middle East, black Africa, and parts of the Americas, but they are irrelevant to the case at hand. Reflections made it clear that I had to stay within the culture zones in which the Soviet Union and Maoist China evolved, and this led to linking the former to the Byzantine Empire and the latter to imperial China. Other justifications for this dual focus are (1) that the two "earlier times" coincided at least for one millennium (Byzantium was extinguished in 1453 when it was "tunneled" into defeat by the Turks); (2) that both traditional empires were hard-pressed—and greatly influenced—by the Mongols, and (3) that Russia and China are jointly responsible for the evolution of present day Vietnam and North Korea. Imperial China tutored them as its hedge-guarding satellites while the Soviet

Union converted them into totalitarian surrogates that have specialized in deploying terrorism as state policy.[11]

III

The Byzantine Empire[12]

(1) A PROFILE. The chief reasons for selecting the Eastern Roman Empire as the first case study are these: it excelled in developing and deploying most but by no means all of the political techniques that we are discussing here these days; and it was the mentor in matters of statecraft on the one hand for Venice, which then set the tone for Europe, and on the other hand for Kievan Russia, the first of several Russias to come. The legacies did not turn out to be alike, however, because the two apprentices did not learn the same lessons from the master sorcerer, and because they were subject to different non-Byzantine influences.

Other but closely related determinants for the choice of the Byzantine exemplar can be briefly summarized as follows. The empire endured from the sixth to the sixteenth century A.D. by dint precisely of its management of indirect political warfare and low-intensity conflicts, and it did so in an exceedingly complex multicultural environment. From the fateful division of Christianized Rome onward, relations between the Eastern Christian or Greek Orthodox realm, centered in Constantinople, and the Christian commonwealth of Western Europe, anchored in the Roman Papacy and the German Nation, were marked by chronic psychopolitical tensions, territorial rivalries, and diplomatic intrigues, as well as by occasional wars and a memorable crusade.

Next, Byzantium was a superpower in terms of world affairs throughout its history, even though its boundaries were to recede steadily under the onslaught particularly of Islam. Its government thus had to administer and defend vast areas in Europe, Africa, and Asia, which were not enclosed by natural geographical frontiers. And within this far-flung domain it had to deal with a host of nationalities widely separated from one another by racial, linguistic, or cultural differences. It should be remembered, furthermore, that Byzantium was "a middle kingdom," not unlike China in this respect. Beyond its periphery lived a great variety of lesser nations some settled, others nomadic, which gravitated toward Constantinople as a result of complex centrifugal or centripetal forces. How should the empire treat such restless and aggressive northern folk as the Avars, Bulgars, Petchenegs, Russians, and Seljuk Turks, who transgressed its boundaries, laid waste its provinces, and threatened its capital? Defensive military actions were usually successful in checking intrusions after they had occurred. But the experience of these encounters made it clear that the interest of the empire required not only military vigilance but also long-range policies that would control the population movements on the periphery and, if necessary, accommodate those foreign elements that seemed intent upon settling in the close vicinity of the imperial state. Byzantium responded to these conditions by creating gradually an intricate system of political controls in which secondary and culturally inferior states came to exist in various degrees of tutelage and dependence.

Beyond this circle of lesser states was a broader circle of aggressive and expansive great powers—Western Rome, Persia, and, from the seventh century onward, the Islamic caliphates. Byzantium's strength varied in the course of their mutual relations. But there was no moment when Constantinople was not the junction as well as the target of rival imperialisms. And since the empire's own destiny was expansion also, its statesmen were forever confronted with the necessity of warding off assaults, loosening the noose around the imperial heartland, and taking due advantage of any opening that would permit a more direct initiatory action on behalf of its own security and greatness. Here, as in the case of the lesser neighboring states and tribes, Byzantium could not rely solely on its military forces as an adequate shield against its foes. Aggressive moves on the part of one or several foreign nations had to be anticipated, forestalled, or weakened whenever possible if the Eastern Christian Empire was to gain mastery over the adverse elements of its geographic and political position. Byzantine statesmanship therefore implied the mandate to exploit the rivalries of enemies, transform the ring of satellites into a system of protection and defense, and generally to cultivate policies short of war that would assure some possibility of coexistence with one or the other of the empires in the outer ring of encirclement.

This orientation toward the environment was not only a product of political and strategic considerations, but also a manifestation of certain involuntary communications that had long linked "the middle empire" to the adjoining orbits. After all, Byzantium occupied an area that had been the crossroads for more than a millennium of diverse cultural forces emanating from all directions. By virtue of its geographic associations alone it was therefore particularly receptive to influences from Persia, Egypt, the Arab regions, and the great Oriental realms lying beyond the circle of Central Asian and Middle Eastern civilizations. The empire was thus conditioned by its very situation as well as by the cultural heritage of classical Greece, Rome, and Christianity to develop an acute awareness of other nations, religions, and value systems. In short, several factors combined to compel the imperial administration to distinguish beneficial or innocuous forces from those threatening the integrity of the state, and to regulate the impact of all cultural influences from abroad by developing appropriate policies for each case.

These were formulated and deployed by a corps of scholarly bureaucrats (comparable to China's mandarinate) who represented all governmental services, including the Church, the treasury, the army, and above all a comprehensive foreign intelligence system. They were the people who found the ways and means of making the central government generally respected within the orbit of imperial power, who assured the stability of the nation's social life by maintaining the rule of law, and who protected the mystique of the imperial establishment by controlling an elaborate court ceremonial. Further, it is interesting to note that they were recruited from all ethnic and cultural components of the cosmopolitan state.

Just as the civil service included officials who were Italians, Bulgarians, Arabs, and Turks, so did the army employ generals of Armenian, Persian, and Slavic origin and hold its ranks open to aliens without much regard to their original provenance. One of the regiments of the emperor's bodyguard, for instance, was composed almost entirely of Russians, Scandinavians, and Chozars, while the Varangian guard was successively recruited from among Russians, Scandinavians, Northmen, and Anglo-Saxons. In the tenth century Armenian contingents were numerous as well as highly esteemed; in the twelfth century, by contrast, Latin troops were regarded as the best.

Quite in contrast to the Holy Roman Empire of the German Nation, where theory and policy converged on clear distinctions between peace and war, Eastern Rome was conditioned to regard war as an ever-present possibility and to trust the standing army as the chief instrument for assuring the survival of the state. Yet the army was deliberately kept small, the theory being that its real strength did not lie so much in its numbers as in the intelligence with which it faced the empire's enemies. It was the business of military administrators to learn each opponent's particular method of warfare and to assemble a whole arsenal of stratagems and tricks that could be employed to demoralize, weaken, or outmaneuver possible antagonists. Only when the enemy's defenses had been thoroughly undermined would Byzantium employ its fighting forces. And the army then would be guided by elaborate instructions outlining techniques for the feigning of flights, staging of night attacks and ambushes, and the conduct of truce negotiations for the purpose of winning time. Similar principles guided the operations of the navy until the eleventh century, when the Byzantine naval strength was permitted to decline.[13] This interpretation of the uses and limitations of warfare explains why a relatively small Byzantine force was often able to defeat a much larger enemy force and why the state could hold its own against the odds of a permanent encirclement.

All Byzantine conceptions of the function of war and the uses of the armed forces were made possible by the empire's successful establishment of a money economy and a permanent fisc with an apparently inexhaustible capacity to make payments. As one authority explains it:[14]

> In the period of eight hundred years from Diocletian to Alexius Comnenus the Roman government never found itself compelled to declare bankruptcy, or stop payments. Neither the ancient nor the modern world can offer a complete parallel to this phenomenon.

This achievement explains why the emperor could pay salaries, i.e., why he did not have to remunerate his vassals for their military aid by granting them land.

(2) INTELLIGENCE, DIPLOMACY, AND WARFARE. Whereas the imperial government was most economical in the use of the military, it was lavish in its expenditure on the arts of diplomacy. Vanquished nations—whether Bulgaria or conquered parts of southern Italy—were treated with calculated mildness and given latitude in self-government, albeit under the strict control of imperial commissioners. Except for extreme cases, where the defeated proved to be entirely intractable and were removed to other districts, the government ruled by indirect and devious means, skillfully exploiting such human foibles as ambition, pride, cupidity, and jealousy. New tribes invading the domain were appeased by grants of territory or of political status, while settled nations were often kept from rebellion and aggression simply by annually paid subsidies, or by fixed remunerations in return for some useful political function. For example, Justinian subsidized the Utigurs as long as they kept the Huns from attacking Cherson and Bosporus. Nor were such arrangements restricted

to so-called barbarians. In the tenth century Byzantium paid Venice for policing the Adriatic, Syria for protecting the eastern frontiers, and various Armenian states for replenishing the ranks of the imperial army. This particular political method of utilizing lesser nations proved profitable also when Byzantium had to cope with great powers that could be neither bought nor defeated. When Justinian wished to divert Persia's attention from the imperial boundaries, he found ways of persuading the Huns and Arabs of the desert to harass this enemy. Indeed the Byzantines discovered in the course of their international dealings that most people could be induced to quarrel with their neighbors. This inexpensive diplomatic tactic proved particularly effective among the unsophisticated barbarians whose predatory designs the government had reason to fear. Byzantine diplomats were therefore continuously engaged in sowing the seeds of suspicion and discord among the lesser nations in the immediate vicinity.

However, the general diplomatic record shows that the imperial agents were acutely conscious also of the intellectual and cultural vacuum that existed in most border regions. They were therefore committed to the task of filling this vacuum by diffusing Byzantine jurisprudence, literature, and art, and by conducting special orientation programs for kings and other leaders. Under the terms of this policy (it was initiated by Justinian), young chiefs arrived at the imperial court either as guests or as hostages; others, exiled from their home country, were granted asylum or educated as pretenders to native thrones. Quite contrary to the miserable treatment usually meted out to envoys from great powers who were enemies by definition, those from the satellites were befriended, protected, educated, and entertained during their sojourns in Constantinople.[15] Also, and since the Byzantines were masters in the art of evolving forms—whether in architecture, liturgy, court etiquette, or diplomacy, the lesser emissaries or chiefs were deliberately drawn into the empire's courtly system where they were decorated, titled, given crowns,[16] scepters, and, if their services were deemed especially desirable, even Byzantine princesses in marriage. Indeed, as employed by the Eastern Empire, symbolism became an international political language through which the government could convey the power and the unity of the empire to its multifarious component groups, whether literate or nonliterate.

This policy of acculturation reached its greatest moral and intellectual depth in the missionary activities of the Eastern Christian Church, which penetrated the interior of all surrounding areas, specifically those inhabited by Slavic peoples. The missionaries seemed to have known as well as the empire's secular intelligence agents that the leadership principle was the pivotal point in the political organization of most barbarian nations. Their proselytizing efforts were therefore usually initiated by attempts to convert the native chief and his entourage. A sixth-century king of the Huns received baptism, with the emperor himself acting as his sponsor. Other monarchs who entered the fold included Czar Boris of Bulgaria (864), Princess Olga of Kiev (957), and Vladimir of Kiev, who received baptism after his capture of Cherson (988). This last conversion was followed by Vladimir's marriage to the Byzantine princess Anna and the collective baptism of his pagan subjects.

Most carriers of the Orthodox faith did not confine their efforts to the titled and illustrious. Indeed their commitment centered on bringing the illiterate simple folk into the protective orbit of the Church. This is well illustrated by the so-called apostles to the Slavs (ninth century), who invented an alphabet for the natives, translated the Holy Scriptures for their use, preached in Slavic, and tried to create a Slavic clergy. The widespread diffusion of Byzantine theology, jurisprudence, literature, and art that followed in the wake of these and related educational efforts was tantamount to the creation of a more or less ideologically unified orbit. And, of course, the Byzantine foreign service favored this development since it greatly facilitated their task of administering the empire.

At its apogee, the Byzantine system encompassed great powers and ancient civilizations as well as small nations and culturally undeveloped societies, and it addressed a great variety of goals. Most of these pertained to that inner ring of nations that separated the state from the other great powers of the world. Here Byzantine diplomats had the mandate of maintaining the empire's existing spheres of influence, and of coping with the steady pressure of barbarian tribes by drawing the new arrivals into the circle of hedge-guarding imperial client states that was meant to serve as an outer line of defense.[17] This design was translated into fact by the establishment of a whole constituency of vassals that included at one time or another the Arabs of Syria and Yemen; the Berbers of North Africa; Lazi and Tsani in the farthest reaches of Armenia; and Heruli, Gepidae, Lombards, and Huns on the Danube. Other satellites in the north and east were Caucasians, Albanians, Croats, Serbs, Bulgars, and Russians. In the western Mediterranean the Byzantine protectorate was long accepted by the republics of Venice, Naples, Gaeta, and Amalfi, and by the princes of Salerno, Capua, and Beneventum.

Within the fluctuating boundaries of this great orbit, Byzantine diplomacy was required to ascertain the degree of control that could be exercised over each separate community and to supervise the evolution of each particular relationship. Also, it had to counter whatever competitive appeals rival great powers might address to these lesser states or tribes, to keep abreast of native movements toward independence, and, if need be, to modify or discard outworn terms of suzerainty. These were the general terms of reference, but as indicated earlier in this essay, the particular diplomatic objectives varied from region to region. A summary view of the entire diplomatic record shows that the Byzantines were able to execute most of these complex assignments. Indeed, in regard to culturally inferior and politically weaker nations they displayed such an ingenuity in finding patterns of both accord and control that one is justified in defining their statecraft as the science of managing the barbarians.[18]

Byzantine political theory assumed that the emperors themselves were most qualified to deploy this science. But even the most proficient emperors needed assistants if the empire's foreign policy was to be systematically transacted. This service was rendered by a special department of external affairs and an elaborately organized body of agents whose status and prestige in the society were fixed in all details.[19] The trained envoys and negotiators had to pass rigid examinations and receive detailed instructions before they could be entrusted with foreign missions. While on duty abroad, they were supposed to collect as much information as possible about the domestic affairs of the host country. Envoys to barbarian courts had particularly complex assignments. They were to study the habits, morals, and institutions of all tribes in the vicinity, ascertain their military strength and weakness, follow the flow of commerce and the trends of intertribal and regional relationships, watch for and investigate internecine quarrels, and identify existing and prospective leaders in the district. Also, they were supposed to analyze the personalities of the barbarian chiefs in order to find out whether they would be susceptible to flattery or threat, to women or to wealth.[20]

The Second Rome declined steadily even as it celebrated some of its greatest triumphs. Its power was sapped on each of its frontiers because it was locked in conflicts with the rival Christian commonwealth in the West; because it could not cope militarily with the stream of determined Islamic conquerors;[21] because it was unable to manage all of the incoming aggressive barbarians all of the time; and because many satellite states composed of erstwhile barbarians had themselves become ambitious aspirants for superpower status. The end came in 1453 when the Islamic Ottoman Turks succeeded, after numerous attempts, to take possession of Constantinople.

(3) BYZANTIUM AND THE RUSSIANS. As preceding references have indicated, Byzantine influences had by that time permeated all neighboring nations. However, most of these—and they included the Turks and other Islamized peoples as well as Venice—proceeded to fashion their own identities and techniques of statecraft, often in stark counterpoint to the legacies received from the Second Rome. In that context we can therefore not speak of meaningful continuities between "then" and "now." The situation is altogether different when we turn to the Russians, a steady presence in Byzantium's orbit.

Prominent as mercenaries, surrogates, and in later times even as "surrogate allies," Russians were also feared as aggressive unprincipled traders who routinely engaged in piracy and plunder when they were thwarted in their designs. This preoccupation or set of mind became markedly apparent from the eighth century onward when the Varangians were tributaries of the mighty commercial empire of the Chozars (a nomad race of Turkish origin that eventually shifted its religious commitment from Greek Orthodoxy to Judaism). But it came to constitute state policy after the Russians took control of Kiev and then established their first state. The focus of their militant commercial expeditions was Constantinople. At least six such semiwars, or "high-intensity operations," were staged against the city of their desires between 860 and 1043, and some of them had devastating effects upon the imperial capital where the Russians continued to be viewed as inferior barbarians while their princes were deemed to be vassals. Some treaties were nonetheless concluded in the course of this ambivalent relationship.[22] One of them (945) committed the Kievans to protect the empire's interests in the Crimea against the aggressions of the Black Bulgars, but it was definitely subsidiary to the commercial understandings reached in the tenth century as a result of Kiev's bellicose insistence upon a share in the empire's trade. These entitled the Great Prince of Rus, his boyars, government traders, and private merchants to send to Constantinople each year as many ships as the prince might desire. They conferred extensive privileges, stipends, and even services upon the visitors during the allotted time of their sojourn. However, they also made it clear that the host country would never cease being suspicious of its trading partners. The Russians had to give the contractual assurance that they "would come in peace," be unarmed, and that they would specify the identities of all officials, vessels, and so forth that constituted the party.

These ever-latent animosities and conflicts were offset by mutual goodwill when it came to the legal resolution of disputes. After all, the Russians had become thoroughly "Byzantinized" in this respect, and Kievan jurists collaborated effectively with their imperial counterparts in formulating legal provisions for the treatment of civil and criminal offenses as well as a clause binding the contracting parties to aid shipwrecked merchants. Yet nothing in the records on either side suggests the acceptance of an international law that distinguished between "peace" and "war."

The linkage with Byzantium ceased officially when the first Russian state was subjugated by the Mongols. However, it revived after the overthrow of the Tartar yoke in the fourteenth and fifteenth centuries, the establishment of the Muscovite Czardom, and the extinction of the Second Roman Empire when the Czars conceived their own imperial designs.

And these, not surprisingly, were in many respects modeled on Byzantine precedents. Two spiritual principles in particular appealed to the Russians as techniques for empire building: the idea of the church-state and the idea of the unity of the Orthodox world. Both could be used to justify and sublimate the territorial and personal aspirations of the Czars. Further, and since it was being realized that the Russian people had become deeply susceptible to the myths, symbols, and rites associated with policies of the fallen empire, the leadership became adept practitioners of the art of manipulating these phenomena on behalf of its own ambitions. Indeed, several legends and symbols were invented—and history distorted—so as to bolster trust in Moscow's divinely ordained mission to become the new Constantinople.[23]

Nor was this the ultimate goal. Dissatisfied with its historical status as the successor or equal of Byzantium, Moscow's statesmen claimed (after falsifying a family tree and inventing other historical episodes) that Russia was not only the leading Orthodox state but also the legitimate heir of the First (imperial classical) Rome, and that the Czar of Moscow was therewith superior over the rest of the European kings and rulers. These claims were announced in doctrinal form in the early part of the sixteenth century when an Orthodox monk proclaimed that Moscow was the Third Rome, charged with the sacred mission of saving mankind—a mission in which both Western Rome and Eastern Rome had failed.[24] This doctrine could become the principal consolidating force in the early Russian state as well as one of the chief determinants of the Russian orientation toward other states and peoples because it was linked from the beginning of the country's history with the power of the national state and the ambitions of its autocratic rulers. It is in this essentially nonspiritual rendition that the idea of Moscow the Third Rome found expression first in the Czardom of Moscow, thereafter in the empire, and lastly in the Third International.[25]

Most scholars of pre-Communist Russia have acknowledged the continuance of Byzantine traditions of statecraft and diplomacy in their homeland,[26] whereas Soviet studies affirm the influence of both Byzantines and Mongols on the evolution of the Russian state. M. V. Levchenko stresses that of the Second Rome in the following passage:

> Russia received Christianity from Byzantium. Along with Christianity the Slavs received writing and some elements of higher Byzantine culture. It is clear that the working masses of our country are right in becoming interested in the history of the Byzantine empire and the Soviet historian must satisfy this interest and give a scholarly history of Byzantium erected on the foundation of the Marxist-Leninist methodology.[27]

R. Vipper, on the other hand, extols the centralized military monarchy of the Mongols in which all social forces were effectively organized for war, but he also pays tribute to Byzantium:

> Although owing to the difficulties of communication with Western Europe, the Moscow state lagged behind the latter in technical inventions, it far excelled it in its harmonious and mighty military administrative organization and skillful carefully thought-out and consistent diplomacy. This was the effect of the peculiar culture of the Great Russian people, which, as comrade J. V. Stalin expressed it, was disciplined by the requirements of self-defense, and was fostered by the traditions of Byzantine scholarship which was zealously studied in Moscow.[28]

Indeed, and as Kluchevsky confirms,[29] the Russians of the Mongol era were adept practitioners of the Byzantine art of influencing people. Muscovite princes thus never dreamed of openly resisting the Mongolian overlord, since they knew very well that the Horde could be dealt with more easily by "peaceful cunning"—"détente" in our times—than by force of arms. Liberation was achieved because the Muscovites managed the Mongolian himself as the instrument of their schemes.

IV

Comparative studies of Byzantine and Russian modes of statecraft suggest the following answers to the questions raised at the beginning of this essay:

(a) Although the Eastern Christian Empire can certainly not be described as "a traditional-closed society"—a term more appropriate to its different Russian progenies—it did employ "political warfare." In fact, its mastery of this diplomatic method has in my opinion never been surpassed or even equaled. "Resort to extreme forms of violence against foreign adversaries," by contrast, was avoided.

(b) The use of surrogates and mercenaries constituted the essence of Byzantine statecraft.

(c) The records are replete with guidelines for the utilization of political and military techniques.

In reply to the fourth, and main, question—"What continuity exists between the ways in which traditional rulers employed these techniques and how they are exercised by present-day governments?"—I have come to the following conclusions:

There are indeed definite parallels or near analogies between Byzantine and Soviet techniques of political warfare, low-intensity operations, the use of surrogates, and so forth. However, the significance of these affinities or continuities cannot be estimated unless one remembers that orientations to foreign affairs are everywhere reflections of a given society's basic internal norms and values.

In the case at hand it is unquestionably true that Russians have sought and cultivated the Byzantine connection for over one thousand years, and that Kievan Russia is the root from which the later czarist empire grew. But as the preceding section of this essay suggests, documentary records of thought and behavior in domestic as well as foreign affairs also show that successive Russian states have deviated substantially from the models set by the Eastern Christian Empire; that the ancient root system of concepts and values was severely disturbed by the Mongols and their immediate czarist successors; and that it was categorically disestablished in our century by Marxist-Leninist rule.[30] (The only order of ideas that withstood destruction is Russia's version of the Greek Orthodox faith.)

In light of the radical transposition of some fundamental principles of persuasion and the eradication of others, it should not be assumed that the two sets of political techniques, however similar in their surface manifestations, originate in similar modes of reasoning or are meant to serve similar strategic purposes. Thus it bears remembering that the Eastern Christian Empire had at no time been a Gulag state (and, as I suggested in Part I of this study, never could have been one), and that governmental power, however authoritarian, was firmly and openly kept in check by several factors that were not to have any equivalents in the totalitarian Soviet empire. For example, in the general context of the Greco-Christian tradition it was assumed that the monarch would always honor the dictates of *philanthropia*—an unwritten moral obligation that required him to serve his subjects in a humane way. And this commitment was buttressed by the classical Roman theory that government is an obligation, not a privilege; by the express precepts of the Greek Orthodox faith, the state religion; and by the ecclesiastical establishment's highly respected "oversight" function in all governmental matters. Now it is true that the imperial policies and actions of the Orientalized Eastern Christian Empire were not decisively affected by the kind of constitutional law that was formulated in the Western Christian Empire on the model of the classical Roman law. However, it was Justinian, after all, who codified the civil law of Rome, and most of his successors—aided by a corps of dedicated jurists—saw to it that Eastern Rome remained a "law state," quite in counterpoint not just to all other contemporary Near Eastern empires[31] but also to the Soviet Russian empire.

Next, whereas Byzantium's strategic design was fashioned to assure the identity, security, and survival of the state in an international society of culturally and politically highly diverse entities, that of the Leninist imperium was built to achieve world domination. However, the two designs are at one—and thus in opposition to ruling Western concepts of international order while in compliance with all Eastern traditions, including those of Kievan, Mongol, and Muscovite Russia—in *not* polarizing the conditions called "peace" and "war." The Occidental law of nations that is rooted in such a juxtaposition has therefore no equivalent in either of the Eastern domains.

This concordance on the interpretation of war and peace explains why political warfare and "irregular" military operations could become leading themes in the foreign policies of two quite disparate imperial societies. Yet it is near-irrelevant for a study of continuities in statecraft because war and all its subspecies were associated with functions in Soviet ideology and practice that would not have been consonant with the self-image, worldview, and strategic design of the Eastern Christian Empire, and that are therefore missing from Byzantine records.

In stark contrast to Marxist-Leninist doctrines, Byzantium was not seized either by hatred for all that is "other" than the party line as defined on a given day, or by lust for total power and trust in total destruction. Nor did it subscribe to theories of permanent war and revolution, or of the absolute need for armed struggle and armed victory. Rather, it sought to reduce the threat of war to dimensions that would allow for the effective management of low-intensity conflicts. Genocidal wars for the total subjugation on the order of those fought by the Soviet Union in Afghanistan or by Sovietized North Vietnam in Cambodia and the rest of Indochina would not have been fathomed in Constantinople. Nor would state-sponsored terrorism have been condoned either as a legitimate or as an effective weapon against foreign adversaries. In these as in many other respects Eastern Christian Rome simply did not become just another Oriental despotism on the order of the Assyrian, Mongol, or radical Islamic prototypes. This may explain why no auspices were provided either for the kind of terrorist fraternities as the Assassins and the Zealots (see *supra*, this essay) that operated in "early times," or for the kind of Leninist terrorist "action groups" and bands of urban guerrillas that proved to be effective instruments of Communist policy-making in "our times."

Other Soviet deviations from Byzantine norms can be isolated if the following factors are borne in mind. Byzantium was an authoritarian church-state. Its governing institutions were what they openly professed to be. All of them were superbly served by intelligence services that had a variety of far-flung tasks, but they were at no time functions or expressions of a covert inofficial system of administration on the order of the Communist Party, its special bureaus, policing organs, local cells, and globe-spanning secret networks. Front organizations of the type set up by Leninist regimes in non-Communist countries singled out for destabilization, revolution, or takeover had therefore no precedents here. On the other hand, it is certainly true that psychological and political warfare was as common in Byzantine as it is in Soviet statecraft. Further, it is incontestable that the different Russias, including the Soviet Union, learned from the Byzantines how to camouflage weakness and wield power inexpensively. The Soviet tactic of intimidating and humiliating emissaries of "great" powers while nursing the egos of the weak through flattery may thus be viewed as a replay of Byzantine statecraft.[32]

Further, and as set forth in earlier pages, one finds in both systems a heavy reliance on satellites, surrogates, and mercenaries. However—and this is in my view the chief area of Soviet deviations from Byzantine patterns—the relationships between the imperial center on the one hand and the latter's satellites and foreign agent nations on the other were fashioned in radically different manners and served entirely different purposes.

Contrary to the Soviet design, which required absolute ideological and political conformity from its political dependencies as well as from its individual subjects at home, the Byzantine called for a form of tutelage or trusteeship not unlike the one instituted first by the West's modern colonial administrations and thereafter by the charter of the United Nations. Being a cosmopolitan civilization and renowned among contemporaries as the foremost center of learning, Constantinople relied on acculturation rather than obedience to heavy-handed controls to keep its hedge-guarding satellites in order. Literacy, Christianity, law, and education were thus implanted in several areas,[33] but policies to re-Christianize Islamic Arabs or turn Catholic Italians into Greek Orthodox Italians were not pursued. Indeed, upward mobility was the theme in the Eastern Roman Empire's orbit of vassalage. Dependencies, whether civilized or barbarian, could retain and develop their own traditions even as they were enriched by Byzantium's deliberate promotion of art and learning, the rise of commerce, and the consolidation of urban life. However, their status of inferiority was not dissimulated nor were the functions they served in the context of Byzantium's strategic design.

All this stands in stark contrast to the administration of the multicultural Soviet imperium. In Eastern and Central Europe—the area of greatest strategic importance for the U.S.S.R.—war diplomacy, coups d'état and low-intensity operations were skillfully managed in the 1940s, 1950s, and 1960s so as to reduce once-independent states to the status of Soviet provinces. Moscow's Communist Party apparat came to recruit and control the leading personalities in each local government, while its armed forces were firmly ensconced along the new long north/south frontier separating the Leninist imperium from what was left of continental Western Europe. Yet each of these dependencies retained statehood as a camouflage on the scene of world politics so that it could cast its pro-Soviet vote in negotiations and debates with non-Communist or anti-Soviet states. This double game had assured the Soviet "bloc" superiority in the United Nations and other international organizations set up on Western constitutional foundations. It also legitimized the Warsaw Pact as an alliance of sovereign self-determining states equal to that of NATO, and it provided the underpinning for such other multilateral but anti-Western compacts as the Helsinki Accords that ratified the Soviet conquests in 1975.

The imperial center's relationship with Eastern Europe has a special poignancy not found in its relations with other satellites. Quite unlike Byzantium, the Soviet Union was culturally inferior to most if not all of its European provinces.[34] Not only did it not have princesses to give away; it had nothing to teach or suggest, either in aesthetics, letters, and art or in urban and economic development. Having left the shores of humanism, cast off the pre-Communist Russian heritage, and opted for totalitarian politics and the garrison state, Moscow rested its case for leadership on providing compulsory education in subversion and all categories of regular and irregular warfare, and on deploying and guiding surrogates—specifically Bulgaria and East Germany—in the transaction of low-intensity operations and terrorist business.

The basic Soviet game plans that were operational in non-Western regions of the world were the same as the ones just reviewed. However, the records accumulated in the Caribbean, Central America, the Middle East, and Africa show that the tactics here employed have some affinities with those put into play by the Eastern Roman Empire in so-called barbarian lands. One of them relates to the technique of inducing convergence in political disposition by selecting a few promising local personages for surrogate status and then shaping their characters and thoughtways in desired ways. However, marked divergences from Byzantine patterns emerge as one reflects on the biographies of several generations of African leadership and their relations with the Soviet master-mentor. For in the Soviet context the task required producing totalitarian regimes subservient to Moscow's brand of Leninism by knocking out traditional loyalties and inhibitions while exploiting such deeply rooted beliefs as trust in magic and ancestral power; stirring up jealousies, suspicions, and above all antagonism to the West; exacerbating ever-latent tribal warring dispositions; and modernizing customary guerrilla warfare.

By and large the Soviet Union succeeded in each of these respects. That is to say, it was well-served by those who came to wield totalitarian power over Ghana, Guinea, Guinea-Bissau, Congo-Brazzaville, Ethiopia, Angola, Mozambique, Zimbabwe, and others. The losers here are the societies that were forced to serve the dual Communist tyranny. Deprived of their African heritage and identity, poorer and more conflicted than ever before, they came to serve: as battlefields for alien causes, often even as "Kingdoms of Death"[35] for their own human kind.

The same brand of "individualization"—and needless to say it is an expression as well as a tactic of Leninist totalitarianism—marked the Soviet play in the Middle East and Central America. The Islamic states of West Asia and North Africa were neither satellites nor surrogates "first-class." Yet Moscow had been successful in conditioning several of the despotic regimes so that they would act reliably in surrogate capacities. Well-served by the KGB and its dense web of international agents, Moscow knew not only how to capitalize on inter-Islamic conflicts and the regionally shared enmity to Israel but also how to latch onto the fanatical hatred of the United States, which has come to consume radical Shi'ites, especially in Iran; how to give covert guidance and support to Colonel Qaddafi's transterritorial designs for murder; in short, how to delegate the task of terrorizing the rest of the world.[36]

The pattern of dependence on ruthless power-seeking personalities to whom active (i.e., unsavory) measures can be safely entrusted also marked Soviet statecraft in the Caribbean and Central America. However, here as in Eastern Europe and the newly Communized states of black Africa (foremost among them Ethiopia), the chief clients were Marxist-Leninist hard-liners. Further, and as revealed by the records documenting the Communist penetration of Grenada, the Soviet Union itself had been calling most of the shots in the entire Caribbean and Central American region because its long-range strategic plan required the transformation of the states adjacent to the United States into Soviet satellites on the model of those in Eastern Europe.

This plan was initiated several decades ago with the conversion of Fidel Castro into an ardent and imaginative propagator of Moscow's brand of Leninism and the concomitant casting of Cuba as chief ideological and military training ground for the Third World's younger generations, supplier of mercenaries for revolutionary battle service in Latin America and Africa, and as the principal base of operations for planning and enacting psychopolitical warfare, guerrilla wars, coups d'état, and all other manner of low-intensity operations in disparate parts of the non-Communist world. Most of these interventions were carried out openly. An interesting exception is the protracted but ultimately successful ideological campaign of transposing Christianity into a subspecies of Marxism during which scores of Jesuit priests and exponents of other Christian orders and churches in the American hemispheres were induced to become willing agents of an atheist principal.

Castro's Cuba occupied a unique position in the Soviet Union's hierarchical imperial order. Although it was never a satellite, it was materially totally dependent on Moscow, received guidelines in policy-making, and fulfilled surrogate, even mercenary functions. Yet it outranked such states as Mengistu's Ethiopia and North Korea. The question whether the Soviet-Cuban connection has an analogue in the history of Byzantine statecraft arises naturally in the context of this paper. Venice comes to mind but must be ruled out because Eastern Rome was not an ideologically unified system and Christianity "then" was not the ideology it appears to be "now." Further, and most importantly, Venice never surrendered its national, religious, and intellectual identity. However, in the limited context of comparing relations between principal centers of power and their surrogates it may be argued that the status of the Adriatic republic resembles that which the Communist Vietnamese empire in Indochina occupied in the Soviet design. For while it served Moscow in important surrogate functions, it retained the characteristics of what used to be North Vietnam and therewith also those that link its long pre-Communist history to that of pre-Communist China.

V

China

(I) HISTORICAL PROFILE. Mainland China today is a totalitarian empire built on Marxist-Leninist-Stalinist principles. But contrary to the Soviet Union, which can be identified only with this political ideology and the operational code it spanned, Communist China is also heir to the Han, Sui, T'ang, Ming, and Manchu dynasties. That is to say, it continues to rest on an authentic, self-contained and creative civilization that had endured for at least twenty-five hundred years before it underwent its transformation in the mid-twentieth century under the aegis of the Soviet motherland of socialism. The theme of continuity is thus being rendered differently here.

Successive generations of Chinese have thought of the space they occupied not as a territorially bounded state but as the abode of "civilization" writ large. As such it fancied itself absolutely and perennially superior to all other societies. However, China was in reality a "middle kingdom." Not unlike Byzantium, it bordered several established realms and had to contend with aggressive or simply nomadic peoples in the porous northern reaches, chief among them first the Mongols and then the Russians. These standing threats explain, in conjunction with the unwavering

Chinese self-view, why all non-Chinese realms were relegated to the inferior status of "barbarian"; why the concept of the enemy was highly developed; and why Chinese dispositions to the many "others" in the Sinocentric universe were marked by suspicion and belligerence.

Contrary to Russia, which began its career in history as an inferior first to Constantinople and then to the Mongol conquerors, China started out as Asia's superpower in 221 B.C. after the victory of the state of Ch'in over all other warring states had led to the establishment of a unified empire.

The intellectual force that determined these political achievements and was ultimately responsible also for the creation of China's renowned bureaucracy emanated from a school of thought known as the Realists, or Legalists. As noted in "War and the Clash of Ideas" in this volume, the essence of its science is the uncompromising recognition that war and organization for war are the mainstays of government, and that people are best subdued by busying them in war and agriculture and by threatening them with punishment. Peace, in contrast, is presented in this literature as a misfortune bound to breed "the Six Maggots," among them detraction of warfare and shame at taking part in it—dispositions that conduce to weakness and impoverishment of the realm.

History instructs us that legalism effectively eclipsed Confucianism in matters of statecraft. The Chinese state has thus always derived its ultimate power from the army—a circumstance that has largely predetermined its authoritarian character up to and including the twentieth century. Dynasties usually came to power through armed force, and revolts—which were commonplace—were staged and smashed by military means. Further, the art of building and besieging walled cities was highly developed from early times onward if only because walled cities were indispensable as headquarters of regional government, storage places for large grain reserves, centers of control over land and peasantry, and staging areas for further conquest.[37]

In the Realist context, then, China is cast in the mold of an imperial despotism in which unity and order are projected by the principle of absolute subordination to the emperor in his role as carrier of Heaven's Mandate and in which lesser peoples were by definition subject to imperial tutelage, chastisement by punitive war, and to conquest when this was deemed necessary and possible. In the Confucian context, by contrast, the empire was experienced and administered as a family of nations on the analogy of the classical Confucian model of the natural family in which "inferior" peoples had assigned roles. Yet, and as Arthur Waley explains, here, too, the emphasis is on the duty to punish badly ruled states or to chastise unruly barbarians on the periphery of the Middle Kingdom.[38] For just as the principle of filial piety could rightfully be enforced by the killing or mutilation of offspring who resisted paternal guidance, so might the art of persuasion in the community of unequal societies be supplemented by the rod of war. It goes without saying in these circumstances that the concept of the "righteous war" often served as a moral cloak for open acts of aggression, and these usually occurred after atrocity stories had been spread concerning the society singled out for punishment.

The steady coexistence or interpenetration of these two schools of thought has several aspects that are directly relevant for a discussion of "continuity" in Chinese modes of managing low-intensity conflicts and waging political warfare. Quite apart from the obvious fact that the latter can raise no serious political and moral problems if war in its general sense is a cultural given, the following characteristics seem noteworthy:

One is to the effect that all Chinese regimes, including the present, have explicitly accepted history as a source of statecraft—a disposition that diverges significantly from the ahistorical bent of the Soviet mind even as it has a tenuous affinity with the history consciousness of the Venetians. However, the two Communist regimes are at one in their commitment to control human understanding of the past and put historiography in the service of strictly ideological purposes. Indeed Mao Tse-tung had an advantage over his Russian counterparts when he silenced millions of thinkers after the "Hundred Flowers Period" and during the "Cultural Revolution" because he could legitimize his totalitarian programs by referring to those of China's first unifier, the Emperor Shih Huang Ti. Further, he could remind his subjects that these policies had been conceived as the logical last step in unification (Derk Bodde's phrasing) by the emperor's Legalist advisers, and that they had also served as models for numerous other "cultural revolutions" in pre-Maoist, dynastic China.

The second—but related—theme that deserves attention in this examination of continuity because it too supplies essential premises for successful political warfare relates to the Chinese stress on ideas and on ways of manipulating human minds.

This is well illustrated by Mao Tse-tung's determination "to examine further the whole course of the controversy between Confucianist and Legalist Schools" so as to bring it into a dialectically satisfying relationship to the ideas promulgated by Engels, Lenin, and himself. As his writings indicate in no uncertain terms, he concluded that "we affirm the progressive character of the Legalist school and criticize the reactionary character of the Confucian school in Chinese history for the purpose of giving . . . history its proper place as a science."[39] In other words, the freedom to falsify and "disinform" in the service of power politics was taken for granted here as in early czarist and Soviet Russia. However, this charge should be mitigated in the case of China by remembering that Western interpreters of Chinese history have gone to unjustified lengths presenting the pre-Maoist realm as an exemplary Confucian state. We should have known that China never was just that. For as Kung-chuan Hsiao has explained it in an essay[40] on the interpenetration of Confucianism and Legalism, imperial China began as a Legalist state. In the periods during which China was officially a Confucian state, Confucianism served largely as a useful supplement to autocratic Legalist practices. Even emperors who sincerely subscribed to Confucianism did so selectively and thus came close to being Legalist in practice.

Also, and as Jean Escarra tells it convincingly in his pioneering study of Chinese law, Chinese governments returned deliberately to their Legalist/Realist wisdom whenever they were in trouble or felt threatened by foreign influences, as, for example, between the mid-nineteenth and early twentieth centuries, when they felt impelled to accommodate Western concepts of law and government.[41] In respect specifically of the law of nations it is significant that the Chinese officially "received" Martin's translation of Wheaton's text on the subject. However, they provided it with an interesting foreword announcing that the practices and propositions set out in the work would not be followed by China, but that the book might nonetheless serve as a useful aid to Peking in planning "border defense," e.g., as a manual on how to deal with Western barbarians.

In short, it was as obvious in the nineteenth century as it had been in the seventeenth, when most of the "red headed" barbarians were induced to relinquish their own commitments to the principles of state sovereignty and equality and to comply instead with the requirements of the Chinese tribute system, that China would not compromise the integrity of its basic norms and institutions. Further, each of these episodes suggested that European and Chinese concepts of statecraft could not be reconciled persuasively without letting the cause of "continuity" go by default.

China's subsequent conversion to Marxism-Leninism stands in marked contrast to these earlier experiences in political and intellectual history. It has had the effect in this writer's view of canceling the integrity of China as a civilization, but it did assure continuity, albeit in a new key, because Marxism-Leninism was Sinified effectively in terms of Legalism.

(2) THE CHINESE ART OF WAR. As readers of Mao Tse-tung's works know well, this transposition is anchored in Realist theories of military and political warfare. It draws on well-known historical episodes illustrative of ingenuity and failure in war and diplomacy as well as on traditional novels such as the *Romance of the Three Kingdoms* (thirteenth century) that are replete with tales of intrigues, ruses, and deceptions.[42] And it communicates the Leninist wisdom thus distilled in the prose of traditional lore, which includes the apt use of traditional allegories, metaphors, and aphorisms. Many of the latter, again, are borrowed from the vocabulary of Chinese boxing, and many more from that of Wei-ch'i, the ancient Chinese game of strategy.

The traditional Chinese philosophy of the Legalist School has consistently maintained that it is necessary to wage indirect as well as direct warfare if the country and the people are to be in shape. The key witness on these matters of statecraft is Sun Tzu (fourth century B.C.), whose testimony is embodied in the treatise *The Art of War*.[43] This classic work contains numerous intricately reasoned guidelines for military and political warfare, among them the following.

All warfare is based on deception. (Chapters 1: 17; 5: 22; 7: 12)

Thus, those skilled at making the enemy move do so by creating a situation to which he must conform. (5: 20)

He who knows the art of the direct and indirect approach will be victorious. (7: 16)

Of all those in the army close to the commander none is more intimate than the secret agent; of all rewards none more liberal than those given to secret agents; of all matters none is more confidential than those relating to secret operations. Take precautions against the spy having been turned around. (13: 5, 12, 23)

But, and as noted earlier in this volume, the core of the work is no doubt Chapter 3, "Offensive Strategy," which ends with the following general maxims:

> When you are ignorant of the enemy but know yourself, your chances of winning or losing are equal.

> If ignorant both of your enemy and of yourself, you are certain in every battle to be in peril.

> Therefore I say: Know the enemy and know yourself; in a hundred battles you will never be in peril.

Only double knowing of this kind can assure successful strategic deception on the interlocking planes of psychological, intellectual, political, and military operations, and therewith maximum victory at less expense than is incurred in all-out total military war. As Scott A. Boorman reminds us, attack by stratagem is not merely outwitting an enemy—whether in internal or external statecraft—but attempting to break his will without fighting; to manipulate his view of the world to the point where he does not fight at all—in short, to know the "indirect" approach.[44] And this, of course, includes the varieties of unconventional warfare, cold war, covert war, low-intensity operations, and so forth with which the United States has not come to terms in our times.

As mentioned in an earlier essay, the Chinese idea of war has found eloquent expression in Wei-ch'i. Quite unlike the Occidental game of chess, Wei-ch'i involves a complex set of well-coordinated attempts to extend control slowly over dispersed territory. The basic strategy here is encirclement and counterencirclement—all aimed at setting up spheres of influence within enemy territory in order to undermine the opponent gradually by attacks from within. The similarity between this pastime and Maoist guerrilla warfare is quite obvious: the aim in both, as in *The Art of War,* is to "enclose" or "form" territory, in the psychological as well as the geographic sense.[45]

(3) DIPLOMACY AND INTELLIGENCE IN CHINESE STATECRAFT. Traditional China could expand and sustain itself in ever-changing circumstances because successive dynasties knew how to apply the precepts of direct and indirect warfare. In fact, these were operational already in the long Period of the Warring States. Contemporary accounts thus tell us how to create false impressions, use divination as a ploy in psychological warfare, and exploit the vanity of opponents. We also learn that trusted defectors served as intelligence collectors, that alliances in the enemy camp were skillfully disrupted, and that states were neutralized. In one significant episode an aggressive large state gets at its real opponent by striking at the most accessible satellite of that opponent.[46]

As these "times of trouble" drew to a close, and as the Chinese heartland moved southward, dependence on semi-barbarian or barbarian border peoples increased because China proper—whatever its geographic or demographic configuration—simply could not cope with its numerous external adversaries and with endemic internal disorders while at the same time engaging in expansion and consolidating conquests. The cause of a single unified Chinese empire thus remained embattled in early Han times, mainly because of incessant pressures by the Hsiung-nu tribes. The record of battles won and lost during the seesaw relationship with this inner Asian confederation of peoples shows that Emperor Wu-ti (141–87 B.C.) and his administration knew well, already in this early, historically significant era, how to deploy a variety of "direct" and "indirect" policies and tactics.

When efforts to bolster defenses by the establishment of new commanderies, watchtowers, or fortifications outside Chinese frontiers proved ineffective, China was often forced to "purchase" security by other means, as Loewe illustrates in the following passage:

> When weak, Han had to submit to the demands of the other party and to purchase peace at the price of valuables. When strong, Han was ready not only to launch large-scale campaigns but also to take other violent measures, for instance, the butchery of the population of Lun-t'ai (ca. 100 B.C.) or the instigation of plots to murder or replace the kings of the oasis communities.[47]

Moves in the diplomatic game included the demand for the presence of hostages, or the agreement to send an imperial princess to wed a local leader, as, for example, in 110 B.C. when that was expedient for the establishment of close relations with a strategically placed tribe. The reverse had to be arranged, however, after a Hsiung-nu victory when the Chinese representative received a Hsiung-nu wife, only to be put to death later as a sacrifice to the gods worshiped by that society. Quite a few of these matrimonial alliances also served the purpose of assuring vital communications, especially in later decades when Han was attempting to coordinate its policies along the Silk Roads where oasis communities controlled water supplies and were able to provide the services of local guides. To separate potential enemies and states that would support the Hsiung-nu was a natural goal in these far-flung operations, and it was approximated not only by founding commanderies but also by wedding a princess to that king who could separate supporters of the Hsiung-nu.

Early precedents for tapping military manpower in non-Chinese societies were also set in this period. Foreigners served Han even as senior military leaders, among them one of the Hsiung-nu kings who then fought against his own people. But the best-known example, Loewe notes (p. 89), is that of a son of a Hsiung-nu king who had been taken into the service of the Han palace as a groom and eventually rose to be a member of a triumvirate that ruled the empire. Also, Han forces occasionally included volunteers. One force thus seems to have been drawn from the states of the Western regions and to have been commanded by a former Hsiung-nu king.

(4) COMPARISON WITH THE WEST. The essential features of statecraft as recorded in the early centuries of China's existence were to remain intact in the ensuing millennia. A comparison with those that we in the West identify with foreign policy or international order yields the following characteristic traits:

Peace and war were not neatly distinguished. The Chinese did not either "declare" war or proclaim martial law, and international relations were not conceptualized as relations between equal states. In short, nothing on the order of the Occidental law of nations was developed in the Sinocentric universe. "Enemy forces were regarded in the first instance not as those of a rival state that existed on equal terms with the Chinese empire but as those of a leader, community, or confederacy that was bent on injuring China's integrity, its persons or crops, its cities or stores."[48] In fact, there was no conceptual distinction between non-Chinese malefactors and the bandits or robbers who might disturb law and order in the inner provinces of China. Further, and as mentioned earlier, the twin notions of China as a superior sphere or civilization that was floating rather than territorially fixed, and as a family of nations in which members had assigned roles and could be either punished or cajoled as expediency dictated, required and sanctioned freedom in the choice of "indirect" means toward furthering Chinese interests. As Fairbank notes in a survey of sixteenth-century (A.D.) imperial responses to the offensive actions of Japanese marauders, the repertoire of the Chinese commander included offers of pardon, patronizing friendship, subornation of colleagues, poisoned wine, moral principles, false intelligence, procrastination, beautiful women, solemn and fair promises, bribery, banquets, threats, intimidation, lies, assassination, and deployment of troops to undo his opponents. "It is a masterpiece of dirty work, far beyond the unsophisticated capacity of a mere military man, and shows why warfare in this particular Chinese style deserves more serious study."[49]

These understandings of "war" and "peace" explain why warfare was usually attended by what would be called "excessive violence" in the West, and why no orderly system of diplomatic representation evolved. Envoys were sent to "barbarians," it is true, but their missions consisted in scouting, observing, and spying, and their safety was nowhere assured.[50] It goes without saying that China viewed envoys from barbarian lands—and these included, of course, those from Europe—as hostile agents bent on ferreting out Chinese secrets. From Han times to the end of the nineteenth century they were strictly controlled. For example, neither Marco Polo nor the Franciscan friars and the Jesuits who advised the Emperor in the late seventeenth and early eighteenth centuries and helped him negotiate with the Russian "barbarians" were allowed to leave the narrow field of imperial surveillance.[51]

(5) BARBARIANS AND SURROGATES IN THE CHINESE SYSTEM. Chinese diplomacy, then, was rendered in terms of political warfare, an aspect of statecraft that was greatly enhanced by the Chinese habit of taking hostages. This tradition which originated in Legalist theory during Ch'in times, evolved into standard practice during later dynasties, including those identified with the Mongols. What is so interesting about the institution is that it applied to "internal" as well as "external" affairs of state. We thus find that not only were sons of foreign rulers educated at the imperial court, but also sons of chief ministers, generals, and governors. For the latter were as much under suspicion as the "foreign" barbarians, and their loyalty, too, had to be assured. This device, known as "internal hostage," is an emanation of the principle of "joint security" that assured compliance and obedience in Ch'in times as it does in Communist China today. Whether we recall the Maoist use of Tibet's Panchen Lama or that of Prince Sihanouk of Cambodia, the continuity marking two thousand years of history is impressive indeed.[52]

As Immanuel C. Y. Hsu reminds us, "Historically, China never had a positive long-term policy toward the barbarians, except the vague principle of playing them off against one another known as *i-i chih-i.*"[53] Watchfulness and ad hoc management were thus standing Chinese dispositions, and these were activated by the creation of a belt of tributary "states" that was consistently viewed as merely the outer fringe of the Middle Kingdom. All of the outlying societies together constituted the emperor's international family. Being inferior and barbarian by definition, each of them was obligated to pay tribute by undertaking periodic missions to the imperial court and accepting those sent out by the latter. For as the recalcitrant Japanese were told in Ming times toward the end of the fourteenth-century:

"It is the common rule of propriety that barbarians should respect the Middle Kingdom. One principle in both ancient and modern times has been for the small to serve the great. . . ."

When hostilities erupted, whether on the frontiers or in the interior, the government traditionally considered two possible responses: a straightforward military solution, called "extermination" (*chiao* or *mieh*); or an indirect politico-economic solution, called "pacification" (*chao-an, chao-fu*—suggesting "summoning and appeasing"), supported by real, but muted, threats of military action.[54] For example, Annam—the core of what became North Vietnam—was duly Sinified, even incorporated in All-Under-Heaven for some centuries. But in others it was in a state of rebellion, deserving chastisement. This occurred when the founder of the Sui dynasty terminated a revolt that had been going on since 541 by extraordinary military means, as well as in the Ming era (early fifteenth century) when Peking re-established direct rule over Annam with the help of Laotian tribes. Another case in point is Korea. The province of which it was a part in Sui times was invaded four times between 598 and 614, but each expedition met with disaster.[55] Yet Korea seems to have held the Middle Kingdom in genuine respect as a culturally superior "Father" nation. This view is borne out by the fact that the Koreans resisted Sinification when it was administered by "barbarians" (the Mongol conquerors), but again acquiesced when a purely Chinese dynasty (the Ming) regained the throne.

The tribute system, in conjunction with the powerful concept of membership in a culturally superior "imperial family" (of which it was, of course, an integral part), facilitated penetration and observation. Also, it provided the auspices under which imperial administrators of barbarians' affairs could select and control the operatives best suited to guide independent peoples into functions supportive of the imperial cause. Such agents might come from the ranks of the bureaucracy, the army, or the imperial household, but they were also frequently chosen from one barbarian nation for the purpose of subverting or fighting another inferior people. A similar situation existed in strictly military affairs: mercenaries as well as surrogates were carefully selected with an eye to exploiting interbarbarian relations.

Buddhist Tibet posed special challenges in each of these respects. All dynasties beginning with the Han had intricate designs for controlling this geopolitically vital region, or—if the maximum goal should prove unattainable as it usually did—to have Tibet function as China's agent. The Dalai Lama's good offices were thus sought in support of Chinese policies and security interests among Buddhist tribes in Central Asia. Indeed, Buddhism itself appealed to Chinese strategists as a "surrogate" system of ideas in 1570 when a shrewd adviser told the Ming emperor that this "barbarian" religion should be spread deliberately among the troublesome Mongols in the north in the hope of "pacifying" their aggressive instincts.

Neither of these imperialist designs had worked well either in relations with the Japanese and the Mongols or—from the eighteenth century onward—with the Europeans. In regard to Buddhist Japan, which was at times officially recognized as a hedge-guarding satellite and as an inferior, it needs to be kept in mind that *The Art of War* had been steadily used as a text for instructing Japanese warriors since before A.D. 760, and that regular contacts had been maintained with the fully Sinicized Korean kingdom of Paechke. Griffith tells us on the authority of numerous records that the Chinese martial classics never ceased influencing Japanese governments. Commenting on the sixteenth-century history of Japan, he refers to four famous warriors whose martial exploits were due in no small measure to their mastery of these classics.[56] One of them, described as a Shogun whose "militarism was diplomatic" and whose "diplomacy was militaristic," is said to have learned by experience that the arts of war and those of peace were the two sides of the coin of statecraft.

The Mongols presented different problems mainly because Inner Asia simply could not be territorially absorbed into the Chinese empire until very near the latter's end when the Manchu administration chose the military solution.[57] By that time the nomad problem had persisted for more than two thousand years, since at least the fourth century B.C., when the Hsiung-nu tribes on the border of North China started to raid the settled farmlands to the south. During the period from about the fourth to the fourteenth centuries Mongols conquered Persia, South Russia, and China—with the Sung empire, though closest at hand, holding out the longest. By 1279 it, too, fell completely under the domination of Mongol tribesmen, and it was clear that the nomads could not be destroyed but had to be lived with. This explains why nomads usually served as components of Chinese border forces, and why successive dynasties viewed inner Asia as a constituent sector of the Chinese military scene. In these complex circumstances it is not surprising that Sino-Mongol syncretisms evolved naturally. Imperial institutions, including direct and indirect modes of inducing compliance with ceremonial acknowledgments of China's superiority, were adjusted to Mongol traditions, and Mongol leaders, in turn, accepted responsibilities toward the Chinese state.[58]

The process of Sino-barbarian cooperation reached its apogee under the Ch'ing dynasty (1644–1912). However, the latter's tribute system was as severely tested in relations with Russia and the Occident as the Western States System proved to be in the Sinocentric universe. All Western states and trading companies that sought to open East Asia to commercial relations viewed China as an incipient nation-state. But this identification was not accepted by the Chinese, who insisted on perceiving the Portuguese, the Dutch, and Russians, and the English—the first "red-haired barbarians" they encountered—as yet another flock of tributaries. And indeed, these Europeans (with the exception of the English at a somewhat later date) accepted the status assigned them as well as the ritual of the kowtow that went with it. The Netherlands, the most active of the Western countries to participate in the Ch'ing tribute system, were perhaps also the most clear-sighted in recognizing already in the seventeenth century that the values and worldviews here in contention were too contrasting to allow for easy compromise: on the Ch'ing side, the strict bureaucratic control of foreign contacts and proper ritual so as to preserve order and culture in the empire; on their own side the concept of a community of equal states adhering to a common code of intercourse that was becoming increasingly formalized in international law.

A breakthrough in the matter of treaty making occurred in relations with the Russians when Peking, advised by resident Jesuits and the Dutch ambassador as intermediaries, engaged in negotiations with these red-haired barbarians. The Peace Treaty of Nerchinsk, which was eventually concluded in 1689, purported to settle the boundary question and other controversial issues "forever." However, neither this pact nor subsequent Sino-Russian accords effected a narrowing of discords on fundamental matters. And the same was to be true in the nineteenth century of the so-called unequal treaties with Western European states under the terms of which China committed itself to accede to the Western principle of "the equality of states" and allow foreign envoys to visit the capital without having to perform kowtow. Yet signing the treaties did not mean that the Chinese had in any way changed their basic view of the world. Rather, they viewed each treaty as a necessary but temporary evil that had to be endured in order to keep the Western barbarians within bounds until China was again strong enough to drive the foreign devils out, cease pretending that it was a nation-state, and resume its appointed role in the world.

(6) CONTINUITY OR CHANGE. Most of traditional China's basic dispositions to foreign relations could be, and were, reactivated by the Maoist revolution because they were supportive of the Leninist commitment to power, conflict, and war even though they lack the latter's totalitarian dimension. This was well-illustrated already in the early 1950s when Mao Tse-tung prepared his design for the total subjugation of Tibet by "encircling" and "neutralizing" Jawaharlal Nehru and his India. The instruments deployed in this typically Legalist psychological operation were Buddhism and international law—two systems of ideas that carried no substantive validity for dedicated Asian Marxist-Leninists.

A Western-type agreement on trade with Tibet was nonetheless concluded in April 1954, and explicit obeisance was pledged in its preamble to the *panca sila,* five precepts of interpersonal Buddhist ethics that have no relevance to the political matters in issue. This maneuver in deceiving a somnolent Indian neighbor was promptly followed by mainland China's genocidal takeover of Tibet, the humiliation of India, and soon thereafter by the Sino-Indian "border war." However, and as in "earlier times," "elimination" worked in tandem with "pacification." Peking had set up a Chinese-Buddhist Association for the purpose of courting foreign Buddhists just before unleashing state terrorism onto Tibet. Soon after this success, it proceeded to rally Buddhists in a Pan-Buddhist Congress.[59] And similar low-intensity operations were staged some years later in Sinicized Vietnam with a view to penetrating the Buddhist "apparatus": according to captured documents (September 1964), Communist cadres were ordered to join Buddhist organizations after severing party links—temporarily.

In short and by way of summation: China's conversion to Marxism-Leninism stands in marked contrast to its earlier experiences in political and intellectual history. It has had the effect, in this writer's view, of canceling the integrity of China as a civilization, but it did assure continuity, albeit in a new key, because Marxism-Leninism was Sinicized effectively in terms of Legalism. "Scratch a Mao and you find one of the better-known traditional Ch'in despots" is thus, in this context, a justifiable conclusion.

NOTES

1. Compare Richard Shultz, "Low Intensity Conflict," in *Mandate for Leadership II,* Stuart M. Butler, Michael Sanera, and W. Bruce Weinrod, eds. (Washington, D.C.: Heritage Foundation, 1984), p. 264, to the effect that LIC "includes guerrilla war, revolution, insurgency, civil war, and coup d'état. Terrorism, which often is targeted as a separate subject, also can be considered as a type of low intensity warfare."
2. See nineteen basic "rules" in *Army Field Manual, Ranger Training and Operation* (1756). I am indebted to Senator Barry Goldwater for this reference.
3. William Safire, *Safire's Political Directionary* (New York: Ballantine Books, 1978).
4. For further comments on these themes see *infra,* this essay. The Safire definition refers to the Jewish Zealots, the Shi'ite Assassins, and the Indian Thugs as three sects whose resort to terrorism has become synonymous with "violence or irrationality." The suggestion here is that terrorism exists when it is "irregular," that is, not consonant with established custom. See David C. Rapoport, "Fear and Trembling: Terrorism in Three Religious Traditions," *American Political Science Review,* Vol. 78 (1984), pp. 658–77 for a lucid comparison of these three sects.
5. Here I find myself in agreement with Aleksandr Solzhenitsyn when he writes: "Communism is a force such as the world has never known. It is anti-human and even metaphysical: its very defects, absurdities, and failures tend to strengthen it the more." See "Three Key Movements in Modern Japanese History" (*National Review,* December 9, 1983); and, with Alain Besançon, *The Rise of the Gulag: Intellectual Origins of Leninism,* trans. Sarah Matthews (New York: Seabury Press, 1981), who write that it is ideology, namely Leninism, that make the difference between the present Gulag state and classic dictatorships or bureaucratic despotisms.
6. Frantisek Silnitzky, *et al.,* eds., *Communism and Eastern Europe* (New York: Karz Publishers, 1979), pp. 25–32.
7. From Fox Butterfield, *China Alive in the Bitter Sea* (New York: Times Books, 1982), p. 405.
8. The well-coordinated assassinations and terrorist policies recently identified with Communist action groups in France, Germany, Italy, Belgium, Portugal, and Greece persuaded Italy's interior minister that "terrorism is no longer guerrilla fighting. This is war, fought in another way." See *Wall Street Journal,* February 4, 1985, p. 27. Commenting on the problem of estimating enemy strength during the Vietnam War, which was "part conventional, part terrorist, part psychological and part political," Paul Nitze noted that he was as uncertain in 1967 as he was in 1984 what importance to attach to forces "that could be one thing one day" and "the next day be something else" (see *New York Times,* December 5, 1984, for excerpts from testimony in General William C. Westmoreland's libel suit against CBS).
9. Michael S. Radu, "Terror, Terrorism, and Insurgency in Latin America," *ORBIS,* Vol. 28, no. 1 (Spring 1984), pp. 31ff., identified the Shining Path as "the most brutal of all contemporary Latin American groups." Founded in the 1960s by Peruvian philosopher-teacher Abimael Guzman Reynoso Sendero who proclaimed himself the "Fourth Sword of Marxism" (the others being Marx, Lenin, and Mao), the Shining Path has a large and fanatical following among students. All accept the founder's message, which combines Mao's personality myth with the God-Sun adoration for the Inca rulers, the promise of a utopia modeled after the Inca state with the projection of himself as the maximum leader worthy of adoration. As totalitarians who admit that human life is irrelevant since only ideology

counts, members of the group also proclaimed it their right to speak and act in the name of the non–Spanish-speaking Indians of the Peruvian highlands. If the latter did not understand or accept Sendero's aims (which seems to have been generally the case), punishment or death could follow.

10. For one of the best evocations of Cambodia's past, see Christopher Pym, *The Ancient Civilization of Angkor* (New York: Mentor Books, 1968).

11. See preceding and subsequent essays on the tangle of these issues; also Bozeman, "The Impact of Terrorism on American Conceptions of War, Law, and Political Intelligence" (unpublished paper).

12. See Bozeman, *Politics and Culture in International History,* Chapter 9, "The Byzantine Realm," pp. 298–356, and authorities there cited for an examination of Byzantine history and statecraft.

13. See *ibid.,* p. 321, note 59, for the suggestion that the Fourth Crusade might have been directed against Egypt and not against Constantinople had the Eastern Empire maintained a fleet in being. See also *infra* this paper for equivalent Chinese principles.

14. M. Gelzer, *Studien zur Byzantinischen Verwaltung Egyptens* (1909), as quoted in Norman H. Baynes, *The Byzantine Empire* (London: William & Norgate, 1925), pp. 130–31.

15. The parallel to Soviet diplomatic techniques is obvious.

16. In order to conciliate the Bulgarians when they were particularly threatening, the czar was even given permission to call himself "Basileus."

17. Cf. this political arrangement with the organization of China's imperial orbit.

18. See J. B. Bury, "Roman Empire, Later," in *Encyclopaedia Britannica* (1944), p. 444.

19. Their qualifications were first enumerated in the fifth century during the reign of Theodoric, the Ostrogothic king of Rome who had been imbued with Byzantinism while a hostage at the imperial court in Constantinople. See Bozeman, *Politics and Culture in International History,* pp. 329f., for particulars. It must be noted that Byzantium did not maintain permanent embassies abroad.

20. For these notations see S. Bakhrouchine, A. Ephimov, E. Kosminski, A. Narotchnitski, V. Serguiev, S. Skazkine, V. Khvostov, and E. Tarlé, *Histoire de la Diplomatie,* Vol. 1 (Paris: M. Potiemkine 1947), pp. 86ff., hereafter cited as Tarlé, *Histoire.* The fact that the authors are Soviet historians is relevant for comparative studies of the Byzantine and Soviet empires.

21. For a poignant record of relations between the two Romes and the conflict's weakening effect on Christendom's relations with Islam see *Memoirs of a Renaissance Pope: The Commentaries of Pius II, an Abridgment;* trans. Florence A. Gragg, ed. Leona C. Gabel (New York, 1962).

22. For a discussion of this relationship see Bozeman, *Politics and Culture in International History,* pp. 340–56, "The Continuance of the Byzantine Tradition in Diplomacy: The Russian Realm," and authorities there cited.

23. See *ibid.,* pp. 351–54.

24. *Ibid.,* pp. 354–55, for excerpts of the text.

25. For this conclusion see Nicholas Berdyaev, *The Russian Idea* (New York, 1948), p. 9.

26. See for example A. A. Vasiliev, *History of the Byzantine Empire, 324–1453,* English edition, revised (Madison, Wis., 1952), pp. 32ff., for a review of Russian historical opinion; V. O. Kluchevsky, *A History of Russia,* tr. C. J. Hogarth, 3 vols. (London and New York, 1911–12), particularly Vol. I, p. 84, for comments on the cultural significance of Byzantine tutelage over the evolution of Kievan law. Nicholas Berdyaev, *The Origins of Russian Communism,* (London, 1937) and *The Russian Idea, op. cit.,* as well as Russian authorities cited in Bozeman, *op. cit.,* p. 342. See also James A. Duran, Jr., "Russian Nationalism in the Cultural Policy of Catherine the Great" (unpublished manuscript), which concludes: "To the Empress and contemporary intellectuals, the recovery of the pre-Petrine Russia was a mission executed in defense of the Fatherland. To them, Kiev Rus was a key element in establishing an antiquity for Russia comparable to that of Western European states" (p. 8).

27. M. V. Levchenko, *History of Byzantium* (Moscow and Leningrad, 1940), p. 4.

28. R. Vipper, *Ivan Grozny* (Moscow, 1947), p. 169. See also Tarlé, *Histoire,* pp. 100ff.

29. *Op. cit.*, Vol. I, p. 285.

30. See Part I of this essay.

31. I have developed some of the ideas here in play in "Decline of the West? Spengler Reconsidered," *Virginia Quarterly Review*, Vol. 59, no. 2 (Spring 1983), pp. 199ff.; and in "Do Educational and Cultural Exchanges Have Political Relevance?" in *International Educational and Cultural Exchange*, Vol. V, no. 2 (Fall 1969), pp. 7–21.

32. See earlier references in this essay and Bozeman, *Politics and Culture in International History*, pp. 302ff., for an account of Constantinople's treatment of Bishop Liutprandt, who came to the rival Christian capital in the mid-tenth century as a special envoy of Otto the Great, charged with negotiating a marriage of Otto's son to the Byzantine princess Theophano. Indications are not missing in the 1980s that the legacy of Byzantium's Roman law has remained intact while buried underground, and that it—not unlike Greek Orthodox Christianity—might well be recovered and revitalized in some post-Leninist times to come, specifically in Russia proper and the Ukraine. See *supra*, Introduction.

33. See *supra*, this essay. It is noteworthy that Ethiopia was Christianized in the fourth century A.D., several centuries before the advent of Islam, and that the missionary effort issued directly from Egypt, then part of Eastern Christian Rome.

34. Bulgaria is an important exception because, like Serbia and Russia, it belongs to the Slavic ethnicities that were Christianized by Constantinople and did not participate actively in the Renaissance. Poles, Czechs, Slovaks, Croats, Hungarians, Lithuanians, Letts, and Estonians, by contrast, were Christianized by Rome and remained provinces of the culturally unified West until they were politically conquered by the Soviet Union. This historically most significant "divide" in the Eurasian space—which has been steadily overlooked by U.S. statecraft and intelligence (see *supra*, Introduction)—is the major cause of many so-called ethnic conflicts, as, for example, those marking relations between Serbs and Croats in modern Yugoslavia.

35. See Francis X. Maier, "Kingdoms of Death: A Reporter's African Journal," in *This World*, no. 8 (Spring/Summer 1984), pp. 27–46.

36. See *supra*, this essay and "Covert Action and Foreign Policy in World Politics" and "Statecraft and Intelligence in the Non-Western World" in the present volume.

37. See Edward L. Dryer, "Military Continuities: The PLA and Imperial China," Chapter 1 in William W. Whitson, ed., *The Military and Political Power in China in the 1970s* (New York: Praeger, 1972), p. 15; see also "War and the Clash of Ideas" in this volume.

38. *Three Ways of Thought in Ancient China* (London: Allen & Unwin, 1939), p. 248; also pp. 141, 175.

39. See "On New Democracy," *Selected Works* (English ed.), Vol. II (Peking, 1967), p. 381.

40. See King-chuan Hsiao, "Legalism and Autocracy in Traditional China," in Li Yu-Ning, ed., *Shang Yang's Reforms and State Control in China* (White Plains, N.Y., 1977), pp. 125ff.

41. See *Le Droit Chinois* (Paris: Libr. du Recueil Sirey, 1936) pp. 69ff., 106ff. On this issue see also Bozeman, "On the Relevance of Hugo Grotius and *De Jure Belli ac Pacis* for Our Times," *Grotiana*, Vol. I, no. 1 (1980), pp. 65–124; and "Human Rights and National Security," *Yale Journal of World Public Order*, Vol. 9, no. 1 (Fall 1982), pp. 40–77.

42. See Edward L. Dryer, "Military Continuities: The PLA and Imperial China," in Whitson, ed., *op. cit.*, pp. 3–24, for a brief survey of special themes.

43. Trans. and ed. by Samuel B. Griffith (New York: Oxford University Press, 1963). See the editor's remarks on the diffusion of the work and the relation between Sun Tzu and Mao Tse-tung, pp. 45ff., and Appendix III. For an American comment on these two issues see Vernon A. Walters, *Silent Missions* (Doubleday, 1978), p. 546. Reporting on his meetings with the Chinese ambassador to France in January 1971, when President Nixon's trip to China was being prepared, Walters writes: "We then discussed the famous Chinese writer on the art of war, Sun Tzu, and the Ambassador told me that his writings were required reading in all Chinese military schools." Walters summarizes *The Art of War* on pp. 614ff.

44. See his essay on "Deception in Chinese Strategy: Some Theoretical Notes on the Sun-Tzu and Game Theory," in William W. Whitson, ed., *The Military and Political Power in China*

(New York: Praeger, 1972), Chapter 16, pp. 313–37. Mao Tse-tung's works are replete with citations or paraphrases of *The Art of War*. However, as noted earlier in this book, it is significant for studies of "continuity" in Chinese thought to recall that Sun Tzu—contrary to Mao Tse-tung—does not believe either in annihilating enemy states and armies, or in *protracted* military warfare. See *supra*, "War and the Clash of Ideas."

45. For an interpretation of the game and its relevance in Chinese politics see Scott A. Boorman, *The Protracted Game: A Wei-ch'i Interpretation of Maoist Revolutionary Strategy* (New York: Oxford University Press, 1969). See pp. 6f. and 208, note 8, for the suggestion that Sun Tzu's theories bear a distinct similarity to Wei-ch'i. His thesis is significant: Chinese Communist policies and the game are products of the same strategic tradition— one without parallel either in Occidental military tradition or in the game of chess. He views Wei-ch'i as an important, if little recognized, model of the Maoist system of insurgency.

46. See Frank A. Kiernan, Jr., "Phases and Modes of Combat in Early China," in Frank A. Kiernan, Jr., and John K. Fairbank, eds., *Chinese Ways in Warfare* (Cambridge, Mass.: Harvard University Press, 1974), pp. 37–66.

47. Much of the following information is based on Michael Loewe, "The Campaigns of Han Wu-ti," in Kiernan and Fairbank, eds., *op. cit.*, pp. 67–110; see in particular p. 78.

48. Michael Loewe, *loc. cit.*, p. 102.

49. John K. Fairbank, "Introduction: Varieties of the Chinese Military Experience" in Kiernan and Fairbank, eds., *op. cit.*, pp. 1–26, see especially p. 23. For in-depth studies of these tactics see Charles O. Hucker, "Hu Tsung-hsien's Campaign Against Hsu Hai, 1556," *ibid.*, pp. 273–307; and Herbert Franke, "Siege and Defense of Towns in Medieval China," *ibid.*, pp. 151–202.

50. On the biography of one Han envoy see Burton Watson, trans., *Courtier and Commoner in Ancient China* (New York: Columbia University Press, 1974), in particular pp. 34ff.

51. See Jonathan Spence, *Emperor of China: Self-Portrait of K'ang-hsi* (New York, 1974), p. 81, and *The Memory Palace of Matteo Ricci* (New York: Viking, 1984), for much valuable information. Also see Essay 6.

52. See Lien-sheng Yang, "Hostages in Chinese History," in *Studies in Chinese Institutional History,* Harvard-Yenching Institute Studies, Vol. XX (1963). See p. 45 to the effect that "taking hostages was a standard practice of the Han Dynasty for controlling small barbarian states," and p. 43 on the exchange of hostages between Chou and Cheng recorded in the *Tso chuan* and the sending of Korean hostages to the Manchu rulers between 1637 and 1645. See also Loewe, *loc. cit.*, p. 102, to the effect that Han generals were rewarded for their services by their success in capturing important personages, such as kings, members of royal families, or other leaders.

53. *China's Entrance into the Family of Nations: The Diplomatic Phase 1858–1880* (Cambridge, Mass.: Harvard University Press, 1960), p. 115. See also Essay 1 in this volume.

54. Charles O. Hucker, *loc. cit.*, p. 274.

55. See L. Carrington Goodrich, *A Short History of the Chinese People* (New York: Harper, 1951), pp. 11–113; and Melvin Frederic Nelson, *Korea and the Old Order in Eastern Asia* (Baton Rouge, La., 1945).

56. See Samuel B. Griffith, *op. cit.*, Appendix II, pp. 172–73. See also Essays 1, 2, and 6 in this volume.

57. John K. Fairbank, "Varieties of the Chinese Military Experience," in Kiernan and Fairbank, eds., *op. cit.*, p. 12.

58. See Frederick W. Mote, "The T'u-mu Incident of 1449," in Kiernan and Fairbank, eds., *op. cit.*, pp. 243–72, particularly p. 244 on the rise of the Mongol nation.

59. For further comments on issues related to Tibet, see Bozeman, "India's Foreign Policy Today: Reflections Upon Its Sources," *World Politics,* Vol. X (January 1958). On the role of deception and terrorism in Chinese and Korean statecraft, see also Bozeman, "U.S. Intelligence and the Problem of Assessing Deception in Leninist and Non-Western Statecraft," and "The Impact of Terrorism on American Conceptions of War, Law, and Political Intelligence" (unpublished papers).

Statecraft and Intelligence in the Non-Western World

Reflections on American foreign policy and intelligence failures in the last decades lead to a variety of questions. This essay is grounded in an analysis of the well-documented record of erroneous assessments and policies in many areas of the world, specifically in Central America (beginning with Castro's advent in Cuba); Southeast and Northeast Asia; Central Asia (notably Tibet and Afghanistan); the Middle East (including Israel); and black Africa.

Based on the assumptions, first, that foreign systems of statecraft and intelligence have to be identified and understood if our system is to be effective, and second, that American citizens must be fully aware of non-American approaches to statecraft if they are to render informed judgments on the merits or demerits of their own government's foreign policies, this essay concentrates on the following questions:

1. Can American foreign policy and intelligence failures be traced to our inability to understand foreign cultures and systems of statecraft?

2. Do non-Western concepts of statecraft and intelligence differ from Western systems, and if so in which respects?

3. What do the findings suggest in terms of needed research and education, especially in the context of comparative studies?

I

The task of understanding others is everywhere and on all levels of human relations experienced as a challenge. In our times this understanding is particularly complex on the level of world politics where each government must take the measure of hundreds, even thousands of other politically distinct organisms if its foreign policies are to be successful.

These standing problems in statecraft are aggravated in the United States by a bent of mind that shies away from identifying and assessing others on their own terms. The particular dispositions that account for this evasive approach are examined in several other essays in this book. Here they can be briefly summarized as follows.

(1) Modern Americans have come to believe that the norms and values encapsuled in their form of government and their ways of conducting foreign relations are the birthrights and open options for men everywhere. In accordance with this

This essay originally appeared in *Conflict,* Vol. 6, no. 1 (1985), and is printed with the permission of the publisher.

persuasion there simply can be no "others." It follows that societies still stuck with traditions of statecraft deviating from what we consider universally valid should be pushed to discard their defunct or erroneous heritage of beliefs so as to align themselves speedily with ours. In other words, today's educated, politically savvy Americans assert in rhetoric as well as action that all peoples are essentially alike and that culture is a nonconcept or nonreality when statecraft is an issue.

What is odd and ambiguous about all this is that Americans generally continue to be avid students of foreign religions, philosophies, ideologies, art styles, social institutions, and literary forms, and that they have no difficulty acknowledging each of these foreign springs and expressions of life as unique and therefore different from equivalent phenomena in the United States.

(2) This ambiguity in modern American thinking about "others" is confounded by a neglectful disposition toward the past and history. Generations of European and American scholars have gone out of their way to assemble and analyze the multifarious records of the world's cultures and political systems—and they cover millennia, not just centuries. One would think, therefore, that they would be prized as data banks for purposes of foreign intelligence. Yet they are definitely deemed irrelevant today, seemingly swept away by a fanatically ahistorical utopianism about the future.

Earlier in this century this used to find expression in doctrines of "progress" and "development," which held that, given the opportunity, the many others in the world would become like us. Knowledge that time perspectives in the thought worlds of Asian, African, and numerous Latin American societies accentuate the past rather than the future did not impede this American confidence. Our trust in futurism is even bolder now. A popular thesis has it that the past has no meaningful connection with the present and the future, and that it should therefore be overcome so as to make room for some unspecified newness. This simplistic cult is bound to have decidedly negative effects on U.S. statecraft at home and abroad if it is permitted to settle and spread. For not only would it sap the roots of national identity— "ours" as well as "theirs"—thus conducing to misrepresentation and misunderstanding in foreign relations; it would also undercut scholarship and therewith the kind of knowledge without which "intelligence" cannot even be fathomed.

(3) The third aspect in modern American approaches to other political systems and cultures—and it is closely related to the first two—is a pronounced tendency not to take ideas or concepts seriously as determinants of national identity but to treat them as mere functions of material forces. This attachment to one or the other gospel of economic determinism explains why we have been poor custodians of our own sustaining values—among them "liberty," "development," "law," "the independent state," and "peace"—and why we did not watch out when others— adversaries as well as friends—began to tamper with these strategically most important Western concepts.

Further, this weakness—and it is a seriously disabling weakness in statecraft— also explains why we are so slow and often so wrong in our appraisals of Marxist-Leninist norms, and why we fail to take account of the dramatic resurgence of non-Western, non-Communist ideas and belief systems.

(4) Other facts in the American mind-set that are apt to induce failure in intelligence and policy planning are an inadequately developed appreciation of the need to protect geographically vital space, a standing inclination to seek short-term pragmatic solutions, an inordinate suspicion of secrecy, and insistence on "openness" in the conduct of foreign relations.

Taken together these elements help explain why the United States was slow in the decisive post-Yalta decades to acknowledge and assess the following changes in our present world environments:

- that Westernization had run its course in the non-Western world, especially in administration, law, and the conduct of foreign affairs;
- that the West's power and influence was generally perceived as having declined;
- that the Marxist-Leninist power realm had expanded significantly and was therefore feared and respected in less powerful states of Asia, Europe, and Africa;
- that the United States had lost credibility as a superpower; and
- that de-Westernization has been a characteristic of thought and behavior in all non-Western societies for quite some time.

It should be admitted that these new realities were effectively screened from casual view by a United Nations organization that contains familiar Euro-American concepts in its constitutional charter. But again, it is hard to understand why it did not occur to us long ago that the majority within the UN membership was bound to consist of Communist and non-Western states whose systems of statecraft, different as they are from one another, stand in stark counterpoint to "the law" of the United Nations as this had been devised by the West in 1945. In this context, too, our foreign policy elites—whether in government, the media, or academe—did not choose to look for what is hidden under surfaces.

In short, "intelligence writ large" has been conspicuously stifled for quite some time, and this has meant that "intelligence lower case" could not even be expected to become fully operational anywhere. This, I think, is the intellectual and psychological malaise that accounts for the fact, cited by Paul H. Nitze among others, that strategic thinking has ceased to be conspicuous in the United States.

II

So much for that innate and ever-latent tendency *not* to differentiate between cultures and societies.

The answers to the second question—namely, whether and, if so, how non-Western cultures and systems of statecraft differ from others—begin as follows.

Comparative studies, first of a great variety of non-Western civilizations, and then of non-Western and Western civilizations, support the conclusion that non-Western cultures are in substantial accord on the following views of life, all of which diverge from those associated with the West, specifically the United States:

1. Time perspectives accentuate the past.

2. The accent in organizing life is decidedly on the group—not on the individual human being.

3. Mankind is not a meaningful concept. Rather, the "communal self" and the "communal other" are experienced as distinct entities. In fact, the concept of "the other" as an enemy is highly developed everywhere.

Taken together, these elements explain why "development" and "progress" are not traditional values either on the individual or the social level of earthly existence, and why change is generally resisted. In sum, they explain why the historical survival rate of Oriental and African cultures is decidedly higher than that of Occidental cultures—a finding that led Richard N. Frye to suggest that the latter may well be abnormal in international history whereas the former exemplify the norm.

As I suggested earlier, none of these culture-related traits have been or are being considered relevant in our policy and intelligence planning.

Further, and forgetting "culture" for the moment, it is possible to illustrate differences between Western and non-Western systems by focusing only on "the state" and on "war." Indeed, these two concepts deserve to be singled out as measures of comparison because they still supply the mainstays of what we continue to call "the international system," and because this system still comprises—officially at least—Western, non-Western, and Communist states.

We begin with *our* understanding of the two terms. The state's main attributes in Euro-American history, political science, and law are sovereignty, territoriality, and an organically close relationship to secular law. However, the present American insistence that states must have specific democratic or constitutional forms of government is decidedly an innovation that conflicts with the basic principle of respect for state sovereignty and domestic jurisdiction.

Next, within the nuclear, originally European States System all states are presumed equal. Relations between them are subject to a law of nations and a code of diplomacy that rest on the foundation of classical Roman and Christian principles of law and ethics. According to these shared understandings, war is recognized as a legitimate policy option for the sovereign state, provided that it is conducted lawfully for lawful ends. Also, we need to remember that war and peace are distinct, not interpenetrating conditions in Western thought and practice. This means that the law of war has always been different from the law of peace.

The main onslaught on this regional international system came with Marxism-Leninism toward the end of the nineteenth and in the early twentieth centuries. A thorough discussion either of this ideology and its ongoing thrust or of the Communist system of statecraft to which it gave rise is not within the purview of this study. Both have long been standing topics of intense research and analysis in the United States. However, the point needs to be stressed that it is not possible in our time to understand non-Western systems—those taken over by Communist regimes and those which remained free—as well as to isolate differences between Western and non-Western statecraft and avoid failure in policy and intelligence contexts if one does not have Marxist-Leninist ideology and Soviet statecraft and intelligence firmly in mind.

The following Communist, specifically Soviet, approaches to "the state" and to "war" must therefore not be overlooked as we deal with non-Western or half-Western societies.

Everyone probably agrees that Marxism-Leninism is a totalitarian combat doctrine that explicitly denies validity to the norms and institutions that together make up the West's civilization and political order. Everyone knows, too, that this ideology provides clear and well-publicized tactical guidelines on just how to discredit and disestablish Western norms of the state, the law, and the entire war-peace syndrome. Also, we are familiar with the factual and irreversible evidence that has been accumulating from 1918 onward. This is to the effect that scores of states throughout the world—among them many that had gained statehood under the aegis of the Wilsonian commitment to the principle of national self-determination—have either been wiped out or reduced to provincial dependencies of the new Communist imperialism. In other words, the traditional Western norm of the state is today a casualty of the Leninist revolution in many regions of the world.

War has been and continues to be the decisive Leninist method for subduing, communizing, or extinguishing sovereign states. But, as illustrated in several other parts of this book, "war," too, carries meanings in Communist statecraft that it does not have in the West. These new realities are camouflaged effectively in accordance with the established Leninist practice of manipulating Western, half-Western, and non-Western mind-sets through the fraudulent use of the West's own normative references to the state, democracy, war, peace, and international law.

Soviet command structures in military and political decision-making are thus routinely dissimulated through reliance on the global network of Communist parties and the surrogate status of dependent Communist governments. Likewise, interstate war is habitually downgraded as being a purely local insurgency, revolution, or civil war—that is, belonging to categories of violent disorder that are traditionally assigned by our international law to the domain of "domestic jurisdiction."

It goes without saying that this leisurely destruction of the state system is an unmitigated defeat for the United States. In reviewing the monotonously repetitive failures in American strategic foresight and foreign policy-making, one must ask: Why was the process not arrested long ago? And why was the nation's educated citizenry so reluctant to assess the new realities even when they were being clearly set out by those responsible for the conduct of foreign affairs? For surely it cannot be denied that the nature of the Vietnam War had been lucidly explained by President Kennedy when he addressed the graduating class of West Point on June 6, 1962, in the following terms:

> This is another type of war, new in its intensity, ancient in its origins—war by guerrillas, subversives, insurgents, assassins, war by ambush instead of by combat; by infiltration, instead of aggression, seeking victory by eroding and exhausting the enemy instead of engaging him. . . . It requires in those situations where we must counter it . . . a whole new kind of strategy, a wholly different kind of force, and therefore a new and wholly different kind of military training.[1]

And the same lesson was repeated in February 1965 when a State Department White Paper ("The Aggressor from the North") presented a detailed analysis of just what war had come to mean in the wake of the bloody conflicts foisted upon Greece, Malaya, the Philippines, and Korea, and how these Communist onslaughts differed from the one visited upon South Vietnam. The specific message here was that the Vietnam War had been carefully planned by Marxist-Leninist tacticians of strife as a series of interdependent but well-disguised covert operations.

Analyses and guidelines such as these did not lead to a "wholly new strategy" and "a wholly new kind of military training" in the United States. In fact the record of the last twenty years shows persuasively that the United States has not been able either to foresee or to cope successfully with Soviet or Soviet-sponsored subversive warfare in non-Western states—whether in Central Asia, Africa, or Central America.

Further, the record suggests that this has been due in considerable measure to lethargy or intellectual inadequacy on the part of low-level governmental bureaucrats who simply failed to analyze the nature of the Soviet connection. As William J. Casey noted in the summer of 1982 when he dealt with the Central American situation, the estimates program was "way down" when he took charge of the Central Intelligence Agency: "I asked for an estimate on the Cubans and their activities. I got it after two months—and it neglected to mention Cuba's relationship with the Soviet Union."[2] Further, Casey found at that time that the agency's "data bank" did not even contain general comprehensive assessments of Soviet intelligence threats. Chief among them, he explained, are (1) the Soviet Union's ability to project its power in Western as well as non-Western regions through subversion, insurgency, the adept use of proxy forces, and the planning and funding of terrorist operations via client states like Libya, Cuba, South Yemen, and the satellites of Eastern Europe; and (2) the ability to "insidiously insert its policy views into the political dialogue in the U.S. and other foreign countries."[3]

As President Kennedy had explained two decades earlier, each of these threats had been successfully activated by Hanoi and Soviet strategists in the Indochina wars. Yet here we were in 1985, still theorizing, still torn by bitter internal discord as to whether the nation's security was really threatened and whether we were morally and legally justified in thinking that an ongoing war was a "real war" just because some in our midst cannot figure out how that would square with what they once were told was "international law."

And the same type of confusion continues to hamstring American understanding of "the state"—the second of my two measures in this comparative study of statecraft. Casey thus found in 1982 that estimates were still done on a country-by-country basis, noting that intelligence researchers would do one on Nicaragua, one on Honduras, one on El Salvador, and so forth, and that no one was looking at the regional interplay between these countries—or for that matter between them and Marxist-Leninist headquarters in remoter areas.

This particular weakness in the estimating process was corrected with the introduction of new agency sections organized along geographical and topical lines. But as indicated by the record of near-hysterical congressional debates on administration policies and intelligence operations in Central America, as well as by the media coverage of this subject matter, the problem of the modern state and therewith of the twentieth-century system of states is still as little understood in our nation as the phenomenon of modern war. Somehow we thus manage to avoid coming to terms with the chief maxims of the Soviet "doctrine of limited sovereignty," even though they have been explicated and applied openly year in and year out by Moscow in each province of the vast "camp of socialism." Briefly put, these maxims are to the effect that the revolutionary process is a single process, knowing no frontiers; that the notion of state sovereignty may never stand in the way of the struggle of progressive forces; and that the law of the class struggle and of social development must always override bourgeois nonsocialist laws and legal norms.

This oversight in "intelligence writ large" is in my view the chief failure in American foreign policy. As suggested earlier, it is due primarily to that heavily cultivated disposition to rationalize—and accept—the political systems of our antagonists as credible equivalents of the one espoused at home. How else can one explain such astonishing examples of scholarship in comparative politics as the thesis that the Supreme Court is the American equivalent of the Moscow Politburo, or that the KGB is a mirror image of the CIA? And how else can one understand the outrage expressed by scholars and news people during the Vietnam War over the fact that the military forces of their own nation did not respect the boundaries separating Laos, Cambodia, and Vietnam when they attempted to counter North Vietnam's sweeping violations of precisely those territorially separate jurisdictions and to frustrate the enemy's maintenance of control over such infiltration routes as the Ho Chi Minh Trail? We were defeated in that war mainly because the nation had in effect become confused and war-weary as a result of these well-publicized American misconceptions; and sometimes it looks as if we are being goaded by the same atmospherics into losing the same kind of "war" in Central America.

Next, and as discussed in several other essays in this book, the integrity of "our" kind of state and state system has been gravely impaired in the last decade by terrorist invasions from without. This type of irregular revolutionary warfare that consists in the main of several species of carefully plotted assassination, and the destruction of strategically vital establishments, has been planned, sponsored, and funded by a few leading totalitarian states, chief among them Iran and the Soviet Union with their assorted surrogates, satellites, clients, and subordinate "hit" squads.

Conceived as state policy, international terrorism, too, is meant to violate politically and territorially fixed frontiers. Its principal aim is to cut down adversary states outside the military battlefield by destabilizing targeted governments and terrorizing civilian populations. In short, it is meant to hold independent non-Communist nations—be they great or small—in the grip of humiliating fear and impotence.

This objective has been attained frequently and in particularly dramatic fashion by carefully plotted assaults on embassies and diplomatic personnel—the chief symbols of the sovereign state abroad. A closely related mode of impugning the internationally established diplomatic code is the practice of anti-Western regimes such as those of Libya and Iran to transform their own embassies in the West into conspiratorial centers for plotting irregular warfare.

The ultimate result of this type of terrorist statecraft is obviously the obliteration of traditional distinctions between war and peace and of that part of international law purporting to guard diplomacy from the incidence of warfare so that it can serve as the major agency for mediating and resolving conflicts between states. Further, and with special reference to the overtly staged attempt to kill Pope John Paul II—the highest representative of Christendom—and to the equally overt massive military assault on the Mosque of Mecca—the holiest symbol of Islam—we were forced to acknowledge that "the new war" is designed to strike at the moral and cultural core of all states that resist the revolution.

III

The case continues to be made—rightly, I think—that our intelligence collection is weak in non-Western societies and that this is due chiefly to our heavy intelligence concentration on the Soviet Union. In 1982, Admiral Bobby Inman went so far as to say that our major weaknesses include "a minimal effort both in collection and analysis" about many of these non-Communist societies, and that "we lack the encyclopedic effort that will let us understand trends before we get to the level of a crisis."[4]

I have some reservations regarding Inman's arguments. First, the Soviet Union was rightly the principal object of our attention. And second, the information at our disposal continues to be impressive—witness the dense intelligence bibliographies on this subject. Yet, and judging the situation as reflected by American elite opinion, congressional opinion, and public opinion, it cannot be denied that all the information we have collected and analyzed has not made a whit of difference in actual foreign policy contexts. In other words, we lost the wars we fought to the Soviet Union, and they included the Second World War, the Korean War, and the Vietnam War; and we were unable, throughout these crucial decades, to predict, preempt, contain, defy, or roll back the expansionist advances in territorial as well as ideological respects that the motherland of socialism had registered in Eastern Europe, East Asia, Central Asia, West Asia, Africa, and Central America.

A major reason for these foreign policy failures vis-à-vis the Soviet Union has been our failure to come to terms with non-Western states. To put it positively, unless we have a thorough understanding of non-Communist countries, more particularly non-Western, non-Communist countries, we cannot even hope to understand and deal effectively with the Soviet Union's global strategy. This is so, I suggest, because the so-called Third World is the stage on which the Soviet Union had chosen long ago to fight and defeat the United States and the West.

Therefore it is useful, even necessary, today to distinguish two groups of non-Western states: (1) non-Western, non-Communist societies—and as we know, these have been greatly reduced in number during the last decades; and (2) those states that are either officially Communist in persuasion, or are deeply penetrated by Marxist-Leninist and Soviet influences.

In regard to the first category, it should be the task of U.S. intelligence as well as of academic research to identify and then strengthen indigenous values and institutions that make for national self-confidence and independence. The same assignment holds for the second category of non-Western states, but here it cannot be carried out until the Communist cover has been identified and lifted so as to reveal the non-Communist essence of the conquered state. In neither case are we apt to be successful as long as we go on trying to implant our norms and values in lieu of those we wish to weaken or remove. Rather, the challenge in each non-Western state requires reliable knowledge of just what it is in the substratal culture that has made or can make a society tick independently in its own way.

This we have not even attempted to do in the last sixty years as the following references illustrate: our zeal to transform defeated Japan into a docile nonwarring political democracy was so obsessive that the victorious United States chose to strike at Shintoism, Japan's ancient state-sustaining religion. General Kenneth R. Dyke, who administered that program after 1945, thus announced that Shintoism had too long been used "as a tool for militarism" and that Japanese textbooks would therefore have to be reduced to pulp. Japan was permitted to have pro-Japanese histories, he explained, but only "as long as Japanese scholars put the early 'history' where it belongs—under the category of folklore."[5] And the same bias pervaded American attitudes toward embattled Asian allies, foremost among them South Vietnam[6] and South Korea.[7]

Our discontent with these and other friendly Asian states has invariably been due to the existence of a form of government that makes inadequate provision for our secular model of democracy. As suggested in several other essays, this American disposition stems from a pronounced disinclination to acknowledge religions and other belief systems as constitutive elements of political order. The notable exception in this syndrome of preconceptions seems to be our positive alignment with Israel's Judaic statecraft. What is puzzling here is that our commitment to the Old Testament has not led us to a close examination of Islam (which is grounded in the Bible). It is this "intelligence gap" that accounts for our policy disasters in the Middle East,[8] chief among them our inability to cope with Shi'ite Iran.

Where does responsibility rest for failures such as these? In my view, it cannot be pinned on any one branch of government or special agency. In a democracy such as ours it rests rather on all educated citizens—those in actual charge of policy-making as well as those in charge of education and communication, specifically the universities, the churches, and the media.

Ellsworth Bunker made a poignant comment on this issue. Reminiscing on his ambassadorship in South Vietnam during an interview with B. Drummond Ayres, he had this to say:

> I think experience has shown that in the age of television you have to have some sort of press control, as the British did during the Falklands War. Television, naturally enough, goes after the dramatic. And that's what the American people saw from Vietnam. After the Tet offensive in 1968, I reported back to Washington that we had won a military victory. But I feared a psychological defeat.[9]

Further, no one can complain that knowledge requisite for political analysis has not been available to every one of us. It is therefore disconcerting to find that self-criticism is generally avoided by shifting responsibility for our policy failures onto the state we are no longer able or willing to defend. In 1975 when President Thieu's government in Saigon was disintegrating; in 1978–79 when the Shah of Iran lost out to the Ayatollah Khomeini; and more recently when the governments of Lebanon and El Salvador, for example, were undermined by adversaries from without, American defeats or withdrawals were commonly rationalized by the argument that "given the collapse of the state's armed forces," or "given" poor leadership in the beleaguered state, the United States could do little if anything to influence the situation.

Implicit in such explanations is the admission that American and not local standards for leadership, diplomacy, and the role of armed forces in society were employed, and that we knew as little about culturally different types of ruling personalities and attitudes to armed conflict as we did about religions, laws, and orientations to the past.

In short, in the places alluded to, as well as in Mao Tse-tung's China, Castro's Cuba, Sandinista Nicaragua, Mugabe's Zimbabwe, Nkrumah's Ghana, or Sékou Touré's Guinea, we did not and do not yet understand the "mind-set."[10]

IV

How, then, do non-Western conceptions of "the state" and of "war" differ from ours?

This question—which receives some attention in most essays of this book—is of general importance if only because non-Western states constitute the majority of states today. Some of them—for instance, India—were carefully tutored in this role during colonial times. All acceded voluntarily to the European States System and subscribed, *mutatis mutandis,* to the West's law of nations and its provisions regarding the rights and responsibilities of states and the rules of conduct in war and peace. Further, and equally voluntarily, they accepted Western forms of constitutionalism as core principles of administration.

None of this did, could, or should have been taken to mean that non-Western states had acceded to the Western heritage of accepted principles encapsulated in references to "the state" and "war." In short, non-Western states were not and—as we know today—are not Western states. Rather, a study of postindependence developments shows incontrovertibly that non-Western peoples everywhere have steadily been reactivating their own cultural and political legacies without discarding the new protective umbrella of modern Western-style statehood. Indeed, it shows that they exist consciously in two different worlds and that their political representatives operate equally consciously within two conflicting frames of reference and in accordance with two disparate codes of thought and conduct. This was confirmed and illustrated by an African judge during a colloquium at The Hague on "The Future of International Law in the Multicultural World."[11] African states— my Senegalese colleague explained calmly and lucidly—thus play two totally separate games: one on the international level of the UN and in relations specifically with the West in which they draw deliberately on Western norms, and another on the level of their own society and culture zone that is in counterpoint to the former, being openly attuned to local or regional values, norms, and expectations.

In light of these shared traits and problems, it may not be off the mark to suggest that non-Western states are complex covert societies. Neither can be understood unless we can fully assess both their overt and covert identities and find the key to their combination. What I find particularly interesting about this challenge to U.S. statecraft is the following. On the non-Western side, it is the ease with which states and their human agents shuttle from one plane of intelligence and action to the other and the adeptness with which they play the different roles assigned them. On the American side, by contrast, it is the placid disposition to look only at surface manifestations of statehood and expect non-Western states to comply with contractual commitments to be peace-loving and democratic.

As I suggested in the first section of this essay, the basic reason for this American stance is no doubt the fact that Western national and international political systems are straight derivatives of Occidental culture, and that earlier generations of our political elites—in contrast to those in the Orient and Africa—were therefore not caught in a standing conflict between politics and culture. The other reason, also mentioned earlier, is the typically American disinclination to take the past and culture seriously.

Comparative studies of the new prototype "state" in Asian, African, and some Latin American regions reveal diverse blends of traditional and modern patterns of statecraft. Some have been concretized most effectively in the context of twentieth-century requirements, as, for example, those fashioned in Japan, Thailand, South Vietnam before its extinction, Singapore, the Republic of China on Taiwan, Turkey, Egypt, and pre-Khomeni Iran. By contrast, others, among them particularly black African, Arab-Islamic, and some Latin American states, go on contending with the challenge of making orderly statehood work.

The divergences are admittedly great, yet non-Western states come close to convergence on the following themes that deviate from Western norms.

To begin with (or to recapitulate), it has to be stressed that the concept of the modern Western state is conceptually and historically alien or uncongenial to the majority of the world's societies mainly because they have not produced trusted systems of secular constitutional law of the kind exemplified by the Roman civil law, the Anglo-Saxon common law, and their modern Euro-American derivatives. In such conditions the state cannot be conceived as a partnership in law meant to bind successive generations throughout time, and the idea of citizenship as we know it is bound to remain remote and unfamiliar.

All this explains why modern non-Western states composed of pluralities of ethnic, religious, or linguistic folk societies—among them specifically those in black and Islamized Africa—have not been able to evolve into unified nation-states held together by mutual trust and shared convictions and commitments. Accumulated African records show instead that most states are actually fields of "foreign" relations among contending parties.[12] Indeed, none comes to mind in which tribally induced apartheid is not the general norm of coexistence outside urban centers. Nor can one think of a new state that has not been rent by internal tribal warfare and other forms of violent disorder.

Similar conflicts have come to mark relations among different ethnic, linguistic, and religious communities in India, Sri Lanka, and Bangladesh. Here colonial Europe's legacy of the unified nation-state is being contested—and in some places overtaken—by resurgent ancient traditions of communal, religious, and political divisiveness and by frenzied flights into near-uncontrollable violence. In the culturally unified Arab-Islamic Middle East, by contrast, the state is precariously grounded for two very different reasons. In the Islamic context—which is being resurrected and reestablished by fundamentalist regimes as the only permissible context for all of life, including politics—the cause of the modern Western state is being refuted as categorically today as was that of the Persian/Turkic power *mulkh* in the early Islamic centuries; the reason is that all such forms of organization are deemed absolutely incompatible with the Prophet's idea of the universal *umma* of all believers. In the Arab context, meanwhile, long-established theory continues to insist on an all-Arab nation, not on separate Arab nation-states called Syria, Iraq, Saudi Arabia, Jordan, Kuwait, Oman, or Lebanon. Here, too, then, as in South Asia and Africa, reality is so contested that it is readily viewed as illegitimate by adversaries within as well as beyond state boundaries.

These widely shared orientations make for chronic unrest, strife, and insecurity—in short, for the heavy incidence of conflicted societies. In conjunction with the absence of an objective stable legal system and the pronounced present-day remembrance of premodern traditions of political organization, they help explain three aspects of non-Western statecraft with which we in the United States do not seem able to come to terms. The first relates to the preponderance of authoritarian forms of rule; the second to the paramountcy of secret societies and clandestine or covert activities; and the third to the widespread predisposition to resort to war.

In addressing the task of distinguishing between the varieties of non-Western patterns of authoritarian rule, it is useful to bear in mind that despotism has been the administrative norm in all multicultural or multinational Oriental empires, among them those of the Chinese, the Mongols, the Turks, and the pre-Islamic Persians. It was so also in the imperial domains of the Aztecs, Mayas, and Incas; of the Islamic conquerors in North Africa and the Sudan; and in the African regions dominated by the Amhara, Zulu, Matabele, Ashanti, Yoruba, Mossi, Kikuyu, and scores of other ethnicities. Further, but in more restricted terms, authoritarianism assured the cohesion of Hindu and Buddhist kingdoms in South and Southeast Asia as well as of the Tibetan theocracy in Central Asia.

Different as these traditions of authoritarianism were, they converged on the idea of associating ultimate political power with personalities. However, in premodern times personalized power was blunted in most of the political systems just mentioned by the general understanding that it served to symbolize, even to hallow, the identity of the entire society in space and time.

Such reservations, however, have given way under the growing stress of having to keep disparate human elements together in the modern state and under the auspices also of alluring totalitarian doctrines of rule, more particularly those developed by the Soviet Union. Power today is thus generally conceived of as naked power. Throughout Africa and the Middle East (but see exceptions cited earlier) one finds that the operative "state" is not so much the expression of a unified nation as the extension of power-holding individual men.[13] However, whether conceived as personal property or trust, as a personalized religious mandate from on high, as a hostage in power games between contending factions and individuals, or as a local surrogate power base for distant foreign principals, the conclusion is irrebuttable that most new non-Western states are as fragile as the particular biographies with which they happen to be linked.

A new psychological dimension has thus accrued to the task incumbent upon American scholarship and statecraft: intelligence now must assess not only the mind-sets of complex non-Western nations but also—in some cases chiefly—those of the power people running them. Further, rather than continuing the present tendency to lump authoritarian states together, we need to distinguish and evaluate them carefully in terms of the cultures and ideologies that condition their political structures and that help shape their orientations to foreign affairs. Reliance on Western norms of "good government," that is, democracy, may justify Freedom House to place King Hussein's Jordan in the category of "half-free" states while judging the Gulag states of Pol Pot's Kampuchea and Sékou Touré's Guinea as not free at all. But it does not follow that such a mode of measurement can capture the basic differences between these states and their respective regimes.

The second theme upon which most non-Western states converge—the predilection, namely, for clandestine political action and organization; secrecy in decision-making, communication, and negotiation; and confidentiality among the likeminded—is a corollary of the first. Indeed, none of the scores of modern coups, plots, counterplots, insurgencies, counterinsurgencies, civil wars, or revolutions could have taken place in Asia, Africa, and Latin America were it not for these deeply rooted predispositions. For whether one reads about the lives of traditional Chinese emperors and warlords; Mongolian autocrats; Hindu India's kings; Southeast Asia's Buddhist devarajahs; Persian shahs; Islamic prophets, sultans, caliphs, and ayatollahs; and African tribal chieftains; or about the policies and destinies of their present-day successors, one cannot fail to note that mistrust and fear of the human environment are dominant motifs everywhere. How to discover and control dissidence; guard against treason, overthrow, and assassination; ferret out fifth columns within; and trace their connections with enemies outside the realm have therefore been paramount preoccupations in all ruling establishments.

Threat perceptions such as the ones here mentioned have seldom been figments of paranoid imaginations. Rather, they were and are justified by social and political realities. For example, traditional as well as nineteenth- and twentieth-century China has been honeycombed with secret societies that often came to constitute states within the state. Some were conceived as benevolent associations, others as expressions of the criminal underworld. Most, however, existed for the purpose of opposing existing authorities in the ranks of the imperial administration, the mandarinate, the army, religious circles, and merchant classes, as well as stirring up revolts in diverse strata of society and spearheading a variety of xenophobic movements. Highly disciplined as covert martial orders that could maintain identity and cohesiveness through reliance on a system of passwords, magic rituals, oath taking, and so forth, they functioned effectively for centuries, often in clandestine cooperation with other revolutionary elements and aspirants to power.

Further, it is relevant for purposes of this inquiry that secret society leaders became pioneers in China's Communist Party and that numerous clandestine associations were held in great esteem by Sun Yat-sen, the Kuomintang, and Mao Tse-tung. Impressed with their revolutionary potential, especially in mobilizing the countryside, and with their capacity for disciplined and protracted struggle in guerrilla warfare, Mao thus made a place for the Red spears in the 1925–27 strategy by assigning them the task of directing peasant uprisings against landowners.

Regime responses to these as to all other disorders in the "celestial empire" have consistently focused on systematic espionage and the meting out of severe punishment. Contrary to other non-Western and Western states in which this political craft was developed as a practical necessity, China was also educated in the theory of intelligence as formulated by the Legalists who provided the rationale for this art in psychological, military, and political terms as well as the tactical guidelines for its deployment at home and abroad. Not coincidentally, Legalist texts also expounded on the absolute need to punish infractions of the social order as harshly as possible. Both themes were to remain prominent in the administrative policies and legal codes of subsequent dynasties and, as we know today, in China's contemporary Communist order.

The patterns of covert thought, organization, and action as recorded in Chinese history are equally well documented in the long annals of other Oriental autocracies. As my earlier assessments of Persia, India, and the Islamic empires of the Moguls, Afghans, Turks, and Arabs[14] indicated, intelligence collection and analysis as well as actual intelligence operations such as "active measures" were cultivated assiduously throughout these realms because they provided the requisite underpinning for the proper functioning of the administrative bureaucracy and the military, and because they supplied the indispensable protective shield for the imperial ruler who symbolized the state.

The classical case for the virtue of espionage had been made in West Asia by Persia's Achaemenid and Sassanian dynasties, which institutionalized "the King's Eyes and Ears" in exemplary manner, and in South Asia by sacred Hindu texts that explained authoritatively that a kingdom must have its roots in spies and secret agents if it is to prosper and survive. All later Oriental despotisms accepted this wisdom and saw to it that their realms were covered with networks of spies, so that the sovereign would know the secrets of the people.

"The people," meanwhile—be they rival royal families, Islamic sectarians, Christian Armenians, Zionist Jews, or simply adventurist aspirants to power—did indeed have their secrets and were often able to keep and then activate them in successful revolts, assassinations, and regime changes. On their level, too, success was invariably a function of intricately organized secret societies and programs of covert action.[15] In short, the long records of Asian history up to and including the present century indicate clearly that we are dealing here with closed societies and with peoples that were conditioned throughout the millennia to endure all manner of conflict and insecurity.

Last, a few comments on the place of secrecy, dissimulation, deception, and indirect controls in African approaches to communication and administration. Here where the Occidental norm of the territorial nation-state is not accommodated by history and culture and where the communal unity of greater societies was traditionally symbolized by kings or paramount chiefs, effective power usually emanated from occult organizations. These included such secret societies as the far-flung Poro in Liberia, Sierra Leone, the Ivory Coast, and other West African regions; the Egba society in southern Nigeria; and the intricately organized "spirit provinces" linking different Shona peoples in the Zambezi region.

The majority of these organisms issue from religious or metaphysical convictions. Based on the belief that the dead continue to live and take an active interest in the affairs of the living, and that nature is peopled by spirits and ghosts, these organisms are there to control human behavior and maintain the existing order by the exercise of ultimate sacred sanctions. Their statecraft is thus essentially magical, for it relies on the administration of a body of esoteric knowledge, communicated in conditions of secrecy through the medium of masks, occult words, signs, and rites; it also relies on disciplines—usually including the taking of oaths—that are designed to rally the membership into absolute obedience to the purposes of the society as interpreted by a hidden government.

Furthermore, the cause of dissimulation and covert organization is enhanced in many instances by the belief that the human realm is related inextricably to that of the animal world. To imitate the habits, particularly the modes of killing peculiar to a locally paramount beast—as, for example, the leopard, the panther, the lion, the crocodile, or the python—and in so doing increase the sense of awe and mystery by disguising the human will or action, could thus become the constitutional source, as it were, for such far-flung secret societies as the leopard men and, during the UN Congo war, the Simbas ("lion guerrillas"). Attention should also be drawn in this context to a highly developed art of dissimulating human identities and intentions as illustrated by Africa's near-countless comprehensive agency patterns in terms of which principals can be shaded or altogether hidden by surrogates and intermediaries.

The following trends are noteworthy today in light of the fact that modern state structures are particularly fragile in Africa. First, interactions between covert and overt regimes have been and continue to be more pronounced here than in West and East Asia. And second, many of Africa's secret societies have been degenerating steadily into unprincipled and often terrorist bands, thus further destabilizing intergroup relations and processes of administration.

The chief underlying reason for this set of developments is no doubt the spontaneous activation, in the stressful circumstances of postindependence insecurity, of traditional beliefs in such supernatural forces as witchcraft and sorcery and in the efficacy of such magical proceedings as the casting of spells and death-inducing curses. What is new today, however, is the ruthless exploitation of these beliefs by scores of modern Africa's absolutist leaders who were in no way inhibited by either traditional or borrowed Western norms from turning the states they personified into "kingdoms of death."[16]

The contrary is indicated. Kwame Nkrumah, Idi Amin, and Sékou Touré were esteemed as hero figures and occupied positions of trust in Pan-African affairs. Much the same is true in the Middle Eastern Islamic zone of the reputations enjoyed by such totalitarian leaders as Muammar Qaddafi of Libya, Hafez al-Assad of Syria, Saddam Hussein of Iraq, and the Ayatollah Khomeini of Iran.

The characteristics of the non-Western state as they have been identified so far in this paper account in considerable measure for the widespread predisposition to resort to war—the third aspect of non-Western statecraft with which Americans do not seem able to come to terms. My general thesis here is that norms and values observed in a society's inner order—be it Western or non-Western—will inevitably be operational also in that society's relations with the outside world.

Thus it is difficult to imagine that such established domestic norms as one-man or one-party rule, warfare within the state, and reliance on unlimited military and policing powers can be turned into their opposites when a line in territorial space is reached that demarcates the existence of another state. Indeed, even theory in the context of non-Western belief systems would bar such restraints. For contrary to a widespread persuasion in our midst that mankind's religions are essentially at one in favoring peace and pacifism, war is an accepted, even hallowed norm in Oriental and African creeds.

These cultural traditions and present-day human dispositions in regard to war are accentuated by the circumstance that territoriality has traditionally not been an attribute of non-Western polities. As explained in several essays in this book, frontiers have been geographically and politically indeterminate and porous in China (the Middle Kingdom), which conceived of itself as the abode of a superior civilization and as entitled therefore to educate neighboring peoples in the art of government, if necessary through wars of punishment or conquest; in India, where kings, being members of the warrior caste, were supposed to harass and conquer other kingdoms; in Africa, where a community's identity hinged on ethnic unity rather than territory, and where warfare of one sort or another summed up the meaning of masculine life; and in the Arab/Islamic realm, where the plurality of modern Arab states is being challenged continuously by traditional concepts of an undivided Arab nation and of an Islamic *umma* of all believers.[17]

In short, the mind-set responsible for war and violence within the state extends automatically to areas viewed in the West as the jurisdictions of foreign states, quite without regard to Western notions of international law.

Reflections on the different species of overt, covert, and cold wars that are being fought year in, year out in the vast conflicted regions of Asia, Africa, and parts of Latin America suggest that these conflicts are authentic expressions of newly resurgent non-Western views of statecraft. However, it is doubtful whether the latter would have surfaced as strongly as they did had it not been for the strong recent impact of Marxist-Leninist doctrines of war (see *supra,* this essay) and the political influence of powerful Communist regimes on the mind-sets of modern non-Western elites.

The interpenetration of these fundamentally belligerent persuasions—those related to Marxism-Leninism and those native to a given culture—explains why war, not peace, is uppermost in the consciousness of our contemporaries in the multiple war-torn regions throughout the non-Western world. After all, what can a young Lebanese fighting man in the fractured state of Lebanon be expected to say except "I am born to war" or "War is my friend—in peace I only feel fear."[18] Likewise, no one can doubt the sincerity of the belief, expressed by Hussein Moussawi (the leader of a fundamentalist Muslim organization in Lebanon), that "This path is the path of blood, the path of martyrdom. For us death is easier than smoking a cigarette if it comes while fighting for the cause of God."[19] These dispositions deserve sympathy, understanding, and accommodation in the United States.

Our responses should obviously be wholly different when we hear Colonel Qaddafi to the following effect:

> We tell the agents in the Sudan that we are allied with the popular revolution in the southern Sudan for the sake of liberating Sudan inch by inch, just as Lebanon was liberated.
>
> The United States cannot save that mean man who is hiding in Khartoum. This is because, with the revolutionary forces in Ethiopia, in the Arab homeland, the revolution in Libya has decided to ally itself with the revolution in the southern Sudan. The peoples will march forward and will develop a people's war of liberation in Sudan, and tomorrow in Egypt and in every area that America seeks to dominate.
>
> We must force America to fight on a hundred fronts all over the earth. We must force it to fight in Lebanon, to fight in Chad, to fight in the Sudan and to fight in El Salvador.[20]

V

What is the relevance of these comparative studies for present-day American statecraft and intelligence and for scholarly research in the field?

My findings support the general thesis that the world is a manifold of mindsets, cultures, and political systems and that worldviews and modes of relating to "others" in foreign affairs are therefore more likely to differ than to be the same.

In regard specifically to non-Western societies this suggests that our norms of statecraft are not theirs, and that our understanding of the nature and function of intelligence is therefore apt to deviate significantly from theirs. Yet reflections on the well-documented record of our policies and intelligence services show that we are not prepared to acknowledge these diversities.

By and large Americans appear persuaded today that intelligence is extraneous to the nation's security interests and governing institutions and that it is "undemocratic" because some of its work is not open to daily public inspection. Indeed, influential segments of opinion in academe and the media tend to view the entire intelligence complex of ideas, institutions, and operations, more particularly the Central Intelligence Agency, as an "enemy within" the nation, more threatening than any enemy without.

This particular bias, which evolved in the last decades, has had the effect of accentuating the traditional American disposition (see *supra*) to level differences between cultures and political systems. The assumption has thus become widespread that non-Western nations are, or ought to become, as dubious and scornful regarding their modes of coping with enemies as we are in respect of ours, and that they, too, should be inclined to view covert and clandestine intelligence operations as aberrations of statecraft.

Research certainly supports contrary conclusions. What to us is a small contrived part of political life pervades all of life in the Orient and Africa. That is to say, we are dealing almost everywhere in the world with covert societies, covert thought, and covert actions.

Further, and not coincidentally, we are dealing with societies that accept the constancy of conflict including war within society as well as in international relations without losing their bearings in life. These orientations—and we should admit that they stand in stark contrast to ours—explain why peace and war are not polarized but allowed to fade into each other, and why so much of non-Western warfare falls short of what we call regular all-out military war. In short, they explain why the cold war or the psychological war of nerves and ideas is and always has been a highly developed form of statecraft throughout the Orient and Africa. (This theme is developed in the Introduction and the last essay of this book.)

Next, comparative crosscultural studies establish the fact that cold wars (including those in which Europe has been involved) are covert and protracted wars. This circumstance, which is anathema to American thought, explains why we today simply do not seem to understand cold wars and why we cannot cope with them successfully. Together with certain other innate dispositions (see *supra*) it also explains why modern scholarship in the political sciences has kept aloof from the rich non-Western literature on statecraft in general and on espionage and intelligence in particular. Had we been as diligent and objective in our explorations of other cultures as European and American scholars were in the nineteenth and early twentieth centuries we would have discovered before reaching the political crisis point in our time that non-Western peoples and ruling institutions do not share our self-inflicted disabilities.

Instead their record shows this: the chief target of attack in intelligence games as played for centuries, even millennia, throughout literate Asia and the nonliterate societies of the American Indians and black Africa has invariably been the mind of the opponent, whoever and wherever he is. To "shape" the enemy, inducing him to contribute to his own encirclement and annihilation (Sun Tzu's phrasing), is the tactic, and to win or prepare victory by nonmilitary means is the aim.

The ammunition in such engagements is therefore not confined to poison, silken strangling cords, laserlike umbrellas, daggers, explosives, guns, and hand grenades. It includes also, indeed mainly so, ideas, stratagems, and ruses, all carefully crafted to weaken the enemy's will power and integrity; to catch his mind in nets of illusions, falsehoods, fears, and threats—in short, to confuse and deceive him with what is known today as "disinformation."

Affinities between these traditions of waging wars of nerves and those perfected by Leninist statecraft are obvious. Indeed, they no doubt account for numerous joint ventures in transnational cold wars, acts of terrorism, and programs of "active measures." Nonetheless, it is in our interest to remain aware of differences in this arena of statecraft as we begin to refine our own understandings of the relation between covert and overt wars on the one hand and between all warfare and peace on the other.

This effort is overdue. For at a time when covert action is the name of the game in the rest of the world, we are seized by an irrational unstudied dread of it. It is in this context of failing statesmanship and scholarship that one must welcome the initiative that was taken by Robert C. McFarlane, President Reagan's national security adviser.[21]

In the course of analyzing Cuban and Nicaraguan-backed guerrilla violence in Central America, notably El Salvador, McFarlane called for educating the American public to the recognition that there is a "gray area" between "total war" and "total peace" in which we shall increasingly encounter determined Soviet efforts to subvert non-Communist governments. For in this gray area—which we continue to exclude from our definition of "international war" but which is being cultivated by all Leninist regimes as the focus of political and military statecraft—covert activity is in his view the needed policy alternative between going to war (our style) or doing nothing when friendly nations are attacked.

The ideas here put in play should be guidelines for academic research, at least if one subscribes to the proposition that good statesmanship depends upon good scholarship. And the same holds for Paul H. Nitze's observation that strategy no longer relates to military affairs only.[22] Rather, a grand strategy is needed in which all elements bearing on the evolving situation are taken into account, and that over long periods of time, be they marked by war or peace. As in the praxis of statecraft and intelligence, so also in research that is meant to be politically relevant or useful. Scholars have to assess the world chessboard as a whole even as they distinguish between its component elements and sectors, be they regions, cultures, states, or nonstate bodies. Further, and also as in practice, the validity range of scholarly analyses should encompass ten to fifty years, not just the immediate aftermath of the crisis that provoked the examination.

Research goals of this kind can be attained only through multidisciplinary and comparative studies. They cannot even be approximated through exclusive reliance on information supplied by the social, political, or behavioral sciences where attention to uniqueness and hence to differentiation is eclipsed today by a strong urge to locate uniformities. Rather, and emphatically so in the context of non-Western statecraft and intelligence, the accent should be shifted back to the humanities, foremost among them history, religion, philosophy, literature, and language. Here where authenticity cannot be easily overlooked, comparative transcultural research comes naturally. It is not surprising, then, that specialists in the humanities have long known the classical Oriental theories and manuals of statecraft—be they Chinese, Mongolian, Indian, Persian, Arabic, or Turkish—whereas political scientists are just beginning to discover the foreign texts as translated and analyzed by their academic colleagues.

A quickening of pace in the planning of close interdisciplinary cooperation is thus required if the world's multifarious systems of statecraft are to be mapped reliably. Such an intellectual and educational reorientation would in all likelihood also contribute to the dissipation of another serious impediment to successful exploration. This relates to the common but erroneous expectation that the study of non-Western intelligence can follow the course charted by studies in Western intelligence contexts and that one's findings abroad can be neatly identified and distributed in accordance with schemes of definition and classification constructed in our academic and political bailiwick.

Such presuppositions stand in counterpoint to two sets of interrelated realities. One centers on the fact—set out in the following essay—that non-Western civilizations, whether traditionally literate or nonliterate, have not brought forth equivalents to the open, secular, all-encompassing universe of higher learning that is symbolized by the West's universities. True, the literate Orient was renowned in early medieval Europe as the abode of superior wisdom. But as learning shifted westward and as the profiles of Europe's first universities became discernible after circa 1200 A.D., it was soon realized that culturally different modes of thought would reveal themselves also in conceptions of higher education.

Thus it bears remembering that knowledge in the East was cultivated as a privileged domain open only to a few chosen segments of society, and that much of education—in fact most of it in Hindu, Buddhist, and Islamic contexts—consisted of imparting accumulated religious and metaphysical truths that were deemed incontrovertible. Centers of learning, then, were essentially closed both thematically and methodologically even though some of them could boast of spectacular libraries.

Modern universities on European and later on American models were inconceivable in literate Asian and North African societies before the onset of Europeanization and modernization in the nineteenth century. And the same was true of nonliterate black Africa where knowledge was communicated orally and behaviorally and where Western specialists on Africa were candidly advised by their educated local informants in the mid-twentieth century that "if you systematize in Africa, you are bound to lose," and "if you want to know how we think, watch how we live."[23]

In short, and quite in accord with other manifestations of non-Western modes of thought to which allusion was made earlier in this paper, we have to reckon with attitudes to learning and education and with ways of organizing and utilizing knowledge that have always been different from ours and continue to be so today. For contrary to the expectation five decades ago that the Western academic universe was as meaningful in Africa and Asia as the West's democracy, law of nations, and the United Nations organization, it was soon apparent that Western-educated elites in Africa and Asia had as ephemeral a hold on the cause of learning and education as they had on government and the conduct of foreign affairs. Hence the present heavy accent on the continuity of tradition in all non-Communist, non-Western regions of the world.

One of the implications of this development for our studies of statecraft and intelligence is the need to recognize that just as the essence of knowledge is not as split up into academic disciplines as it is in our academic universe, so can intelligence not be set apart from statecraft and society or subdivided into elements that parallel the ones we have extrapolated recently under such headings as analysis and estimates, counterintelligence, clandestine collection, covert action, and so forth. Rather, and as suggested earlier in this essay, intelligence is a scheme of things entire. And since it permeates thought and life throughout society, Western scholars must understand all aspects of a state's culture before they can assess statecraft and intelligence.

NOTES

1. *U.S. Public Papers of the Presidents: J. F. Kennedy (1962)* (Washington, D.C.: U.S. Government Publications, 1963), pp. 452–54.
2. Suzanne Garment, " 'Capital Chronicle' on 'Casey's Shadows: A Greater Emphasis on CIA Analysis,' " *Wall Street Journal*, July 16, 1982.
3. See Casey's August 24, 1982, speech at the Sixty-fourth Annual Convention of the American Legion, as discussed by Newton S. Miler in "Counterintelligence at the Crossroads," in Roy Godson, ed., *Intelligence Requirements for the 1980's: Elements of Intelligence*, rev. ed. (London/New Brunswick, N.J.: National Strategy Information Center, Inc., 1983), pp. 60ff. For a comprehensive analysis of the present world's main wartorn regions and of U.S. strategy in Central America and the Middle East, see an interview with Casey in *U.S. News and World Report*, April 23, 1984, pp. 27–29.
4. *New York Times*, July 5, 1982.
5. Obituary of General Dyke, *New York Times*, January 18, 1980.
6. For some poignant illustrations in intelligence-related contexts, see William Colby and Peter Forbath, *Honorable Men: My Life in the CIA* (New York, 1978), pp. 270–98.
7. For a lucid discussion of this case, see Robert Myers, "The U.S. and Korea: Values in Conflict," a CRIA symposium reported in *World View*, October 1981, pp. 13–15. For a comprehensive analysis of this matter, see also Bozeman, "Human Rights and National Security," *Yale Journal of World Public Order*, Vol. 9, no. 1 (1984); and Bozeman, "Conflicting Cultural Perspectives on Human Rights," keynote address at Symposium on Cross-Cultural Aspects of Human Rights: Asia, Foreign Service Institute, U.S. Department of State, 1988.
8. See "Covert Action and Foreign Policy in World Politics" in this volume. See also "Iran: U.S. Foreign Policy and the Tradition of Persian Statecraft" *ORBIS*, Vol. 23, no. 2 (Summer 1979), pp. 387–402.
9. *New York Times*, May 11, 1984.
10. See Daniel O. Graham, "Quality in U.S. Intelligence," in Godson, ed., *Intelligence Requirements for the 1980's: Elements of Intelligence*, pp. 23ff, for the comment that failures of perceiving "the mind-set" led policymakers to support the formation of left-wing governments in Italy and Chile in the early 1960s. At that time planners proceeded from the belief that only socialist governments stand in the way of Communist ones. For an important source of American misperceptions of Castro, see Herbert Mathew's insistent reportage in *The New York Times* during the decades following Castro's ascendancy to power.
11. The colloquium was held under the auspices of the Academy of International Law and the United Nations University in Tokyo, with the participation of judges from the International Court of Justice.
12. For excellent reporting on the African scene, see the essays by Clifford May in *The New York Times*, 1983–85. For the relation between traditional statecraft and modern administration, see Bozeman, *Conflict in Africa: Concepts and Realities* (Princeton, N.J.: Princeton University Press, 1976).
13. In this respect it is relevant to note that the regional organization of African states is officially constituted as a union of African *heads* of state.
14. See "Covert Action and Foreign Policy in World Politics" in this volume.
15. For an exposition of this syndrome in the Middle East, see *ibid.*
16. For well-documented accounts, see, among many others, the recent histories of Guinea-Bissau, Ghana, Liberia, Guinea, Uganda, Zimbabwe, the Congo, and Ethiopia, and the biographies of their respective leaders. Particularly poignant records include: Francis X. Maier, "Kingdoms of Death: A Reporter's African Journal," *This World*, Vol. 8

(Spring/Summer 1984), pp. 27–46; Eric Pace, obituary essay on Sékou Touré, *New York Times*, March 28, 1984; and Clifford May's references to Camp Bioro in Guinea, the prison where Sékou Touré's opponents were kept, tortured, and usually executed, *New York Times*, 1983–85. For analyses of different themes in African covert thought and action, see Bozeman, *Conflict in Africa*, pp. 80–294.

17. See *supra*, this essay; also "War and the Clash of Ideas," in this volume, and "The Nuclear Freeze Movement in Conflict: Moral and Political Perspectives on War and Its Relation to Peace," *Conflict: All Warfare Short of War*, Vol. 5, no. 4 (1985), pp. 271–305.

18. *New York Times*, March 12, 1984.

19. Review of an ABC documentary "War and Power—The Rise of Syria," *New York Times*, June 14, 1984.

20. *New York Times*, March 20, 1984.

21. *New York Times*, May 14, 1984.

22. Paul H. Nitze, "Strategy in the Decade of the 1980s," *Foreign Affairs*, Vol. 59, no. 1 (Fall 1980), pp. 82–101.

23. For African comments on African modes of thought and communication, see Bozeman, *Conflict in Africa*, pp. 69–99, and the chapter on "Nonliterate Thought and Communication," especially p. 79.

Knowledge and Method in Comparative Intelligence Studies of Non-Western Societies

KNOWING THE SELF AND THE OTHER: "COMPARISON" AS CONCEPT, METHOD, AND PREREQUISITE FOR STATECRAFT AND POLITICAL INTELLIGENCE

Every comparison carries the assumption (1) that the phenomena up for juxtaposition are comparable and (2) that they are probably dissimilar. Further, all comparisons are initiated and guided by the researcher's explicit or implicit choice of norms for measuring relations among phenomena A, B, C, and so forth. And in that phase of the intellectual process it stands to reason that the measure of comparison will be provided by the society or culture that the scholar knows best. In fact, no comparison—whether in the context of philosophy, theology, history, economics, the social sciences, or the arts—can get off the ground unless this kind of extended self-understanding is firmly in place.

Next, it is axiomatic that one cannot proceed to comparisons without having reached an understanding of "the other" on its own terms—be it a social institution, a mind-set, a nation, a language, a form of government, a way of war, or the totality of a foreign civilization. This intellectual and political challenge was often met successfully in the politically divided but morally unified European world. For example, Hugo Grotius knew that he had to compare the laws, ethics, and customs of the continent's diverse peoples before he could single out affinities and accords that could be trusted to sustain order in relations among Europe's newly independent states. Indeed, the truth bequeathed by the "Father of International Law" is to the effect that good international law is a function of good comparative law.[1] (Little heed has been paid to this thesis in our times.)

Also, and as illustrated by the *Federalist Papers* and other historical documentation, the Founding Fathers of the United States were not ready to draft a federal constitution until they had conducted comparative studies of European forms of constitutionalism, the English common law, and classical jurisprudence, specifically of the Roman law.

The demands implicit in crosscultural comparisons are obviously more complex than those related to intracultural comparisons if only because the scholar cannot

This essay originally appeared in *Comparing Foreign Intelligence: The U.S., the U.S.S.R., the U.K. and the Third World,* Roy Godson, ed. (McLean, Va.: Pergamon-Brassey's International Defense Publishers, Inc., 1988), and is printed with permission of National Strategy Information Center, Inc.

expect to find innate affinities such as shared religious, linguistic, ethnic, or historical legacies. Here the task of understanding "the other" usually calls for starting from scratch as the following allusions to the West's early relations with non-Western societies suggest.

Herodotus reminds us forcefully in *The Histories* that Greece was not Persia and that both knew the measure of that "otherness" throughout the protracted conflict during which neither tired of holding out for the integrity of its self-view.[2] Likewise, we know from the well-kept records of classical Rome that generations of jurists were as committed to preserving Rome's cultural integrity as they were to understanding the beliefs and institutions of multiple other human groups with which Rome had come to coexist. The main purpose of the comparison here was to distinguish, and then to link, the *ius civile* and the *ius gentium*.

It is important to bear in mind that these precedents in comparative research had not been set in academic enclaves by scholars concerned with theory building but by learned elites serving the internal and external needs of statecraft. Further, and not surprisingly, it was recognized in precisely this context that close studies of other societies were prerequisites for strategic thinking and the conduct of political and cultural relations, and, therefore, that it was imperative to develop systematic methods of collecting and analyzing foreign data—in short, to ground diplomacy in what we have come to call "foreign intelligence."

The archival records of three cosmopolitan Christian power centers—the Byzantine empire, the papacy, and the Republic of Venice—show convincingly that these goals were concretized impressively during medieval and early modern times. Also, one learns much about what has come to be called "methodology" from this literature as well as from the biographies and narrative accounts of a host of scholarly European explorers, missionaries, diplomats, and agents of influence who were committed by choice or mandate to the cause of understanding societies in the Orient and in Africa.

Whether one follows the two ninth-century Byzantine apostles to the Slavs, who invented alphabets for native languages, translated the Holy Scriptures for their use, and preached in Slavic; or the two sixteenth-century Dominicans, Bartolomé de Las Casas and Francisco de Vitoria, and the seventeenth-century Quaker William Penn—all three equally determined to comprehend the nature of American Indians; or Marco Polo, Matteo Ricci, and Sir William Jones, who pioneered in intellectual explorations of China, India, Central Asia, and Abyssinia; or La Cerda e Almeida, Robert Moffat, David Livingstone, Richard F. Burton, Mary Kingsley, Johann L. Krapf, Henry Barth, Robert S. Rattray, and Leo Frobenius, who worked ceaselessly to map Africa's human panorama, one finds an overwhelming consensus on the need to identify the foreign springs of thought and mental processes that might account for institutions, customs, beliefs, and modes of comportment that were found to differ radically from European "home" norms.

The particular purposes or reasons for these European journeys of discovery were infinitely various, whether self-set or assigned by European governments, churches, religious orders, geographic societies, medical associations, trading companies, or philanthropic enterprises. But whatever the auspices, the quests for foreign intelligence were generally uniform in aiming at opening lines of human as well as technical communication with non-Western regions; identifying politically cohesive entities—be they tribes, nations, or empires—in terms of location, language, and form of administration; gaining insight into the character traits of ruling personalities and elites; and uncovering basic values, social customs, and orientations toward the outside world.

Specific objectives ranged from propagating Christianity to improving health and education; introducing writing and literacy (as, for example, in the Slavic regions north of the Byzantine empire and in later centuries throughout black Africa); stimulating commerce and economic reform; abolishing the Arab and European slave trade (specifically as it related to black Africa); inducing compliance with Western-type laws and modes of treaty making; settling regional disputes at the behest of local non-Western principals; attracting friends, surrogates, or clients; and extending spheres of influence or control.

Knowing the self, knowing the other, and knowing how to measure the distance between the two were prerequisites in all ventures of this kind. The relevant questions in the present inquiry are, therefore, the following: How did early Western collectors and analysts of foreign intelligence go about their business? Where and how did they find the information they were looking for? What can be said about research methods in both collection and analysis throughout the centuries that preceded the advent in the mid-nineteenth century of the modern European university with its dense variety of separate academic disciplines and methodologies and its well-stocked libraries? A reading of biographies and histories suggests convincingly that Alexander P. Martin, an American Protestant missionary in nineteenth-century China, actually spoke for many generations of Western diplomats, agents, and scholars when he noted simply, "With no book or vocabulary to guide me, I was left to form my own system."[3]

Collecting, Analyzing, and Using Information: Case Studies in China and Africa

CHINA. In regard to China, the majority of these "personalized systems" converged on the ultimate aim of Christianizing the Chinese people. However, each emissary seems to have realized soon after his arrival that first, he could not possibly reach the people's minds unless and until he had succeeded in penetrating those of the emperor's bureaucratic elites; and second, he would not even reach this subsidiary goal if he would openly speak about the superior qualities of a non-Chinese faith and culture.

Prolonged observation and study persuaded all Jesuit and most other Christian missionaries that indirect approaches would have to be designed in order to win confidence, respect, and official status in the empire's ruling circles. And this was indeed achieved after Matteo Ricci and his successor, Adam Schall, concluded that they would have to overwhelm the educated Chinese imagination with the wonder and precision of Western science and technology if they wanted to condition it for the reception of the most sublime of Europe's gifts. And indeed, the Jesuits' learning in mathematics, cartography, and such mechanical skills as repairing clocks, spinets, and cannons convinced the Chinese that they were dealing here with men of unrivaled learning and expertise.

But, and as Ricci had rightly fathomed, it was the impact of Occidental astronomy that convinced Ming elites and China's Manchu conquerors that they were dealing here with the sources also of unrivaled power. Ricci's correction of the Chinese calendar thus had great psychopolitical importance, for almost all facets of life, including political decisions, ran to the rhythm of the lunar months, auspicious days, and authoritative predictions as recorded in Peking. And since the emperor was the mediator between heaven and earth in Chinese belief as well as the paramount father figure in the Sinocentric family of nations, Chinese calendars were followed unswervingly also in the tributary border states.[4]

Success in these respects earned Ricci and later Jesuits admission to the highest ranks of the bureaucracy.[5] But Ricci realized early that more was required if he was ever to attain his ultimate goal. And since he knew that his ideas would only be taken seriously if he was able to present them in Chinese and do so with literary elegance, he learned to master the language in just that measure. More important, he immersed himself in China's culture, history, and literature, specifically the Buddhist and Confucian classics, so that he could understand the Chinese mentality, communicate with the learned on an equal footing, and qualify as an instructor for their sons.

The following episode illustrates Ricci's phenomenal learning and the uses to which he put it in crosscultural research and diplomacy. Drawing on Chinese conceptions of the past and traditions of memorization and on his own highly developed theories of memory training, Ricci wrote a short book in Chinese on how to foster advanced skills in remembrance. The purpose of this "memory palace"[6] was probably dual. He presented the work to a powerful Chinese governor whose sons were candidates for important government-sponsored examinations in the evident hope that success in passing the tests would enhance official interest in Christianity—the manual's ultimate mental and moral source. But this worldly calculation is offset by the substance of the work, which consists of intricate designs for fixing the meanings of Christian symbols, images, and ideas "permanently" on Chinese minds.

Hopes for permanent achievement were difficult to sustain. Both Ricci and Schall had discovered in the course of acquiring knowledge of Chinese matters that in order to convert China to Christianity they would first have to convert themselves to China. And this they had accomplished not only by reaching great depths in penetrating the foreign civilization but also by adopting the surface appearance and comportment of Chinese-ness as represented by the literati. Indeed, in the judgment of some of the latter, the two Jesuits had come to look and even think like them—an impression also relayed by Ricci when he chose the Buddhist attire while absorbed in studying that faith. It is noteworthy, however, that Ricci failed to gain the identity as a Confucian that he had ardently sought.

Disappointment deepened when the Jesuits realized that Christianity itself would have to be Sinified to a degree and that they would have to be satisfied with winning only an "accepted place" for their religion. Further, anti-Christian and generally xenophobic reactions developed in late Ming and early Qing times—to gain momentum in subsequent centuries. In 1664 Schall was accused by his Chinese adversaries of high treason. The charge as memorialized was that he had come to Peking secretly and had posed as a calendar maker in order to engage in spying out the secrets of the imperial court.[7] The original penalty of death by dismemberment was modified to flogging and banishment, and this again was eventually commuted to house arrest until death—a destiny earlier assigned also to Ricci. (Twentieth-century equivalents of this penalty probably include "hostage status" and the Communist practice of "internal exile.")

I chose Matteo Ricci and his immediate successors as proponents of early modern European designs for that process of getting to know China, which is commonly called "the opening up of China," because they were pioneers in the art of examining a complex foreign literate society systematically (and sympathetically), and because they left records that tell us reliably just what they did in that business of collecting and assessing foreign data and just how and why they ultimately failed.

These records introduce the Jesuits as intelligence officers working for an ulterior ideological cause under the ultimate direction of distant principals. Yet they also, even primarily, establish them as self-directed, self-reliant scholars and personalities. Indeed, had it been otherwise, Ricci and Schall could not possibly have penetrated to the deep recesses of China's cultural and political identity while at the same time withstanding "acculturation" without morally and psychologically cracking up.

Parallels with modern Soviet and Western techniques of training and running intelligence agents abroad suggest themselves but cannot be sustained readily. In regard to "acculturation," for example, operatives today—whether native or foreign-born—also assume "new" identities and professional associations when serving abroad. But these are programmed covers and acts of dissimulation, all closely monitored by political superiors. In short, they are not open expressions of a scholar's individually felt need to know what Confucianism is all about; why Western-type law is irrelevant; why the calendar is so important; how China profits from technical assistance; or when and why a mission had to be deemed a failure.

Ricci and Schall found the answers to questions such as these. Both were thus aware of China's deep-seated hostility toward foreigners and the creeds they brought even as they valued Chinese friendship in interpersonal relations, and both came to realize that Christian missionaries were actually being appreciated mainly for their technical skills. Insights and experiences such as these were confirmed by the biography of the Belgian Jesuit Ferdinand Verbiest (seventeenth century), who ended up serving China by tutoring the K'ang-hsi emperor in astronomy; the *Elements of Euclid* (which Ricci had translated into Chinese); and spherical trigonometry, besides executing an imperial order to cast "light but effective cannons."[8]

It is relevant for the particular purposes of this discussion to note that the Jesuits were also asked to act as technical advisers in matters of law and foreign affairs. Some served as multilingual interpreters in relations with the Dutch and other European governments. Others played a decisive role—thus qualifying as agents of influence in the "intelligence" meaning of that term—in negotiating border conflicts with Russia and drafting the Treaty of Nerchinsk in 1689, which purported to settle the vexing disputes "forever." However, neither this pact nor subsequent Sino-Russian accords were instrumental in narrowing existing disputes—a reality that Matteo Ricci had accurately foreseen:

> There are no ancient laws in China under which the republic is governed in perpetuum, such as our laws of the twelve tables and the code of Caesar. Whoever succeeds in getting possession of the throne, regardless of ancestry, makes new laws according to his own way of thinking. . . . The extent of their kingdom is so vast, its borders so distant, and their utter lack of knowledge of a trans-maritime world is so complete that the Chinese imagine the whole world as included in their kingdom. Even now, as from time beyond recording, they call their Emperor . . . the Son of Heaven.[9]

This was written when Hugo Grotius, Ricci's contemporary, composed a European code of international law by relying on the same scholarly disciplines and comparative techniques. Neither text was remembered or fully understood in the mid-nineteenth century when Alexander P. Martin, a Protestant American missionary, took time off from religious concerns to translate Henry Wheaton's *Elements of International Law* (originally published in Boston in 1836) into Chinese to help bring Chinese education and Chinese ways of conducting international relations into line with Western norms.[10] These lofty purposes were not achieved. Rather, China's imperial officials made it incontrovertibly clear that they would not follow the principles set out in the Wheaton volume even though they attached tactical usefulness to the work in their traditional scheme of planning "border defense," specifically as this related to controlling the red-haired barbarians from the West. In this context, foreign affairs administrators were able, for example, to force the Prussians to relinquish a Danish ship that they had captured in China's territorial waters.

By the end of the nineteenth century it was rather clear that Westerners had ceased trying to understand China on its own terms and were no longer able to function effectively as political agents of influence and gatherers of intelligence. Instead, they were as content to serve China as agents dispensing technical assistance as they were prepared to endure China's open and often violent persecution of the Christian faith that had brought them to the Orient in the first place. In short, they had forgotten the major purpose of the mission.

AFRICA. The foregoing case study illustrates orientations to the collection, analysis, and usage of information about "other," or foreign, societies that I have found to be typical of all groups of European explorers. (Constraints of space prevent the inclusion of additional case studies in this essay.) But the most productive and innovative among them—at least in the context of comparative studies of intelligence—may well have been the men and women who uncovered Africa in its full geographic and human diversity. Their collective accomplishment is of singular and lasting importance—whether recorded between the fourteenth and eighteenth centuries by the Portuguese, the Dutch, and the Order of the Capuchins, or in the eighteenth and nineteenth centuries by French, German, Scottish, and English nationals—for one main reason: it was carried out in a world in which writing was unknown. This meant that European explorers had to make their particular, usually lonely ways in the uncharted continental vastness without meeting people who could read or write. Further, it meant that they had to learn how to compensate for the absence of written literary and historical records by cultivating oral sources and by learning local languages through reliance only on speech. Lastly and mainly, it meant that they could not hope to master the standing task of identifying, understanding, and assessing scores of linguistically distinct communities without knowing how to gain insight into nonliterate modes of thought and communication.

Our libraries today are dense with well-kept journals and other original source materials that attest to the attainment of these objectives and to the efficacy of near-countless "personalized systems" of interpreting, projecting, and organizing the information so assembled.

Further, we learn from the data banks left by those early Occidental Africanists what we also learn from the legacies of the early Occidental Orientalists, namely, that explorers had a way of intuitively upping the stakes of their self-set or mandated tasks and of embarking on revolutionary causes. In the case of Africa, this disposition found paramount expression in determined attempts to bring writing to approximately one thousand linguistically discrete communities that had resisted literacy as represented by Egyptian, Arabic, and Coptic influences for the preceding millennia.

This revolutionary program[11] was predicated on finding and accurately assessing information about the mental, social, and political implications of orality on the one hand and writing, on the other, which was not required for the task of tracing the course of rivers like the Niger, the Nile, the Congo, or the Zambezi. Close cooperation with centers of administration, both indigenous and European, was needed, especially when it was realized by governing authorities that self-government and modern statehood were absolutely dependent upon the firm installation of writing.

The following illustrations must suffice. The first relates to the Christian Kingdom of the Kongo, where the Christian sovereigns of the African Kingdom and of Portugal, the Capuchins, and the papacy had decided in the fifteenth century to embark on a program that would introduce literacy and education and strengthen Christianity, thereby establishing the African Kingdom as a member of the international Christian society of states.

It is relevant to note that the kings of Portugal and Kongo were equals in the sense that both were subservient to the universal church; that Kongo was drawn into diplomatic relations with other European powers; and that "acculturation" between the Portuguese and the Kongolese was openly promoted by intermarriage, dispatches of diplomatic missions, exchanges of persons, and programs of technical assistance. Yet sizable segments of the populations became resentful of the inroads made by Christianity and literacy, and anti-Christian movements arose with increasing frequency. By 1700 the Kongo had lost its status as an Afro-European state and had been reabsorbed into the African nonliterate, non-Christian scheme of things. Indeed, a twentieth-century review of this extraordinary international relationship led a leading African historian to conclude that the European presence had not left any significant traces, even though it had been experienced for four hundred years.[12]

Commitments to implant the written word so as to further such causes as education, historiography, national consciousness, statehood, and pacification were carried through in record numbers throughout the nineteenth and early twentieth centuries. One of the most productive English scholars was Robert S. Rattray, a British colonial administrator who engaged in tireless linguistic research before he was able to give written renditions and assessments of the proverbs, folk tales, religious beliefs and rituals, and laws and constitutions that together represented the formidable Ashanti Kingdom in what is Ghana today. Another was Dr. Henry (Heinrich) Barth, who spent years studying the composite societies of tributary systems that had evolved in Islamized central Africa on the basis of conquest, slavery, slave raiding, and the exaction of tribute. In regard to the role of writing in these essentially nonliterate areas, Barth concluded in the course of his explorations and negotiations that he was dealing with zones of "restricted literacy" where Arabic had been drawn into the Negro host culture in which the written word was esteemed more or less exclusively for its magical qualities.[13]

Conclusions such as these were obviously of great importance for such requirements in the conduct of Euro-African relations as the selection of allies and agents, the interpretation of incoming information, and the structuring of agreements. It is not surprising, therefore, that most European colonial administrators discriminated carefully between literate and nonliterate, Muslim and native African customs when they initiated bargaining procedures, and between verbal assurances and written pacts when it came to concluding accords.[14]

Early Multidisciplinary Approaches to the Collection and Analysis of Information

The Europeans who pioneered in Africa and Asia as collectors of intelligence on behalf of the West converged on the following dispositions and ground rules for research and operation.

Most were self-directed individuals whose commitment to learn about foreign lands and peoples was basically personal and voluntary, far exceeding the needs of government in whose services they often stood.

The ultimate source of their steadfast interest to understand the "others" they encountered was humanism in its classical and Christian connotations. This explains why comparisons with "the self" did not automatically establish "the other" as the "enemy"; why information was collected and assessed in accordance with observations of reality rather than by following preconceived theories; why the explorers were after original sources; why crosscultural communications in matters of both collection and analysis were preferably cast in terms of interpersonal relations; and why the quests for intelligence invariably centered on the need to understand the workings of individual foreign minds and the mind-sets identified with their societies.

Reflections on the work done by this innovative breed lead to the conclusion that the explorers reached this central target of their intellectual activities by developing what we are now accustomed to calling multidisciplinary research. The disciplines that disengage themselves from the maze of these early operations as indispensable guides for the penetration of foreign societies and their ways of thought are language studies and literature; religion, theology, philosophy, and ethics; ethnography and general anthropology; geography and history.

An overview of recorded achievements shows a consensus also on two other points: first, the humanities were deemed the most valued sources of insight for an understanding of Asian and African societies (quite contrary to what contemporary Chinese surmised, namely, that the West's inventiveness and learning were rooted in mathematics); and second, no discipline in the humanities was cultivated as assiduously and profitably as history.

Several reasons explain this focus. It was recognized by scholarly European explorers in the last five hundred years as it had been by their classical forebears that non-Western perspectives on time differed radically from their own inasmuch as time's weight was supposed to lie heavily on the past. To preserve traditional thoughtways and institutions, not to change them, has, therefore, been the standing orientation in both literate and nonliterate cultures. This meant that serious European researchers could neither assess nor deal effectively with an Asian or African society unless they had succeeded in reconstructing its past and in identifying the constant or unwobbling principles that made it "tick."

This way of digging for intelligence explains the successful identification of certain semi-covert yet effective non-Western forms of political organization and decision-making that would have eluded research in pure political science because they were not sufficiently concrete or adaptable to norms known in the West. The Jesuits in China could thus come to terms with the intricacies of Peking's celestial statecraft, while European Africanists had no trouble "reading" the historical and political meanings of mythical and symbolic "constitutions," understanding the past as relayed by the dreams of their informants, and assessing the actual relevance of such magical commonwealths as the conglomerate of "spirit provinces" that some Shona peoples had called into being on the Zambezi.[15]

Last but not least it should be noted in this summation of early European designs for the collection and analysis of information about foreign peoples that those in quest of intelligence were not working in academic enclosures and that they were not adverse to close cooperation with policy-making officials and institutions in their own society. Rather, the opposite seems to have been the norm. After all, and as mentioned earlier, the modern European university—upon which later American, Asian, and African universities were modeled—did not emerge before the middle of the nineteenth century. This meant that learning was not the monopoly of the academically educated but a shared legacy on which all could draw and to which all could contribute, whether they were explorers, missionaries, government officials, envoys, agents of influence, or travelling citizens.

As noted earlier in this book, nowhere in Europe were the themes sketched here exemplified more persuasively than in the long history (eighth to eighteenth centuries) of the Venetian intelligence system.[16] At the core of this establishment were erudite, highly disciplined envoys and secret agents who knew how to evaluate the long-range significance of events, whether recorded in Europe or Asia; how to recruit reliable informants; how to size up the character traits and political dispositions of influential personages, whether in the papal court in Rome, the Byzantine Christian empire, the capitals of Europe, or the far-flung domains of Mongols, Turks, Persians, and Arabs; and how to compose their official ambassadorial reports (*re-*

lazioni) to the Venetian government. These were carefully preserved over the centuries in well-organized, readily accessible archives that had the ultimate function of conditioning successive generations to understand foreign societies realistically on their own terms and to develop unifying time-transcendent perspectives on the republic's national interests in world affairs.

This unusual conception of strategic intelligence and statecraft greatly impressed Leopold von Ranke, probably Europe's foremost historical analyst of foreign affairs and a pioneer in modern comparative studies. The theme for international history that preoccupied him throughout his life was the seemingly endless counterplay between Occident and Orient, specifically Europe and the Islamic Middle East, which was dominated in the nineteenth century by the Turkish empire. It was in this context that Ranke had occasion to reaffirm the time-transcendent function of the Venetian *relazioni* as the only reliable data bank of intelligence about critical developments in sixteenth- and seventeenth-century Turkey; and its contents presaged decadence.[17]

POLITICAL INTELLIGENCE IN AMERICAN THOUGHT AND POLICY

The United States is historically and culturally an offshoot of Europe. Yet it is clear today that American thoughtways in the domain of statecraft and intelligence diverge significantly from those identified with all of Europe in the preceding twenty-five hundred years.

What are the determining factors in this development? Which new norms or concepts have been shaped in American scholarship and statesmanship? How do they "play" in today's world environment, specifically in relations with non-Western non-Communist societies? And how effective is the U.S. political intelligence system in coping with foreign ways of conceptualizing, organizing, and using this complex matter called "intelligence"?[18]

Questions such as these should be addressed by scholars and government officials since the evidence indicates that the United States has not been as successful as it had been expected to be in dealing with nations in the so-called Third World.

The point was thus often made in the course of the American Consortium for the Study of Intelligence's colloquia that the United States does not really know how today's non-Western nations "tick." And indeed, a stock-taking of intelligence and policy failures directly attributable to misperceptions and wrong assessments suggests strongly that something is askew in the nation's thoughtways when different administrations and successive generations of congressional representatives, public policy elites, and officers in the intelligence community continue to be unprepared for such developments as the Leninization of Cuba, Ethiopia, and strategically important parts of black Africa; the Yom Kippur War; the Arab oil embargo; the North Vietnamese offensives of 1968 and 1975; the Shi'ite transformation of Iran; the Soviet Union's open military takeover of Afghanistan; and the dramatic open revolt against Soviet occupation throughout Eastern Europe in 1989.[19] The chief underlying reasons for U.S. intelligence failures in such contexts seem to be the following:

1. The nation as a whole has come to commit itself to a simplistic or reductionist version of the Declaration of Independence, which is to the effect that mankind is essentially undifferentiated and that the world society is therefore meant to be unified both morally and politically.

2. In this spirit Americans have gradually come to believe that the United States is a "lesson" and a guide for mankind and that it has a mandate to help democratize all others.[20] In short, U.S. views of the world and of the national self appear to converge today in the certainty that culture is a nonconcept when statecraft is the issue.[21] The need to assess an African, Asian, or Latin American society does not really arise in such premises. Comparisons become pointless and "political intelligence" evaporates as a concept, a process, and a set of institutions.

3. Next, modern American thought about relations between "the other" and "the self" is confounded by a neglectful disposition toward the human experience of the past. This orientation deviates from the legacy of Western civilization but is congruent with an indigenous American persuasion that all relevant history begins in 1776 and that it is actually only with the future and the very recent past that policymakers need to be concerned.

It goes without saying in light of these assumptions that present-day Americans know little about Europe's history and its organic linkage with that of the United States and even less about the millennial past of Asian and African peoples and its extraordinary hold upon the thoughtways of present generations. True, the case of the "missing historian" is officially recognized today by U.S. schoolmasters as a grave calamity for its educational system. But the fact remains that "he" or "she" was not on the job in critical times to help direct the work of collecting and analyzing intelligence data on behalf of the government's foreign affairs establishment.[22]

The records thus show indisputably already in the nineteenth century that American dealings with non-Western societies are marked by great weariness with others' dispositions to respect the past. American missionaries in nineteenth- and twentieth-century China are a case in point. Martin was thus decidedly irritated by that "constant harking back to the past" in which the Chinese engaged during negotiations pertaining to one or the other plan for improving or changing a customary life-style, institution, or set of beliefs, and so were most of his countrymen.[23] All were concerned with fashioning China's future by "doing good" in terms of supplying technical assistance and modern educational facilities including medical schools; and all were destined for disappointment because the imports were resisted and at times brutally dismantled.

4. Not much had been learned from the accumulation of such experiences when the United States embarked on extensive worldwide economic aid policies after the end of World War II. The standing expectation continues to be that material improvements in living conditions will automatically spark political developments favorable to U.S. versions of freedom, democracy, and peace. Even these goals are being conceived rather mechanistically today for the United States is obviously satisfied when the foreign governments—be they non-Communist, non-Western, or Communist—provide their nations with constitutions modeled on Western norms

and when they sign UN charters, resolutions, and declarations. How else can one explain the State Department's assessment that scores of long-established African and Asian societies had actually put away their past and acquired a new identity in 1948 when they affixed their signatures to the Universal Declaration of Human Rights?

The stress on materialism, economic determinism, and current events in this projection of "development" in times-to-come explains why the collection of foreign intelligence has been generally confined to recording recent economic, social, and, in some instances, military data. Altogether missing are commitments to identify the foreign nation's own values and idea systems; to find out how its people feel, think, and reason; and to determine whether or how the preexisting cultural infrastructure can accommodate the American norms pressed upon them now.

In short, the fourth and, in my view, most critical aspect of American dispositions toward non-Western societies—and it is obviously closely related to the preceding three—is a pronounced inability or unwillingness to come to terms with religions, philosophies, ideologies, and other bodies of belief that have decisively shaped the foreign mind-sets but which continue to baffle Americans. As I had occasion to point out in earlier papers on comparative studies and non-Western cultures—some of them included in this book[24]—numerous strategically significant intelligence and policy failures could have been averted if we had assessed the psychological, intellectual, and political relevance of Confucianism; Legalism (also known as Realism); Buddhism; Shinto; Hinduism; Sikhism; Islam; Judaism; Africa's diverse renditions of Christianity, Islam, and Animism; and Southeast Asia's complex syncretisms of a variety of creeds.[25]

A survey of non-Western societies in our era reveals incontrovertibly that all had acceded voluntarily to the European States System and to the West's law of nations, and that all had freely accepted Western forms of constitutionalism as core principles of administration. None of this should have been taken to mean, however, that non-Western states had suddenly become Western states. It is thus one of many puzzling blind spots in U.S. diplomacy and intelligence that scant, if any, attention was being paid on the one hand to the gradual waning of trust in panaceas offered by the West and, on the other, to the steady resurgence of confidence, even pride, in traditional ways of coping with life's insecurities on political, moral, and mental levels. Overlooked altogether, therefore, was the fact that the legacies of the past were being reactivated without discarding the new protective umbrella of modern Western-type statehood. Indeed, comparative studies show that non-Western peoples exist consciously in two different worlds and that their political representatives operate equally effectively within two conflicting frames of reference and in accordance with two disparate codes of thought and conduct.[26]

The other self-inflicted impediment in U.S. relations with non-Western peoples is the proven U.S. incompetence to predict, contain, and assess the impact of Marxism-Leninism and totalitarian statecraft upon their destinies.[27] This failure is partly due to faulty readings of Communist strategies, but it is a function also of the stubborn American disposition to identify non-Western states in terms of their nominal Western appearances rather than in those of their authentic substance. Yet it is the latter, not the former, that supplies the countervailing forces to the intruding alien power, and these differ greatly from one case to the next as do the tactics of Leninist principals and surrogates. Since Americans do not know the basic or sub-stratal configurations of non-Western mind-sets, they are obviously not equipped in intelligence terms either to isolate these "contra" forces or to anticipate, preclude, and actually cope with Communist-controlled insurgencies.

5. My last comments on present-day American orientations to comparative in-telligence studies in regard to the non-Western world bear on the state of the art in U.S. academic institutions and on the relationship between these institutions and the nation's policy-making agencies. These relations have often been described as decidedly adversarial, but a juxtaposition of intelligence-related policies and intel-ligence-related academic research shows a near-total convergence of views on major issues. The question whether this is so because the professoriate's input in terms of personnel and therewith of information has been so great as to be decisive or be-cause it is so small as to be inconsequential may therefore be irrelevant.

Not irrelevant are the following facts: (1) academic programs made scant, if any, allowance for national security studies; they made their appearance slowly in the 1970s under the auspices of private research centers, such as the National Strat-egy Information Center, Inc.; (2) political intelligence was conspicuously missing in the curricula until the Consortium for the Study of Intelligence succeeded in making a convincing case for honoring this age-old phenomenon of statecraft; (3) multidisciplinary approaches have been strongly advocated by the International Studies Association in earlier years, but they remain anchored, by and large, in political science, the behavioral sciences, and economic theory; and (4) compara-tive studies on the level of world affairs are wanting in depth and significance. As I suggest in an earlier part of this essay, this is so for a variety of reasons, among them neglect of the humanities and therewith absence of vital data from non-West-ern societies.

Where, then, is the academic—and therewith the educational—focus in com-parative research? Professional literature indicates that it continues to be on theory building. True, some excitement seems to have been "lost," as relayed in the pro-ceedings of a conference in 1985,[28] but the consensus was that comparative political analysts are more rigorous and scientifically sophisticated than their predecessors. Little was made of the undeniable fact that non-Western cultures and societies have not brought forth academic establishments, disciplines, and theories of the kind the United States takes for granted[29] and that the United States allowed its theories to take off as universal givens even though they had evolved almost exclusively from working Western data. In short, much needs to be done by way of understanding the real world before U.S. analysts are ready to formulate internationally tenable theories.

The modern professoriate's commitment to the primacy of theory in interna-tional relations research is the counterpart of the U.S. government's present-day commitment to uphold at all costs the universal validity of some internationally untested American ideals of human life on earth. This correspondence is not sur-prising, since most government officials, congressmen, and senators received their education in the nation's colleges and universities. In recent times, therefore, there has been a striking convergence of inclinations not to perceive new realities, especially when these are obviously inimical to the national interest. Indeed, the very notion of the national interest has been eroding in the last critical decades during which academic institutions cast themselves in the role of value-neutral, quasi-supernational monitors of their country's behavior in foreign affairs.

When the president of the University of Minnesota was asked by the State Department in 1981 to cooperate with its policy of imposing security restrictions on the research activities of mainland Chinese scholars (then guests on the campus), he replied curtly: "Our mission is teaching, research, and public service, and neither our facility nor our administrators were hired to implement security policies."[30]

Likewise, and in a similar vein, the University of California refused to allow the Department of Defense to use fifty beds at each of its five hospitals for the treatment of military casualties in the event of a war.[31] As Alvin H. Bernstein concludes in his illuminating essay,[32] there is a good deal of evidence that this kind of pronouncement is echoed approvingly throughout the groves of academe and that the assumptions underlying such rebuffs represent a wide consensus among the professoriate.

The targets singled out consistently for the deepest antagonism have been on the one hand "the military" and its "fascist mind-set," and, on the other, the intelligence community, specifically the Central Intelligence Agency. Some of this ire in the ranks of our educated elites may well be due to an inadequate understanding of modern species of irregular, protracted, and political warfare and of the nullifying effect they have had on traditional American conceptions of war and its relation to peace.[33] However, the public case against political intelligence in general and its covert dimensions in particular, as it was steadfastly made in classrooms until recently and as it continues to be made in Congress and the media, appears to stem from an unresearched but culturally congenial assumption that "intelligence"—a word that had come to stand for plain old espionage and dirty tricks in the ivy halls of academe—is incompatible with an open democratic society. This, too, was poignantly illustrated when over one hundred law professors protested a bill in 1981 by the Senate subcommittee on terrorism (S.2216) that was designed to ban the publication of the names of U.S. intelligence officers. Unmoved by the knowledge that such publishing would gravely imperil the lives of U.S. government agents, they stuck to their objection that the legislation in question would limit the freedom of speech and press guarantees of the First Amendment.[34]

In the vacuum of civil ethics and concern for national security that resulted from academic actions such as these, it is no wonder that leaking state secrets and classified information is today not generally viewed as treason but rather as its opposite, an exercise in true democracy. This metamorphosis of norms and values definitely conduced not only to a breakdown of security—here viewed as concept and reality—but also to a breakdown of the concept and reality of national consensus policy. In this respect, then, I agree with James A. Schlesinger, who observed during a discussion of the uneasy relationship between freedom and security that "to preserve secrecy, especially in a democracy, security must be part of an accepted pattern of behavior outside of government and inside."[35]

Americans may have come closer to a national consensus on these grave matters of state in the last few years and may even have started to do something about the depleted state of U.S. intelligence capabilities. But I doubt that U.S. achievements to date would meet the standards set by George Washington (the Founding Father personally supervised intelligence operations during the Revolutionary War) when he insisted in a speech in 1777 on "the necessity of procuring good intelligence" and on "secrecy" as its indispensable requirement.[36] In fact, I think this nation-state has steadily regressed in the art of statecraft, mainly because it could not count on the civic support and scholarly contributions of its most highly educated elites and because its principal foreign-policy–making institutions—Congress, the State Department, and the Central Intelligence Agency—have gradually become too close extensions of these elites.[37]

Robert A. McCaughey has taken a sharp look at all this in a recent volume, *International Studies and Academic Enterprise: A Chapter in the Enclosure of American Learning*.[38] There he defines "international studies" as a specific collectivity of intellectual pursuits through which Americans have sought greater knowledge and wider understanding of the world beyond their national boundaries and those of culturally akin Western Europe—those parts of the world, namely, that they have traditionally regarded as having histories, cultures, and social arrangements distinctly different from their own. Quite in contrast to other intellectual enterprises that were "academized" soon after the emergence of the university in the United States in the last third of the nineteenth century, the study of foreign cultures and societies was not monopolized or "bounded" in this fashion until around 1940, when it, too, became an academic enterprise.

Among many central questions raised in this illuminating volume, the following as presented by McCaughey are particularly pertinent to the themes here under discussion:

> Could the achievements that characterized international studies as an academic enterprise have come except at the relative if not actual expense of international studies as an intellectual enterprise?
>
> Might not the talent and energies that academic enclosure concentrated within the university have had a more beneficial impact on American society had they been more widely dispersed?
>
> Did enclosure advance or hinder the formulation of an enlightened American foreign policy and the education of an internationally informed electorate?
>
> Need the flourishing of international studies within the university in the 1950s and 1960s have been attended by the withering of nonuniversity components of the enterprise that seemed so vital as late as the 1930s?
>
> Should international studies be viewed today as "a saturated activity"?[39]

Whether U.S. intelligence studies stay within the academic enclosure or take distance from it by following in the footsteps of earlier explorers, it is probably evident to many that the nation's intelligence arteries are seriously clogged today. This challenge implies the following tasks: to refine or correct public conceptions of the meaning and function of intelligence, to reassess the curricular base for studying intelligence in all its segments, and to evaluate existing techniques of research.

Unless these needs are met expeditiously, comparative studies of intelligence will not be developed since "comparison" cannot get off the ground as long as the home norms are defective.[40]

POLITICAL INTELLIGENCE STUDIES IN NON-WESTERN SOCIETIES

As the title of this essay indicates, I set out to investigate general approaches to comparative studies so as to get a handle on the task of understanding and comparing non-Western practices in the field of political intelligence.

Communist non-Western countries are usually excluded from the non-Western category either because they have been officially extinguished as sovereign states or because they have voluntarily opted to be Communist rather than non-Western, or because Western scholars and statesmen are as yet unsure of their actual identity. However, the point needs to be made that it is not possible in *our* time to understand non-Western systems (those taken over by Communist regimes and those still free), to isolate differences between Western and non-Western systems of statecraft, and to avoid failure in policy and intelligence contexts, unless one has Marxist-Leninist ideology and statecraft firmly in mind. Also, and specifically in the context of comparative studies, it should be mandatory to compare Communist and non-Western thoughtways so as to be able to estimate the impact of the former on the latter on political, mental, and psychological levels, and identify linkages, affinities, and deviations.

The Question of What Is a State

One of the main problems in such an undertaking relates to the unit of comparison. We speak today either of "the non-Western world"—even though we know that it consists of hundreds of very different political entities—or of "non-Western societies"—even though we know that the word "society" may stand for village, state, city, tribe, clan, secret fraternity, bazaar, empire, a group of assassins, or the world entire. This set of uncertainties may explain why we are reluctant to let go of that tidy Occidental concept of the territorially defined nation-state that has long served as the globally valid norm or measure of political identification and comparison. But as suggested earlier in numerous and different contexts, this unifying principle, too, is shaky and embattled today, nowhere more so than in non-Western and Communist regions of the world.

For example, most states in black and Islamized Africa consist of pluralities of ethnic, religious, or linguistic folk societies that have not been able to evolve into unified nations. None comes to mind in which tribally induced apartheid is not the general norm of coexistence outside urban centers. Nor can one think of a new African state that has not been beset by internal tribal conflicts and warfare.

In the culturally unified Arab-Islamic Middle East, the Western model of the state is refuted as categorically today as was that of the Persian/Turkic power *mulkh* in the early Islamic centuries because it, too, is absolutely incompatible with the prophet's idea of the universal *umma* of all believers. In the Arab context, mean-while, long-established theory continues to insist on one all-Arab commonwealth, not on separate Arab nation-states. Needless to say, none of these are reliably de-fined in territorial terms. Further, here as elsewhere in the non-Western world, one also finds that the state has degenerated into a protective cover for the dissemination of contra-state ideologies and power centers.

Next, and as illustrated in other essays in this volume, the integrity of the con-cept "state" is critically impaired also because it is applied to political establish-ments that are too different to be comparable or equal in terms of either international theory or power politics.

The state, then, is not the decisive working unit for intelligence studies, com-parative or otherwise.[41] And the same holds *mutatis mutandis* for Western under-standings of war and its relation to peace as incorporated in international law be-cause the rights of war and peace were conceived from Grotian times onward as functions of the territorially defined sovereign state.[42] In short, we do not have a globally meaningful international system. Therefore, we cannot count with a pre-cise or bounded political framework capable of hallowing all of our comparisons; to put it differently, we cannot systematize studies of intelligence in terms of a state system that is defunct.

This realization has served to confirm my view that the world society consists today as it did before the nineteenth century of a plurality of diverse political sys-tems, and that each of these is in the final analysis the product of culture-specific ideas and modes of thinking rather than of particular political and economic ar-rangements. The challenge in my view of comparative studies is therefore to iden-tify the structuring concepts and values that lend uniqueness or distinction to "the other" society, region, or culture—namely those that provide moral and mental security because they stubbornly resist compromise under the impact of interna-tional and intercultural relations.[43]

The Widened Field of Inquiry

Another major question in studies such as the present relates to the choice and use of academic disciplines and research techniques.

On the assumption that I am proposing a somewhat different, perhaps an "al-ternative" approach to intelligence research, I should begin by saying that the gen-eral study of cultures, belief systems, and modes of thinking—most of them trans-territorial in conception and reality—is more time-consuming and comprehensive in scope than that of territorially bounded states or political systems. In my expe-rience, it cannot be undertaken in the narrow context of social or political science but simply requires multidisciplinary work. Further, and as explained earlier,[44] the humanities are the best guides in these endeavors, foremost among them language, literature, history, religion, philosophy, and philosophical anthropology.

For example, I could not come to intellectually satisfactory terms with the na-ture and incidence of war and conflict in black Africa or with African ways of absorbing or managing these phenomena until I had immersed myself in the belief systems and historical traditions of about one hundred separate African communities. Most Sinologists feel the same way about the task of understanding China on its own terms. Simon Leys explained this recently in the following passage:

> Specialization is impossible. China is an organic entity, in which every element can be understood only when put under the light of other elements; these other elements can be fairly remote from the one that is under consideration—sometimes they do not even present any apparent connection with it. If he is not guided by a global intuition, the specialist remains forever condemned to the fate described in the well-known Buddhist parable: as they wanted to figure out what an elephant really looked like they groped, one for the trunk, one for the foot, one for the tail, and respectively concluded that an elephant was a kind of snake, was a kind of pillar, was a kind of broom.[45]

The Chinese case is a particularly instructive example of the need to study particular phenomena in the extended general framework of culture. Thus it is noteworthy that the Chinese themselves have traditionally conceptualized the Middle Kingdom not as one bounded state in the company of others, but as a civilization so uniquely superior that it cannot be presumed to have frontiers. This self-view spawned China's insistently Sinocentric worldview; sanctioned imperial schemes of military and political expansion; and sustained several politically and culturally potent ideas of imperial administration, chief among them the notion of the emperor's "heavenly mandate" and the concept of a family of unequal and inferior nations held together by the "Imperial Father"—images persuasively concretized throughout the centuries by the tribute system and the well-organized dependence on hedge-guarding satellites and surrogates.

The advantages of a widened field of inquiry for issue identification (in our case "intelligence") are illustrated also by studies of China's greatly various schools of thought, philosophies, and religions, which have been contending with each other from about the sixth century B.C. onward. I do not think it is possible to understand any norm, institution, or policy, either in traditional or in modern China, without being at least on speaking terms with Confucianism, Legalism (and their often contentious interactions), Taoism, and Buddhism, while remaining keenly aware in particular of the decisive impact that Legalism has had on dynastic as well as on Maoist and post-Maoist statecraft.[46] Further, it goes without saying that knowledge of these idea systems and their different syncretisms is required for any intelligence-centered research in the rest of the Orient, perhaps specifically in the Sinified societies of Northeast, Southeast, and Central Asia.[47]

In sum, crosscultural comparative studies of such topics as time perspectives and history; philosophy, religion, and ideology; law, ethics, and jurisprudence; political organization, government, and statecraft; international law, diplomacy, and intelligence; conflict and conflict management; and of the relation between peace and war have persuaded me that the whole of a given society or culture must be explored before one can reach tenable conclusions about the meaning content of one particular manifestation of "the whole."

The first segment in my scheme for the comparative study of intelligence in the non-Western world consists, therefore, of extended examinations and comparisons of non-Western cultures and societies. Since I obviously cannot append my published work on this matter to the present chapter, I decided to extrapolate the main findings in an "Inventory of General Propositions" (A) upon which I find non-Western cultures to converge. This is designed as background for the second segment dealing specifically with non-Western orientations to intelligence, which are abstracted in an "Inventory of Propositions" (B) that focuses on concordance or affinity—thus justifying our summary reference to "The Non-Western World." (Most divergences are explicitly marked under each of the two headings.)

A.   Inventory of General Propositions That Determine the Meaning and Function of Intelligence in Non-Western Societies

1. In non-Western as in Western societies, "understanding" means insight into the workings of the human mind. However, conceptions of mind differ and so do the purpose of gaining insight into it.

Asian and African pronouncements on this subject as recorded in millennia of history and explicated in religions and philosophies of timeless significance are at one in taking a dim view of human nature. The task incumbent upon government and education, therefore, has been to know how to mold and socialize the human mind so that people would stay pliant and subservient in the stations to which they are assigned, whether by religion and birth as in India's caste system, by the Confucian dogma of the five classic human relationships as in China and most Sinified societies; by tribal and intertribal customs as in black Africa; or by simple fiat of a ruling establishment. Nowhere are individuals presumed free and equal, destined to develop independently on their own. Rather, what one detects in all non-Western records is mistrust of the individual human being and fear of the moral, social, and political implications of individualism as this concept has been understood in the West in the last millennia.

These factors, often in conjunction with the religious requirement to eliminate the ego altogether—as in Hindu and Buddhist societies—help explain the paramountcy of authoritarian rule in the diverse provinces of the non-Western world and that striking stress on harsh punishment and internal espionage or surveillance commonly found in traditional Asian and African empires, kingdoms, caliphates, sultanates, chiefdoms, and folk societies as well as in most of their present-day successor states.

The same set of basic persuasions and ruling norms provides the reason why "the other"—namely, the one who does not "belong"—is almost automatically regarded as an enemy. The following additional circumstances help explain the orientation.

2. Non-Western societies and political systems were not designed either as nations of equal citizens or as melting pots of people. Rather, order was maintained by keeping classes, factions, and racially different groups in conditions of apartheid.

This is well-illustrated in traditional China by dense catalogues of gradations in the class system, as, for example, regulations regarding "the mean people" (slaves, entertainers, beggars) and "the good people," and the elaborate prohibitions attending relationships between members of these different categories.[48] Further, the logic of the Chinese self-view demands uncompromising hostility against non-

Chinese. These were, therefore, routinely regarded and described as "devil slaves," "ghosts," "inhabitants of the nether world," "animals," or "issue of union with animals," and, of course, as "barbarians"—epithets also heaped upon Europeans and Americans in the nineteenth century as in modern Communist times.[49]

African cultures differ in numerous significant respects from those associated with the Orient, but homogeneity is society's commitment here as there. Indeed, here it is an absolute requirement. For contrary to the situation in ancient literate civilizations where it was always possible, with the aid of writing and adjunct intellectual skills of communication, to extend the boundaries of the politically unified or unifiable groups, nonliterate societies had to be small and self-sufficient if they were to be effective and enduring. Furthermore, each had to be composed exclusively of people who spoke the same language, actually and figuratively, since cohesion and order cannot be assured in conditions of orality unless all people think in terms of the same symbols, identify with the same ancestral spirits, and obey the same taboos.

The order of the folk society, upon which modern Africa continues to rest, has ensured this type of closely knit, kinship-centered solidarity and conformity for millennia. The man who did not belong simply could not have a standing here (unless he became a fictitious relative through adoption). Outside such exceptional circumstances, the stranger has invariably been a calamity and an object of extreme suspicion. Frequently cast in the ritual role of scapegoat, or "carrier," he was saddled with all the evil that had accumulated in the community and driven out or killed so as to allow the in-group to survive in its authenticity.[50]

In sum, literate and nonliterate non-Western societies originated as closed, tightly controlled societies, and most have continued to be just that. Most are also conflicted societies where mistrust and hostility mark the coexistence of diverse religious, linguistic, racial, social, or ideological groups today as they did in the past, while relations between the central government and all it governs are chronically informed by reciprocal antagonisms and fears.

3. Dissidence, subversion, internecine feuding, and conspiracy have been endemic occurrences according to the records, as are harsh responses by ruling establishments. How to discover and control conspiracies; guard against treason, overthrow, and assassination; and ferret out fifth columns within and trace their connections with enemies outside the realm have, therefore, been paramount preoccupations of rulers everywhere. A comparison of the modalities upon which pros and contras in all categories of association—whether governmental or nongovernmental—relied shows conclusively that covert thought and covert action constituted the indispensable essence of political existence throughout the non-Western world.

A pronounced predilection for clandestine political action and organization; secrecy in decision-making, communication, and negotiation; and insistence on absolute confidentiality among the like-minded emerges in this context as yet another theme upon which non-Western societies have converged for centuries. Indeed, none of the scores of modern coups, plots, counterplots, insurgencies, counterinsurgencies, revolts, and civil wars could have taken place in Asia and Africa had it not been for these deeply rooted predispositions and their foremost manifestations: secret societies and secret systems of internal intelligence or espionage.

As I had occasion to note in earlier publications and other essays in this volume, Islamic empires were layered societies, composed of numerous essentially self-sufficient corporations, guilds, bazaars, sects, and religious brotherhoods. These, too, were closed societies in the sense that they were beholden to their own social codes and customs. And since they were usually hostile to state authority as well as to other nonstate associations, they often engaged in clandestine and covert operations. Further, and more to the point of this discussion, flights into subversive association were so commonplace between the seventh and twentieth centuries that "the secret dissimulated society" became the normative organizational model for religious and political activism, especially in Persia and the Arab lands.[51]

Analogous patterns emerge from the histories of East Asian civilizations. As noted in the Fourth Essay of this book, China was honeycombed with secret societies, and many of them came to constitute states within the state. Some were conceived as benevolent associations, others as expressions of the criminal underworld. However, most existed for the purpose of opposing existing authorities in the ranks of the imperial administration, the mandarinate, the army, religious circles, and merchant classes, and were active also in stirring up revolts or spearheading xenophobic movements. Highly disciplined as covert martial orders, which could maintain their identity and cohesiveness through reliance on a system of passwords, magic rituals, oathing, and so forth, they have been functioning effectively for centuries, often in clandestine cooperation with other revolutionary elements and aspirants to power. Secret society leaders thus became pioneers in China's Communist party and were held in considerable esteem by Sun Yat-sen, the Kuomintang, and Mao Tse-tung.

A related yet somewhat different secret-society syndrome evolved in culturally homogeneous Japan. Here it was patriotism, not its opposite, that motivated Japanese citizens in the nineteenth century and thereafter to form secret associations to support the cause of imperial expansion. The precedent for this kind of service was set in the context of preparing the war against China when Genyosha (the Black Ocean Society) was founded in 1881 for the purpose of gathering intelligence through undercover espionage. Described by Richard Storry (a noted English historian of Japan) as a terrorist organization and school for spies, it yet contributed greatly to Japan's dramatic victory over China. Also, it spawned another ultranationalist secret society—the Black Dragon Society, or, more correctly, the Society of the River Amur (founded in 1901)—that prepared the equally successful war against Russia by collecting intelligence in Manchuria and Siberia and relaying it to the Foreign Office and the military, by organizing Chinese guerrillas to harass the Russians, and by establishing links with Muslim secret societies in the Czarist realm.[52]

Nowhere in the world are the themes of secrecy and dissimulation as highly developed and as deeply rooted in thought patterns, worldviews, and political systems as in black Africa. They are not set out here because I had occasion to discuss them in the preceding essay.[53]

4. The foregoing survey of concordances among non-Western cultures and societies provides some explanation for the common incidence of internal, or domes-

tic, intelligence. The classical case for the necessity of keeping subjects under surveillance and of "learning the secrets of the people" was developed between the fifth century B.C. and the eleventh century A.D. by two great Asian empires.

In West Asia the practice was initiated by Persia's Achaemenid dynasty when "the king's eyes and ears" were institutionalized in an exemplary manner. As discerned from Hindu texts, the precedent was followed by India's Hindu kingdoms (many of them had been included in the original Persian empire). As elaborated by Persia's Sassanian dynasty, it was accepted by all Islamic caliphates, albeit in versions strictly inferior to the original mode.[54] The theater of most intelligence operations, including covert actions, was everywhere in the immediate entourage of the governing personality since it was he who personified the state in the past as he does now.

In East Asia it was China that set the example beginning with the period of the Warring States. In fact China may well be *hors concours* in comparative studies of intelligence because it is the only politically unified region in the world in which policy-making has always been closely and consciously aligned with political theory. It is, therefore, difficult to imagine how the period of the Warring States could have come to an end had it not been for the impact on statecraft of that Realist (Legalist) science that began evolving in the seventh century B.C. to reach its apogee in the writings of Lord Shang, Han Fei Tzu, and Sun Tzu. In regard to matters of internal intelligence, it is noteworthy therefore that Mao Tse-tung chose to follow carefully in the footsteps of the first and second Ch'in emperors.

For example, the Communist system of grouping families or households in city dwellings and rural communes in such a way that reliable cadres can assure close surveillance of their thoughts, words, and actions recalls the precedent of a Ch'in decree on "Household Registration System." This provided that people had to be organized into groups of five and ten households that would spy on each other and expose "evil persons" so that they could be made to share in each other's crimes and penalties. Further, the parallels are close between the Maoist tactic of allowing a hundred schools of thought to bloom in order then to have them wilt and the Ch'in policy of "surveillance and castigation," which provided that all books of poetry and history had to be burned and Confucian scholars buried alive.[55]

According to my findings in studies of Asian systems of intelligence or espionage, it is the human mind in its totality that is targeted rather than the actual evidence of willed wrongdoing. However, the studies also indicate that methods of tracking and punishing the movements of the mind differ considerably, even in the East Asian context. This is illustrated by a juxtaposition of China and Japan.

As the records of the cultural revolution show, the Chinese regime is not satisfied unless it succeeds by means of tightly organized mass "struggle sessions," extreme humiliation and physical aggression to decompose or liquidate the minds of those it has identified as traitors.[56] Their counterparts in Japan, by contrast, were usually confined to prison during the stressful 1930s. There they were pressured to think about the aberrations of their thoughts; to deconvert from positions taken earlier; and to compose a detailed, well-reasoned, and sincere *tenkosho* (recantation), even when execution was a foregone conclusion of the case. Also, they, like all other Japanese for that matter, were watched routinely in those times by the "Thought Police" (Tokko), which had been created in 1911 as an instrument of the government for the purpose of coping with left-wing thought and enforcing national security laws.[57]

Japanese deviations from Chinese norms are of special interest for scholars of comparative intelligence because they combined, in the course of many centuries, to constitute a unique "system," not just in non-Western but in global terms. What is noteworthy here is that Japan's system has indeed been shaped decisively by Sun Tzu in military as in civilian terms. The records not only tell of battles and protracted military campaigns, which were planned and executed in conformity with Sun Tzu's guidelines, but also are replete with accounts of teams of officially appointed spies who were constantly on the move in the country, watching and listening for any signs of revolt or criticism of the government, of experts in "divination"—a skill regarded throughout Asia (and Africa) as indispensable for intelligence work on human minds—and of elite corps of samurai who had mastered techniques of dissimulation so completely that they could make themselves invisible.

However, and in counterpoint to Chinese conceptions and practices of internal and external intelligence, spying was acclaimed openly in Japan as a noble and patriotic duty that was doing honor to Japan. In this respect, then, Japan resembles Venice rather than China. Both were island states and empires, and it is unlikely that either could have survived had it not been for a national dread of treason and a confidence in intelligence. It is in this sense that one should probably understand the following boast attributed to Major General Fukushima after Japan's victory over Russia at the opening of the twentieth century: "Sun Tzu would have been proud of this operation. He would have said we had followed his textbook to the very last sentence. But we know that we did better than that. We started a new book where he left off."[58]

The striking convergence of non-Western societies upon the need to know and control the human mind has numerous interlocking causes. In the context of this inventory of propositions, it also has a few interesting if somewhat discomfiting connotations for the West that deserve mention. Paradoxical as it may appear to be, one learns from a comparison of non-Western and modern Western intelligence systems that the former—which are culturally not conditioned to subscribe to individualism—pay far greater heed to the workings of the mind than the latter, which pride themselves on their commitment to the cause of the individual and are renowned for their know-how in psychology and psychiatry, yet often fail conspicuously when challenged to deal wisely with treacherous operatives of their own or defectors from an enemy camp.

The chief source of this focal non-Western concept is the deeply ingrained disposition to perceive "the other"—be he at home or abroad—as an actual or potential enemy. For whether contenders are active or dormant, non-Western common sense suggests that one cannot cope with their existence unless one always knows just what and how they think. To discover, thwart, or retool the "other's" intentions; guess or forestall his likely moves; and neutralize, trick, or turn—and, if necessary, entirely undo—his intellectual processes is thus obviously a greater, more serious challenge than understanding the "other" whom one does *not* identify in this way.

Further, but in the same context of comparative psychology, Asian biographies and histories of ideas teach that individuals in educated circles do not strive for that total integrity in commitments to causes and beliefs with which moral and mental achievements are commonly associated in the West. Rather, they tend to be at ease belonging to different schools of thought that would be viewed as mutually exclusive in the West, and representing a plurality of identities that individuals in the West would find confusing, to say the least. Yet in the perspective of intelligence concerns, there are definite merits in such dispositions. For example, the enigmatic Japanese traitor Ozaki was at one and the same time a Marxist-Leninist, a Communist internationalist, a Japanese nationalist, a member of the government's Showa Research Association, a serious scholar, a spy serving the Soviet Union, and a journalist. He, not unlike other intellectuals known in East Asian history, was a covert personality whose "true" identity was usually disguised.

Studies of Islamic patterns of thought and communication reveal closely similar variations on the theme of dissimulation. For instance, and as William S. Haas points out in a pioneering analysis of the Persian mind,[59] the Shi'ites countered the Sunni faith of Persia's Arab conquerors by making allowance for faith by "mental reservation" (*ketman*). Under the protective cover of this religious dispensation, a Shi'ite was allowed to pretend that he was a Sunni, or even a Christian or a Jew, whenever he felt he was in danger of being found out by his mortal enemy. This custom gradually came to dominate other life contexts as well. In that of statecraft, *ketman* thus supplied techniques of cunning, simulation, and ruse that generations of Shi'ites within and outside of Persia/Iran have deployed successfully in the management of both domestic and foreign affairs.

As Americans and Europeans have had occasion to discover in recent times, it is difficult for the West's open societies to contend with this particular dimension of psychopolitical warfare in the Middle East.[60] Here as throughout the Orient, rulers and ruled have traditionally recognized that deception and dissimulation are the essence of statecraft and that, as the ancient Hindus put it, a kingdom has its roots in espionage. A tightly organized network of agents and informants (the *bārid*)—all masters in the art of disguise—thus spanned each caliphate or empire in the domains of the Islamic Persians, Arabs, Turks, and Mongols. The ruling principle in these counterintelligence establishments was a total commitment to confidentiality and secrecy. And, as comparative historical studies of this Asian ethic show, it was honored almost two thousand years ago in India's *artha* world, where he who divulged a secret as by talking in his sleep "was to be torn to pieces,"[61] just as in this century's Near East, where the highly influential Bairut Society—which had begun as a whispering campaign of like-minded opponents to the Turkish regime—was dissolved voluntarily when it was discovered that its secret had not been kept.[62]

In short, communication throughout Asia calls not for openness but for allusiveness, indirection, and a host of secret modalities in speech and behavior. In explaining his rejection of interviews with American journalists, an Arab OPEC official said simply:

> What you have here are two different cultures. In the United States, communication is a virtue. You come home and can't wait to discuss the day's events with your wife. People who communicate well are respected. But in the Arab world, the opposite is true. Communication is a vice. Secrecy is a virtue.[63]

The West has only fragmentary knowledge of explicit intelligence arrangements in Africa's traditional nonliterate societies. One of them relates to Mzilikazi, an early-nineteenth-century warrior king in the tradition of the Zulu chief Shaka, whose conquests established a far-flung Ndebele empire south of the Limpopo River in an area once part of Southern Rhodesia, now of Zimbabwe. Since intelligence was of the utmost importance for Mzilikazi's military campaigns, diplomatic exploits, and scheme of administration, the chief relied heavily not just on usual go-betweens and scouts but on specially selected spies charged with collecting information about the movements of all enemies. Further, Mzilikazi made extensive use of literate white traders and hunters and established unusual personal relationships with the celebrated explorer and missionary Robert Moffat and several other missionaries (among them three Americans). The major compelling motive behind these contacts seems to have been Mzilikazi's speculation that missionaries would be ideal mediators in his relations not only with white men but also, perhaps mainly, with his native enemies.[64] However, all categories of agents were supplemented and outclassed by the ruler's wives. Stationed at every major kraal, they shared power with the district commanders and provided the king with continuous information on local developments.

More relevant for an appreciation of typically African methods of collecting information, communicating with others, and exerting influence are on one hand the structured palaver, in which talk is meant to be protracted, discursive, and roundabout, and, on the other, a vast array of overt and covert intermediaries, deputies, and ritual agents. These traditional intelligence operatives include the West African bards (*griots*) who are highly esteemed as masters of the spoken word; such "outcasts" as the smith whose potent curses are among the most feared sanctions; and the prophets, diviners, rainmakers, medicine men, witch doctors, and other parties with connections to the domain of the occult who are not presumed to operate on the side of order, peace, goodwill, and mutual understanding and who occupy their positions of trust precisely because they are capable of operating beyond good and evil. What is considered "active measures" in our midst was certainly an accomplished skill throughout nonliterate traditional Africa.[65]

The foregoing survey of shared culture traits suggests that non-Western societies are complex covert, not open, societies, and that they are culturally and politically comfortable being just that. Not one of the modern non-Western states can be understood on its own terms unless one fully assesses both the present officially overt identity and the traditional covert identity and unless one finds the key to this combination.

Next, comparative studies make it clear that non-Western societies are internally conflicted by virtue of basic culture-sustaining belief systems, and that relations between government and the governed are marked by standing mistrust. Cold wars of minds and nerves are thus integral aspects of the social order here; and this explains why they tend to be protracted, even endless, quite in contrast to the common American assumption that a "cold war" has somehow been "declared" and can, therefore, also be "deestablished" by an act of will.

This difference between non-Western and modern American orientations explains why internal intelligence and espionage are accepted as a must in the former and as a regrettable deviation from the Declaration of Independence or the Constitution in the latter. It also explains, in conjunction with the absence or irrelevance of the principle of territoriality in political jurisdiction, why it is at times difficult in non-Western societies to distinguish clearly between wars against individual minds and social mind-sets on the one hand, and irregular, indirect political warfare—including such so-called low-intensity conflicts as terrorism, highjacking, and assassination—on the other. Indeed, since the concept of "the enemy" transcends all boundaries, and since war and peace interpenetrate in non-Western thought, it is even difficult to draw reliable lines of distinction between any of these war-related species and outright formal military war.[66]

Whatever the captions that Western theorists have supplied for non-Western modes of waging internal and external warfare, the actual non-Western rules of engagement are essentially the same for all types of war and conflict. They were set out clearly over two thousand years ago by Sun Tzu in the context of Chinese culture and politics, but comparative studies strongly suggest that the following maxims are in fact valid summations of all non-Western practices:

> All warfare is based on deception.
> Thus, those skilled at making the enemy move do so by creating a situation to which he must conform.
> He who knows the art of the direct and indirect approach will be victorious.

The philosophy underlying these and numerous other instructions as presented in Sun Tzu's section on "offensive strategy" centers in the norm "Know the enemy and know yourself; in a hundred battles you will never be in peril."[67]

The Chinese and other Asian peoples learned early that only double knowing of this kind can assure successful strategic deception. However, and as Scott A. Boorman reminds us,[68] the art of attacking by stratagem is not merely outwitting an enemy—whether in internal or external statecraft. Rather, it aims at breaking his will without fighting by manipulating his view of the world and inducing him to contribute to his own encirclement. Accounts from the long period of China's Warring States thus relate in great detail how to create false impressions, use divination as a ploy in psychological warfare, exploit the vanity of opponents, and disrupt alliances in the enemy camp. Further, the records of all Oriental despotisms tell what it takes to recruit surrogate societies that would be fit to manage other "inferior" polities, how to find reliable individual agents while avoiding security risks, and when to entrust defectors with the task of collecting intelligence. In regard to the all-important matter of inducing and sustaining loyalty, one notes a remarkable concordance on favoring eunuchs and slaves.

B. I. Inventory of Concordant Non-Western Orientations to Intelligence

This comparative study of orientations to intelligence in the non-Western world allows for the following conclusions or propositions:

a. Intelligence pervades and dominates statecraft. Internal and external intelligence interpenetrate. All intelligence stands for "knowing the enemy." Since knowing the enemy is tantamount to fighting him, the conclusion is tenable that intelligence stands for warfare of one kind or another.

b. These circumstances, together with the absence of a politically independent academic establishment, explain why definitions of intelligence are not provided explicitly. Those who want definitions must extrapolate them from the facts.

c. Western definitions and classifications of the separate elements of intelligence are not readily applicable; they require adjustment.

Collection and analysis are institutionalized processes in most literate societies, but it should be borne in mind that perception and estimate are usually near-instant mental operations.

Counterintelligence is subsumed in all statecraft, and covert action is the name of the game in domestic and international affairs. Neither is adequately covered by our distinctions and definitions, which derive from premises not acknowledged in Africa and Asia.

B. II. The Relevance of Non-Western Concordances on Approaches to Intelligence for Western Scholarship

The following notations are abstracted from the foregoing analyses because they bear directly on the standing task to further the scholarly development of intelligence in the United States:

Comparative culture studies of the West, the Communist realms, and the non-Western non-Communist regions show incontrovertibly that norms and values dominant in a society's inner order are inevitably operational also in that society's relations with the outside world. This organic linkage explains why orientations to political or strategic intelligence are everywhere reflections of a culture's disposition to domestic government and surveillance.

Today's political systems as associated, respectively, with the West, the Communist realms, and the non-Western regions are too diverse to constitute a meaningful international system. This factor, in conjunction with other data assembled in this chapter, make it unlikely that there can be one theory that would do justice to the world's varieties of intelligence.

An African scholar observed not long ago: "If you systematize in Africa, you lose." This cautionary advice applies in my view also to most literate, non-Western non-Communist nations. As matters stand today, U.S. intelligence is far removed from the goal of understanding the latter on their own terms. To systematize and internationalize present U.S. versions of "the truth" would, therefore, be irresponsible in the context of both scholarship and statesmanship, since it would mean simplifying or misconstruing the very ideas that make the difference in foreign affairs. (Just look at the damage done in recent years to such strategically vital Western words and concepts as democracy, law, individual rights, and peace.) What the agenda calls for in the present era is restraint in internationalizing the little we know and determined efforts to revitalize comparative multidisciplinary studies on behalf of all that we do not yet know.

NOTES

1. This theme is developed in A. Bozeman, "On the Relevance of Hugo Grotius and *De Jure Belli ac Pacis* for Our Times," *Grotiana,* Vol. I (1980), pp. 65–124; and in "Does International Law Have a Future?," banquet address at the annual meeting of alumni from the New York Law School, March 1984, as published in the *New York Law School Journal of International and Comparative Law,* Vol. 6, no. 2 (Winter 1985) pp. 289–99.
2. For an extended discussion of this theme, see Bozeman, "Understanding 'The Other': The Missing Link in U.S. Foreign Policy," in Marshall Hayes, ed., *Book Forum,* Vol. VII, no. 1 (1984), pp. 21–24.
3. Jonathan D. Spence, *To Change China: Western Advisers in China 1620–1960* (Penguin Books, 1980; reprinted in the 1969 ed. publ. by New York: Little, Brown and Company, 1980, 1984), p. 129.
4. *Ibid.,* pp. 5–22. Also see Simon Leys, "Madness of the Wise: Ricci in China," in *The Burning Forest* (1st American ed., New York: New Republic Books, 1985), pp. 35–46.
5. For example, Jesuits were regularly appointed to direct the Bureau of Astronomy.
6. See Jonathan D. Spence, *The Memory Palace of Matteo Ricci* (New York: Viking/Penguin, 1984), particularly Chapters 1–4.
7. Spence, *To Change China,* pp. 20ff.
8. *Ibid.,* p. 41.
9. *China in the Sixteenth Century: The Journals of Matthew Ricci, 1583–1610,* trans. Louis J. Gallagher, S.J. (New York: Random House, 1953), p. 43. On this general subject, see also Vincent Chen, *Sino-Russian Relations in the Seventeenth Century* (The Hague/Boston/London: Martinus Nijhoff Publishers, 1966); John E. Wills, Jr., "Ch'ing Relations with the Dutch, 1662–1960," in John K. Fairbank, ed., *The Chinese World Order: Traditional China's Foreign Relations* (Cambridge, Mass.: Harvard University Press, 1968); *A Documentary Chronicle of Sino-Western Relations* (1644–1820), comp., trans. and annotated by Lo-Shu-Fu, 2 vols., published for the Association for Asian Studies (Tucson: University of Arizona Press, 1966). See Bozeman, "On the Relevance of Hugo Grotius and *De Jure Belli ac Pacis* for Our Times," *op. cit.,* pp. 74–80, for a juxtaposition of the European and Chinese international systems. And see *infra,* this essay, section III.
10. Spence notes in *To Change China,* p. 134, that Martin had studied Ricci's skills. See *supra* and *infra,* this essay.
11. Nothing like this was attempted by the Arab-Islamic imperialisms in Africa. As Sir Henry Maine and others have pointed out, Oriental empires were tax-taking, not legislating empires of the European kind. For this comparison, see also in this volume, "International Order in a Multicultural World."
12. Diedrich H. Westermann, *Geschichte Afrika's: Staatenbildungen suedlich der Sahara* (Cologne: GreVen-Verlag, 1952), p. 390. For other historical accounts and analyses, see Jan Vansina, *Kingdoms of the Savanna: A History of Central African States Until European Occupation* (Madison, Wis.: University of Wisconsin Press, 1966); Ian George Cunnison, *The Luapula Peoples of Northern Rhodesia: Custom and History in Tribal Politics* (Manchester: n.p., 1959); and by the same author, "Kazembe and the Portuguese 1798–1832," *Journal of African History,* Vol. II, no. 1 (1961), pp. 61–76. For a general assessment of

the relationship, see Bozeman, "Transcultural Diplomacy: The Case of Portugal" and authorities there cited in *Conflict in Africa: Concepts and Realities* (Princeton, N.J.: Princeton University Press, 1976), pp. 334–46.

13. Henry Barth, *Travels and Discoveries in North and Central Africa, Being a Journal of an Expedition Undertaken Under the Auspices of H. B. M.'s Government in the Years 1849–1855,* 3 vols. (New York: Harper and Brothers, 1857–1859). For excerpts and other references from this work that are relevant to the present chapter, see Bozeman, *Conflict in Africa,* pp. 194ff; 328ff; 347; 360ff.

14. Barth's conviction that European forms of treaty making evoked suspicion everywhere was shared by traders, travelers, missionaries, and other explorers (among them Matthews, Moffat, Livingstone, Kingsley, and Bishop Tucker). For an overview of English responses to this problem, see Bozeman, "Transcultural Law: The Case of England," in *Conflict in Africa,* pp. 346–68.

15. For case illustrations and references to source materials, see Bozeman, Chapter 6, "Mythical Vision, History and Society," pp. 100ff, and Chapter 7, "States, Empires, and Society," pp. 118ff, in *Conflict in Africa.*

16. The Eastern Christian Byzantine Empire rates first place in a comparative study of European intelligence systems. It is not discussed here even though it apprenticed Venice because its influence on Western European statecraft was negligible. But see "Traditions of Political Warfare and Low-Intensity Conflict in Totalitarian Russia and China", "Covert Action and Foreign Policy in World Politics" in this volume; and Bozeman, "The Byzantine Realm," in *Politics and Culture in International History, op. cit.*

17. For an interesting commentary on this issue, see Hans Heinrich Schaeder, *Der Mensch in Orient und Okzident, Grundzuege einer eurasiatischen Geschichte* (Munich: R. Piper & Co., 1960), pp. 407ff.

18. As a faithful member of the founding directorate of the Consortium for the Study of Intelligence, I accept the latter's definitions of "intelligence" as a complex of ideas, a process, and a set of institutions as well as its distinctions between components of intelligence— each the subject matter of specialized publications. See Roy Godson, ed., *Intelligence Requirements for the 1980's* (1979–1986). Yet I confess to being pleased to find a note in the seventh volume of the Godson series entitled *Intelligence and Policy* (Lexington, Mass.: Lexington Books, 1986), p. 106, that tells us that, in practice, covert action and counterintelligence are intimately connected with collection, since the human infrastructure for covert action is often scarcely distinguishable from that of collection, while collection is intimately involved in counterintelligence. In the context of the present essay, this comes close to saying that political or strategic intelligence is knowledge of "the other."

19. See Malcolm Wallop, "Speech to the Veterans of the OSS," September 25, 1979. Also B. Hugh Tovar, "Covert Action," in Roy Godson, ed., *Intelligence Requirements for the 1980's: Elements of Intelligence* (Washington, D.C.: National Strategy Information Center, Inc., rev. ed., 1983), pp. 72–79.

20. This orientation marked policy pronouncements in the Carter administration, notably in respect of "human rights," and it had become prominent also in the Reagan administration, where the stress was on "democracy." For a much publicized expression of this policy commitment, see Secretary of State George P. Shultz, "New Realities and New Ways of Thinking," *Foreign Affairs,* Vol. 63, no. 4 (Spring 1985), pp. 718, 709, 710, 705. The ambiguities of "the new thinking" appear clearly when these pages are read in the sequence indicated. For extended examinations of these matters, see "American Policy and the Illusion of Congruent Values," in this volume; also see Bozeman, "U.S. Foreign Policy and the Prospects for Democracy, National Security, and World Peace," *Comparative Strategy,* Vol. 5, no. 3 (1985), pp. 223–67; "The Roots of the American Commitment to the Rights of Man," *Rights and Responsibilities,* copyrighted proceedings of a November 1978 conference sponsored by the Center for Study of the American Experience, the Annenberg School of Communications, University of Southern California, 1980, pp. 51–102; and "Human Rights and National Security," *Yale Journal of World Public Order,* Vol. 9, no. 1 (Fall 1982), pp. 40–78.

21. See "American Policy and the Illusion of Congruent Values" in this volume for further comments.
22. For distressing evidence of bungled historical facts and misunderstandings of political developments, see, for example, *Country Reports on Human Rights Practices for 1982 and 1983* as issued by the Department's Bureau of Human Rights and Humanitarian Affairs. These publications were officially distributed by the Foreign Service Institution in 1985 as background for the symposium "Cross-Cultural Aspects of Human Rights in Asia." They are discussed in "American Policy and the Illusion of Congruent Values" in this volume.
23. See Part I of this essay and Spence, *To Change China*, pp. 129ff., 161–83, for an illuminating account of Dr. Edward Hume's service and the "Yale for China" complex.
24. Cp. Bozeman, "The Nuclear Freeze Movement: Conflicting Moral and Political Perspectives on War and Its Relation to Peace," *Conflict: All Warfare Short of War*, Vol. 5, no. 4 (1985), pp. 271–305; "Foreign Policy and the Prospects for Democracy, National Security and World Peace," in *Comparative Strategy*, Vol. 5, no. 3 (1985), pp. 223–67; and a number of essays in this volume.
25. See Bozeman, "Iran: U.S. Foreign Policy and the Tradition of Persian Statecraft," *ORBIS*, Vol. 23, no. 2 (Summer 1979), pp. 387–402, and compare the Introduction and "Covert Action and Foreign Policy in World Politics," in this volume.
26. René-Jean Dupuy, ed., *The Future of International Law in a Multicultural World*, Proceedings of a Colloquium November 17–19, 1983 (The Hague, Boston, London: Martinus Nijhoff Publishers, 1984), for these and other comparisons, among them Bozeman, "A Preliminary Assessment of the Future of International Law," pp. 85–104. See also "Statecraft and Intelligence in the Non-Western World" in this volume.
27. For a brief but lucid reminder of this record, see Professor Marvin Alisky's letter to the *Wall Street Journal*, January 10, 1986: "Chiang Kai-shek had to go and China got Mao Tse-tung. . . . Batista had to go and Cuba got Castro. . . . Diem had to go and Vietnam got enslaved. . . . Somoza had to go and Nicaragua got Ortega. . . . Ian Smith had to go and Rhodesia-Zimbabwe got Robert Mugabe. . . . The Shah had to go and Iran got the Ayatollah. . . . Marcos must go. But awaiting power are Filipinos antagonistic to long-range U.S. interests." For Southeast Asian reactions to U.S. interferences in the Philippine elections, see Barbara Crossette, "Asian Nations Alarmed," *New York Times*, February 15, 1986.
28. See James A. Bill, "Area Studies and Theory-Building in Comparative Politics: A Stocktaking," *PS*, Fall 1985, pp. 810ff., for an interesting account of academic views.
29. But see Victor LeVine's reservations, *ibid.*, p. 811. See also Herbert Simon, *Models of Man: Social and National* (New York: Wiley Publishers, 1957), as noted by Richard J. Heuer, Jr., "Strategic Deception and Counterdeception: A Cognitive Process Approach," *International Studies Quarterly*, Vol. 25, no. 2 (June 1981), pp. 294–327; see p. 295: "We behave rationally within the confines of our mental model, but this model is generally not well adapted to the requirements of the real world."
30. *New York Times*, November 27, 1981, Barbara Crossette reporting. See Alvin H. Bernstein, "The Academic Researcher and the Intelligence Analyst: How and Where the Twain Might Meet," in Bruce W. Watson and Peter M. Dunn, eds., *Military Intelligence and the Universities: A Study of an Ambivalent Relationship* (Boulder, Colo., and London: Westview Press, 1984), pp. 37ff., for references and interpretations of the evidence.
31. *Chronicle of Higher Education*, January 16, 1982, p. 3.
32. Watson and Dunn, eds., *Military Intelligence*, pp. 37ff.
33. This issue is analyzed in Bozeman, "The Nuclear Freeze Movement: Conflicting Moral and Political Perspectives on War and Its Relation to Peace," *Conflict: All Warfare Short of War*, Vol. 5, no. 4 (1985), pp. 1–35.
34. W. Jackson Stenger, "The Perspective from Academe," in Watson and Dunn, eds., *Military Intelligence*, pp. 1ff., notes on p. 10 that academic opposition to a military connection is now deeply embedded in the universities.
35. *New York Times*, December 22, 1984. See Senator Barry Goldwater to the effect that "[we]

have the fourth-best intelligence system in the world—behind Israel, England, and Russia. We could do better. . . ." (*U.S. News and World Report,* December 17, 1984).

36. These reminders were made by former Attorney General William French Smith in a speech (December 18, 1981) that dealt with the depleted state of U.S. intelligence capabilities before the advent of the Reagan administration.

37. For the most constructive critical analysis of this dilemma, see two papers by Senator Malcolm Wallop, "The Role of Congress," in *Hydra of Carnage,* (Lexington Books, 1986), pp. 251–57, and "U.S. Covert Action: Policy Tool or Policy Hedge?" *Strategic Review,* Summer 1984, pp. 9–16.

38. *International Studies and Academic Enterprise: a Chapter in the Enclosure of American Learning* (New York: Columbia University Press, 1984). See in particular preface, xvi. For the definition of "enclosure," see preface, xiv, and Part I, "In the Land of the Blind, 1810–1940." The section on the founders of American East Asian studies (pp. 82ff.) relates directly to section I of the present essay where nineteenth-century American emissaries to China are discussed.

39. Robert Rossow addressed a similar challenge in the 1960s when he examined the needs of "the new diplomacy" that was evolving at that time. The agenda for recasting the training of diplomats (he likens them to crosscultural interpreters), which he submits in a paper on "The Professionalization of the New Diplomacy," *World Politics,* Vol. XIV, no. 4 (July 1982), pp. 561–75, is of great relevance also for us today. Rossow warns against overdoing "pure" social science because it would lead to disciplinary parochialism, to the conversion of methodologies into ideologies, and to the widening of the gulf that exists between the world of science and scholarship and the world affairs of state. The main objects of study in his view are culture patterns, social processes, and value systems. The culture concept should be the starting point of professional training, and the needed disciplines here are anthropology, history, psychology, and linguistics. A subgroup of methods comprises those that deal with the comparative analysis of value systems and ideologies—a field (he notes) that is aptly called "philosophical anthropology" but is not being adequately covered by the standard disciplines.

40. This was recognized by William F. Casey when he took charge of the Central Intelligence Agency: "I asked for an estimate on the Cubans and their activities. I got it after two months—and it neglected to mention Cuba's relationship with the Soviet Union." Suzanne Garment, "Capital Chronicle," on "Casey's Shadows: A Greater Emphasis on CIA Analysis," *Wall Street Journal,* July 16, 1982.

41. See preceding essays.

42. I have developed these conclusions in several earlier books and papers, among them *The Future of Law in the Multicultural World* (Princeton University Press, 1971); "The Future of International Law," in Dupuy, ed., *The Future of International Law in a Multicultural World;* "The Nuclear Freeze Movement: Conflicting Moral and Political Perspectives on War and Its Relation to Peace," in *Conflict: All Warfare Short of War,* Vol. 5, no. 4 (1985), pp. 1–35; and in most of the essays in this volume.

43. For an extended version of this theme, see Bozeman, "Civilization Under Stress: Reflections on Cultural Borrowing and Survival," *Virginia Quarterly Review,* Vol. 51, no. 1 (Winter 1975), pp. 1–18.

44. *Supra,* this essay, Parts I and II.

45. Simon Leys, *The Burning Forest,* p. 4.

46. This has been overlooked by many Western Sinologists who chose to focus on Confucianism as the molding force.

47. The same general case for the analysis of belief systems is here made, albeit by implication, in respect of Christianity, Judaism, and Islam.

48. See T'ung-tsu Ch'u, *Law and Society in Traditional China* (Paris and The Hague: Mouton, 1961), pp. 128; also the "Penal Codes" identified with the T'ang and other dynasties. *Supra,* this essay, Part I, with observations by early European researchers, including Ricci.

49. See H. R. Isaacs, "Group Identity and Political Change: The Role of Color and Physical

Characteristics," *Daedalus,* Spring 1967; and other references in Bozeman, *The Future of Law,* pp. 140–60. For a recent exposition of this type of bias in the rest of Asia see Barbara Crossette, "Prejudice Is One of Asia's More Common Afflictions," *New York Times,* December 29, 1985, "The Week in Review."

50. See Bozeman, *Conflict in Africa,* pp. 95–99, and notes 69–76 for references and illustrations. The pronounced hostility for all things Western that pervades African rhetoric and policy today can be understood as a modern enactment of this stubborn old theme.

51. See "Covert Action and Foreign Policy in World Politics," in this volume, for the organization of secret societies and their role in politics. Also Essay 5 on "Statecraft and Intelligence in the Non-Western World."

52. See Richard Storry, *A History of Modern Japan* (Penguin Books, 1979), pp. 145ff., and *The Double Patriots: A Study of Japanese Nationalism* (Boston: Houghton Mifflin, 1957). See also Richard Deacon, *A History of the Japanese Secret Service: Kempei Tai* (New York: Berkley Books, 1985).

53. These themes are developed in Bozeman, *Conflict in Africa,* Chapters 5, 6, 7, 9, and 18.

54. I have presented the Persian, Islamic, and Indian intelligence systems in considerable detail in "Covert Action and Foreign Policy" in this volume, and in *Politics and Culture in International History.* The best explication and rationalization of the system is found in Nizām al-Mulk, *The Book of Government or Rules for Kings,* trans. Hubert Darke (London: Routledge & Kegan Paul, first publ. 1960; 2nd ed., 1978) under such titles as "On Intelligence Agents and Reporters" and "On Sending Spies for the Good of the Country" and, in regard to India, in the *Arthasastra* and other original literature.

55. Li Yu-ning, ed., *Shang Yang's Reforms and State Control in China* (White Plains, NY: M. E. Sharpe, Inc., 1977), pp. 35ff., 42, 48, and 91.

56. See also Ti Chiang-Hua, "The Physical and Mental Destruction of the Ping-Pong Team—A Sports Horror," trans. Emily Wang, *Free China Review,* January 1986, pp. 29ff. The champion athletes who had made great contributions to Chou En-lai's "Ping-Pong" diplomacy were subsequently persecuted as traitors in so relentless a manner that one after the other was driven to commit suicide. This experience, the author notes, recalls the old Chinese saying: "Once the birds are gone, the bow can be cast away; once the hares are bagged, the hounds can be killed for food."

57. See Chalmers Johnson, *An Instance of Treason: Ozaki Hotsumi and the Sorge Spy Ring* (Stanford, Calif.: Stanford University Press, 1964); Richard Storry and F. W. Deakin, *The Case of Richard Sorge* (1966); and Richard Deacon, *Kempei Tai,* for close analyses of the Japanese system and some internationally significant modern cases of treason, espionage, and retribution.

58. Deacon, *Kempei Tai,* p. 79. For other instructive information in regard to these psychopolitical issues, see Truong Nhu Tang, *A Vietcong Memoir,* with David Chanoff and Doan van Toai (San Diego, New York, London: Harcourt Brace Jovanovich, 1985).

59. See William S. Haas, *Iran* (New York: AMS Press, 1966), and Ann K. S. Lambton, "The Spiritual Influence of Islam in Persia" in A. J. Arberry and Rom Landau, eds., *Islam Today* (London; n.p., 1943), pp. 163–77, on the doctrine of *taqiya,* a dispensation from the requirements of religion under compulsion or threat of injury.

60. See Angelo Codevilla and Roy Godson, "Intelligence (Covert Action and Counterintelligence) as an Instrument of Policy" in Roy Godson, ed., *Intelligence Requirements for the 1980's: Intelligence and Policy* (Lexington, Mass.: Lexington Books, 1986), p. 102, for a searching discussion of the problems that the United States faces in this area of statecraft.

61. Heinrich Zimmer, *The Philosophies of India,* Joseph Campbell, ed., Bollingen series XXVI (New York: Pantheon Books, 1951), p. 83; also "Covert Action and Foreign Policy in World Politics," in this volume.

62. Ibid.

63. *New York Times,* November 3, 1984.

64. Bozeman, *Conflict in Africa,* pp. 290ff.

65. *Ibid.,* Chapter 18; pp. 259–303; also pp. 9ff., 366ff. and notes.

66. See Ernest R. May, ed., *Knowing One's Enemies: Intelligence Assessment before the Two World Wars* (Princeton, N.J.: Princeton University Press, 1984), and "Strategic Intelligence in Cold Wars of Ideas" in this volume.

67. Sun Tzu, *The Art of War,* trans. Samuel B. Griffith (London: Oxford University Press, 1981), p. 84.

68. Scott A. Boorman, "Deception in Chinese Strategy: Some Theoretical Notes on Sun Tzu and Game Theory," in W. Whitson, ed., *The Military and Political Power in China* (New York: Praeger, 1972), pp. 313–37; also his important volume on *The Protracted Game: A Wei-ch'i Interpretation of Maoist Revolutionary Strategy* (New York: Oxford University Press, 1969).

American Policy and the
Illusion of Congruent Values

The world's rich records of literature, history, art, religion, and philosophy tell us that human beings do not live by bread alone. Rather, they are eloquent witness to the fact that men love to think, and to generate, communicate, and play with ideas. In fact, they tell us that human beings live by ideas, and that some of those ideas come to structure life and thought in society. It is in this category of ideas that we deal with politically significant values—those that lend identity, integrity, and internal security to a given community.

Americans tend to be both conscious and proud of the values that have inspired, attended, and emblazoned the "great American experiment." Yet pride, no matter how justified, becomes pernicious if it leads to distorted vision. Increasingly American perspectives have become blurred by the assumption that our paramount values are shared by human beings everywhere, and that the United States is therefore justified—even entitled—to insist that the governments of foreign sovereign states (at least the weaker ones) must install these values promptly in their respective societies.

Thus, for example, Secretary of State George Shultz tells us that American foreign policy is driven by the commitment to "peace, democracy, liberty, and human rights; racial justice; economic and social progress; the strengthening of cooperation and the rule of law"; and that "we have a duty" to transform the world environment in accordance with those primary goals, values, and ideas.[1] The conceptual core of the value-laden terms is not set out either in this or in any other authoritative text. Yet definitions are surely needed at a time when all states in the world—be they Communist totalitarianisms or non-Communist, non-Western despotisms—claim to be "peace-loving democracies" or "people's republics" and are in fact officially recognized as such in the United Nations as well as in American public diplomacy.

Also missing is a well-reasoned explanation of why it is necessary or in our best interests to implant our primary values in all other nations of the world. Secretary Shultz starts out with the plausible thesis that "civilizations thrive when they believe in themselves; they decline when they lose faith." But he ends the argument in the very next sentence when he switches from the plural of "civilizations" to the singular American culture: "it" must retain "this bedrock self-confidence that its values are worth defending" and propagating.[2] No "others" are even mentioned in this context. In fact, the article by Shultz leaves the impression that other cultures either do not exist, or—if they do—that they do not count.

This essay originally appeared in *Strategic Review* (Winter 1987); it is printed with permission of the United States Strategic Institute.

Given these conceptual premises, it is imperative to begin at the beginning and to ask just what the old Greek word "democracy" has come to mean today. To which of the scores of fancy modern "human rights," as these are listed in the UN Universal Declaration of Human Rights, the Helsinki Accords, and other pacts we signed, do we assign paramount value? And just what do we mean by "peace" at a time when it is surely tempting to conclude that the world is a vast theater of diverse, often interconnected wars? Questions such as these require answers if American citizens are to be enabled to think constructively of the moral and political commitments expected from them, and if the many "others" in the world are to understand what the United States would like them to underwrite.

As noted in another essay, we act as if there exists a universal common logic of thinking shared by all thinking people, as if there is one metaphysical pool of universal human thought upon which all can draw, and as if we can count on some elementary objective spirit. But such predispositions screen the irrefutable fact that perception is guided by culture, and in culture especially by language.

After all, ways of thinking are aspects of different speech communities and different moral orders. What is possible in one thought world may therefore be impossible in another. For example, if "law" is embedded in religion, as it is in Islam, Judaism, Hinduism, and most of black Africa's tribal communities—or if a language provides one and the same word for "state," "power," and "dynasty," as it does in Arabic—it is obviously not safe to assume that the idea of secular constitutional rule is sufficiently congenial to be realized effectively.

In short, mankind is not all of one kind; rather, it consists of a plurality of speech communities and civilizations. Each of these is sustained not so much by particular political arrangements as by its own substructure of paramount values. Indeed, and as we know from the histories of the Greeks and the Romans, the Persians and the Arabs, the Chinese and the Indians, a culture's survival is a function of the basic ideas and persuasions that lend uniqueness to the culture complex in the first place and that are not compromised in times of internal or external stress.[3]

THE CORE OF WESTERN VALUES

As explained in the preceding essay, all comparisons, including those relating to values, have to start with one set of norms, and there is nothing wrong with choosing the standard one knows best—in our case, that of the West. However, "democracy" and "human rights" do not sum up this standard. It follows that no crosscultural comparison and no value-related foreign policy can possibly get off the ground as long as we continue shortchanging our civilization into empty code words to which it has been negligently reduced in the last twenty years.

What is at the core of Western political values? It has been obvious for over two and a half millennia that man is conceptualized in Western civilization as an individual being who can think on his own. Indeed, the assumption rules that his mind is the only source of thought and inventiveness. Further, since the person is the measure and main subject of life and society, he is presumed to have rights as well as obligations in his functions as a citizen or resident of the state.

It is a noteworthy aspect of our own civilization that all basic orientations to life have traditionally been encased and communicated in the language of secular law, nowhere more so than in the fields of internal and external politics. Classical Roman jurists in the pre-Christian era thus defined the state as a partnership or a bond in law, while the common law in England accepted Burke's definition of the state as a compact between successive generations meant to endure through time.

Contract, as illustrated by these two instances, as well as by the medieval Gruetli Oath—an accord that bound a few liberty-loving Swiss cantons in a common political destiny and has ever since been the rock on which Switzerland's model democracy rests—thus emerges from the West's long history as the core concept of the state. Also, and in tune with the same sentiment and logic, contract is the core of constitutional democratic government, and therewith the condition precedent for legally enforceable civil liberties.

On the level of foreign affairs, meanwhile, "contract" rendered in the form of treaty is trusted in the West as the main agency for stabilizing interstate relations. In this context, it is relevant to note the linguistic circumstance that even the word "peace" is a close relative of the word "pact."

In short, the West has brought forth a magical but very complex cluster of ideas. The primary supposition is the focus on the individuality of a person's mind and its capacity to make decisions and conclude voluntary accords. The second, perhaps equally significant presupposition ensues from the mutuality of promises, implicit in such contract, to do or refrain from doing something later on. In this sense contract projects confidence in the future as well as confidence in the good faith of the other party, be this another human being, a corporate entity, or a state.

In a masterful comparison of Western and Eastern cultures, Sir Henry Maine explains that only societies capable of relating to contract with all its implications and demands can "progress" in the sense of being prepared to effect future-directed change, legislation, and development.[4] Suffused with this Promethean spirit, the Occident has brought forth numerous "progressive" societies. These, however, have definitely been a minority in world history. The majority—whether in Africa or Asia—subscribed to the opposite principle, namely that of holding on to status. For here, where the individual mind has traditionally not been accepted as the activating principle in society, the past was supposed to carry over to the future.

This explains why non-Western societies were sturdier than their Western counterparts in retaining the kind of internal communal security that compliance with time-honored values provides. For example, it explains why China, Persia, and Egypt outlasted classical Greece. However, the same factor also explains why the Promethean principle of development simply did not have a chance in the Orient and in Africa.

This set of issues is very much with us today, and it illustrates well some of the illusions and misperceptions that have marked American foreign policy in the last decade. Thus it continues to be common to distinguish developed states—and they are mainly of the West—from less-developed or undeveloped states; to identify "development" with industrialization, wealth, or some other strictly economic causes and effects; and to argue strenuously that the developed "rich" have a moral duty to "develop" the undeveloped "poor" states, whereas the latter have a "human right" to development and therewith also to economic aid and all manner of other assistance. (The category of economically malfunctioning states includes, incidentally, most Communist states.)

American foreign policy has underwritten this set of assumptions, even though all of them are based on theories of economic determinism that surely are not the source of the American genius and have little to do with the commitment to freedom and democracy. American policy has also accepted international covenants and declarations in which legally meaningless rights to life, health, education, and development are listed alongside the right to fight wars of liberation and the right to promote a people's traditional culture. Questions about the congruity or incongruity of these demands are not being raised. For instance, no one asks whether the right to culture is always compatible with the right to development.

THE MEANING OF DEMOCRACY

If contract, at the core of Western values, is progressively future-oriented, this tends to be carried to extremes in American society. Indeed, especially in a year in which we celebrated the bicentennial of the American Constitution, one was baffled by the pronounced ahistorical bent of mind that marks our foreign policies, as well as of our scholarship and our educational system.[5] Apart from remembering the glory of 1776, we seem to be weary of our past as a known sequence of two hundred years and a store of accumulated yet distinct ideas and events. Quite naturally, then, we are even wearier when it comes to thinking about time spans of one thousand or two thousand years—time spans from which the United States was nominally absent but in which most other states and cultures, including those identified with Europe, feel at home. In either case the disposition seems to dominate that the past should be overcome as speedily as possible so as to make room for a future of our present choice.

This time perspective and the ignorance of reality, specifically of foreign cultures and thoughtways, that it fosters hover over our policy-making. In fact, by blotting out America's European legacy, these factors have gradually made for a crippled, decidedly unconvincing national self-image. What is any intelligent person, at home or abroad, to make of the following propositions that appear prominently in the *Country Reports on Human Rights Practices* for 1983 issued by the Bureau of Human Rights and Humanitarian Affairs of the Department of State?

> . . . Any efforts we make on behalf of democracy . . . are sustained by democracy's gradual expansion since the days of the American Revolution. In 1790, there existed only two democratic republics: the United States and part of Switzerland. By 1909, there were a number of constitutional monarchies, but the tenacity of the old order was shown by the fact that there were still only three democratic republics outside the Western Hemisphere: France, Switzerland, and Liberia. Today, there are fifty genuine democracies, comprising about a third of the world's population. . . .[6]
>
> Today, with the exception of a handful of remote monarchies, all governments claim to base their legitimacy on the consent of the governed. . . . Our times display a re-

markable paradox: the victory of democracy is virtually complete in principle, but still limited in practice.[7]

The only alternative to democracy as a contemporary system of legitimacy is Marxism-Leninism. Developing countries, when they choose their institutions and officers, choose either the forms of democracy or those of Marxism-Leninism.[8]

How true are any of these allegations? And how do they square with the next series of propositions under the title "Three Fallacies About Democracy," where one learns the following?

Perhaps the most widely held fallacy about the democratic form of government is that it is an exclusively North Atlantic phenomenon. The facts, of course, are otherwise. Neither India nor Japan, Costa Rica nor Botswana, Senegal nor Fiji belong to the North Atlantic constellation of states; all are thriving democracies.[9]

Nor is democracy in such countries necessarily an import from the North Atlantic area. Many peoples have some form of democracy as part of their heritage. In 1700 there were more extensive areas of democracy in Africa than in Europe, because the societies called "primitive" by colonialism carried on their decision-making by democratic means. Conversely, there was probably never as great a loss of human freedom in a short period of time as in the years 1884 to 1900, when these societies came under colonial administration from outside. Yet the tenacity with which the North Atlantic nature of democracy is held suggests that it is based on an underlying presupposition: the relativist assumption that freedom's appeal does not derive from something inherent in human nature, but is merely the result of a particular form of cultural conditioning.[10]

A reader of these official policy statements learns nothing about the presumed value content of "democracy" and "human rights." Satisfied with a new, stridently formulated thesis that nothing meaningful has ever occurred in any civilization before the United States began its existence as an independent state on the European model, our government spokesmen obviously feel relieved of any scholarly commitment to survey the evidence.

The linguistic, legal, philosophical, and historical roots of Western—i.e., European—values and governmental institutions are thus studiously bypassed, even though there never could have been a United States of America without them. Indeed the ignorance and bias displayed in this regard border on the comical. What is one to make of the reference to Fiji as a "thriving democracy," a pat on the back for "parts of Switzerland" for being decently governed in the eighteenth century, and total silence when it comes to the British House of Commons, where President Reagan chose to announce his concern with democracy?

Democracy is not a value either in the West or in non-Western societies if its core meaning is simplistically identified with elections, held regularly American-style in accordance with the one-person, one-vote principle. It is a value in the Euro-American society of states because it is inextricably and organically linked to two other primary values: namely the rule of law and the independent state—concepts seldom advanced in this context by our policymakers today. However, it should not be lightly assumed that either democracy or the rule of law are necessarily primary sustaining values in the non-Western, non-Communist societies, since these may be held together by other value commitments. Therefore, it is both wrong and unstatesmanlike to proclaim, as the State Department's Bureau of Human Rights does, that "the only alternative to democracy as a contemporary system of legitimacy is Marxism-Leninism."

Further, we seem to believe that "democracy," as we think of it, was somehow mislaid not only by Asians, Africans, and Latin Americans but also by Europeans, and that the "new" American thinking can somehow revive or otherwise install it. The thought that democracy of the American kind may not have a past in the regions under our considerations has no currency in our preoccupation with "the future." But can "a future" really be conceptualized without full acceptance and understanding of the past? And in terms of statecraft is it possible to recompose an ancient foreign nation without knowing just what the structure and the substance are that one intends to tamper with?

In short, it is high time to recognize that history is the foremost tool for political analysis, especially when dealing with cultural and political formations that are older than the United States by thousands of years. It is through sheer historical ignorance that policymakers seem not to recognize that most political systems in the world have existed without benefit of contract and of equivalents for the Roman civil law and the English common law—both presuppositions for the kind of liberty and constitutional democracy we take for granted and therefore wish to establish abroad.

VALUES OF COMMUNIST SOCIETIES

In short, non-Western states are not Western states and Communist states are not democracies; there would be no need for the agonies of foreign policy-making if it were otherwise. Rather than continue indulging the illusion that values are shared—when all that is actually being shared is a set of words—we should admit that radical contrasts of values exist, especially in human understandings of the individual and his rights, the nature and function of the state, and the meanings assigned to such central concepts as peace and war.

In the last six years we have slowly come to acknowledge the existence of value-related incongruities in regard to the Soviet Union, but by no means yet in regard to such other Marxist-Leninist states as mainland China, Vietnam, Cuba, Nicaragua, Ethiopia, Angola, Zimbabwe, and North Korea. Thus we know that the individual mind is not accepted as the source of thought and inventiveness in the Soviet world and that the human being has no rights to free thought, speech, and movement. The logic of the Marxist-Leninist dogma stipulates instead that evidence of an independent mind is a serious threat to political authority and regime security, and that those in charge of administering the totalitarian creed and the society it called forth are obligated to silence nonconformist speech, throttle nonconformist thought, and do away with nonconformist people—a mandate carried out faithfully for more than seventy years.

We also have recognized by now that the concept of the state in Communist society translates into the reality of the Communist Party's power apparatus, specifically that of the all-encompassing KGB. Indeed, surveys of the latter's internal and external activities fully support the thesis developed by John Dziak that the Soviet Union is best defined as a "Counterintelligence State."[11] However, compliance with the borrowed Western vocabulary of "the state," "constitutionalism," and "democracy" is favored for the purpose of gaining advantage in interstate relations and international organizations; for as Lenin had observed, "democracy" facilitates destabilization and takeover.

Next, no one today denies that Marxism-Leninism is a combat doctrine. Rooted in uncompromising enmity toward all that exists outside its own firmly set context, it is irrevocably committed to the primary cause of overturning the West's legal and political order and of undoing the West's cultural infrastructure of values.

Yuri Andropov thus reminded us during his tenure as head of the KGB in 1979 that "Marxism-Leninism is the textbook for achieving socialist revolution and the building of a new society throughout the world."[12] The dense record of successful Moscow-led insurgencies, revolutions, and open wars of aggression is irrefutable evidence that this mandate is being carried out methodically.

Further, the Leninist-Soviet code for conducting international relations, as made manifest in government documents and actual behavior, is explicitly to the effect that Western understandings of peace and war are incompatible with Soviet values and interests. In fact, nowhere in Marxist-Leninist literature are "peace" and "war" objectively distinguished. The former Secretary of the CPSU Central Committee, Boris N. Ponomarev, contributed this definition of peace: "An international peace is one which best allows the realization of the goals of Communism."[13] And Leonid Brezhnev wrapped it all up—including the relation of the future to the past—by saying in 1973: "Trust us, comrades, for by 1985, as a consequence of what we are achieving by means of détente, we will have achieved most of our objectives in Western Europe. . . . A decisive shift in the correlation of forces will be such that by 1985 we will be able to exert our will whenever we need to."[14]

This prognosis has come true on many levels. As noted earlier in this book but in another context, the modern State System and its corollary, the International Law of War and Peace, have been reduced to shambles, mainly as a result of the Soviet Union's steadfast adherence to its "Doctrine of Limited Sovereignty." The major tenets here are: (1) the revolutionary process is a single process, knowing no frontiers; (2) the notion of state sovereignty may never stand in the way of the struggle of progressive forces; (3) the laws of the class struggle and of social development must always override bourgeois nonsocialist laws and norms.

Western and non-Western states—be they democracies or moderate dictatorships—have thus been eliminated as independent states by means of conquest or reduction to dependency status as colonies, provinces, satellites, proxies, or surrogates. This destructive process was in full swing already during the Second World War, and its momentum quickened in each of the ensuing decades to which we summarily refer as "peace." Yet it cannot be said that we ever did much to forestall, roll back, or oppose Communism's territorial and ideological advances. Indeed, at times it became quite clear that our concern with the verbal propagation of "peace," "human rights," and "democracy" far outweighed our concern with that other elementary political value: namely, national integrity and security, and therewith the integrity and security also of friendly non-Communist states, be they Western or non-Western.

This was dramatically illustrated by foreign policy pronouncements during the Ford and Carter administrations, the records of the Helsinki Conference in 1975, and the texts of the Helsinki Accords. All converge on our willingness to cancel the territorial, political, and moral integrity of Europe and compromise the basic security interests of the West in return for Soviet promises to honor what President Ford listed as "the most fundamental human rights": namely, liberty of thought, conscience, and faith, and the exercise of civil and political rights, as well as certain corollary, secondary rights such as the free flow of information, ideas, and people, and "the protection of the priceless heritage of our diverse cultures."[15]

It was as evident in 1976, as it proved to be throughout the ensuing decade, during which compliance with the Helsinki human rights provisions of Basket Three was assiduously monitored, that the Soviet rulers were not about to forsake their ideological norms or values and dissolve the Gulag empire so as to transform it into a faithful copy of "constitutional democracy." Rather, they have demonstrated explicitly by word and deed that they were determined to expand the Leninist domain by all modes of warfare including military conquest, and that they would at no time cease terrorist statecraft both at home and abroad. True, constitutions and treaties continued sprouting within Communist domains, for as Santiago Carillo, the leading Spanish Communist, reminded us in 1977, "we are going to play the game of legality,"[16] because it is tactically necessary in this era of history to accommodate constitutionalism so that it can be eliminated later.

BLURRED PRISMS OF THE OUTSIDE WORLD

American failures in the conduct of foreign affairs must thus be ascribed in no small measure to slipshod treatment of values. Our estimates of the Soviet Union's system of ideas and its strategic significance have been tragically mistaken. The same judgment holds for our analyses of European, Asian, and African value systems. Had our policymakers been more diligent and astute in examining the standing value priorities and security concerns of Poles, Czechs, and Hungarians, they would probably have chosen to act decisively in 1948 or 1956. Likewise, had we been intellectually prepared to identify the essence of pre-Maoist China, pre-Communist Vietnam, and dynastic Iran, we would probably not have been taken in by the advertised image of Mao Tse-tung as an "agrarian reformer," of Ho Chi Minh as an "Asian Washington," or of the Ayatollah Khomeini as a "saint."

In deciding whether the installation of democracy and human rights should be the primary goal of U.S. foreign policy in non-Western states, it is important to remember that democracy is, in the final analysis, a form of government. As such it has the same elementary function to discharge as other forms of government. This consists in preserving the state and assuring if not its greatness, then at least its integrity and durability in time. Loss of territory, of authority, of international credibility, or of self-respect, by contrast, has everywhere and always been considered as evidence that a form of government has miscarried.

It is probably not a matter of dispute that democracy is by far the most difficult of all forms of administration. Nor will many contest the judgment that democracy, being popular or populist and hence subject to changing electorates and changing human representation, can scarcely avoid being plagued by disunity, inconsistency, and shifts in internal and external policy-making.

Unpredictability then has always been a built-in weakness in democracies. But in the European democracies it was kept under control by a permanent apolitical civil service of highly educated citizens—an element entirely missing in the American system. Further, also in contrast to the European scene, consistency and reliability in foreign affairs are being frustrated on the American scene by a constitutional conflict in which the legislature insists on defying the principle of the separation of powers by usurping the powers of the executive, usually for the purpose of gaining short-range local advantages on behalf of causes that have nothing to do with long-range national interests in the conduct of international relations.

Lastly, Americans are handicapped when it comes to structuring their relations with non-Western peoples because, unlike generations of Europeans, they have not coexisted with Asian and African societies for over two millennia. These factors explain, in conjunction with a standing lack of interest in history and geography, why we do not take foreign value systems and modes of thinking seriously, and why there is reason to fault our present drives on behalf of democracy and human rights.

THE VALUES LANDSCAPE OF EAST ASIA

The late President Mohammed Zia Ul-Haq of Pakistan remarked, "Democracy is a bitter pill to swallow."[17] Must it be swallowed, in the knowledge that the given state cannot digest it and endure? And is it really in our best interest to try to force-feed friendly nations (the only ones thus victimized) at the risk of destabilizing and estranging them?

These are urgent questions, for the evidence is overwhelming that the uneasiness exhibited by President Zia has afflicted all of neighboring Southeast Asia's remaining independent states. None of them wanted to go the Vietnam way, but each has had to contend with aggressive Communist forces. As an astute American reporter remarked, all are distrustful of American-style democracy with its stress on opposition parties that would force a state's government to share power with enemies trying to bring it down.[18] The alternative upon which such diverse states as Thailand, Malaysia, Indonesia, Singapore, the Philippines, and perhaps even Burma appear to agree is a commitment to seek "consensus politics" by drawing all politically relevant parties and interests together while phasing out the combative opposition.

Similar dilemmas confront us in East Asia, specifically in regard to the Republic of China on Taiwan and South Korea. Both are truncated in original physical and political identity and self-image, and both have reason to link their diminished destiny to American foreign policies in the region. Each was marked for extinction, yet each succeeded by dint of talent, discipline, and industriousness not only in overcoming adversity but in fashioning societies whose intellectual and economic productivity far outdistance the achievements of other non-Western, Communist, and many Western states. Further, each continues to be a staunch ally of the United States. What, then, is so wrong about the value system underlying the governments in the ROC and South Korea to justify ceaseless American prodding to get close to the "models" set by the United States in recent years? Why not respect and sustain the states of Southeast and Northeast Asia for what they are?

The main issue barring such accommodation appears to be noncompliance with present-day American interpretations of our nation's First Amendment rights, notably those to freedom of expression and equality. Rather than go on deriding South Korea, Taiwan, Singapore, Malaysia, and Indonesia for not living up to our standards or ideals—a tactic conducive only to alienation—we should study and evaluate theirs so that we can integrate them into a long-range policy design for this entire, geopolitically most important region.

The basic truth in this context is that Asian societies derive their cultural and political strengths, and therewith their primary sustaining values, from religious or quasi-religious belief systems that are comprehensive in the sense that they address life in its entirety rather than in some of its selected manifestations, e.g., as jurisprudence does in the West. Equivalents for Western-type constitutional and criminal law—the prerequisites for civil liberties and political freedoms—are thus missing in Hinduism, Buddhism, Confucianism, Islam, and Shinto. Different as these great norm-setting moral orders have always been, they converge on not viewing the individual human being as separable from the group he belongs to or represents—be it the family, the caste, the race, or the profession—and in identifying government and public order with authority and power.[19]

GRAFTED AND BORROWED WESTERN VALUES

What is so very interesting about southeast and northeast Asian states, including Japan, is this: being maritime nations for the most part and existing on the periphery of the Asian landmass, on peninsulas and islands, they have been "street-wise," as it were, to the ways of trade and war, accommodation and resistance for at least a millennium. This explains why this vast region has brought forth some of the world's most talented, historically experienced, and cosmopolitan peoples. All were chronically challenged to relate to greatly varied value systems and international political orders, among them those fashioned by Hindu and Buddhist India, Confucian and Legalist China, a plurality of ethnically diverse Islamic conquerors and traders, and an equally various host of Christian Europeans. In the process of these encounters they learned to borrow and assimilate alien ideas without losing their cultural and political identities.

Hinduism was thus successfully implanted—for example, in Cambodia and parts of Indonesia—during that pseudo-imperialist phase of India's foreign relations known as the "Indianization" of Southeast Asia, but Hinduism was made to shed the caste system. The original Buddhist message was blunted and effectively nationalized in provinces of Southeast Asia, as well as in Japan, where it was made to cede to Shinto, specifically in matters of state. Confucianism has supplied core values to parts of Vietnam, Korea, and other so-called Sinified societies, but it, too, appears in different incarnations, as do Islam and Christianity.

The relevance of these records in cultural borrowing was acknowledged by European colonial administrations when they set out to introduce legal and political reforms. The Dutch, for example, studied Indonesia's indigenous norms known as Adat law before associating them with Roman-Dutch law, and analogous preparatory work was done by the French and the British before determining which concepts of the Roman civil law and of the English system of common law and equity to graft upon the native orders.

Although most of these grafting operations were successful, it is probably fair to say that the cause of the independent nation state in these regions has continued to rest with native infrastructures of norms and values—a proposition well illustrated by Thailand (Siam) and Japan. Neither had been a colonial province of modern Europe, but both proceeded on their own to study continental Europe's legal codes and constitutional systems so as to select norms that they could integrate securely. Also, both were officially admitted to the modern European States System at the beginning of the twentieth century because they were found to be sovereign states willing to accept European norms of international law.[20]

THE CONTRADICTORY U.S. APPROACH TO CHINA

Asian belief systems and internal structures of government have been accepted and avidly studied by Western scholars and extensive comparative treatises abound. But questions about their legitimacy in terms of select abstract principles held dear by Occidentals, or their nonconformity with actually functioning Western institutions, were not raised officially in the context of diplomatic relations until this became the vogue in the Carter, Reagan, and Bush administrations.

It is relevant to note that the State Department expressed itself quite differently as recently as 1975 when it explained American decision-making in regard to friendly states that derogate from international legal commitments to respect political rights:

> . . . In view of the widespread nature of human rights violations in the world, we have found no adequately objective way to make distinctions of degree between nations. This fact leads us, therefore, to the conclusion that neither the United States security interest nor the human rights cause would be properly served by the public obloquy and impaired relations with security-assistance recipient countries that would follow the making of inherently subjective United States government determinations that "gross violations do or do not exist" or that a "consistent" pattern of such violations does or does not exist in such countries.[21]

In this respect it is relevant to recall again (see also the Introduction to this book) that a strategically coherent American policy doctrine for East Asia had been in the making in the last years of World War II, when the then–Secretary of the Navy, James Forrestal, identified Formosa as "the whole key to the future in the Pacific." . . .[22]

Instead of following and fulfilling this vision U.S. policymakers "rewarded" us with the Shanghai Communiqué, several "openings" to Communist mainland China, the downgrading of the ROC (i.e., Formosa), and a bizarre "adjustment" of the democracy-human rights doctrine. It is in this context that Taiwan, a modern, moderately Confucian, resolutely anti-Communist state is being routinely reprimanded (and thus internationally humiliated) either for retaining martial law or for not having the kind of political party system we prefer. The People's Republic of China, by contrast, a totalitarian system in which civil liberties and political freedoms are excluded by definition, is systematically excused.

It is evident, then, that the democracy–human rights syndrome is not considered pertinent today either for "upgrading" the values and institutions of the PRC or for strategic planning on behalf of American security interests. Nor is it likely that democratization of the kind we desire will set in if and when Leninism is dislodged. For as experienced Sinologists have pointed out time and again, the focus of Chinese, specifically Confucian, ethics and politics has never been on the individual person, but rather on the web of human relations in which each mortal is presumed to be enclosed.

The Legalists, by contrast, who laid the foundations for Chinese statecraft when they assured the country's unification after the Period of the Warring States in the third century B.C., stood for an egalitarian public "law." However, as explained elsewhere in the present volume, this set of norms was rooted in the conviction that human nature is intrinsically evil and utterly untrustworthy. It is therefore identified almost exclusively with harsh penalties and rigorous policing practices—aspects that explain why Mao Tse-tung's writings are peppered with highly complimentary references to the Legalists.[23] Further, policy projections in regard to a possible future China would be remiss for reasons noted in earlier essays if we were to forget that the Western idea of "the state" is entirely alien in this culture realm.

In short, China's Asian orbit has never been a system of equal sovereign states—a worldview that explains why international law of the Western type could not be accepted. Nor can U.S. policy count, either now or in the future, on mainland China's compliance with the norms and values that we espouse on individual, social, and national levels.[24]

ROOTS OF ISLAMIC VALUES

Peace, law, democracy, and individuated rights have received particularly reductive versions in the Islamic Middle East and North Africa—regions that adjoin Europe and had been part of the Greek, Hellenistic, Roman, and Christian culture world for centuries before being conquered by Islamic forces. Here as elsewhere in the non-Western world it was and continues to be common to borrow the West's norm-setting words when describing locally prevalent values and institutions. Indeed it is often being maintained that "law" and "democracy" are uniquely Islamic creations. However, even cursory comparisons of theory and society show readily that the pivotal legal and organizational references—those that have survived metamorphosis and change—are wholly at variance with those carried by the Western vocabulary.

The Islamic commonwealth is at one with the West in acknowledging the supreme importance of law, but law here is "knowledge of the practical rules of religion" and knowledge also "of the rights and duties whereby man is enabled to observe right conduct in the world, and prepare himself for the future life." Despite bitter divisions in the interpretation of the *shari'a,* all believers converge in the confidence that Islamic law is the only ideal, unalterable law in the world, and that Allah alone knows it.

"Law" in the Western sense simply could not have arisen in these intellectually confining conditions; and, as suggested in several preceding essays, a legitimate secular form of political organization on the order of the state was as unfathomable in medieval as it is in modern times.

Directions on how to concretize the Islamic ideals of the *shari'a* and the "Community of all believers" are altogether missing, even when allowance is made for the office of the prayer-leader, out of which the caliphate gradually evolved. For as the records show convincingly, each acting Arab caliph was fenced in by unattainable theoretical models, deprived of legitimate powers to lead and legislate, and therefore forced to rule pragmatically. Because of these premises, he was always at the mercy of civil strife and the prey of rival thrusts for power usually marked by violence and assassination. Quite in contrast to the traditions of the pre-Islamic Arabs in trading cities and the desert, government simply had to evolve into despotism in this region.

This innate tendency was confirmed, and in an interesting way legitimized, when real power gradually passed to representatives of defeated non-Arab, but newly Islamized Near Eastern empires, foremost among them that of the historically prestigious Persians. Their neatly recorded maxims of statecraft—together with those enacted by the Eastern Christian Byzantine empire between the fifth and fifteenth centuries and thereafter by conquering groups of Turks from inner Asia— served to redefine the multiethnic Dar al-Islam in the mold of what became known as the Perso-Byzantine-Turkish power state (*mulkh*). As represented by the Ottoman empire in the ensuing five hundred years, this was an effective centralized despotism, since the power of the Muslim establishment was deliberately held in check by a comprehensive secular bureaucracy and by the armed forces—both heavily staffed by slaves from the empire's Christian provinces and Africa.

A unifying system based on constitutional law and the concept of citizenship could not and did not arise here. But the Ottoman version of the *umma* did give some scope to freedom, on the one hand by allowing vassal kingdoms, sultanates, and sheikdoms autonomy in local matters, and on the other by delegating powers to a variety of corporate structures, each representative of a special set of personal commitments. In fact, it was actually only through membership in such groups or guilds that the individual could gain any status in the empire.

VALUES AND VIOLENCE IN THE MIDDLE EAST

The wide range of differences separating Western and Islamic understandings of law, the state, and government was not narrowed in substance either after the dissolution of the Ottoman empire at the end of World War I or after World War II when the mandate system was terminated and when all Arab and Arabized societies, excepting the one identified with Palestine, were recognized first as independent states and in due course as peace-loving democratic members of the United Nations.

The tenuousness of these developments in the "Westernization" process was clearly recognized by H. A. R. Gibb, the renowned Arabist, when he noted in 1956 that "violence is not less violence because clothed in incomprehensible legal forms,"[25] as well as by Richard Nolte, who wondered in 1958 "whether the modern Islamic states of the Middle East by establishing constitutions and bills of rights based on Western models have been able to establish in fact the substitute rule of law thus implied." His conclusion was essentially negative; for by thrusting the *shari'a* into the background, the influence of secular conceptions from the West was bound to have the effect of dissolving the qualified rule of law imposed during the centuries of classical Islam. "Never fully controlled, the ruler now appears to be fully uncontrolled from a *shari'an* point of view."[26]

This judgment continues to hold for the Arab sector of the Middle East. In fact, the political and psychological plight of Islam's heartland has steadily worsened in the last thirty years as "fully uncontrolled rulers" proceeded to devalue and dismantle their own states. This movement, which is fuelled by Islamic fundamentalism and was long prodded by Leninist ideologues and operators, has so far not seriously affected either Turkey (which overcame the traumatic experience of losing its imperial identity by methodically building a "nation-state") or Egypt (the statehood of which is grounded in a sturdy infrastructure bequeathed by Pharaonic, Roman, and Christian legacies). However, by easing the norm of the territorially bounded state, therewith removing major conceptual impediments to war, it has been instrumental not only in consigning a geopolitically crucial area to anarchy and violence, but also in invalidating norms of international law that we consider basic in the conduct of foreign policy—those, namely, that distinguish between "peace" and "war."

TOWARD AN ESCAPE FROM SHALLOW MORALISM

It has been the thrust of the foregoing that the policymakers of the United States have been intellectually unprepared to foresee or cope not only with Middle Eastern developments—be they ideological, political, or military—but also with the broader reality of the world at large. The question is in order therefore whether our value-oriented foreign policy, shallow and limited as it is, will see us through the next decades. Should we really go on reminding friends and enemies that "we want to promote and defend human rights everywhere," as Secretary of State Shultz told a news conference at the time of the Geneva summit meeting?[27]

Time may be running out for us, but should not our foreign policymakers finally take some of that time to study the vital regions of the world on their own terms, rather than simply fit them into the illusion of "the American age"? If they did, they might come to confront the following disconcerting but compelling conclusions:

1. The primary normative commitments of all Marxist-Leninist hegemonies are not reconcilable with ours, and we must therefore contain and contest them by all

available means if we wish to retain our integrity and to survive as a state capable of carrying out policies of our own.

2. The value systems of non-Western states—different as they are from one another—are nearly at one in not being able to accommodate Western concepts of constitutionalism, individual rights, and peace as securely as we wish they would.

3. The norms that traditionally assured communal consensus, security, and continuity in the literate and nonliterate civilizations of the Orient and Africa have traditionally been social constraint, inequality, and cultural homogeneity—not personalized liberty, equality, and the melting pot.

4. Recent American calls for drastic revisions of long-trusted moral orders come at a time of unprecedented peril to the very existence of independent non-Western states. Most of these have long been threatened and destabilized from within and without, and no end is in sight for this kind of aggressive thrust.

5. U.S. policies have had the effect of fostering destabilization. Our track record of weakening small non-Western and Western states and of bringing ally after ally to fall, because we found them morally flawed, has clearly not served our security interests or our prestige in the world.

6. Shallow moralism of the kind we choose to stand by nowadays is no substitute for historical understanding and political realism. It should therefore cease to be our guide in the conduct of foreign affairs, thus making possible a return to John Quincy Adams and a wiser reading of the Declaration of Independence than has been common in the last decades. Adams has this to teach us: "America goes not abroad in search of monsters to destroy. She is the well-wisher to the freedom and independence of all. She is the champion and vindicator only of her own."

NOTES

1. George P. Shultz, "New Realities and New Ways of Thinking," *Foreign Affairs*, Spring 1985, pp. 705ff.
2. *Ibid.*, p. 720.
3. For a substantiation of this approach, see Bozeman, "Civilizations Under Stress: Reflections on Cultural Borrowing and Survival," *Virginia Quarterly Review*, Winter 1975, pp. 1–18.
4. Sir Henry Maine, *Ancient Law, Its Connection With the Early History of Society and Its Relation to Modern Ideas* (New York: Henry Holt & Co., 1879).
5. For a remarkably clear analysis of this predicament, see Soven Eggerz, "Emphasis on Social Studies Leaves Students Ignorant of History and Geography," *Human Events*, June 21, 1986, pp. 12ff.
6. Bureau of Human Rights and Humanitarian Affairs, Department of State, *Country Reports on Human Rights Practices for 1983*, February 1984, p. 8.
7. *Ibid.*
8. *Ibid.*
9. *Ibid.*, p. 9.
10. *Ibid.*
11. John F. Dziak, "The Study of the Soviet Intelligence and Security System," in Roy Godson, ed., *Comparing Foreign Intelligence: The U.S., the U.S.S.R., the U.K. and the Third World* (Pergamon-Brassey's International Defense Publishers, 1988), pp. 65–89. See also the first and third essays of this book.

12. Albert L. Weeks and William C. Bodie, eds., *War and Peace: Soviet Russia Speaks* (New York: National Strategy Information Center, Inc., 1983), p. 32.

13. *Ibid.*, p. 20.

14. *Ibid.*, p. 18.

15. For textual references and analyses, see Bozeman, "Interference or Legitimate Concern: The Human Factor in U.S.-Soviet Relations," *Proceedings of the National Security Affairs Conference–1977, Toward Cooperation, Stability and Balance* (Washington, D.C.: National Defense University, August 1977), pp. 167ff; reprinted as *How to Think About Human Rights* (New York: National Strategy Information Center, Inc., 1978). See also the Introduction to this book and "The Roots of the American Commitment to the Rights of Man," *Rights and Responsibilities; International, Social, and Individual Dimensions* (conference proceedings) (Los Angeles, CA: University of Southern California Press, 1980), pp. 51–103.

16. Santiago Carillo as quoted by *The New York Times*, January 16, 1977. To the same effect, see the so-called Brezhnev Constitution of the Soviet Union, 1977.

17. *U.S. News & World Report*, September 22, 1986, p. 10.

18. Barbara Crossette, "A Region Edges Away from Democracy," *New York Times*, May 4, 1986.

19. For extended commentaries on these amalgams of interlocking value references see Bozeman, *The Future of Law in a Multicultural World* (Princeton, NJ: Princeton University Press, 1971), pp. 14, 21f., and pp. 121–39: "India and Indianized Asia."

20. See L. Oppenheim, "Non-Christian States," in *International Law, A Treatise*, 2 vols. (London: Longmans, Green and Co., 1905), Vol. I, p. 147.

21. *New York Times*, February 25, 1977.

22. Vernon Walters, *Silent Missions* (Garden City, NY: Doubleday, 1978), p. 111.

23. For references to texts and other authoritative analyses, see Bozeman, "China," *The Future of Law in a Multicultural World*, Chapter 5, pp. 140–60. See also Bozeman, "Conflicting Cultural Perspectives on Human Rights," Keynote Address, *Symposium Cross-Cultural Aspects of Human Rights: Asia, Proceedings No. 1* (Linda L. Lum, ed.), Foreign Service Institute, U.S. Department of State, March 1988, pp. 49–63; "Human Rights and National Security," *Yale Journal of Public Order*, Vol. 9, no. 1 (1984) and various essays in this book.

24. For an extended comparison of European and Chinese systems of international order, see Bozeman, "On the Relevance of Hugo Grotius and *De Jure Belli ac Pacis* for Our Times," *Grotiana*, Vol. I, pp. 65–124, and bibliographical notes 5–14. See Jonathan D. Spence, *The Memory Palace of Matteo Ricci* (New York: Viking/Penguin, 1984), and by the same author, *To Change China: Western Advisers in China 1620–1960* (New York: Penguin Books, 1969, 1980), for a close examination of many frustrating projects "to change China."

25. H. A. R. Gibb, "Social Reform: Factor X—The Search for an Islamic Democracy," in *Perspective of the Arab World: An Atlantic Supplement* (New York, 1956). See also various essays in this volume.

26. Richard Nolte, "The Rule of Law in the Arab Middle East," *Muslim World*, Vol. XLVIII, no. 4, 1958.

27. *New York Times*, November 1, 1985.

Strategic Intelligence in
Cold Wars of Ideas

I

Leninist and Islamic Cold Wars Against The West

The Euro-American West has been contending with two "cold wars" in this century: one with the Leninist Soviet imperium that was prescribed by the Communist ideology and has been fought relentlessly since 1914; and the other with a group of radical Islamic states, foremost among them Iran, Iraq, Syria, and Libya, that has the imprimatur of the Islamic faith but did not go into high gear before ca. 1950. The engine driving both cold wars is hatred of the West. The tactics and modalities of fighting them are different, however, except that both enemies rely heavily on deception and terrorism.

The West, led since 1920 by the United States, has been on the losing side in each of the contests up to 1989–90. But the question of whether either of the protracted psychopolitical conflicts can now be pronounced "over" just because the Soviet Union's power and prestige were cut down in 1989 by successful anti-Communist revolutions and secessions, or because the U.S.-led coalition had handed Iraq a smashing military defeat in 1990 while liberating Kuwait, can be answered only after one has assessed the reasons for the dense record of European and American policy failures *before* 1989. After all, Americans in particular will probably not be allowed to forget that their policymaking governmental and academic elites were totally surprised and unprepared when they learned one day in 1989 that the Soviet economy—which had been praised to the skies the year before—had collapsed; that Marxism-Leninism was pronounced bankrupt in its homeland, finished as ideology, as economic theory, and as political system; that the citizenry was in open rebellion and the Soviet empire's satellites in different stages of insurgency, autonomy, or independence.

In the context of U.S. political intelligence one must surely say, What a Waterloo! And that judgment deepens with reflections on the gasps of astonishment throughout the nation when the East Europeans led by the East Germans simply sacked their Communist governments and returned to their Roman law roots of constitutionalism.

Is the Leninist Cold War Over Now?

This successful continental European revolt in the cold war between freedom and totalitarianism may well rate in international history as second only to some battles in the eight-hundred-year-long *guerra fria*[1] between Islam and Christendom that was won for the West by Spain in 1492. But not much was done under U.S.

auspices to support the Eastern European freedom fighters, solidify the newly recovered frontier that separates the West's law states from the East's despotisms, and
exploit the stunning cold war victory over the Soviet Union. The Soviet Union was
not pressured to remove its military forces from Germany, immobilize its resident
KGB agents in the region, deconstruct its Communist Party apparatus, and cease
its espionage and terrorist activities. The nerve centers of the Soviet cold war system thus continue to be in place.

The end of the cold war then is clearly contingent on the liquidation of the
Soviet system. It is dependent also on the actual evolution of long-captive nations
into independent states and on how successful generations of individuals in East
and Central Europe will be in coming to terms with the residue of Leninism that
remains lodged in their minds and psyches. After all, it is relatively easy to open
prison doors, close slave labor camps, and dismiss Communist rulers but very difficult to lay aside modes of thinking and patterns of behavior that have been carefully implanted and administered by the enemy for over five decades. And lastly,
it should be recognized that the efficacity and duration of the Leninist cold war for
control of continental Europe are in great measure functions of flawed Anglo-American policies in the region.

As noted in the introduction to the present volume, the United States and the
United Kingdom knew little about the geography and history of Central and Eastern
Europe and nothing about the complex cultural North-South frontier separating the
West from the East when they arranged for the demolition of the German, Austrian,
and Ottoman empires between 1914 and 1920 and the creation in the space thus
vacated of a belt of small independent but defenseless states. The same policy was
followed during and after the Second World War when these small but geostrategically vital outpost nations of the West were assigned to satellite status in the Sta-
linist Gulag empire. Further, but in the same context of time and space, Anglo-
American policy was instrumental in weakening the West's next line of defense in
the region by keeping Germany demilitarized, splitting that state's western part into
zones of occupation by American, British, French, and Soviet forces, surrendering
its core northeast provinces to incorporation by the Soviet Union and Poland, and
by consigning Austria to political irrelevance.

In these circumstances it is not surprising that little if anything was done by the
United States to arrest or impede the expansion of the Soviet dominion or to checkmate the formation of Communist Party networks and the spread of Marxist-Leninist doctrine. Indeed, an overview of the nation's policies and actions in the last
seventy years indicates that its administrations did not recognize the Soviet Union
as an enemy and did not really understand the "cold war" and our stake in it.

It goes without saying that the inability to diagnose hostile cold-war offensives
is matched by the inability to mount, organize, or support appropriate counter–cold
war measures. This was illustrated early on in the 1920s when the American policy-
making establishment was deaf to multiple signals from German and East European
scenes of Communist-staged putsches and insurgencies that announced the nature
of Soviet cold war tactics and intentions in no uncertain terms, as well as in 1936
when the United States was deceived into perceiving the "low-intensity conflict"
in Spain as a genuine civil war even though it had actually been carefully pro-

grammed by the KGB as "cover" for the Soviet scheme to dismantle the Spanish nation-state, thus undermining Europe from the South.

A survey of U.S. statecraft and intelligence during the decades leading up to 1989–90 allows for the conclusion that the United States still does not understand the Leninist mind-set and that Central, Eastern and Southern Europe are still *terra incognita* to its policymakers and intelligence services. As long as this condition persists we shall obviously not know whether or when the cold war is over, nor will we know how to cope with it effectively.

The Significance of the Persian Gulf War for Issue Identification

The United States left the European cold war battle scene abruptly when it decided in August 1990 to engage in an all-out military war against Iraq, which had just seized Kuwait. The Persian Gulf war was fought brilliantly, successfully, and— as it was to transpire during and after the fighting—for very good reasons. However, it was fought without the guidance of good political and military intelligence and without knowing just what we were going to do in the Middle East once the war was over.

Iraq's invasion of Kuwait was a total surprise, as was its state of extraordinary military preparedness. We did not know either Saddam Hussein's war plan or his personality. Had the government's Middle East experts been better read in Arab history and the biographies of Arabdom's illustrious leaders (and they include the Prophet), they would surely not have suggested the naïve comparison to Adolf Hitler with whom this Iraqi leader has no connection.[2] If they had wanted to draw parallels with well-known twentieth-century totalitarian dictators, they should obviously have chosen Stalin, with whose political system Saddam Hussein has long been linked. But here again a critical intelligence gap was bared in the course of the Gulf war. The United States had evidently not known that the Soviet Union had been deeply engaged for three decades grooming Iraq for its regional wars and its probable encounter with American forces even though the accumulated evidence of joint terrorist operations has long pointed clearly in that direction. It took the open "briefing" by the chief Soviet general in charge of this program to tell Americans in considerable detail how long he had worked grooming the Republican Guard and what its characteristics were, and in his estimate continue to be.

Thus we learned *ex post facto* that the U.S.-led coalition had actually fought two enemies and won two victories. Not only was Saddam Hussein's design to unify Arabdom, gain control of the Middle East, and eliminate Israel and the United States from the area stifled,[3] but the Soviet Union's prestige was greatly cut, and that not only in military terms. This double victory certainly rates satisfaction but does not make up for the double failure in strategic foresight that attended it: namely, the failure to study the thoughtways of two self-professed enemies of the United States before engaging them in war. Had our policymakers done their homework they would have discovered without difficulty that Leninism and Islam— different as they are from each other in most respects—yet converge on viewing all foreign relations as war relations, on not accepting the twin ideas of the state and its frontiers as ultimate norms of statecraft, and on being deaf therefore to Western entreaties charging breach of law or treaty. Such concordances—and they are developed and qualified in preceding essays—explain why Leninist and Islamic societies are by definition conflict systems and why the genus "cold war" is deeply entrenched in both. In brief, it could have been expected that Leninist and Islamic cold war tacticians would find ways of combining their moves in psychopolitical as well as geostrategic contexts.

This new alignment of forces suggested at the time that the whole West, but specifically its continental European core province, would have to reckon henceforth with a historically new Eurasian fault line—one that connects the vast Soviet-controlled bicontinental landmass with the Southwest Asian heartland of Islam. The subsequent dissolution first of the Soviet empire and thereafter of the Soviet Union itself, and the concomitant evolution of scores of successor states had the effect of transforming established *political* identities and frontiers. However, it is not likely to conduce to a blurring of the great *cultural* divide between the Eastern European peoples Christianized by Rome and the adjoining Slavic, specifically Russian societies Christianized by Byzantium. Indeed, a hardening may be expected here since the historic fault line will henceforth be perceived and administered by multiple, ideologically disunited governments.

These new geostrategic challenges to the security of newly liberated East-Central Europe are compounded by developments in the former Soviet Union's sector of Asian Islamic republics that adjoins the Russian sector. All were Leninized and are now independent. As in the different Russias so also here: no one can foresee in which—if any—measure these nations will de-Leninize, but it is evident already in the early 1990s that they will be drawn ineluctably into alignment with the Islamic homeland in the Middle East.

The North-South fault line in the Eurasian culture world has thus become about as complex as it used to be before Czarist Russia's conquests of inner Asian Islamic khanates. Now as then it also joins the East-West line that separates continental Europe from Islamic Africa. This intercontinental and cultural boundary connecting West Asia with the Atlantic Ocean has been worked to great advantage in recent times by Libya's Muammar Qaddafi and leaders of Islamic fundamentalism with a view to consolidating Arab/Islamic policies all along the southern Mediterranean coast as well as horizontally across Saharan Africa.

Continental Europe, then, was effectively encircled throughout most of the twentieth century by two longtime adversaries of Western civilization—a condition that has had decidedly crippling effects on policy planning throughout the West. Since it can be ascribed in considerable measure to a general neglect of geopolitics and culture history, it is reasonable to hope that the West's policy strategists in the post-1990 era of world society will be more attentive in these respects and more alert therefore to the existence of invisible yet permanent cultural frontiers.

In the strictly Western or European perspective it is possible to experience the dramatic actualities of the 1990s as a replay of history that began with the birth of Europe in the throes of the Greco-Persian wars twenty-five hundred years ago and continued with Europe's expansion and consolidation in Roman and early Christian times in order then to be challenged and partially arrested by Islam between the seventh and fifteenth centuries A.D.

How pertinent are historical records for present-day processes of policy formation in North-South and East-West relations specifically as these bear on the coexistence of Islamic and Christian societies in the Mediterranean region? In this writer's opinion they constitute an invaluable data bank in the context of intelligence and statecraft that allows for the extrapolation and assessment of all that has proved to be enduring in behavior patterns and is likely therefore to be recurring also in the future. In other words, this kind of knowledge or intelligence is valuable because it can provide information as well as foresight in policy-making and tactics.

Constant Themes in Mediterranean Culture and Politics

The return to the Mediterranean region as history's major proving ground in rival Christian and Islamic operations is apt to reactivate the following general themes in European consciousness.

Southern Europeans gained a profound understanding of the Mediterranean Sea and its geographic function on one hand as an irreversible link between Europe, Asia, and Africa, and on the other as a lasting divide between the numerous, strikingly divergent cultures and political systems that evolved on the edges of these three continents. Further, they were persuaded in the course of eight hundred well-chronicled years of close coexistence with various Islamic groups on both land and sea that while mutually tolerable, even agreeable terms of accommodation are possible in social and intellectual matters,[4] Christianity and Islam are indeed antipodes when it comes to conceptions of political organization and warfare.

These two propositions have received attention in several essays, but they require annotation in the context of the present discussion, which addresses the ultimate effects of their protracted interaction.

(1) The pivotal reference in all Muslim relations with non-Muslim peoples has always been the *jihad,* even though this doctrine of permanent military, political, and psychological war was traditionally compromised in actual relations with the two other scriptural peoples, that is, the Christians and the Jews. Some allowance for peace was thus made throughout premodern times albeit with the explicit proviso that it be viewed as a temporary cessation of hostilities. That is to say, the *jihad* was often muted into a state of "dormant" or "protracted" war during which amicable relations with non-Islamic nations could be cultivated more or less at will.[5]

The Christian faith, by contrast, does not allow for a doctrine of permanent war. Medieval notions of "the just war" and "the crusade" were therefore neither scripturally ordained nor did they imply a state of permanent belligerence. However, in Western Christendom they were activated by ecclesiastical and secular authorities when overt military wars were designed either to withstand invaders or to reconquer what they had taken earlier, as, for instance, in the crusades for the recovery of the Holy Land in the Near East.[6] In Eastern Greek Orthodox Christendom (Byzantium), by contrast, where centuries of close coexistence among European, Asian, and African peoples had fostered cultural affinities, and where the Christian power center was surrounded by hostile counterplayers, "crusading" was muted into low-intensity contests. Indeed, as illustrated in the fourth essay of this volume and by au thorities there cited, Byzantine statecraft excelled in psychopolitical operations, "cold wars," and the diplomatic arts of managing less-developed peoples in its environment—aptitudes that were also highly developed in the Catholic Adriatic Republic of Venice, which had begun its illustrious millennial existence as a surrogate of Constantinople (see essay 3).

(2) Contradictory dispositions toward war and peace also explain why Christians and Muslims differed sharply on how to administer the lands they had come to hold. The primary mandate incumbent on Islamic rulers and their armies was the religious duty to spread the faith by steadily advancing the geographic and political frontiers of the Dar al-Islam so as to make it eventually coterminous with the inhabited world. Less effort was invested in evolving and implanting institutions of public order that would solidify what arms had won. And here the chief impediment has always been the irrevocable *shari'a* prohibition to fathom or support secular forms of government.[7]

Christianity, too, evolved as a universalist, hence expansive faith. But as mentioned earlier, the warring mandate was effectively controlled in both Christian empires by the strong commitment to peace that sets the New Testament apart from the Old Testament and the Koran. And this restraining principle was complemented in the Byzantine empire by geopolitical circumstances to which reference has already been made. In short, medieval Christians were disadvantaged in strictly military terms. For whereas war against them and all unbelievers had been officially declared by the prophet's original message to last throughout all earthly time, they were conditioned by religion to view each war as a singular interruption of normal peacetime life. Yet, and perhaps paradoxically, it is precisely this disposition that animated Christians to firm up and pacify the frontiers that had been reached; consolidate the territory and the human community that had become theirs to administer; and do all that in the manner of the Romans in reliance on Rome's civil law.[8]

The Function of Frontier Zones in European Statecraft

The objectives here listed were furthered throughout medieval Europe by developing municipalities and staking out frontier zones in disputed territory for service on one hand as barriers against hostile inroads from without, on the other as farthest outposts of the established cultural and political order. Such gatekeeping borderlands—known as *marches* in England and France, *marcas* in Spanish, and *Mark* in German—played strategically significant roles in the histories of many European countries[9], particularly along the North-South and East-West lines dividing Europe from Asia and Africa while linking the Baltic with the Mediterranean.

Some of these marches were destined to be contested throughout time. For example, Estonia, Livonia, and Courland in northeast Europe started out as forward bases of the medieval "Holy Roman Empire" and the Hanseatic League of trading cities, having been Christianized under the auspices of Roman Catholic bishoprics and ecclesiastical orders. In the age of nation-states, however, they were returned to the status of bitterly contested borderlands. Other frontier territories, by contrast, evolved either into core provinces of the nation-state, as instanced by the "Mark

Brandenburg" in Germany, or into embryonic states like the "Oestermark" that foreshadowed Austria (Oesterreich).

The challenge of holding and possibly advancing embattled cultural frontiers was even greater along the East-West line in the Mediterranean region where the Greek city-states had set the precedent when they contained the Persians, and where a millennium later Christendom and Islam were to remain locked in combat and conflict from 700 to 1500 A.D. The stage of their historically fateful interactions was the Mediterranean Sea in its entirety. Perceived by many as an "Islamic/Christian Sea," it may also be likened to an immense, perennially contested water *marca* that is unlikely to yield to bids for absolute dominion. The stage that really counted, both for the Islamic offense and the Christian defense, was Europe's southern coast lands (its "soft underbelly" in twentieth-century semantic usage). And here the contest remained focused for seven hundred years on the Byzantine empire, heir to classical Greece in its gatekeeping functions in the extreme east of the continent, and on the Iberian peninsula in the extreme west of the Mediterranean where Portugal and Spain were to stand steady guard first as culture-conscious *marcas* and thereafter as politically highly accomplished states.

II

The *Guerra Fria* in Spain: 711–1492

The momentous centuries during which most of Spain was occupied by Islamic forces were circumscribed by a thirteenth-century Spanish writer as a *guerra fria*— a cold war between cultures, mind-sets, ideas, and operational tactics that provided the underpinning and penultimate cause for the ferocious military encounters between the Islamic invaders and their Christian European target peoples, but never stopped even after battles had been either lost or won. As noted earlier, numerous parallels can be drawn between the West's twentieth-century cold wars, armed wars, and low-intensity conflicts and those fought by Europeans against Asian and African Muslims in the Mediterranean area. In fact, there is little in the dense historical accounts of these international relations that is not relevant for Western statecraft today. Yet the purposes of this particular book are served best by limiting the inquiry to the following themes.

In which ways did Spain and Portugal cope with the near-ceaseless overt and covert invasions by different Islamic groups? How did medieval Spain's different principalities and municipalities manage to retain their essential identities while living in close quarters with culturally and politically hostile communities that were firmly settled in their midst? Which spiritual and tactical resources made it possible for this divided and embattled nation to go on resisting foreign domination for eight centuries without cracking up while simultaneously staging a protracted *reconquista* that was to culminate in 1492 in the total liberation of the Iberian peninsula? True, Muslim forces continued to probe, harass, and at times even cross Europe's new *marca* in the South; but in long-range geopolitical and historical perspectives it is fair to say that the epochal Spanish accomplishment sealed the security of Europe north of the Pyrenees, and that it is comparable only to that registered by the Greek city-states in the fifth century B.C. in the eastern Mediterranean.

The Scene as Set by Islam

Spain had been a province of the classical and early Christian Roman Empire until it was invaded first by the Vandals and the Suevi, and in the fifth century A.D. by the western Goths. However, since cleavages and frictions among the different Germanic peoples and between all of them and the indigenous Spanish-Roman population had not been eliminated by the governing Visigothic kingdom, Spain was divided, weak, and unprepared when struck by an avalanche of Islamic invasions in the eighth century. The first, in 711, brought newly Islamized Berber forces from Umayyad-controlled North Africa and led a few months later to the destruction of the Visigothic kingdom. The next (712), conducted by Musa, the governor of Islamized North Africa (who was allegedly jealous of the phenomenal success recorded earlier by his underling), resulted in the capture of all significant towns and strongholds, including Seville, the intellectual center of Spain and once its Roman capital, as well as Saragossa in the north. Thereupon Muslim forces reached the highlands of Aragon, Leon, the Asturias, and Galicia, and Spain was transformed into a province of the caliphate under the name al-Andalus. Now only the Pyrenees were left to bar entrance into the coveted "land of the Franks." The mountain range was crossed by Musa's third successor in 718, but attempts to take Toulouse and Aquitaine were foiled by fierce Germanic resistance.

The third and most ambitious expedition northward was led by Abd-al-Rahman, then Spain's ruling emir, and struck through the western Pyrenees in 732. Bordeaux was stormed and its churches set on fire. After burning a renowned basilica outside the walls of Poitiers, Abd-al-Rahman pushed toward Tours, where he was met and decisively defeated by Charles Martel, the powerful major-domo of the Merovingian court, and his Frankish warriors who—in the words of a seventeenth-century French historian—had formed a hollow square, standing shoulder to shoulder, firm as a wall, inflexible as a block of ice.[10]

After several decades of anarchy during which twenty-three governors followed each other in quick succession, Islamic Spain was consolidated by a talented member of the Umayyad dynasty. When the Abbasids announced their ascendancy to the caliphate in the East (A.D. 750) by massacring the members of the Umayyad caliphal family, this survivor escaped; reached Spain after five years of wandering in the Near East and North Africa; captured Cordova and Toledo; suppressed successive Shi'ite and Berber revolts, and succeeded in 773 in establishing Spain as an emirate that was wholly independent of the Abbasid caliphate (773). The eighth emir or sultan in the new dynasty (Abd-al-Rahman III, 912–961) was the first to assume the title of caliph, and Cordova was developed into a resplendent capital that could hold its own in relations with Baghdad.

The Umayyad era (756–1031) marks the apogee in Islamic Spain's history. However, the caliphate began waning already by the end of the tenth century, and its total collapse set the scene first for renewed anarchy and fratricidal warfare in the conglomeration of petty Islamic states, and thereafter for the methodical ransacking and conquest of Spain by the fanatical Berber dynasty of the Almoravids (1090–1147). The land was soon inundated by semi-Islamized tribal Africans who were interested solely in war and booty and thus proved wholly unprepared to absorb and administer the civilization they had conquered.[11] Weakened by decadence and disintegration, the Almoravids fell easy prey in the mid-twelfth century to the Almohads, another North African Berber dynasty. It, too, had started out as a religiopolitical movement, but contrary to the Almoravid establishment it soon evolved into a vast caliphate empire that joined the whole Muslim part of the Iberian peninsula with the entire North African coastland from the Atlantic to the borders of Egypt.

The most vexing problem facing all Almohad caliphs and among them particularly Al-Mansur (1184–1199) issued from their fanatical determination to finish off the Christian north. A *jihad* was eventually launched by Al-Mansur's son (1199–1214). But it was cut short in 1212 by a disastrous defeat of the Islamic troops. The historic battle was fought some seventy miles east of Cordova against a Christian army led by Alfonso VIII of Castile, whose forces also contained French crusaders. It included contingents from Aragon and Navarre, both represented by their kings, and from Portugal, represented by Templars and other knights. The overthrow of the Almohads was complete: for they were expulsed from the peninsula.[12]

The Christian *reconquista,* then, was in full swing at the beginning of the thirteenth century. However, its completion was to take 280 additional years, since Islam continued to hold out in the Spanish south under the auspices of the Nasrid dynasty (1232–1492) in Granada.

Which Salient Points Can Be Abstracted from the Tangled Spanish Cold War Records?

(I) THE CAUSES OF SUCCESS AND FAILURE ON THE ISLAMIC SIDE. The basic patterns of Islamic statecraft in Western Europe were analogous to those developed in the Middle East. As discussed earlier in this book, they center on authoritarian personalized rule and strong moral and political commitments to expand territorial dominion by waging war, and to propagate and sustain the faith by means of the *jihad.*

Reflections on the Spanish records thus justify the conclusion that the conquest of the Iberian peninsula was conceived and carried out by all Islamic invaders as a set of outright military rather than "cold war" operations, and that wars for the propagation of the faith were fought throughout the centuries with undiminished religious fervor, nowhere more so than in the Christian strongholds of the northern marches. Here it became the practice of a tenth-century caliph to conduct holy war campaigns each spring and autumn against Leon, Castile, and Catalonia. Among the recorded achievements are the capture of Zamora in 981, the sacking of Barcelona in 985 (his thirteenth), and the razing of the city of Leon in 988.

External warfare, then, was as incessant in the Muslim West as it was in the Muslim East of the Mediterranean region. Further, here as there its incidence and its ravages were confounded by ceaseless internecine or civil wars and a great variety of high-intensity conflicts. In Spain and North Africa these were set off by standing religious or sectarian divisions between Shi'ite and Sunni believers; pervasive ethnic or racial conflicts among Arabs, Berbers, and tribal African blacks on one hand, and between all of these groups and Spanish Muslims and Jews on the other; by mass insurrections and revolts as well as by continuous, usually violent contests between rival aspirants to personalized power, rival dynasties, and rival petty states or emirates.

Islamic Spain was neither unified nor effectively linked to Muslim power centers in North Africa. These circumstances, most vividly illustrated by perennial feuds between Arabs and Berbers, are often cited by way of explaining just why *jihads* against Christianity—and it remained enemy number one throughout the centuries—had to be halted so often; in short, why they did not end in speedy total victory.

There is merit to this conclusion provided one recalls that significant Iberian/ North African variants of basic Islamic beliefs and norms of governance were also determined by these circumstances. For instance, the mere fact that Arabs were greatly outnumbered by Berbers and blacks from inner Africa helps explain why such complex concepts as the *umma,* the *shari'a,* the *imam,* or the *jihad* were inadequately understood, or why they got so mixed up with non-Islamic African creeds and traditions of rule as to forfeit much of their clarity and authenticity.

In light of these intellectual and ideological confusions it is not surprising that no ruling establishment in the Islamic West was able to create even the semblance of an enduring transcultural *umma* by unifying Arabs, Berbers, Numidians, Goths, and Gallic Romans; and that no sustained efforts were ever made outside the *jihad* context to link Christians, Muslims, and Jews in politically effective and viable associations. Further, and more to the point of this particular discussion, the annals of Islamic statecraft in Spain suggest strongly that one of the oldest and least primitive provinces of Europe's classical and Christian civilization was held captive most of the time—the brief Umayyad period being the exception—by a rather primitive Islam, and that in condition of unrelieved anarchy and violence.

All Islamic imperialisms differ from those brought forth by Europeans in classical as in later times because *shari'a* norms do not set reliable bounds for the exercise of despotic power, and because they do not accommodate the twin concepts of the self-determining individual and the citizen. In fact, the term "citizen" was totally outside the Muslim experience, and the idea of equality was severely compromised.

Three inequalities in particular were established by law and developed through centuries of usage: the unequal status of master and slave, of man and woman, of Muslim and non-Muslim.[13] The status of humans in each of these categories—and they obviously often overlapped—was carefully circumscribed by jurists in terms of privileges and obligations. But all people assigned to them were identified as permanently inferior beings—with the non-Muslim female slave occupying the lowest rank in the Islamic setup.[14]

Although the law regulating life for subject peoples was in theory the same wherever Muslim dominion had triumphed, it proved to be malleable under the influence of local traditions and was apt therefore to affect societies in different ways. For instance, Islamic power centers in Spain and North Africa were as active in enslaving, capturing, buying, and selling African blacks and European Christians for service in mercenary armies, harems, and bodyguards as Eastern caliphs and sultans were. But comparative surveys suggest that western Mediterranean regimes were more capricious and abusive in administering the rules than governments in the Arab homeland of Islam. This was so partly because the Iberian peninsula—a relatively limited space—had become crowded with just too many culturally incompatible peoples, but mainly because Spain was viewed by all Islamic arrivals as a province of the Dar al-Harb (the domain of war). As such it was destined to remain subject to rule by *jihad* as long as unbelievers—and they rank throughout the Dar al-Islam as primary foes of the faith—had not been totally subjugated. Other enemy categories also consigned to eradication cover bandits, rebels, and apostates. Needless to say, they could always be identified in abundance in the Iberian region.

(2) THE RECONQUEST OF SPAIN. It is doubtful that the splendors of Islamized city life—and they turned out to be ephemeral, too—ever made up for the multifarious negatives of the Islamic conquest. Rather, the records suggest that all who lived in Spain between the eighth and fifteenth centuries were disoriented or harassed by the continuity of oppression, war, fear, and, above all, insecurity. In such circumstances it is not surprising that scores of malcontents, be they segments of ruling Muslim establishments or African slave armies, chose to express their frustrations and special grievances in violent revolts, uprisings, and insurgencies. Most of these were short-term ventures that did not lead to systemic changes either in Spain's identity or in its administration.

The Spanish *guerra fria,* by contrast, was conceptually and politically in a class by itself. Its protagonists were nationalists determined to defend or recover the land that was rightfully theirs, and Christians who were morally committed to the maintenance and defense of their faith. Their chief long-range objectives did not waver over time; when they were achieved it was clear also that Europe was saved and the whole world totally transformed.

A just appreciation of this feat requires remembering that the mental and political processes of holding to and furthering the Spanish objectives were infinitely convoluted and protracted throughout the centuries. After all, these early "freedom fighters" started from the lamentable nothingness of what looked like total defeat. But I believe I am right in supposing that the outlines of the *guerra fria* were embedded in the minds of those who found themselves checkmated all of a sudden, and that the idea was passed on mysteriously year in, year out to like-minded countrymen who learned through threatening experiences how to flesh it out in actual programs and practices that matched the needs and opportunities in their particular districts of the divided war-torn homeland.

How then should one view the *reconquista*? The term is usually employed to denote the sum total of all strictly military operations that eventually were to prove decisive in assuring the liberation of the Iberian peninsula. Seen in this light, the battle data are indeed chronologically reliable indicators of the actual correlation of forces at a given moment. And in this narrow context it certainly makes as much sense to say that the reconquest began in the eleventh or the twelfth or the thirteenth century, when major Christian victories could be recorded, as it does when one concludes that the *reconquista* (and therewith the *guerra fria*) came to an end with the recovery of Granada in 1492.

However, such a view needs correction in light of the fact that the Spanish cold war was, like any other cold war, an ongoing contest of mind-sets, ideas, and objectives played out on all levels of existence. Seen in this multidimensional context, it was a maze of interlocking low- and high-intensity conflicts whose beginnings and ends could not be dated as events. The reconquest should therefore be accepted as the military dimension of this complex process as well as the culmination of the *guerra fria*.

The *guerra fria* began in the minds of Spanish Christians as a near-automatic sequence to Islamic victories in the eighth century. It was not initiated as a counteroffensive, nor was it articulated as an all-Spanish policy since there was no central authority in the divided and occupied land. What early records convey instead are two pronounced but not necessarily compatible dispositions: the will to resist further Islamic encroachments that was pervasive in the North, and the inclination to seek the best possible terms of accommodation with the enemy, long dominant in the South. Christians in both regions seem to have been prepared to convert to Islam, under pressure as well as by choice. But the new religious and political alignment was naturally experienced as less problematical by those who lived in relative freedom in still-independent Christian cities and kingdoms than it was for those who had become inferior subjects of Islamic authorities.

These were the most numerous and most discontented classes of subject peoples. And among them again the identity problem weighed most heavily on the Mozarabs, that element in the population of Spain, Hitti writes,[15] that had assimilated itself in language and ways of living to the conquering Moslems but retained its Christian faith. These "would-be Arabs" came to constitute a large proportion of the population and were therefore the special object of restrictions in the large cities where they were frequently the majority. Thus they lived in quarters of their own, kept (under the Umayyads) their special magistrates, and wore no distinctive clothes. However, they usually bore double names: one Arabic and familiar, the other Latin or Spanish and more formal. They even practiced circumcision and kept harems. Most Mozarabs were bilingual, their native tongue being the Romance patois that was to become Spanish, but even in such cities as Toledo they continued in the use of Arabic as the written language of law and business for two centuries after Alfonso VI had reconquered the town in 1085.[16]

In short, Mozarabs had to cultivate split personalities and lead double lives if they wanted to survive or "make it" under the psychopolitically stressful and everthreatening auspices of the *guerra fria*. This motif of the double personality was dramatically personified in the eleventh century by the Cid, the most colorful of Mozarabs, who is celebrated in Spanish history and literature as the exemplar of chivalry and resistance to the infidel, but who had also covered himself with glory while serving an Islamic dynasty at Saragossa.[17]

The burden of moral, mental, and political ambivalence rested probably even more heavily on Christian converts to Islam who had secretly remained Christians or who chose to return to their native faith. In their case governmental surveillance

was naturally intensified since such subjects might be guilty of apostasy and treason—an eventuality that had the natural effect of raising levels of anxiety or fear in
the ranks of those who might then have to opt for either recantation or death.

The Muslim treatment of Spain's numerous Jews was similar to that meted out
to Christians. In accordance with classical theory as developed in the Arab East,
they, like Christians, might qualify for *dhimmi* status as long as they remained
unbelievers and permanent residents who clearly submitted to Muslim rule and paid
the poll tax to the Muslim state. The major disability attached to this condition was
that such individuals remained forever outsiders who were granted some legal protection but no political rights whatsoever.

Although even these privileges were compromised by anarchical Islamic practices in the Iberian peninsula, Andalusian Jewry did enjoy at times considerable
prosperity, political influence, and freedom, nowhere more so than in the cities.
For example, the inhabitants of Lucena (termed by al-Idrisi a Jewish city and considered the wealthiest of their coreligionists in the Muslim world) were called upon
by an Almoravid ruler of Spain to meet out of their pockets the deficit in the public
treasury.[18] More important, Jewish immigrants from the Mediterranean East were
able to establish a Talmudic school in Cordova that soon became the center for the
unfolding of Spanish-Jewish culture. These were singular events, however, that did
not make up either for the massive record of institutionalized and arbitrary oppression or for the equally massive record of insecure and conflicted Jewish lives. Much
like the Mozarabs who outnumbered them greatly, Jews preserved themselves morally and politically by using the language and dress of the Arabs, by following their
manners, and above all by cementing their own togetherness in the separate city
quarters to which they had been relegated, as, for example, in Cordova.

All of the aforementioned groups and their individual memberships remained
objects of deep, often justified suspicion as fifth columnists or traitors. And some
of them, as for instance the Neo-Muslims, were naturally mistrusted also by Spanish Christians in whose eyes they were reprehensible renegades. Yet conflicted,
confused, and persecuted as most of them were, it is in their ranks, specifically
those of the Mozarabs, that mere dispositions to resist the Islamic establishment
hardened into fighting power.

Uprisings after uprisings gradually coalesced into chronic revolution, nowhere
more poignantly so than in Cordova. Some of the conspiracies schemed in this
important enclave of the *guerra fria* cut across religious and ethnic lines of division.
For example, some of Cordova's Christians were so outraged about the tendency to
Arabicization that they countered it with a movement that climaxed in the voluntary
martyrdom of several men and women. Islamic punishments, which included the
execution of a Christian priest, only served to crystallize this cause. Other separate
but related insurrections were staged by Christian slaves, renegades, Jews, and even
liberal Muslims. One of the more dramatic in this group involved a Muslim de-
scendant of a Visigoth count who led a well-organized rebellion against Islamic rule
in the Spanish South. After he failed in his ambitious plan to get the governorship
over Spain, he made a point of openly professing the religion of his forefathers that
he had long concealed.

The paramount theaters of the early *guerra fria* were Spain's old occupied cities and the territory they controlled. Apart from Cordova these included Toledo, the most important royal city in the eyes of all conquered natives and the one that was more often in rebellion than at peace; Saragossa; Tudela and other frontier towns in the northern marches that had been incorporated by independent Aragon, then administered by an old Visigoth family that had embraced Islam; and Seville, the chief center of Roman culture under the Visigoths, which had a population mostly descended from Romans and Goths. The rulers of these places represented an odd admixture of Christians and Muslims, of Visigoths and anti-Arab Berbers. All of them were in league with their neighbors to the west, the Christian kings of Leon.

Separatism was the code word also in the Galician Southwest where an Islamic renegade brigand founded an independent principality "whence, with the aid of Alfonso III, king of Leon and natural ally of all anti-Arab rebels,"[19] he spread terror far and wide. And at the southwestern corner of the peninsula (the modern Algarve of Portugal) yet another renegade was able to shake off Arab suzerainty.

Resurgence of the Roman Christian State in the Northern Marches

While whole provinces and states were breaking loose under the continuous pressure of Mozarab insurgencies,[20] the northern kingdoms of Leon and Castile had united, Galicia and Navarre were added, and Islamic communities and sovereigns became tributary to Christian states in virtue either of conquest or of treaty arrangements. In short, the Christian reconquest of Spain was near completed by the mid-thirteenth century (see *supra,* this essay), and the outlines of Spain as a European Renaissance state were clearly discernible.

The following aspects of Spanish statecraft and intelligence are in my view noteworthy for two different yet connected reasons: First, they explain why the Christian leadership in the North was able in the two ensuing centuries to complete the military war as well as the *guerra fria,* to liberate and pacify the rest of the country, district after district, while simultaneously also transforming it into a unified nation-state. Second, they are suggestive for those American and European policymakers who were able, at the threshold of the twenty-first century, to register spectacular military victories against overt aggression in the strife-torn Islamic Middle East, but who did not have even the semblance of a blueprint for settling the different chronic cold wars and high-intensity conflicts that invited the aggression.

Thirteenth-century Spaniards in the newly unified North knew what they wanted. They had to recover Spain in its territorial integrity; they had to reunite the parts that had so long been separated, and they had to restore national consciousness. This meant not only that they had to oust ruling Asian and African establishments from the rest of Spain and disestablish the Islamic dominion but also, indeed mainly, that they had to recover or reactivate the two comprehensive systems of ideas that buttressed the reality and authenticity of Spain: Christianity and Roman law.

Next, but in the same general context, Spain's northern wardens were consciously engaged not only in nation-building but also in state-making. And in that capacity they knew what Europeans seem to have experienced throughout classical and early modern times, namely that Rome's civil law and the Christian faith were also exemplary support systems for "the state" and public order because they had the effect of unifying and pacifying men.[21]

For reasons noted earlier in this and other essays of the present book, Islam had no equivalent for Spain's "new" thirteenth-century political vocabulary of internal statecraft. Complementarity was therefore also missing in what Spaniards—along with other Europeans—distinguish as the vocabulary for external statecraft. Indeed, Islam shuns the juxtaposition of these two categories except when they relate to believers versus unbelievers, just as it does not accept the idea of boundaries. The revolutionary Spaniards, by contrast, were decidedly frontier-conscious from the beginning when they planned and developed their embryonic states, the *marcas,* as well as later when the gradual reunification of states and provinces required redrawing and reinforcing boundaries with a view to secure the new sovereign state and the new local peace that had been attained.

In assessing these policies and activities it should be borne in mind, first, that Spanish objectives were set, reached or approximated while the military and the cold war against Spain's Islamic societies was in full progress; second, that the Islamic counterplayers did not subscribe to the Christian differentiation between war and peace; and third, that the Spanish nationalists upped the ante in their fight for the Europeanization of Spain by insisting on a frontier also between "war" and "peace." All of this meant by implication that they had to find a way of living at peace with sizable Muslim communities that had been defeated or were to be defeated, while remaining resolutely at war with those who continued to hold the south.

The "Surrender Constitution" and Its Function in Spain's Internal and External Statecraft

It is interesting that incessant warring and its associated concerns for security did not have the effect of distancing Christian Spanish mind-sets from the traditional commitment to cultivate law as this had been inculcated throughout Spain when it was a province of the Roman Empire. The cities and townships continued to take care of their municipal charters; the kings and their administrative agents—all steeped in jurisprudence—continued to legislate, to structure government in terms of constitutions, and to shape relations as well as unions with other states in accordance with the same trusted norms of Rome's contract law. Above all, perhaps, scholarly life in cities and at royal courts continued to buzz with studies of law—just as it did during precisely those centuries in neighboring nonoccupied Italian states.[22] In short, Rome's constitutional law fortified the Spanish spirit because it carried the whole agenda for the postwar future of the nation, and because it provided this beleaguered *marca* of the Christian West with indestructible links to the rest of continental Europe, and therewith to the revolutionary movements of the Renaissance and humanism.

It is under these auspices then that the Council of Magnates in the state of Leon was developed into the Cortes, and that this body came up in 1020 with the Great Charter of Leon that was to become the model for constitutional government throughout Spain.

It was in this context also that serfs were emancipated, and that charters were given to towns with a view to calling forth a class of burghers who were self-governing, armed, and prepared to defend themselves. In short, traveling in symbiosis with the reconquest, Roman constitutional law helped solidify the advancing frontier by supplying the new frontier communities with a firm framework for maintaining peace and order.

Although there was nothing automatic about this particular process in medieval Spain's *guerra fria* with a variety of Islamic peoples, it merits the attention of those in the modern West who seek new ways of securing states and boundaries all along those geopolitically critical North-South and East-West fault lines to which reference is made at the beginning of this essay. The core of early Spanish statecraft in these respects is symbolized by a special arrangement with conquered Islamized frontier communities which was known from the eleventh century onward as "the surrender constitution." This device emerges from the records as the major long-term Spanish stratagem for peacemaking and state-making. As designed by Aragon-Catalan kings, such pacts conceded constitutions to surrendering Islamic districts that were loosely modeled on Leon's model *magna carta*. That is to say, they provided for extensive self-government and civil liberties; recognition of the *shari'a* as applicable law; and for the services of Islamic go-betweens in relations with central Christian authorities.

The general objectives implicit in all such grants to sizable enclaves of defeated Muslims included the following: to assure the security, recovery, productivity, and consolidation of the territory and its human settlements; to control the local peace and forestall strife, dissidence, treason, and insurgency; to safeguard and accommodate the Islamic subject population in the context of its cultural heritage; to tone down the *guerra fria* and encourage interactions between Muslims and Christians; and to call forth conditions that would promote assimilation and a return to Christianity.

Such purposes were consonant with the norms of the traditional Roman law of nature and the *ius gentium*, which circumscribed the status and rights of persons who were not Roman citizens, as well as with Christian ethics and the canon law. Indeed the papacy gave full and explicit support to royal initiatives in matters relating to "surrender constitutions," at no time more so than in the thirteenth century, when the Church (headed by Innocent IV in 1243–54), ecclesiastical lawyers, and members of the reformist Cluny order of monks[23] were deeply engaged in rethinking Christianity's relations with non-Christian societies. In regard to Spain's relationship with the "guest" communities left over by its erstwhile Islamic invaders and governors, the church people seem to have been at one in deep compassion for the defeated Muslims. Their pronouncements thus stipulated that these so-called Mudéjar communities had a *right* to full autonomy and a *right* also to freedom from conversion by force, and that Christians could not expulse them under any circumstances without offending charity[24]—never mind that no such rights or exemptions were granted by victorious Muslims to defeated Christians. In sum, an early projection of twentieth-century "Liberation Theology" can be detected here.

It cannot be denied that Christian Spain's war for independence and unity was adversely affected by the revisionist Catholic stance when policymakers had to deal with the large, essentially hostile Mudéjar communities in Valencia and Granada (see *infra,* this essay). However, a retrospective view of the whole endeavor between 711 and 1492 leaves no doubt in this writer's mind that the ultimate hard-won success in reconquering Spain and in restoring law and Christianity must be ascribed to Spanish statecraft and intelligence, specifically to Spain's highly developed capacity to understand the Islamic counterplayer realistically on his own terms.

Apart from being fully familiar with Islamic religious convictions, laws, social mores, political institutions, and norms of warfare, Iberian Christians knew well how to distinguish the mind-sets of Arabs, Berbers, and black Africans on one hand, and of Shi'ite and Sunni believers on the other. Those who negotiated surrender terms, truces, and other accords were therefore able throughout the centuries to gauge what or who could be assimilated or accommodated, and which blocs of alien humans and institutions had to be kept at a distance; to assess latent or covert dispositions to hostility; and to decide in the final countdown which European values and interests could not be compromised.

The surrender constitutions were thus significantly different from their Islamic equivalents, the *dhimmi* system and the Covenant of Umar, which assured general tolerance and privileged treatment to Christian and Jewish settlements in Muslim territory provided that these enemy scriptuaries complied with rather stern obligations to all Muslim authorities. In this respect, then, one is justified in likening Spain's surrender charters for Mudéjars to the Byzantine Empire's model for granting apartheid and protection to the large community of Orthodox Jews in its midst.[25]

Several other successful variants on the apartheid theme were recorded in the histories of Middle Eastern empires, but the original Arab-dominated Dar al-Islam experienced chronic difficulties in these respects because it had been conceived— and was being activated throughout its allotted time—as an empire whose political dynamic found expression in relentless movement, not in consolidation. As such it proved to be a successful religious union, that is, one that knew how to attract and convert, but an ineffective political union. For not even its most talented leaders were able to controvert or circumvent the prohibitions of the sacred law so as to establish trustworthy and viable secular structures of political organizations of the kind brought forth, for example, by the Persians and the Turks.

The Limits of Transcultural Peace and Unity

In dealing with its Islamic settlements, Christian Spain had to contend mostly with this particular Arab factor and its fanatical adjunct, the Berber/black African complex. That is to say, Spanish authorities had to persuade their would-be citizens to overcome their innate antagonism not just to European norms of rule but to the very idea of governmental order and control. In this they succeeded with the help of "the surrender constitution" when the alien community was numerically small: Muslims converted, forgot their Arabic, and allowed for political assimilation. The exceptions here were those who continued to practice Islam secretly and who thus developed the same type of dual personality that was noted earlier in discussing the status of the Mozarabs.

The charter stratagem was ineffective, however, and in this writer's view even counterproductive, when Mudéjarism was represented by large compact blocs of uncompromisingly hostile peoples, as it was in the kingdom of Valencia and in Granada.

In Almohad Valencia,[26] which had received its first surrender constitution from the Cid at the end of the eleventh century, Mudéjars soon outnumbered Christians as masses of defeated Muslims from other districts began flocking to the Valencian refuge. Resistance stiffened in these conditions, and the ever-present cold war merged with open military war. Revolt after revolt had to be put down; conquest followed reconquest; truces were concluded; but battles and sieges went on and on. Northern Valencia, specifically the Sierra de Eslide, thus remained a military problem for Christian Spain because it had become the habitat for Muslim malcontents and brigands, as well as a breeding ground for conspiracies with distant Muslim sovereigns, fifth-column activities, and treachery.

Surrender constitutions were nonetheless negotiated and renegotiated, and each revolt or war, however violent, seems to have ended with a royal amnesty. One forgave the Saracens of Alfandech Valley (a strategically most important district near the Spanish capital) all offense and damage that had been committed by them, and added the proviso "any Saracen who had taken himself off to the war zone, or outside our realm, can return to the aforesaid valley of Alfandech and remain there safe and secure." Nor can anyone "presume to demand anything from him as ransom-of-war."[27] Indeed, one cannot help but conclude from reading some of the charters, first, that concessions, privileges, and rights were simply heaped upon Valencia's Mudéjar "guest communities," particularly in the thirteenth century when the international Christian church took an active interest in non-Western societies; and second, that the guest communities remained resolutely hostile, militant, and separatist in disposition. A blend of two reasons probably accounts for this stance: One is to the effect that the *jihad* in mind and action—not peace—is the prescribed course for Islamic men, especially when the chance for winning big against infidels is as great as it was in Valencia. The other relates to the fact that European ideas of legally assured rights and obligations are irrelevant for those who are ruled by the *shari'a*. In short, the large community of Mudéjars in Valencia was allowed to evolve into a quasi-sovereign Islamic polity that could not possibly be assimilated by Spain's constitutional ways.

The unification of Christian Spain was a *fait accompli* in strategic planning when Ferdinand of Aragon married Isabella of Castile in 1469. As Hitti notes,[28] this "struck the note of doom for Muslim power in Spain." However, there still was Granada, the southern geopolitically most important province of European Spain. It was ruled between 1232 and 1491 by members of the Nasrid family, an offspring of the Spain-coveting Berber dynasties, who paid homage and tribute to Castile but continued to be stalwart champions of Islam. Moreover, and not unlike Valencia, Granada became an asylum for Muslim refugees fleeing the lands lost to Islam, as well as for great numbers of Arabized Jewish immigrants from Syria and other eastern locations who tended to be on the Islamic side in this protracted *guerra fria*.

The early Nasrid sultans did succeed in developing a wealthy, architecturally resplendent court and capital in Granada that recaptured for a while the reputation of Umayyad Cordova as patron-host to scholars while accommodating about 500,000 inhabitants. However, the political position of the sultanate was precarious to begin with, in both internal and external respects. Chronically plagued by factional and dynastic infighting, it worsened in the 1480s when the nineteenth sultan not only refused to pay the traditional tribute but chose to launch a military attack on Castilian territory. The sultan was taken by surprise and defeated when King Ferdinand retaliated successfully with the capture of the fort that guarded the southwestern entrance into the Granadan domain, and when one of the sultan's sons staged an armed rebellion against his father that resulted in his seizure of the Alhambra in 1482.

But this was by no means the end of intrigues and rival bids for power in the Muslim camp as brothers fought brothers and nephews were pitted against uncles. The Castilians won out finally because they knew how to take advantage of the turmoil in the enemy's ranks while their army advanced, taking town after town, until it encircled the capital. When an invitation to surrender was turned down in 1490, the siege was pressed into a blockade that was instrumental, in December 1491, in inducing the surrender of the garrison within the period of two months. This grace period was requested by the garrison because it hoped that Muslim friends in Turkish and African circles would send relief. Not surprisingly, the period expired without any sign of such assistance, and the Castilians entered Granada on January 2, 1492.[29]

Hitti notes in his account of these transactions that the garrison's 1491 surrender agreement required an oath of obedience by the sultan, his government, and his people to the Castilian sovereigns, and that the Muslims would in return be left secure in person under their laws and free in the exercise of their religion.[30]

Since it has become fashionable in the United States five hundred years later to "indict" Ferdinand and Isabella for not having kept this promise of the "surrender constitution," it is historically and politically necessary to correct available intelligence by providing the following facts:

- A seven-hundred-year war against Islamic invaders and occupying forces ended in 1492 with the military victory of Christian Spain and territorial, political, and moral unification of the country's diverse provinces.

- The Sultanate of Granada ceased existing when the governing ruler and his entourage departed willingly, never to return again.

- The age of surrender constitutions was over if only because no quasi-sovereign foreign governments were left in unified Spain that could have asked for or received such grants. In other words, the frontiers of the state were now settled.

- Surrender constitutions were bestowed upon communities; they were not bills of civil liberties for individual alien residents.

- Individual members of Granada's vast and compact Islamic enclave did not aspire at citizenship and civil liberties because the three determinants of such rights—namely the state, secular law, and citizenship—were not even recognized by the Islamic belief system.

- Being antistate and anti-Christian by religious instruction as well as by choice, Muslims in Granada did not want to be assimilated. Being enemies, they naturally exhausted themselves in conspiracies, revolts, and fifth-column operations.

No evaluations of Spanish statecraft during the *guerra fria* with Islam can proceed on course without steady remembrance of the fact that this historically momentous war of contradictory ideas between Christianity and Islam was fought for seven hundred years on multiple fronts, and that it involved multiple parties. In this perspective, then, the Spanish front was just one of several other fronts in the Mediterranean region. After all, Islamic forces had also wrested the entire Near East, North Africa, and parts of Italy from their Christian occupants. The Crusades, fought by combined Christian forces on behalf of recovering the lost lands, had been failures. Above all, the thousand-year-old Eastern Christian (Byzantine) Empire was extinguished by the Ottoman Turks in the course of the same protracted "unconventional," "low-intensity" conflict as the one unleased upon the Iberian peninsula.[31]

Constantinople was captured in 1453 and the crescent replaced the cross throughout the eastern Mediterranean, including Greece and the Balkan Peninsula, just thirty-nine years before the cross replaced the crescent in Granada. This achievement freed Islamic policymakers and their surrogate retinue to resume their attacks on Spain by stimulating and supporting local uprisings throughout the sixteenth century. Royal decrees (1501, 1526, 1556) that Muslim residents must either comply with the law of the land and desist from playing Muslim politics or leave Spain proved ineffective—hence the final order of expulsion by Philip III in 1609 that was carried out by physically deporting the Moriscos (the name for Muslims and crypto-Christians who had chosen to remain after the capture of Granada) to North Africa. As noted in preceding pages, expulsion and deportation had been common Islamic devices for punishing and eliminating Spanish Christians and Mozarabs throughout the centuries-spanning *guerra fria*.[32]

The Spanish Victory: Its International Dimensions

1492 not only marks Spain's victory over Islam and its resuscitation as an independent Christian European state. It is a big year also in international history because it was then, allegedly in Granada's Alhambra, that Christopher Columbus appealed to Queen Isabella for a subsidy for his maritime adventure—the one that was to result in the discovery of America.[33] Indeed, 1492 symbolizes the whole fifteenth century of explorations and discoveries during which Iberian, predominantly Portuguese seafarers and explorers succeeded in rounding the Cape of Good Hope, penetrating the heart of Africa, and finding a new way to India—a record of revolutionary scientific achievements that climaxed in 1498 when Vasco da Gama dropped anchor off Calicut in India.[34]

All this had been dreamed up, initiated, and accomplished by "two small nations, one but two years reestablished in full possession of its homeland, the other boasting a population of perhaps a million and a quarter."[35] In thus opening the gate to the Atlantic Ocean and providing direct access to Asia and newly discovered America, the West's two gatekeeping *marca* states had succeeded in liberating Europe from the Islamic stranglehold over the Mediterranean region and in linking the continents of the earth. In short, Columbus and Vasco da Gama between them can be said to signify the end of the Middle Ages and the advent of modern times as well as of the modern world society.

Next, 1492 epitomizes the leading roles that both Iberian nations were able to play throughout the era of Europe's revolutionary Renaissance in contexts as varied as the arts, sciences, architecture, letters, philosophy, theology, law, and state-craft—and that even though this was the crucial time span also in Spain's war of liberation from Islam.

It is thus noteworthy, especially when compared with English dispositions in North America, that the Spanish crown, the University of Salamanca, legal schol-ars, theologians, and scores of common educated citizens were deeply preoccupied already in the last years of the fifteenth century with resolving such questions as: Did the king have just title to dominion in the Indies? Was the conquest a just war? Was the Indian inferior by nature or a rational being? And authoritative answers came promptly. The papal bull of 1501 legitimized the right to dominion; a crown committee of lawyers and theologians pronounced the Indian free by nature, not a candidate for slavery, and not subject to the Inquisition; and a 1502 decree placed the Indians under the crown's special protection with provision for severe penalties against those who might restrict their freedom.[36]

Although these principles were upheld by the Crown, the Church, and the jurists during the three centuries of the Spanish-American empire, they proved too lofty for reliable implementation by local administrations in America. But as Bynum E. Weathers notes, they did pave the way for the development of the postindependence nation-state systems in Latin America,[37] even as they greatly stimulated sixteenth- and seventeenth-century Spanish thought about the nature and currency of interna-tional law. Francisco de Vitoria thus concluded in *The Indians Recently Discovered* (1532) that since the discoveries had joined Europe and America, the community of nations was now extended "by natural necessity" to include the "American principalities."[38] The Portuguese, meanwhile, seem to have entertained the same proposition also in Africa, as when the king of Portugal and the king of Kongo (later Angola) were recognized as equals in their subservience to the Universal Catholic Church, and their respective states as near equal participants in the Euro-pean States System.[39]

Neither of the great transnational Iberian designs for unity, peace, and order made much of an impact on the thoughtways of black Africans and American In-dians. One impediment was, of course, the fact that the new designs were brought by strangers under the auspices of conquest and colonial settlement. But the chief barrier throughout these momentous centuries was the chasm separating the indig-enous peoples whose cultures had been fashioned without the benefit of writing from the intruding Europeans who represented the most highly literate of all cul-tures. Clusters of finely chiseled ideas such as those represented by "law" and "Christianity" (the state-making elements in the Iberian peninsula) just did not come across in their authenticity, but the idea of the "state" did, centuries later.

Spanish thought and statecraft were more effective in bringing a measure of order into international maritime relations. As a result of the Iberian openings to the Atlantic Ocean the Mediterranean Sea ceased to be "the central sea," as the

Arabs had liked to call it, and Islamic nations lost their superiority in matters maritime. However, since they remained powerful and held on to the Islamic doctrine that all relations with unbelievers are in essence *jihad* relations, southern Europeans were in no position to reinstate Roman customs or the ancient Rhodian sea law. Piracy, hostage-taking, and ransom payments—activities into which Spanish Christians had also been drawn during the *guerra fria*—thus continued to be scourges, but their incidence was greatly mitigated by Spanish and Italian efforts to develop a maritime system anchored in bilateral treaties and adjudicating courts. Although neither agency proved congenial to Muslim mind-sets, far-reaching agreements were arrived at because the Christian counterplayers had gone to considerable trouble collecting and analyzing Islamic customs of the sea.

International relations on the open sea, over which no single government could claim jurisdiction in Western opinion, were thus regulated from the tenth century onward by locally distinct but functionally interlocking administrative boards and compilations of law (*consulados* in Italian) in Italian and Spanish towns. The most influential among them, scholars agree, was the Consulato del Mare of Barcelona. Probably compiled in the thirteenth century, it was published in Catalan in 1494, two years after Granada had fallen and Columbus had discovered America, and four years before Vasco da Gama reached India.

Early Spanish Projections of Modern Western Statecraft

Like other Renaissance states in southern Europe, Spain was deeply rooted in classical and Christian civilization. However, unlike its neighbors the Spanish state found out under the daily stress of the *guerra fria* that this root system did in fact provide the winning strength for besting its Islamic enemies and for putting its own house in order. It was thus under these essentially adverse auspices that Spain evolved into the first "modern" European nation-state that associated statehood with territorial boundaries and an integral system of beliefs and commitments.

The innovative architects of this state model were Isabella of Castile, who was in charge of building the state's internal structure, and Ferdinand of Aragon, who shaped the contours of the state, set the parameters for the conduct of its foreign policies, and designed the diplomatic and military apparatus for their execution. And in this context it is noteworthy that the Aragonese king was as keenly aware in the mid-fifteenth century of the French threat to Spain's northern boundaries and of the French king's preparations to intervene militarily in Italy as he was of the continuous Islamic machinations in Valencia and Granada. Yet nothing in the records indicates that he ever contemplated abandoning one military or cold war battlefront when a crisis arose in the other. As Garrett Mattingly explains it in his exquisite study of Spanish statecraft,[40] Spain was ready—even though its resources were no match for those of France—because the Granadan wars had trained a tough infantry and able commanders, and because Ferdinand had developed a diplomatic system and an intelligence service that could be activated instantly.

This was borne out between 1455 and 1495 in the course of French invasions of Spain and Italy when Ferdinand of Aragon (then also king of Sicily) succeeded in drawing all major European states together in an anti-French coalition; getting them to meet in Venice under the presidency of the papacy; and having them agree in the Treaty of Venice (1495) to protect one another in the possession of their territories and to defend Italy against the Turks.

Ferdinand's design for Europe's collective security was distinctly new, and so were the support services he called into being for the purpose of shaping both conflicts and accords. Although he had learned much from the records of Italian, particularly Venetian, and papal statecraft and from Spain's experiences with low-intensity operations in the *guerra fria* with Islam, Ferdinand seems to have relied chiefly on his native Aragonese wits when he fashioned his network of diplomats, spies, and other agents in novel ways. It is thus noteworthy that he thought of his resident envoys as servants and symbols of the alliance that was to encircle and hamper the French. All were therefore instructed to persuade their hosts to join the "Holy League"; cement the union by negotiating, for example, dynastic marriages; and stir up anti-French movements in that nation's remoter regions. Each of Aragon's resident embassies—they were stationed in Rome, Venice, London, Brussels, and at the migratory Austrian court—had functions of its own, and so did each of several ambassadors at the Holy See, where resident embassies had been maintained since 1480.

"Knowing the Enemy"—Spanish Style

The whole network was in place by 1490—the only one of its kind among Europe's "new" major powers. Also in place was Aragon's intelligence system. It consisted of special nonaccredited "residents" whose status and function was kept ambiguous, and who were counseled to live and move inconspicuously. One such agent (a personal adviser to Ferdinand and Isabella) was thus sent to Maximilian of Austria in 1487–88, where he remained for several years. Another—a military man with experience from the Granadan wars—served at that time in Brittany with the mission to encourage the party of independence and coordinate prospective military efforts.

The keystone of Ferdinand's scheme was England, and not surprisingly therefore it was host to one of the most important secret missions—namely, that of Dr. Rodrigo de Puebla, special counselor to the Catholic kings, who was to remain in England for more than twenty years (with only one three-year interruption), tasked to lay the foundations of Anglo-Spanish relationships.[41]

Neither diplomacy nor political intelligence prevented the French invasion of Italy in 1494, but both together were the decisive weaponry that defeated France a year later. Further, and perhaps more importantly in the context of present-day intelligence studies, fifteenth-century Spain left a rich legacy in psychopolitical statecraft upon which seventeenth- and twentieth-century Spanish intelligence diplomats could draw when few other strategic assets were available.

Ten years after England had defeated the Spanish Armada, a group of Spanish diplomats received the mandate to salvage whatever was left of Spanish prestige and power so as to enable Spain to influence English policies in the impending Thirty Years' War between Europe's Catholics and Protestants. The hero in this dramatic story—which is admirably told by Mattingly[42]—is the now legendary

Gondamar. He won out, without a threatening army at his back, or a family purse, or even any feeling of common faith and common interests, when he decided to develop his intelligence network primarily as an operation on the highest level. He began by collecting the needed information through conversations and observations in court circles and in close contacts with scholars and scientists, among them Sir Francis Bacon. He ended up by developing a genuine friendship with King James himself after studies of the royal character had convinced him that it was the king, not his ministers, who shaped English policy. No covert action or corruption had been needed to succeed in one of Gondamar's more spectacular coups: obtaining the copy of Walter Raleigh's secret map showing the goal of his Guiana voyage. That document, Mattingly notes,[43] passed into the ambassador's hands from the hand of the king of England.

Gondamar needed this particular relationship with the king so that it would serve as leverage in his all-important task of convincing England of Spain's unique and everlasting prestige as Christendom's major shield, and of inducing the king to keep his nation neutral in the Thirty Years' War. Such a war, with England in it, he reasoned, would end whatever chance for greatness was left in Spain's future as well as have disastrous consequences for Catholicism everywhere. And since he had by that time established his ascendancy "over the spirit of the king,"[44] he was able indeed to immobilize England in the critical opening years of the epochal conflict. As Mattingly concludes: "It would be hard to name an ambassador before or since who had attained such a position, or exerted by sheer personal force such influence upon the affairs of Europe. Only years of daily contacts, of careful study and preparation could have achieved so much."[45]

Spain's influence on the Western states system was to wane in the ensuing centuries but to wax in the mid-twentieth century when the nation, then reduced to its original *marca* identity, proved to be the only member of the European system to take on and beat the Soviet Union in its massive cold war for the conquest, first, of the peninsula and thereafter of Western Europe.

As we have come to know in the last two decades from newly published intelligence files, biographical and autobiographical accounts of Soviet defectors and non-Soviet spies, specifically members of the Cambridge spy ring in England,[46] and from thorough examinations of the Leninist presence in Spain, the country was in fact "occupied" by Leninism when the Franco forces began their *reconquista*. The Loyalist government, including its Defense Ministry, was controlled by the Communist apparat; the police of the Spanish state were fully penetrated; and the Comintern was in total yet well-camouflaged control of the International Brigades. Cadres were trained by Soviet advisers; warfare was organized by "Political Commissars"; and total terror was dispensed by the Cheka. It is not surprising in these circumstances that the Loyalist government was powerless to contest either the workings of secret tribunals in the prisons of the International Brigades or the mass executions in which the Cheka engaged.[47]

However, Spain was not saved from "fascism" by the different Communist brigades and other Western support groups as planned by their Soviet commanders. Rather nationalist Spain fought and won another *guerra fria*—this time against Leninism.[48]

III

How Should We Think of Cold Wars in the Twenty-first Century?

Intelligence services in the West must address a future in which Leninism and Islam, singly or in combination, will continue to affect local, regional, and international politics, and for the following reasons. Marxism-Leninism has been officially declared bankrupt and wholly nefarious to humankind. However, it was so deeply seeded by its propagators in all regions in the world that it will inevitably go on informing collective and individual thought processes and sparking conflicts marked by terrorism and aggression until it withers away or is decisively superseded by other persuasions.

Islam, by contrast, is a time-transcendent vigorous faith and political doctrine that will be with us for ever. Indeed, the German historian Leopold von Ranke (1795–1886) viewed the East-West conflict between Christian Europe and Islamic Asia as the biggest of all historical and political problems—one that would be passed on from century to century, and that Europe could handle only if and when it was united. In brief, it is prudent to assume that the two cold wars will remain agenda items for Euro-American policymakers and intelligence analysts in the foreseeable future.

What should they strive for? is therefore the major question. The U.S. government's answer as announced at the end of the Persian Gulf war and repeatedly confirmed thereafter by President Bush follows precedents set by American Presidents throughout the twentieth century. It calls peremptorily for the establishment of a "new" world order, one that will bring democracy, peace, and order to the Middle East. This by now traditional formulation of American war and peace aims—which implies a *renvoi* to the United Nations Charter, international law, and American norms of government—has won bipartisan congressional approval. As elaborated on May 3, 1991, by Stephen Solarz, a congressional Democrat with pronounced interests in the conduct of foreign affairs, it stands for a renunciation of aggression; a renewal of the "sanctity" of existing borders; a reestablishment of the "sanctity" of states; and a promise to respect the human rights of individuals.

Such propositions are, to say the least, puzzling for the following reasons. Most states—and they include the United States—did not attach "sanctity" either to existing states or to existing borders. States were created and obliterated with abandon between 1920 and 1991, and so were boundaries, sometimes by wanton aggression, other times by equally wanton peace treaties. Also, nothing in the records indicates that the United States has either invariably or often interfered by force in order to restore the independence of victimized states.

Further, and as suggested in several preceding essays, twentieth-century records do not show that non-Western polities have been decisively influenced by these "new" references to "old" Western ideals. True, the UN system and international law have served many useful functions in today's divided multicultural world, but since their norms are internationalized versions of uniquely Western concepts and institutions, they do not help much when such non-Western low- and high-intensity conflicts as the ones discussed in this essay have to be analyzed and controlled. What is needed here is a region-specific focus, and this means in the case at hand that intelligence requirements for diplomatic operations in the Mediterranean theater will not be identical with those needed to secure Europe's eastern marches from penetrations by hostile Eurasian forces.

Preparing a New Order in the Mediterranean Region and the Middle East

Studies of the historical and modern Middle East suggest that U.S. intelligence should accept the following realities. The Western idea of peace has no equivalent in Islam, and *jihad* "in the sword and in the head" is the basic norm in relations with unbelievers at home and abroad. Conflict is therefore accepted in all its ramifications and deep antagonisms are apt to be permanent. However, and as noted in the first section of this essay, these negatives can be muted into a quasi-peace by negotiating long truces and covenants.

The record of U.S. policies in the Middle East does not show much awareness of these predispositions. This factor in conjunction with the abrupt creation of Israel and the concomitant neglect of Arab aspirations and grievances has had the foreseeable effect throughout the last half century of hardening the *jihad* complex that had been near-dormant for some five hundred years, and of converting the low-intensity cold war against the West, particularly the United States, into a chronic terror-ridden LIC.

It is unlikely in these circumstances that any American version of a "new" international or regional order will be acceptable in this multicultural strife-torn area as a reliable and realistic security system unless the United States shows convincingly that it addresses the separate interests of *all* component states. And since the likelihood of such a change in orientation must also be pronounced nil at this time— which happens to be a crucial moment for all security-conscious nations in the West—one must conclude that the United States is politically and diplomatically checkmated here.

An exit from this predicament is best prepared by cooperating closely with the European Community and by accepting southern Europe's Mediterranean *marca* states as lead actors in the confrontation with Islam. And among them again the United States would be well-advised by intelligence analysts grounded in geopolitics, history, and present-day politics to recognize Spain and France as most valuable players.

Preparing a New Order for the Northeastern and Central European Ramparts of the West

A 1991 survey of the old cold war fronts in this region leads to the following findings. The dissolution of the Soviet Empire is not yet a *fait accompli* and did not yet lead to a restoration of full sovereignty for its former satellites because Soviet armed forces continue to be stationed on their territories and in West Germany. Likewise, the transformation of the Soviet Union into a commonwealth of eleven separate republics must still be viewed as process rather than actuality if only because the republics have not yet been able to agree on the command structure, placement, and function of the Soviet forces. Euro-American diplomacy and intelligence as concerted in NATO, for example, should do more to expedite these processes than has been apparent in the early 1990s.

However, the most urgent mandate incumbent upon American intelligence communities consists in taking stock of the ongoing revolution in the former Soviet-controlled space and of its effects upon the thoughtways—not just the economies—of its component peoples. What, apart from economic necessity, is apt to unify them as citizens of the new commonwealth of independent states? Can one conclude that the epochal revolt against Communism originated in the all-Russian sector of the former empire, and that it was nurtured by Russian Christianity, Byzantine Roman law, and Russian nationalism? If so, can the twin causes of statemaking and pacification be furthered from without by activating this cultural infrastructure without alienating the Islamic republics of the defunct imperium and splitting the new commonwealth of sovereign states?

This issue is as portentous for Eurasian as for Euro-American policy planners. The long-range security interests of the latter will in all likelihood be determined by the following geocultural changes in the environment. The waning of Soviet Leninism and the resuscitation of pre-Leninist values is bound to favor friendly, perhaps even close relations between the Slavic, chiefly Russian sector and Western Europe. The simultaneous waxing of Islam in the further Asian sector, by contrast, will no doubt make for alignment with the adjoining established Muslim states, specifically Iran; for radicalization of belief systems along Shi'ite fundamentalist lines, and thus for conflict with the West as well as with the Russian domain. In other words, the North-South fault line has now become also a boundary between Islamic and West European belief systems, and as such it merges with the classical East-West line along the southern Mediterranean coast that Muslim forces had consolidated between 700 and 1500 A.D.

The foregoing study suggests the following general guidelines for dealing with cold wars of ideas:

Think more in geopolitical and less in juristic terms.

Accentuate assessment of cultural rather than official territorial frontiers.

Recognize the North-South and East-West fault lines as continental Europe's and hence the West's geostrategically important boundaries.

Assure the security of the West's borderlands against inroads by adversary cultures.

Keep track of interactions between divergent idea systems: it is they that provide the underpinning for all cold wars.

NOTES

1. The term *"guerra fria"* was coined by Don Juan Manuel, a thirteenth-century Spanish scholar, when he described the situation in his native Spain during the long period of Islamic wars and occupations. See Luis Garcia Arias, *El concepto de guerra y la denominada "guerra fria"* (1956), as reviewed in *Annuaire Français de Droit International,* 1956, p. 925.

2. The same gap in knowledge was conducive to our defeat in the Vietnam War where we failed conspicuously in understanding Buddhism and Confucianism. See earlier essays in this book on Leninist ways of warring and on the different implications of a *jihad*.

3. This is made clear by Saddam Hussein's February 1990 address to the heads of the fourth summit meeting of the Arab Cooperative Council States. See *ORBIS*, Vol. 35, no. 1 (Winter 1991), pp. 117–19, for the text. As abstracted by the editors, Saddam Hussein argues that with the decline of the Soviet Union, Arabs have lost the counterweight that prevented the imposition of a pro-Israeli Pax Americana in the Middle East. Since Arab interests are profoundly in conflict with Western interests he finds that only a strong Arab military stand can prevent the United States from dominating the Gulf. The Bush administration declared at that time that the speech did not represent a shift in Iraqi policy, and that cooperation with Saddam Hussein remained the best policy.

4. For patterns of accord between Muslims and Christians, see Bozeman, *Politics and Culture in International History:* Chapter 10, "The Muslim Realm," and Chapter 12, "The Mediterranean Elites and the Furtherance of Cultural Affinities."

5. On this subject see Majid Khadduri, *War and Peace in the Law of Islam* (Baltimore, Maryland: The Johns Hopkins University Press, 1955) and by the same author as translator, *The Islamic Law of Nations: Shaybani's Siyar* (Baltimore, Maryland: Johns Hopkins University Press, 1966). See Gustave von Grünebaum, *Medieval Islam: A Study in Cultural Orientation* (Chicago, 1946), and Bernard Lewis, *The Political Language of Islam* (The University of Chicago Press, 1988), Chapter 4, "War and Peace," and Chapter 5, "The Limits of Obedience," which discuss different categories of enemies and of *jihads*. See p. 90 to the effect that Anwar al-Sadat, the former president of Egypt, was murdered in 1981 by a group of fundamentalists who charged in court that he was a Muslim only in name. For by setting aside the *shari'a* and introducing a Western, and therefore infidel system of law, society, and culture, he had proved himself to be an apostate. Now the apostate is traditionally viewed as worse than the usurper, the tyrant, and even the infidel ruler (the one who is not Islamic). Similar arguments were used to justify the overthrow of the last Shah of Iran. They were also advanced by Saddam Hussein as justification of the *jihad* against Saudi Arabia.

   Lewis concludes that the principle of war against the apostate opened the possibility of legitimate, indeed obligatory war against an enemy at home, and that this has developed in our times into a doctrine of insurgency and revolutionary war, both officially sanctioned as forms of *jihad*. In this respect it is noteworthy that the rules of warfare against the apostate state or ruler are much harsher than those governing war against the unbeliever. On this subject see *ibid.*, pp. 85ff. and 145–47.

   See Lewis B. Ware, "An Islamic Concept of Conflict in Its Historical Context," in *The International Dimension of Culture and Conflict*, the proceedings of a symposium on this subject (Air University Press, Maxwell Air Force Base, Alabama, 1991), for a richly suggestive analysis of the Shi'ite conflict concept.

6. See Bozeman, *Politics and Culture in International History*, Chapter 8, "The Medieval Western European Realm" (pp. 238ff.), for discussions of the crusades; also, *Memoirs of a Renaissance Pope: The Commentaries of Pius II, an Abridgement*, trans. by Florence A. Gragg, ed. by Leona C. Gabel (New York: Capricorn Books, 1962).

7. For a discussion of this perennial problem in Islamic government and politics see Bozeman, *The Future of Law in a Multicultural World* (Princeton, N.J.: Princeton University Press, 1971), Chapter 2, "The Islamic East," and authorities there cited.

8. See general texts on European history; also Stephen L. Dyson, *The Creation of the Roman Frontier* (Princeton, N.J.: Princeton University Press, 1987), and Walter Goffart, *Barbarians and Romans, A.D. 418–584* (Princeton, N.J.: Princeton University Press, 1987).

9. For a richly suggestive analysis of frontiers and marches and their respective functions and meanings see Antonio Truyol y Serra, "Las Fronteras y Las Marcas," *Revista Espanola de Derecho Internacional*, Vol. X, no. 1–2, 1957. For Byzantine modalities of securing marches and frontiers, see "Traditions of Political Warfare and Low-Intensity Conflict in

Totalitarian Russia and China," in this volume. The role of frontier territories in the evolution of the United States is not dissimilar to that of marches in Europe.

10. André Duchesne, *Historieae Francorum scriptores,* Vol. I (Paris, 1636), p. 786. See Philip K. Hitti, *History of the Arabs,* 3rd. ed., Rev. (London: Macmillan, 1946), Chapter 34 pp. 493ff., "Conquest of Spain," for a somewhat pro-Arab accounting of Spain's history in these centuries.

11. See Hitti, *op. cit.,* pp. 542ff., for a characterization of this dynasty; *ibid.,* pp. 534–35 for the excesses of certain eleventh-century Umayyad rulers. One who held the throne for only a few months found time to have the severed heads of numerous Christian leaders of the northern marches who refused to acknowledge him converted into flower pots and placed on the banks of the river opposite his palace. Tired of all that, Hitti notes, the Cordovans at last decided to abolish the caliphate altogether.

12. *Ibid.,* pp. 549ff.

13. Bernard Lewis, *The Political Language of Islam* (Chicago and London: University of Chicago Press, 1988), pp. 64f.

14. *Ibid.*

15. Hitti, *op. cit.,* pp. 543ff.

16. *Ibid.* Hitti also notes that one of the early kings of Aragon (died 1104) could write only in Arabic script, and that the Mozarabs used Arabic letters even when writing Latin.

17. *Ibid.,* p. 545, for the interesting notation that Philip II (died 1598) presented El Cid to the pope for canonization, and that the epic *Cantar de mio Cid* (composed in the middle of the fifteenth century) has deeply influenced Spanish thought throughout subsequent ages, contributing powerfully to the establishment not only of the native language but also to the consolidation of the national character.

18. *Ibid.,* p. 516.

19. *Ibid.,* p. 518. The most famous "renegade" activist in these annals of Spanish history was the Cid, who won the surrender of Valencia in 1094. See *supra* and *infra,* this essay.

20. Mozarabs were persecuted, massacred, and banished from Spain throughout the duration of the *guerra fria.*

21. See the histories of the early Christian kingdoms of Axum and Ethiopia in Africa and of the two Christian Roman empires.

22. For suggestive insights see Robert I. Burns, S. J., ed., *The Worlds of Alfonso the Learned and James the Conqueror, Intellect and Force in the Middle Ages* (Princeton, N.J.: Princeton University Press, 1987).

23. Bozeman, *Politics and Culture in International History,* p. 255, note 49, on the international Cluniac Order; also pp. 254–67, "The Influence of the Catholic Church on International Government and International Relations," and on the role of Canon Law.

24. See Robert I. Burns, S. J., *Muslims, Christians, and Jews in the Crusading Kingdom of Valencia, Societies in Symbiosis* (Cambridge, Mass.: Cambridge University Press, 1984), p. 59.

25. The Byzantine expedients for administering a vast empire that contained scores of different ethnicities are discussed in Bozeman, *Politics and Culture in International History,* Chapter 9, pp. 298–389. Some of them, including the regulations for Jewish autonomy, were borrowed by Sassanian Persia and, after Byzantium's annihilation in 1453, by the Ottoman Turkish empire, which introduced the most intricate scheme for satisfying the diverse longings for apartheid in the form of the *millet,* a nonterritorial communal formation encompassing the members of each officially recognized religion and sect. See Bozeman, *The Future of Law in a Multicultural World* (Princeton, N.J.: Princeton University Press, 1971), pp. 73f., and authorities there cited. However, the mother of all such discriminatory designs was Achaemenid Persia, the contemporary of classical Greece. See Essay 3 in this volume; Chapter 1, pp. 43ff., in *Politics and Culture in International History,* and the essay "Iran: U.S. Foreign Policy and the Tradition of Persian Statecraft," *ORBIS,* Vol. 23, no. 2 (Summer 1979), pp. 387ff.

26. For a detailed case study and documentation of the acrimonious relations between the Chris-

tian state government of Valencia and its vast settlement of essentially hostile Mudéjars, see Burns, *Muslims, Christians, and Jews in Valencia.*

27. *Ibid.*, pp. 288–91, for textual references to two thirteenth century charters, and pp. 74ff. for a discussion of Alfandech's charters. One of the last Mudéjar revolts in Valencia took place in Eslida in 1526.
28. Hitti, *op. cit.*, p. 551.
29. *Ibid.*, p. 555.
30. *Ibid.*, pp. 554f.
31. See "Traditions of Political Warfare and Low-Intensity Conflict in Totalitarian Russia and China" in the present book where the Byzantine empire is examined.
32. As we have learned from the records of the Persian Gulf war (1990–91), expulsion continues to be a common practice in Islamic/Arab statecraft. See, for example, Elaine Sciolino, "Iraq's Shi'ite Majority: A Painful History of Revolt and Schism," *The New York Times,* March 30, 1991: "Nervous about guerrilla activities and a popular Shi'ite revolution in Iraq, the Baghdad government expelled no fewer than 200,000 Shi'ites, charging that they were an Iranian fifth column threatening the stability of Iraq." When assassins tried to kill Hussein in July 1982 while he visited a stronghold of Shi'ite militancy about forty miles from Baghdad, he ordered the entire population deported and the village razed. It is relevant to recall that Shi'ites were generally held in disrepute by the Sunni majority because they expressed their dissidence not just in intellectual disputations but in violent physical action. This had a pernicious effect on the Dar al-Islam, especially in the thirteenth century when the Order of Assassins was particularly effective. (See "Covert Action and Foreign Policy in World Politics" in this volume.) At that time influential Shi'ites showed themselves ready to receive the pagan Mongols as liberators from the Sunni yoke, for it was a Shi'ite vizier (of the Sunni caliph) who suggested the conquest of Baghdad to the Mongol prince Hulagu, and another Shi'ite dignitary who, following the fall of Baghdad, persuaded the alien conqueror to kill the captured caliph. See von Grünebaum, *op. cit.*, pp. 186–89.
33. Hitti, *op. cit.*, p. 555, note 2.
34. Luis Vaz de Camoëns (d. 1580), Portugal's greatest poet, celebrated his countrymen, particularly Vasco da Gama (d. 1524), in his epic poem *The Lusiads* (1542). See *The Lusiads of Luis Vaz de Camoëns,* Leonard Bacon, trans. (New York, 1950). For a discussion of the work and the themes it treats, see Bozeman, *Politics and Culture in International History,* Chapter 11, "Patterns of International and Intercultural Relations at the Opening of the Modern Age."
35. William C. Atkinson, *A History of Spain and Portugal* (Penguin Books, 1960; reprinted 1961), p. 117. By way of comparison, it is interesting to find the following evaluation of Spain in St. Lane-Poole, *The Moors in Spain* (New York, 1899), p. 280: "The Moors were banished; for a while Christian Spain shone, like the moon, with a borrowed light; then came the eclipse, and in that darkness Spain has groveled ever since,"
36. See Bynum E. Weathers, "Culture and Conflict in Latin America," *Cadre Paper,* Center for Aerospace Doctrine, Research, and Education (Air University Press, Maxwell Air Force Base, 1991), pp. 27ff., for a discussion of these documents and an interesting institution known as "entrustment" that had been originally employed in Spain during the *reconquista.*
37. *Ibid.*
38. See Bozeman, *Politics and Culture in International History,* pp. 289ff., for these Spanish projections of the law of nations, which stood in marked contrast to the Grotian scheme as composed in the mid-seventeenth century.
39. Bozeman, *Conflict in Africa: Concepts and Realities,* pp. 334–46, "Transcultural Diplomacy: The Case of Portugal."
40. Garrett Mattingly, *Renaissance Diplomacy* (Baltimore, Maryland: Penguin Books, 1964), Chapters 13, 14, and 15. He also wrote *Catherine of Aragon* (1942) and *The Armada* (1959).
41. *Ibid.*, p. 122. Ferdinand sent another special counselor (also a veteran from the Granada wars) to the French court, allegedly for the purpose of negotiating closer diplomatic relations, but actually to collect military intelligence. *Ibid.*, p. 123.

42. *Ibid.*, pp. 220–32, "The Game of Chess."

43. *Ibid.*, p. 226.

44. *Ibid.*, p. 228.

45. *Ibid.*, p. 230.

46. Oleg Tsarev, the deputy spokesman of the KGB, said recently that Kim Philby, Guy Burgess, and Donald Maclean (three prominent members of the Cambridge spy ring) had been under the control of Aleksandr Orlov (a Soviet intelligence officer who defected to the United States in 1938) in the 1930s; and that Orlov, with the rank of "special major," was sent as the NKVD's chief clandestine field officer to Spain in 1936. There he was in touch with Philby, who worked as a correspondent for *The Times* of London covering the Franco side of the war. (Philby's code name with the NKVD was "Söhnchen.") *The New York Times*, June 26, 1991, as reported by David Binder. The latest of numerous studies of these three Cambridge spies is Verne W. Newton, *The Cambridge Spies: The Untold Story of Maclean, Philby, and Burgess in America* (New York: Madison Books, 1991). Since the Soviet Union is said to have had sixty-one agents of ninety-three worldwide working in Britain, and since it was able to recruit leading figures of the governmental and literary elites as trustworthy agents in the 1920s and 1930s, it is helpful to read Samuel Hynes, *The Auden Generation: Literature and Politics in England in the 1930s* (New York: The Viking Press, 1977).

47. For an exemplary examination of these records, see R. Dan Richardson, *The Comintern Army: The International Brigades and the Spanish Civil War* (University of Kentucky Press, 1982).

48. In the context of this particular essay it should be noted that the Franco government did not open the Gibraltar gateway to the Axis powers during World War II. Also, it should be recalled that the term "fascist" refers exclusively to Mussolini's conception of the Italian "Corporate State." If Franco must be typed or compared, it is safer to think of him as kin to Ferdinand of Aragon and perhaps even to one of the better Umayyad caliphs.

THE AUTHOR

Adda B. Bozeman, professor emeritus of international relations at Sarah Lawrence College, is a Barrister of the Middle Temple (London), a Diplomée of the Section Diplomatique, École Libre des Sciences Politiques (Paris), and a J.D. from Southern Methodist University Law School. She has studied, written, and lectured extensively on the interrelationship of culture and statecraft. Among her major works are *Politics and Culture in International History, The Future of Law in a Multicultural World,* and *Conflict in Africa: Concepts and Realities,* as well as a series of monographs on the place of intelligence in the world society's culturally different political systems. Professor Bozeman is a founding member of the Consortium for the Study of Intelligence and a member of the Executive Committee of the International Studies Association's Intelligence Studies Section.